Ethical and Legal Issues in Modern Surgery

Introductory Series in Medicine

ISSN: 2045-0346

Series Editor: Nadey Hakim *(Imperial College Healthcare NHS Trust, UK)*

Published

Forthcoming

Introductory Series in Medicine Vol. 2

Series Editor: **Nadey Hakim**

Ethical and Legal Issues in Modern Surgery

Editors

Nadey Hakim
Imperial College Healthcare NHS Trust, UK

Vassilios Papalois
Imperial College Healthcare NHS Trust, UK

Miran Epstein
Queen Mary University of London, UK

Imperial College Press

ICP

Published by

Imperial College Press
57 Shelton Street
Covent Garden
London WC2H 9HE

Distributed by

World Scientific Publishing Co. Pte. Ltd.
5 Toh Tuck Link, Singapore 596224
USA office: 27 Warren Street, Suite 401-402, Hackensack, NJ 07601
UK office: 57 Shelton Street, Covent Garden, London WC2H 9HE

Library of Congress Cataloging-in-Publication Data
Ethical and legal issues in modern surgery / edited by Nadey Hakim, Vassilios Papalois &
Miran Epstein.
    p. ; cm. -- (Introductory series in medicine ; vol. 2)
    Includes index.
    ISBN 978-1-84816-246-4 (hardcover : alk. paper) -- ISBN 978-1-84816-296-9 (electronic)
    I. Hakim, Nadey S., 1958–   , editor. II. Papalois, Vassilios E., editor. III. Epstein, Miran, editor.
IV. Series: Introductory series in medicine ; v. 2.
    [DNLM: 1. Ethics, Medical. 2. General Surgery--ethics. 3. General Surgery--legislation &
jurisprudence. WO 21]
    RD27.7
    174.2'97--dc23
                                                                                2014044355

British Library Cataloguing-in-Publication Data
A catalogue record for this book is available from the British Library.

Typeset by Stallion Press
Email: enquiries@stallionpress.com

Printed in Singapore

Contents

Preface

Over the second half of the twentieth and, even more so, in the twenty-first century there have been indisputably some truly dramatic changes in the overall framework and content of medical practice that also have major ethical and legal dimensions.

The provision of healthcare used to be dominated by a paternalistic attitude where the doctor was the dominant figure: he made all the major clinical decisions, his judgment was never questioned, he was the one making decisions on the allocation of resources, and in a situation when something went wrong it was highly unlikely that his ability or skill would be disputed. Nowadays, the provision of healthcare is based on a complicated partnership between healthcare providers (doctors, nurses, pharmacists, and clinical scientists), patients, administrators, and, last but not least, organizations responsible for providing finance (the government with respect to NHS systems or insurance companies with respect to private healthcare systems). The development of multicultural societies and the fact that decisions regarding the provision of healthcare and assessment of its quality have to be made on the background of so many different ethnicities, religions, cultures, and languages has made matters even more complex. The puzzle becomes even "tougher" if we add to this the ever developing phenomenon of patients travelling to seek healthcare in a country different to their country of origin or residence. Furthermore, the development of new medical specialties, the interdependence of medical specialties (with most decisions being taken not at an individual but at a multidisciplinary level) as well as the rapid development of modern and advance treatments for very challenging patients and the introduction of new technologies in medical practice have dramatically broadened the spectrum of ethical and legal issues related to medical practice.

Modern surgery is of course no exception from the rest of medical specialties when it comes to facing complex ethical and legal issues. Even more, we believe that the challenges in surgical practice are greater than perhaps any other specialty if we consider that surgery is always at the far front of innovation, advanced intervention, and acute care. Surgeons of all ranks feel frequently overwhelmed with the complexity of the ethical and legal challenges and this can have a profound effect for their professional but also personal well-being and, even more so, can negatively affect patient care.

This book aims to address in a systematic and comprehensive way the ethical and legal challenges related to modern surgical practice. The first part deals with the more general issues that set the overall ethical–legal framework and "scene" and the second with more specific issues related to surgical subspecialties. The chapters are written by authors with immense experience and expertise in their respective fields. Chapter 14 on "Ethical Issues in Transplantation" is considered to be a classic and the author and Imperial College Press have kindly agreed to its inclusion in this book.

We are truly grateful to all authors for their truly superb work and to the editorial team of ICP for their precious commitment and support.

We hope that the book will be a helpful and supportive "companion" for surgeons (but also colleagues from all specialties) for their ethically and legally challenging practice in an ever-changing world.

Nadey Hakim, Vassilios Papalois, and Miran Epstein
London
September 2014

List of Authors

Jon Anderson
Consultant Cardiothoracic Surgeon
Imperial College Healthcare NHS Trust
Hammersmith Hospital, London

Kamran Baig
Consultant Cardiologist
Trent Cardiac Centre, Nottingham

Rebecca C. H. Brown
Institute of Applied Health Sciences
University of Aberdeen, Aberdeen

Jeremy Campbell
Consultant Anaesthetist
Imperial College Healthcare NHS Trust
Hammersmith Hospital, London

Priyanka Chadha
Imperial College NHS Healthcare Trust, London

Bernard Morris Dickens
Professor Emeritus of Health Law and Policy
Faculty of Law
Faculty of Medicine and Joint Centre for Bioethics
University of Toronto, Toronto

Miran Epstein
Reader in Medical Ethics
Barts and The London School of Medicine and Dentistry
Queen Mary University of London, London

Andrew J. T. George
Deputy Vice Chancellor (Education and International)
Brunel University, London

Alice Guilder
Oxford Deanery

Nadey S. Hakim
Max Thorek Professor of Surgery
Adjunct Professor of Transplantation Surgery Imperial College London
Imperial College Healthcare NHS Trust, London

Philip Hébert
Professor Emeritus, Department of Family and Community Medicine
Sunnybrook Health Sciences Centre
University of Toronto, Toronto

Richard Huxtable
Professor of Medical Ethics and Law
Centre for Ethics in Medicine
School of Social and Community Medicine
University of Bristol, Bristol

Allyson MacVean
Senior Research Fellow
Bath Spa University, Bath

Christopher Madden
Department of Neurological Surgery
University of Texas
Southwestern Medical Centre, Dallas, Texas

Howard Morgan
Department of Neurological Surgery
University of Texas
Southwestern Medical Centre, Dallas, Texas

Vassilios Papalois
Consultant Transplant and General Surgeon
Renal and Transplant Unit
Imperial College Healthcare NHS Trust
Hammersmith Hospital, London

Shaneel R. Patel
Academic Foundation Trainee in Vascular Surgery
South Thames Foundation School, London

Ivo Pitanguy
The Ivo Pitanguy Clinic and Institute, Rio de Janeiro

Felicity Plaat
Consultant Anaesthetist
Imperial College Healthcare NHS Trust
Hammersmith Hospital, London

Henrique Radwanski
The Ivo Pitanguy Clinic and Institute, Rio de Janeiro

Duke Samson
Department of Neurological Surgery
University of Texas
Southwestern Medical Centre, Dallas, Texas

Aris Sterodimas
The Ivo Pitanguy Clinic and Institute, Rio de Janeiro

Amanda Venters
Lay Member
Clinical Ethics Committee
Imperial College Healthcare NHS Trust, London
Lay Member
Ethics Committee
British Transplantation Society

Louis Whitworth
Department of Neurological Surgery
University of Texas
Southwestern Medical Centre, Dallas, Texas

Ariel Zosmer
Associate Specialist
Centre for Reproductive Medicine
St. Bartholomew's Hospital, London
Honorary Clinical Senior Lecturer
Centre for Primary Care and Public Health, Blizard Institute
Queen Mary University of London, London

Part 1
General

1

Ethical Issues in Surgery: The Patient's Perspective

Amanda Venters

What might an average patient consider to be the ethical issues in surgery? Does a patient even consider that the surgeon might not behave ethically and if not what does an average patient think are the motivations and principles that a surgeon is governed by?

1.1 The Nature of the Relationship between Patient and Surgeon

The very nature of the relationship between patient and surgeon is unique — it is quite obviously not one of two equals in an absolute sense, but instead one where the commitment to the best possible result is, or should be, equal on behalf of both the patient and the surgeon.

For the patient the relationship with the surgeon is particularly unusual and intense — they are required to place an unparalleled amount of trust in someone who they have had potentially very little personal contact with and who they will very likely not interact with much, if at all, after the event. The patient is generally a complete novice with little or no knowledge of the intervention, options, and other variables or indeed what their role could or should be. Uniquely the patient is almost being asked to bare their soul as much as their body because the surgeon may have the potential via their actions to dictate the long-term future of the patient. It is no wonder that major surgery is often judged to be one of the most stressful life events possible.

If one takes this thought further (it is not the most obvious thought process to a patient) surgery is also a somewhat peculiar process. The thought that a relative stranger may literally have your life in their hands, that they have seen you at your most vulnerable, and via their actions they have changed your body (and life) forever is a sobering one.

Clearly (and somewhat uniquely within medicine) the ability to judge short-term success is immediate. The surgeon will have undertaken to repair, add, remove, or even reuse body parts in an agreed procedure and at the end of it the objective will have a definable outcome. Of course that is not the end of the process because the fact that the immediate technical expectations have been achieved might not lead to the desired long-term outcome for many reasons.

1.2 Patient Autonomy

The patient is not an object to be treated at the discretion of the profes-sional — whilst the patient has no right to demand treatment they are certainly entitled to refuse it. However, in order to do this they need to understand the situation and they need to be equipped to make their decision.

It is probably not unusual for patients to appear to be about as engaged with their surgical options as they are when they take their cars in to be serviced. In those circumstances they may be told that various strange parts are wearing out and need replacing at a huge cost and they have no idea what the parts are, let alone if they need replacing, but just agree because they do not know otherwise. This apparent apathy may be borne of a lack of understanding of what, in an ideal situation, their role could, or indeed should, be rather than a lack of willingness to engage usefully.

1.2.1 *Equipping the patient to use their autonomy*

Even if they have researched their symptoms and conditions, the average person has probably managed to have too much data yet not enough information to make a reasoned decision on the facts and circumstances of their particular case without the support and guidance of the surgeon.

Therefore there needs to be a real commitment from the surgeon to the patient to help and guide them through the process. Just as whilst on the side of the surgeon there might at least be the temptation to be quite patriarchal and do what they believe is in the patient's best interests; after all they might need to expend more time and effort on guiding the patient through the process (which might in any case be the same), on the side of some patients there might be hesitation or even fear which prevents them from fully engaging in a process which they feel ill equipped for. This engagement should ultimately ensure that the best possible result is achieved by this participation, rather than the patient merely being there as an object or even perceiving themselves more as a "victim".

The surgeon should take a patient with all their available health information, explain to them all the options and reasonably foreseeable outcomes, and allow that patient to decide on the right risk/reward balance. Then, using their theoretical and practical professional skills, they undertake the surgery with the intention of achieving the most desirable outcome in the circumstances.

If a competent patient chooses not to make a decision then there can be no consent and no treatment, conversely if they choose to make a decision which appears totally irrational then that is their choice.

1.2.2 *Autonomy and outside influences*

A patient alone, if competent, is of course legally entitled and indeed obliged to make an autonomous decision about their treatment options. That does not mean that they cannot seek assistance, it merely means that the individual should decide the extent to which they wish their family, religious leader, or other person(s) to participate in the decision making process.

An obvious place for outside influences to occur would be within the patient's family, and their involvement and its appropriateness might be an issue which needs to be addressed in the process. Is it either appropriate or desirable?

In the course of a brief relationship (however intense) a surgeon cannot possibly understand all the family dynamics which may be as complex and unfathomable in a patient family as in any other. They need to make a judgement call as to the risks and benefits of both their involvement and lack there of, but ultimately they need to do their best to ensure that the decision is not borne of coercion but is actually what the patient wants and not merely what the family or others want.

It follows that the best interests of the patient might be served by giving them the "time and space" to process the information without the family pressures but equally that having the wider family involved might help them understand the information better by allowing the family to assimilate "unfiltered" information — i.e., direct from the surgeon so that they are all operating on the same base information. It is always interesting that the intention of the conveyance and receipt of the information can have major differences in its interpretation.

It is fraught with danger to assume a particular intent on the part of the family when they are involved — in a positive sense they know the patient better, and they would know how the rehabilitation and/or range of outcomes would most likely work and possibly be more supportive of that. In a negative sense they may have their own phobias, beliefs, and emotions, or even agenda, which might not be supportive of or compatible with the patient's best interests.

The other obvious type of outside influence is cultural and/or religious. In this case it can be a more complex dilemma because the consequences of the patient's decision are potentially not just on the way that the treatment decision is made but possibly also on their position and reintegration into their community or religious body.

In many ways the stronger the belief is, based on a specific circumstance or teaching, the easier it is to understand and possibly even rebut. Where there are cultural or religious influences which appear to go outside the patient's best interests then the surgeons should consult and ask for support from chaplains and/or appropriate "experts" to resolve the issue such that the patient has as broad a spectrum of knowledge as possible to deal with.

1.3 Informed Consent, a Process not a Signature

What is the right thing and how do both the patient and the surgeon end up with the proverbial meeting of minds? It is all too easy for patients to not truly participate in the process, to place blind trust in the superior knowledge of the expert, and assume all is well unless the outcome is not what they imagined or were prepared for.

Whose responsibility is that — do the patients have as much responsibility to engage and participate in the process or can they "opt out" of their participation in any of the preparation and decision making? Conversely how much responsibility is there upon the surgeon to ensure that they have done a "reasonable job" of fully engaging the patient and have they really obtained informed consent?

1.3.1 *Information overload*

Some patients will come in having done a great deal of research from a number of sources, potentially both appropriate and inappropriate — what is the surgeon's duty to engage with them in these circumstances?

The obvious idea would be to be able to point the patient to reliable sources of information and explain to them why these are the most appropriate sources (i.e., from a professional association, the NHS, etc.) and also if they have managed to find sources which are not reliable to give an overall indication as to why these sources are not appropriate (i.e., not verified, not factually correct, the flat earth society, etc.) and possibly rebut myths.

Of course it is also possible that the patient may have tapped into sources which publish legitimate concerns but which the surgeon does not necessarily agree. In this case the time and effort should be invested to ensure that the patient understands the basis on which the surgeon's beliefs are held and it will underlie their consent should they choose to give it.

1.3.2 *Devolving decision making*

Every patient is different and the onus lies on the medical team as a whole to ensure that the patient has the appropriate level of detail for them to make the decision to either grant or withhold consent.

What happens if the patient simply says, "I will leave it up to you doctor to do what you think is right"? Is it any more ethical for someone to wish to devolve their decision making to a doctor than to someone else — perhaps a family member or religious or spiritual advisor who may or may not have a better understanding of the situation in its physical and spiritual context than the patient?

The obvious interpretation is that just as a competent patient is allowed to make an irrational decision over treatment options they are able to devolve that decision making to another person — as long as that devolution is made by a competent patient to a competent person who is willing to accept that responsibility.

However, is it ever ethical for a doctor to take over that decision making? It would seem logical that the doctor could go ahead as if with a patient who lacked competence in the patient's best interests, but they would need to be sure that the patient would not be better served by more effort to engage them, rather than taking over. The real risk of accepting this devolution is if the outcome is not what the patient either anticipated or wanted — if all went well it would not be a problem.

1.4 Where the Patient Lacks Competence

1.4.1 *Whose best interests?*

In cases where the patient is not competent to make a decision and there is no Enduring Power of Attorney then the ethical and legal requirement on all members of medical staff is to act in "the patient's best interests"; but what might those be and how do the various parties' expressions of their views of the patient's "best interests" get weighed up?

Since doctors generally go into the profession to heal people they would understandably err on the side of treatment for the individual by inclination, and of course in the case of potential litigation they could feel that to treat would be more desirable than not to.

First, the practicalities of the patient's real life outside the hospital can sometimes be completely outside the experience of the surgical team and/ or wider multidisciplinary team. It is a very human desire to give as much of a chance for a patient to enjoy "life" outside the hospital but sometimes by that very desire they could be condemning the patient to a life that they do not want to lead and which leaves them with no quality of life, but the moment that that could have been avoided was changed by a well meaning, albeit ill-judged, professional intervention.

Whilst various religious groups believe in the sanctity of life, and others believe that outside life there is nothing, it should not be presumed what the patient's view might be without due consideration of all available facts.

It may be true to say that a completely healthy patient cannot possibly conceive how they might have a good quality of life outside perfect health; it does not mean that their stated unwillingness to tolerate that has no validity. Morally what is the greater "sin" — that of commission or omission?

Does an intervention against the patient's wishes which results in a quality of life which they would not seek, but have no real choice but to tolerate, really result in a valid interpretation of the patient's best interests? Even if that quality of life would be perfectly acceptable to another patient or even "most" patients? Of course it depends upon the consequences of the lack of intervention.

Weighing up the evidence of a patient's best interests is clearly harder if the natural physician's response to do their best to "heal" someone (however small that possibility might be) comes up against the family's or loved ones' inclination to do nothing. It is more clouded if the family have not previously discussed with the patient what they might do in certain situations, or even have feelings of guilt because their motivations might not be at all compatible with what the patient would really want.

1.4.2 AND versus DNAR

Most people are familiar with the "Do Not Attempt Resuscitation" (DNAR) order but certain hospitals in the US have another saying of "AND" — "Allow Natural Death" — which would seem to be a much more apposite saying. It gives a dignity and demonstrates the fact that death is inevitable and what most people would prefer is a good death after a good life.

It seems that as a society we have moved further away from death being viewed as part of life and almost that death is the worst thing that can happen to a person/patient. Realistically if one considers that option it cannot be so, even if one does not believe in a life after death. How can even "nothingness" be worse than someone merely existing as a shell of the person they once were? Just as our Western norms have moved us away from truly accepting a person's departure as a natural part of life, we have also moved away from the family structure of the extended family who were able to share the care of elderly and infirm relatives to situations where the burden often falls on a single person whose life becomes a treadmill of caring for a shell and who therefore themselves have no quality of life.

None of the above is intended to suggest or even contemplate euthanasia or assisted suicide, but when one is considering best interests one should not assume that taking a decision to treat rather than not to treat is necessarily the low risk option for the patient or family — in fact it could even be said that it is a morally bankrupt decision because they might ultimately be acting in their best interests, not the patient's.

1.4.3 *Beneficence versus malfeasance*

Ethically it is not enough for someone who has made professional oaths to just not cause harm, but to actually attempt to do some good. The issue is that different people will judge the two options in different ways depending upon their interests, relationships, and values and they may not always align with those of the surgeon, even if they are no less valid and reasoned.

It is easy to give greatest credence to those other parties whose views most closely align with those of the prevailing view of the medical team and not necessarily with the views of those who know the patient best.

It is self-evident that the applicability of certain surgical interventions is very situation-dependent and therefore something that would and "should" be the obvious choice in someone who is otherwise fit and healthy might not be a reasonable approach for certain others who are both in very different physical circumstances and who have expressed views upon what they believed was in their own best interests.

Of course it is difficult to know with any certainty what the particular patient might wish in terms of intervention or otherwise in particular circumstances because ultimately people might change their mind and one can take the decision in line with what "might reasonably be expected" in the circumstances.

Perhaps it might be expected that the "do nothing" option would be the hardest for a surgical team to accept, given that they are trained to try to save lives by action and the prospect of inaction which is bound to result in the death of the patient is not an easy one. But in the same token the action of doing something might actually cause the very harm they would aim to avoid — in which case the action is not for the good of the patient but actually for the benefit of the surgical team.

1.4.4 *Judging motive*

Often when weighing up best interests one has to consider how the motives of the people involved play into their views. Of course there is no simple answer and sometimes the answer is obviously that trust has to be placed in the professionals in acute and emergency situations (though even then a cool and questioning head may be the critical difference).

In other cases of either planned or elective surgery it is the willingness of the surgical team to engage with the patient to ensure that they have given truly informed consent or determined best interests, as opposed to gaining a signature which is universally accepted as not necessarily proof of anything.

In the case of a person lacking capacity the unspoken truths may be the ones really driving the decision — perhaps the family feel guilt at not having been supportive enough or have selfish motives for wanting the person to have a procedure just so they do not feel responsible or similar — whatever the circumstances the motive should be to clearly act in the patient's best interests and not anyone else's.

1.5 The Treatment Roadmap

It might be helpful to break down the treatment process into a number of parts:

1. Diagnosis of issue/condition.
2. Determination of treatment options (surgical or not).
3. Understanding of the range of surgical options (from aggressive to do nothing).
4. Choice of option (informed consent) or best interests.
5. Surgery.
6. Post surgery.

1.5.1 *Diagnosis*

Since the focus is on surgery it might be reasonable to start at "understanding surgical options" but that assumes that the patient understands and accepts that they have a condition in the first place for which the treatment by surgery is an option. Since the surgeon is by nature not the first professional to see the patient it might be assumed that by virtue of the patient's presence they accept the requirement, however it would seem prudent that the first step should be to understand the patient's state of mind and therefore their ability to make rational decisions.

1.5.2 *Understanding treatment options*

The patient generally arrives at a surgical option via referral from a process which starts with some type of ailment or complaint and travels through a referral process until it is established that one of the options is surgery. It is never the only option as there is always the "do nothing" option even if that would result in death.

Where surgery and other treatment are inextricably entwined it is important that the patient has the ability to understand how the various treatments are going to work and an idea of who to refer to at any given point and knows how to slow, stop, or even accelerate the process by referring to a person or team who take overall responsibility for their care. It may be more "efficient" as a process for the "flow" of patients to work in a certain way but patients are human and want some continuity and to feel that they as an individual matter and are not just an anonymous hospital number.

Just as the referring team should contextualise where surgery fits into the treatment options, the receiving surgical team should give the same message from their side so the patient understands that there is continuity and consistency.

1.5.3 *What is the range of possible options?*

Once the patient has a referral to a surgical team it falls upon the surgical team (and ideally the actual surgeon) to take the patient through the option process before any intervention happens.

Simplistically most patients want to understand their condition, to know why they need whatever procedure it is that is recommended, and if there any alternatives or consequences to not doing that specific procedure.

For a simple procedure where the patient understands and agrees with both the need for and the type of intervention, it is a simple process. For more complicated proposals with more options/higher risks it may be more time consuming and laborious. The goal however should be the same — to enable the patient to give informed consent.

The general success of a procedure is not a reason to spend less time on the consent process and also there should be some consideration taken to explaining if and when the particular surgeon's or facility's results are not as successful as the norm — perhaps because the cases have been more complex or inherently risky.

Of course there may be subtle nuances in the options — such as the consequences of delaying treatment to improve outcome (i.e., by the patient having chemotherapy, losing weight, or stopping smoking) — and these should also be discussed in detail.

1.5.4 *Patient assumptions*

In general the patient should be entitled to assume a number of facts:

1. That the proposed procedure is in fact necessary or desirable.
2. That the surgeon proposing it is competent to carry it out (has the necessary training, skills, and equipment).
3. That they are fully informed about whether it is experimental, the inherent risks and the possible outcomes.

1.5.4.1 *Professional competence*

There may be cases where the surgeon's results are less successful than the average and it should go without saying that if a patient asks for that sort of information they should be given the facts. However optimistic the surgeon might be in a particular case it cannot possibly be right to "fudge" the answer to a patient, even if it results in the patient refusing consent.

Regardless of the legal position, ethically, a patient has the right to be provided with as much information as they need in order to determine whether they can put their trust in a particular surgeon.

Just as medical professionals should be protected from vexatious and malicious complaints, there ought to be a situation that equally protects patients from unknowingly being placed in the hands of someone whose skill levels are not "top notch" or whose current results might indicate a question about their more recent competence. Obviously this is situational depending on where the results are in a spectrum — if all surgeons' results are within a tight cluster then "below average" could be marginal, but to look at either the mean or the average in isolation could be very misleading.

It is self-evident that a surgeon who is a real danger to patients should be prevented from operating at all, and it is incumbent upon their fellow professionals and the management body of the hospital to ensure that this is enabled in such a way as not to "shoot the messenger". In more enlightened private sector companies this might include "Speak Up lines" and the like.

However it is equally important that information which might be pertinent to the patient giving informed consent is available, if requested, in an unbiased way, even if receipt of that information might lead to the patient not giving consent. The legal position might be clear but it is also a clear ethical error to withhold information which might lead the patient to a different decision.

1.5.4.2 Full disclosure

Obviously certain procedures are by nature more inherently risky and patients need to be able to understand that, but that does not mean that the patient is not entitled to make that decision.

In especially complex issues, where perhaps the full extent of the situation is not predictable, then the process may be even longer — the various options need to be discussed and the patient needs to understand the "worst case" scenario as well as the "best case" scenario.

Ideally the patient should have time to digest the information and come back and ask more questions if applicable. Patients should also be encouraged to take notes, write important information down, and have access to up-to-date documentation which describes the process if possible. It should also be noted that out of date information can cause undue concern to the patient if the same process is not adhered to. If the particular situation dictates that it is not relevant to conform strictly to the norm that should be clear in the information the patient is given, again to ensure that the patient is not unduly concerned.

The "ideal" surgeon needs two parallel areas of particular skill — the medical/surgical one and the ability to communicate perhaps complicated processes in a manner which the patient and/or their family understand.

This should mean that the surgeon who is to undertake any procedure meets with the patient to discuss the option(s) and what the consequences might be. When a patient entrusts themselves to the trauma of surgery the least that the surgeon can do is to respect that trust by meeting them first (and not in the operating theatre).

1.5.4.3 *Communication styles and methods*

Each patient is different and the inability of a particular patient to understand jargon, large volumes of information, or perhaps language does not mean that the patient is unable or unwilling to make their own treatment decisions; it just means that the communication methods might have to be adapted.

The use of props, tools, and presentation material can make a fundamental difference to making the patient comfortable and to empower them to make the right decision for themselves. There is no reason for this not to be optimised by holding workshops, encouraging patient interaction, or even making use of DVDs, flip cards, or other items which use a variety of methods to engage the patient's understanding and therefore their ability to make the decision.

Aside from the legal requirement to gain consent it seems obvious that a patient who understands and feels that they made their own choice is going to be more likely to be compliant with future treatment and better able to deal with any unforeseen and negative consequences which might arise.

1.5.4.4 *Statistics*

Statistics are routinely used to describe the risk of an operation but in reality there is only one statistic that counts for the patient — did it achieve the desired outcome or not? It is no comfort whatsoever to hear that in 97% of cases the procedure is successful if you end up as one of the people in the 3%.

Also quoting statistics can be downright misleading — as far back as 1954 Darrell Huff wrote the imaginatively entitled book *How to Lie with Statistics*, so the use of them should be simple, appropriate, and relevant to the particular situation. If a new technique is to be used that significantly affects some key process then quoting statistics relating to the "usual" technique is misleading.

Finally what are the consequences of being on the "unsuccessful" side of the statistics? A 95% success rate is not as impressive if the 5% consequence is death, whilst a 50% statistic where the other 50% is "no change" might be an easier choice.

At the end of the consent process the idea is that the patient has made a decision on the course of action, however it does not automatically follow that if the decision is irrational, or the patient refuses to make one, the ethical and moral responsibilities of the surgeon end there. Ethically it is appropriate to attempt to find out why the patient is behaving as they are — is there a phobia, belief, or emotion that drives them to that position? If there is, can it be addressed or treated such that it is removed from the process and the patient has a better basis on which to base their decision making?

1.5.5 *Surgery*

In an ideal situation the surgery is carried out at the right time and in the best interests of the patient and the objective is successfully accomplished. However it may not happen in that way and this can be another area which is fraught with both ethical and emotional issues as well as the obvious physical consequences to the patient.

At this point it should be noted that for various (and possibly good) reasons the surgeon may have delegated much of the consent process to someone else or even that the surgeon has to be changed at the last minute. From a patient's point of view this is not ideal because much of their commitment has to be based on trust and if they have not met the actual surgeon doing the procedure then how can they be expected to place this enormous trust in them?

A basic ethical behaviour and even courtesy should be that the actual surgeon meets and talks to the patient before the operation and allows the patient to reinforce their consent, even indirectly via their actions.

What should always be remembered is that the patient is the one who will truly have to live (or if the issue was fatal, their family) with the consequences. Whatever sanction/personal feeling of accountability might result for the surgeon (whether legal, professional, or personal) it is not going to be the same as the consequence for the patient and the patient should be the person kept at the front of the mind at the time — to help or lessen the consequences even just by moral support.

1.5.6 *Post surgery*

Whilst the surgeon may be supported by a multidisciplinary team it would seem obvious to the patient that the conclusion of the actual surgery ought not to mean the end of the surgeon's interest in that patient. The surgeon should retain responsibility to discuss the success or otherwise of the surgery with the patient, and then explain any handover to other healthcare professionals in such a way that the patient does not feel abandoned and helpless, but rather that the handover is done at the appropriate time and with sufficient communication and notice.

1.6 When Things go Wrong

Generally patients understand that sometimes things happen which were not supposed to — either that the patient has a surprise for the doctor or that a mistake is made by the surgical team. In either of these cases the outcome can be less desirable than anticipated. What should happen then?

The patient is not an object and, in addition to whatever hospital process is required in these circumstances, the surgical team should do the following:

- Explain what happened and what was done about it.
- Ensure that the explanation is done by a member of the team that the patient is familiar with — i.e., not someone junior they have never seen before.

- Do not try to "blame" the patient by asserting that (especially if it is without foundation) it is somehow the patient's fault.
- If the patient has done something which has caused a problem — like eating when they were supposed to be "nil by mouth" — then that should be stated in a matter of fact manner but without "pointing the finger". There is plenty of time for the patient to live with the consequences.
- If it is clear that human error is to blame then an apology or at least an acknowledgement should be made.

In many US states there are either "I'm sorry" laws or laws prohibiting an apology within 24 hours from affecting medical litigation. A University of Michigan study showed the reduction in litigation costs from $3 m to $1m and in the number of cases from 262 to 114 over a four-year period following the introduction of a Medical Error Disclosure Program which demonstrates that not only is this the ethical thing to do, but there are financial benefits to this.

Conversely a Harvard study found that there were fewer trials with Medical Error disclosure but the payouts increased — again on an ethical front it can be argued that to inflict possibly years of litigation on a patient who has suffered harm is intensely unethical and therefore if they are getting a higher payout it reflects more accurately the harm that they have suffered and it is only right morally and legally that they get a fair compensation.

The fact is that an error is no less an error if it is either denied or obscured — for most patients the lack of admission to the facts results in even more harm than may have been done by the error or errors in the first place. Patients should not have to go through trying statutory or other processes to get the facts of a situation and it is disingenuous to try and obscure the facts for fear of litigation.

A good doctor will take on board all the facts, consider what could and should have been done better, and ensure that the same mistake is never repeated. A poor doctor will try to deny responsibility, avoid self-review, and will most likely repeat the mistake. Perhaps, if they are lucky, they will forget that patient because they get lost in a morass of other situations, but a fundamental error will never be forgotten by the patient because they have to live with the consequences of that error for the rest of their lives.

A patient never goes into treatment thinking "never mind if it goes wrong — I can always get cash" because what they want is the best outcome from the procedure and their health, not money — it may be that financial settlement can help ameliorate the damage suffered by the patient, but it is never a substitute for good care. Of course there are patients who are greedy and may seek to unjustly enrich themselves, but in the main it is most unlikely to happen because the average patient is as likely to behave in a fraudulent way as the average doctor is to seek to harm.

In all aspects of life people are rewarded by their economic worth not by their moral worth, hence why bankers get huge rewards and why others in more "worthy" jobs get paid relatively paltry amounts. In the UK in particular, emphasis is placed on compensating for monetary loss rather than quality of life or trauma (both emotional and physical) which does end up with medical settlements giving curious justice. It seems most unlikely that any patient would rather have the compensation, however substantial it might be, rather than the outcome that was desired in the first place. Money does not compensate for a lifetime blighted by error.

1.7 Elective Surgery and Ethics

Increasingly people are turning to surgery to change their lives in a way that was not contemplated even a couple of decades ago. It used to be that surgery was given on a strictly serious need basis — to fix a physical problem for which there was no alternative. Increasingly it has moved from the strictly necessary (where the boundaries are continually being expanded as research opens up new possibilities) to other areas where it can most politely be described as a lifestyle choice.

These tend to be in the areas of plastic and weight loss surgery as well as child birth. Of course they were all developed in response to real physical need but there has been an expansion into vanity — the desire to look like someone else, never age, or lose weight the easy way. The stories of so called "yummy mummies" having tummy tucks at the same time as their elective caesarean (maybe anecdotal but a disturbing concept even in abstract); celebrities having repeated plastic surgery so they look grotesque not youthful — how does that translate into "the patient's best interests"?

As importantly, does the surgeon have a responsibility even in elective surgery to say no, even if a competent patient requests a procedure that they fully understand?

What about those people who start showing signs of treating surgery as part of the body maintenance regime — how much should the surgeon be responsible for counselling caution as these are not procedures without risk? That would be up to the conscience of the surgeon, but they should never forget that potential patients might be just as vulnerable and in need of guidance if they are going for a truly lifestyle choice rather than a life-supporting result.

It is disturbing when, just as with retailer sales, plastic surgeons are emailing or posting out discount vouchers via women's magazines or websites. Since no surgery is entirely without risk, the patient likely has the feeling that the surgeon's innate professionalism will be the same in any circumstances.

1.8 Summary

To return to the questions posed at the beginning of the chapter: What might an average patient consider to be the ethical issues in surgery? Does a patient even consider that the surgeon might not behave ethically and if not what does an average patient think are the motivations and principles that a surgeon is governed by?

The average patient does not necessarily think of these concepts couched in the language of ethics — patients tend to believe that surgery will be undertaken at the right time, for the right reasons, and for their benefit.

Patients generally see medicine and surgery as a vocation and not merely a job, and want to be able to trust that their surgeon's motives are at all times altruistic and not self-serving or money making. Most patients go into surgery wanting to trust and rely on their surgeon, and mostly that works very well.

An "inexperienced" patient soon realises that there are three phases of surgery:

- Preparation/consent.
- Execution.
- The aftermath.

All these are orchestrated by the surgeon and, in an ideal situation, at the end of it the surgeon can reflect on a job well done and the patient on a health benefit.

Even if things do not go according to plan, sensitive and appropriate actions by the surgeon can make the difference between feelings of helplessness and betrayal and mere regret and acceptance.

2

Consent for Clinical Interventions and Medical Research

Miran Epstein

Since the mid twentieth century, the doctrine of informed consent has become the most important tenet of medical ethics worldwide. This chapter provides a systematic critical overview of the doctrine. By means of a structural-contextual analysis, it shows that there is a gap between what the doctrine appears to do and what it actually does. This gap requires us to reassess its social role, history, and morality.

2.1 The Traditional Doctor–Patient Relationship and its Ethics

The discussion on informed consent could benefit from a brief presentation of the *fiduciary ethics* that preceded it, starting rather with the *fiduciary doctor–patient relationships* they regulated.

A fiduciary relationship is a power-wise asymmetrical social relation where in the informed and competent party acts responsibly in the best interests of the uninformed and incompetent party who reciprocates with trust and, if applicable, obedience.

Fiduciary relationships existed, and in some cases continue to exist, for example, between agent and principal, trustee and testator, guardian and ward, attorney and client, partner and partner, director and shareholder, teacher and pupil, parent and child, etc. Just before the mid twentieth century, they prevailed in all countries between doctors and patients as well. The doctors supposedly knew best how to treat their patients and were thus expected to take charge of their care. Correspondingly, the patients were deemed ignorant of their own good and were thus expected to trust their doctors and obey their instructions.

In each of the pertinent areas, the fiduciary relationship was regulated by a corresponding ethic. In European medicine, many of the ethics had first drawn their premises directly from the *Hippocratic Oath* of the late fifth century BC [1]. In the late eighteenth century, medicine in Anglo-Saxon countries embraced modified ethics containing a set of new principles developed by the English physician Thomas Percival (1740–1804) [2,3]. In the US, it took the Percivalean ethic another five decades to be replaced by the *American Medical Association* (AMA) *Code of Ethics* (1847), a code that has since been amended several times [4]. These medical ethics may have differed from one another in certain respects. However, common to all of them were the fiduciary principles of *avoiding harm* (*non nocere*) and *doing good* (beneficence).

Let us note that in the fiduciary era patients agreed to and occasionally refused interventions proposed by their doctors, *as they do now*. Refusal was probably not very common, though, either because patients trusted their doctors or because they feared their reaction. Indeed, refusal was frowned upon, whereas now it is regarded as a basic right of most patients. More importantly, during the most part of the fiduciary era, medicine and its ethic were separated from the state and its ethic, i.e., the law. This meant, among other things, that, unlike the current situation, the patients' choices were subject to no legal conditions and had no legal implications. As a matter of fact, even after US medicine had sworn an allegiance to the state in the mid nineteenth century, it took the state roughly a century until it launched a fully fledged attack on the traditional fiduciary medical order and its ethic.

2.2 The Contractual Relationship and the Doctrine of Informed Consent

Indeed, things changed in the second half of the twentieth century, first in medical research (since the late 1940s) and then in the clinical sphere as well (since the early 1970s). Starting in Anglo-Saxon countries and rapidly becoming global, the change involved three apparent aspects.

One aspect was *critical*: the medical collective has gradually come to perceive the traditional fiduciary order as paternalistic, harmful, and immoral. Describing the primary role of early *bioethics* (the predominantly applied-philosophical clinical-academic discipline that studies issues of ethical interest arising in medicine and related areas, provides advisory and educational services concerning such issues, and is the quintessential institution and social agent of contemporary medical ethics), the American bioethicist Arthur Caplan said,

> The Freddy Kruger of bioethics for the better part of two decades has been the doctor who pushes his or her values onto the patient. This devil has been completely exorcised and a large part of contemporary bioethics scholarship seems to be devoted to the task of assuring that the paternalistic doctor stays dead and buried [5].

Another aspect of the change was *relational*: the medical collective has actually replaced the traditional fiduciary relationships with different kinds of relationships: *contractual relationships*.

Contractual relationships are taken to be power-wise symmetrical. They involve some sort of exchange ("a contract") between seemingly equal parties, each of whom is driven by one's own interest only, each of whom is taking *private responsibility* for one's own choices.

Private responsibility means two things. First, it means that if something went wrong for one party as a result of their own choice, they could blame themselves only. Second, it means that, if their choice resulted in harm to the other party, they might be liable to sanctions that are specified in the law and/or the pertinent ethic and are enforced by an appropriate institution thereof.

At present, there are two kinds of contracts in our society: a *general social contract* and various *private contracts*.

The general social contract is lawful in principle. It involves the state on the one hand and all eligible private parties (individuals, groups, or institutions) on the other hand. To be more specific, it applies automatically to the state, assuming that it is invariably able to take private responsibility for its choices regardless of their nature and irrespective of their lawfulness. On the other hand, it applies only to private parties that are deemed able to take private responsibility for their choices regardless of their nature and lawfulness and irrespective of whether or not they have anything to do with any private contract. The general social contract is not an option for the state and the eligible private parties. None can escape from it.

By contrast, private contracts may or may not be lawful in principle. They only involve private parties that are deemed able to take private responsibility for their choices. They also differ from the general social contract in that they are optional. In other words, the eligible parties may choose either to enter the contract in question on the basis of some common interest, or to not do so if no common interest could be established. In any case, however, they will take private responsibility for their choices. Thus, even if they choose to refuse to enter the private contract, they will still be bound by the general social contract.

The third aspect of the change was *ethical*. The medical collective replaced the local ethics that had regulated the traditional fiduciary relationships with new ethics that fitted the contractual relationships. The new ethics have gradually converged on a single global ethical doctrine. This doctrine defines inclusion and exclusion criteria for entering the contract in question, asserts the tests that are supposed to ensure that these criteria have been met, sets the measures that must be taken when they have not been met, specifies the sanctions and remedies for breach of the contract, establishes oversight and enforcement institutions, and furnishes the corresponding justifications.

The contractual shift warrants several clarifications.

First, it has cut across the entire medical board: at present, contractual relationships feature in most medical interactions. The traditional fiduciary relationships have been elbowed aside and are now confined to exceptional circumstances only.

Second, at present, different medical contracts may involve different parties, e.g., doctors and other healthcare professionals, medical scientists, patients, healthy researchees in clinical and other medical trials, collectives of medical stakeholders (the general public and the state, for example), private healthcare payers, healthcare providers, private suppliers and subcontractors, etc. Some contracts involve neither a doctor nor a patient. For example, a contract may involve a healthcare institution on the one hand

and a private-sector subcontractor on the other hand. Other contracts involve either a doctor or a patient, but not both. For example, in public healthcare systems, one contract typically involves the medical institution *qua* service provider and the patient *qua* service consumer, while another contract involves the institution *qua* employer and the doctor *qua* employee. In such systems there is usually no direct contract between the doctor and the patient. The former enters the contract with the latter merely as a delegate of his or her employer. Direct contracts between doctor and patient exist primarily in private-sector healthcare settings. However, they may be accidentally established in public settings as well, for example, when a doctor makes a therapeutic–prognostic promise to the patient. That making such a promise is currently considered unethical does not in itself affect the validity of the contract in question.

Third, as said, contractual relationships are deemed to be power-wise symmetrical. Thus, the corresponding ethic uses the same criteria of eligibility for all parties involved. For example, both the medical party and the patient must be *competent, informed,* and *free* in order to enter the contract in question. At the same time, however, for each party the ethic uses different tests and different sanctions for breach of the contract. This stems merely from the different contractual terms (conditions) that apply to each. For example, the test assessing the doctor's competence (e.g., graduating from an acknowledged medical school and having no criminal record) differs from the test assessing the patient's competence, because each is subject to different contractual terms and obligations.

Having said that, most medico-ethical discussions that deal with contractual relationships in medicine focus strictly on the doctrines that apply to individuals and collectives that are about to enter a contract with the medical party, and so will we.

The contractual doctrine that applies to individuals has evolved since the beginning of the twentieth century through a progressive series of legal cases. However, it was consolidated first in the US in the early 1970s. It is called *informed consent* (the term has since also come to be used in the context of non-medical contracts involving individuals) [6]. An analogue doctrine, which regulates contracts that involve collectives rather than individuals, evolved in parallel. Let us call it *informed consensus.* At present, its main institutions include oversight committees, public consultations, referenda, and parliamentary elections to the degree that they concern medical and healthcare policy. These collective institutions approve or reject collective medical contracts.

Fourth, both informed consent and informed consensus are currently enshrined in two different ethical systems: *medical ethics*, namely the collective conscience of medicine, and *the law of the state* where it happens to be the collective conscience of the general electorate. Both systems treat the doctrines somewhat differently, though: relative to the law, medical ethics imposes on the medical party stricter terms, whereas relative to medical ethics, the law imposes on the medical party stricter sanctions for breach of the terms as these are defined by its own standard.

Having said that, the law as a whole has now become an integral part of medical ethics (the *ethical doctor* is supposed to be, among other things, also a law-abiding citizen). This means that the law defines the minimum standard of the ethic as far as the terms are concerned and the maximum standard as far as the sanctions are concerned.

Finally, informed consent and informed consensus are the tenets of contemporary medical ethics. They jointly form its quintessential elements, namely the elements that distinguish it from its fiduciary predecessors.

2.3 Informed Consent: General Considerations

The doctrine of informed consent rests on the premise that subjects have a right to choose to enter or to not enter any lawful medical contract, provided that they are eligible, that is, able to take private responsibility for the choice in question.

The doctrine works on the correct understanding that individuals — the patient themselves or their legal representative — may or may not be able to take private responsibility, and that they should take such responsibility only if the necessary and sufficient conditions for taking it have been met. It also acknowledges correctly that these conditions (criteria) are partly internal and partly external to the subject. Accordingly, it defines a set of tests that must be passed in order to establish that these conditions have indeed been met. Passing these tests forms one of the three essential elements of any contract, the other two being giving/refusing consent and, at any rate, taking private responsibility for one's choice. Note that these criteria and tests apply, *mutatis mutandis,* to collectives as well (informed consensus).

While the doctrine of informed consent focuses mainly on the subject who considers entering a medical contract, it imposes on the medical party the duty to ensure, before seeking the consent of the subject, that the criteria of the subject's eligibility have been met. Having said that, it must be emphasized that this is ultimately a legal matter. Thus, in case of dispute, the court will have the final say. Five points need to be made in this regard.

(1) The court's decision is likely to rest on the testimony of an expert witness. Competence, for example, is typically assessed by a psychiatrist.

(2) The party wishing to challenge the status quo has the onus of proving the point in question.

(3) The court does not consider the validity of the evidence in light of the rigorous standard that applies in the criminal law (*beyond reasonable doubt*), but rather in light of the laxer standard that applies in the civil law (*balance of probabilities*).

(4) The contract in question will be regarded as legally valid — in other words, it will receive the sponsorship of the state — if it is lawful in principle, if the parties passed the pertinent tests, and if they actually made their choices. Having said that, a lawful contract may be regarded as legally valid even when some of the tests have not been passed. For example, failure of the medical party to offer the subject adequate information may amount to negligence. However, it is unlikely to render the contract void.

(5) The legal validity of the contract does not depend on the way the consent was given, namely on whether it was explicit, implied, or of an opt-out kind, signed and/or witnessed or just documented. The way the consent is given has bearing only on the strength of the evidence that it was indeed given. For this reason, the medical party tends to insist on the subject's *signed consent* if the patient seems to be litigious or if the medical intervention involves a relatively high rate of litigation, as is the case with surgery, medical research, invasive diagnostic procedures, high risk pharmacological interventions, etc.

2.4 Informed Consent: Criteria of Eligibility

The criteria of eligibility to give/refuse consent — that is to say, the criteria attesting to the ability of the subject to take private responsibility for the consequences of one's choice — are threefold:

(1) The subject must be *competent* to make the choice in question.
(2) The subject must be *informed* about the different options and the expected consequences of each.
(3) The subject must make their choice *freely*.

Let us expand on these criteria.

Competence. To be eligible to give consent, the subject must be competent. Competence, or mental capacity, means having an *abstract will* plus the ability, given the two other criteria, to translate this abstract will into a communicable *concrete will*. It is the set of the task-specific cognitive properties and capacities that are necessary and sufficient for taking private responsibility for one's choice, given that the other two criteria have been met. These properties and capacities are as follows:

(1) Having pertinent values and goals, namely having an abstract will (e.g., to get better).
(2) Having the ability to distinguish between valid/relevant/full and invalid/irrelevant/partial information, respectively.
(3) Having the ability to understand, process, and remember the pertinent information.
(4) Having the ability to tailor the choice to one's values and goals, namely, to make a rational choice expressing one's concrete will (e.g., to have the proposed operation).
(5) Having the ability to communicate one's choice, namely concrete will.

Informedness. The subject must be in possession of all the information relevant to the choice in question.

Freedom. The subject must have more than one option to choose from, and be free from any duress, whether external or internal, in choosing among the different options.

2.5 The Tests

Two general points pertaining to the tests of competence, informedness, and freedom must be emphasized. First, the tests are all *threshold* (pass–fail) tests. They regard their objects (the criteria) not as continua, but rather as binary either/or qualities. This means that different subjects are equally eligible or ineligible to give informed consent, all other things being equal. Second, the tests set the pass threshold very low. In other words, it does not take much to be considered eligible.

2.5.1 *Tests of competence*

There are two kinds of tests of competence, depending on the circumstances.

In the "normal" default case, a *status test* will apply. This test, called *the presumption of competence*, "deduces" the competence of the subject or their legal representative from age and "sound mindedness", i.e., being conscious and not behaving in a way that suggests incompetence. Thus an adult (and, in the UK, minors older than 16 for example) who seems to be of sound mind is taken to be competent as far as medical contracts are concerned.

The exceptional non-default case pertains to the person whose previously established or presumed incompetence (see below) has been called into question either by themselves (attempting to obtain authority to make their own choice, typically to refuse a particular medical intervention) or by the medical party/a relative/the court (attempting to impose private responsibility on the subject). In such case, a *functional test* will apply. It assesses the person's *actual* choice-specific cognitive performance, i.e., the decision making process. According to this test, the faintest sign suggesting choice-specific competence will suffice to establish it [7].

2.5.2 *Tests of incompetence*

The assessment of *incompetence* is a mirror image of the assessment of competence.

A *functional test* of incompetence will apply when the person (wishing to exempt themselves from legal responsibility or to shift it to the medical party), the medical party, a third party such as a relative, or the court (wishing to protect the person) wish to challenge the presumption of competence.

A *status test* of incompetence will apply in two different circumstances. First, it applies to minors. In the UK, for example, minors under the age of 16 are presumed incompetent, although they have a right to try to challenge this presumption (eligible minors are called *Gillick/Fraser competent* [8]). In some other countries younger children do not have this right. Second, the status test applies to those who have already been established as incompetent by means of a functional test in the absence of new evidence of competence. According to this test, the status quo in itself should lead to the presumption that the person continues to be incompetent to give or refuse consent. This presumption is called the presumption of continuance. In effect, the presumption of continuance applies also in the case of subjects who were at some point presumed competent in the absence of new evidence to the contrary.

2.5.3 *Tests of informedness*

In *clinical settings*, the test of informedness regards the competent subject (or their legal representative) as informed if the medical party *offered* them *adequate information* concerning the proposed intervention. This means that refusal of the subject to accept the information or to make a choice on its basis cannot in itself count as failure to be informed. Thus a competent subject who rejected or ignored the information offered by the medical party would be presumed informed nevertheless. Presuming that they made an informed choice to not be informed, they would still have to take private responsibility for their choice.

In *research settings*, the test of informedness has a slightly higher threshold. It regards the competent subject as informed if the medical party offered them adequate information concerning the proposed intervention *and* made sure they understood it (in clinical settings the latter point is an ethical recommendation only, not an obligation) [9].

Although in practice the test of informedness applies to the competent subject only, it has potentially severe ethical and legal implications for the medical party as well. As previously stated, failure of the medical party to offer the competent subject adequate information would not invalidate the contract, but such a failure would be regarded as negligence. By contrast, failure of the medical party to offer the competent subject any information at all would render the contract void and the intervention a battery. In light of these points, we need to consider what counts as *adequate information.*

In the UK, until recently, the adequacy of the information offered to the competent subject by the medical party used to be measured by a general legal standard of medical proficiency called the *Bolam test* [10]. This test meant that, if the medical party reached the standard of "a responsible body of medical opinion", they were not negligent. Thus, adequate information was defined as information that was considered adequate by the pertinent medical body. Historically, this meant that doctors divulged to the competent subjects whose consent they sought relatively little information regarding the nature of the proposed intervention and particularly its *potential risks.*

Now, however, the standard is higher almost everywhere. The medical party is currently required to comply with the *prudent patient standard.* Accordingly, adequate information is regarded as information of amount and detail which the "reasonable patient" would deem adequate. Needless to say, the information may exceed even this standard, if the subject requests.

Regardless of the standard used, different countries require that the information be offered in different scopes. In the UK, for example, the information is normally offered succinctly and in lay terms. By contrast, in the US it tends to be exceptionally detailed and linguistically legalistic, especially in so far as the potential risks of the intervention in question are concerned.

At any rate, to be considered adequate, the information offered to the subject must contain the following minimum: the nature of the proposed intervention, the potential risks involved, potential conflicts of interests, the right to refuse the intervention or to withdraw consent at any time during the intervention without reprisal, and any other relevant information the subject would explicitly ask for. The test of informedness works on the assumption that failure of the subject to ask for any other information implies the subject's lack of interest therein.

It should be stressed that, in general, the standard of informational adequacy that applies in medical research settings is somewhat higher compared to the standard that applies in clinical settings. The difference is attributed to the fact that subjects are not expected to benefit from participating in medical research as opposed to clinical interventions.

Finally, a word about *subject/patient information sheets* (PIS). Medical ethics currently works on the premise that different subjects have different informational needs, all other things being equal. One subject may need more information and in a certain way, while another may need less information and in another way. The law, however, is blind to individual informational needs. For this reason, subjects are routinely given a *standard information sheet*, which is similar in essence to the part of any other standard contract which is called "terms and conditions". Thus, while the subject's declaration of informedness in the consent form is supposed to provide sufficient legal evidence that information has indeed been offered to them, the PIS provides sufficient legal evidence of informational adequacy.

2.5.4 *Tests of freedom of choice*

To ensure that the subject made their choice voluntarily, the tests of freedom check for two things.

First, the subject must have more than one option to choose from. In practice, this means that the medical party must clarify to the subject that the latter has a right to refuse the proposed intervention or withdraw their consent at any time during the intervention without reprisal. This vital element of informational adequacy is thus also a necessary condition of freedom of choice.

Second, the subject must not be coerced to choose any particular option. For example, evidence of explicit threats, which is relatively easy to furnish, is likely to render the contract void. Evidence of subtle pressures — e.g., emotional extortion, financial difficulties, and pressures resulting from interpersonal power relations — could do the same. However, it is more difficult to furnish. At any rate, the medical party must ensure that they do not put any undue pressure on the subject to make any particular choice. For example, doctors who wish to conduct research on their own patients must ask their colleagues to seek the consent of the patients. In order to avoid abuse of their position of power they must not do so themselves.

Ultimately, however, the subject themselves provides the proof of free-dom of choice by ticking the box on the consent form that says, "I confirm that my consent is voluntary".

2.6 Who Can Give Consent and Refusal?

The competent subject must normally make their choice themselves and by themselves alone. However, others may be involved as well.

In both clinical and research settings involving a competent minor, the medical party is strongly advised — not legally compelled — to seek the consent of a legal representative in addition to the consent of the minor. This is in order to prevent unnecessary conflicts. In research settings, a conflict between the decision of the minor and that of their legal repre-sentative should normally count as refusal. By contrast, in clinical settings concerning a critical intervention, the conclusive legal decision in case of conflict should be in accord with the best interests of the minor.

Until recently, different medico-legal systems used to treat the incom-petent adult differently. In the UK, for example, no one could give consent on behalf of an adult patient. In such a case, *the doctrine of best interests* prevailed, meaning that the medical party had the fiduciary duty to decide about the pertinent intervention according to what they considered as best for the patient. Now, however, the medical party may appeal to the doc-trine of best interests only when no personal legal representative of the patient is available.

In elective and emergency clinical settings, the legal representative of an adult may usually refuse any intervention including a life-saving one. Things differ somewhat when incompetent minors are involved. In elec-tive clinical settings, the legal representative may refuse any treatment. By contrast, in emergency clinical settings, the representative may not refuse interventions which the doctor deems vital to the health and life of the patient.

In elective medical research settings, consent must be sought from all competent subjects and legal representatives of incompetent ones.

In addition, a research ethics committee (in the US it is called an *independent review board*) must approve the study in principle (informed consensus). In rare cases, the committee may approve the research without consent at all (consent waiver); for example, when consent is difficult to seek, when consent could introduce bias, or — in emergency research settings — when no personal or *professional legal representative* is available, the research cannot be delayed, and participation in the research is deemed to be in the best interests of the patient (note that the presumption that participation in research can in principle be in the best interests begs the question).

A professional legal representative (PLR) is a person unrelated to the research who is appointed by the hosting healthcare institution. The role of this representative is to give consent on behalf of incompetent patients in emergency research settings on the basis of the presumption that the latter would have consented anyway, if they could [11]. To clarify, such a presumption does not appeal to the doctrine of best interests, but rather to knowledge of the patient's previously expressed wishes or, if such knowledge does not exist, to knowledge of what the "reasonable" patient would have wished in the case in question. The representative is thus supposed to "put themselves in the place of the patient" and deliver a *substitutive judgement* [12].

2.7 Advance Directives

Competent subjects may express their wishes — consent or refusal, not a demand of any particular treatment — concerning any particular future interventions in advance. This means that, if they become incompetent, their previously expressed wishes would have to be respected. In this sense, advance directives are simple extensions of the doctrine of informed consent.

Verbal or written advance directives are equally valid. However, the former are more likely to raise dispute. Having said that, written directives do not preclude the possibility of a later change of mind expressed verbally, or of reporting an alleged change of mind. At any rate, once advance directives are regarded as valid they will be binding on the medical party.

2.8 Assent and Dissent

As said, individuals who lack the mental capacity (competence) needed for entering a certain contract cannot consent to or refuse the intervention in question. Yet, such individuals may occasionally be able to express their *assent* to or *dissent* of that intervention. Assent and dissent are similar to consent and refusal, respectively, in that they all respect the person's *authority* to make one's own choice. However, the former differ from the latter in that they impose no private responsibility on the individual. Assent and dissent thus have no legal implications.

The assent/dissent of an incompetent person should be sought in addition to the consent/refusal of their legal representative. As a rule, in research settings, the person's dissent should prevail over their representative's consent.

2.9 Justifications for Informed Consent

The most common *ethical* justification for informed consent appeals to the assumption that it respects the right of the competent subject to make their own choices (the underlying ethical principle is called respect for the subject's autonomy). Indeed, it is widely believed that the subject who consents/refuses expresses their autonomy. Whether or not this is necessarily the case is, as we shall see, open to dispute.

The most common *legal* justification for informed consent pertains to the fact that contractual relationships privatize responsibilities and thus exempt the doctor from responsibility for the subject's choices. In this regard, the subject's informed consent protects the medical party from litigation concerning anything that may happen to the subject as a result of their own choices.

The most common *medical* justification appeals to the assumption that the act of seeking the subject's consent promotes trust and therefore enhances compliance, improves clinical outcome, and reinforces the social status of the medical professional.

Let us note, however, that fiduciary relationships are more likely to achieve these important goals. True, contractual relationships may involve trust, but only accidentally (and in some sense also inappropriately). Let us bear in mind that the parties to such relationships are driven by their own interests only and must take private responsibility for their choices. This means that none should trust the other. As a matter of fact, contractual relationships require mutual distrust, caution, and self-reliance.

2.10 The Official History of Informed Consent

If the ethical transformation in medicine and the rise of informed consent can indeed be described as the replacement of the paternalistic ethic by an ethic of respect for the patient's autonomy, and if this replacement can be described as *a shift of power from the doctor to the patient*, then the historical causes of this power shift must also have been the historical causes of the respective ethical shift.

This view was best expressed by Ruth Faden and Thomas Beauchamp in 1986:

> [Law] and ethics, as well as medicine itself, were all affected by issues and concerns in the wider society about individual liberties and social equality made all the more dramatic by increasingly technological, powerful, and impersonal medical care. ... [It] seems likely that increased legal interest in the right of self-determination and increased philosophical interest in the principle of respect for autonomy and individualism were but instances of the new rights orientation that various social movements of the last 30 years introduced into society. The issues raised by civil rights, women's rights, the consumer movement, and the rights of prisoners and the mentally ill often included healthcare components: reproductive rights, abortion and contraception, the right to healthcare information, access to care, human experimentation, and so forth. These urgent societal concerns helped reinforce public acceptance of the notion of rights as applied to health care.
>
> At the same time, the Nazi atrocities, and the celebrated cases of abuse of research subjects in the United States raised suspicions about the general trustworthiness of the medical profession. The rise of interest in informed consent in medical care in the second half of the twentieth century may have been as much a result of complex social forces changing the role and status of American medicine as a reaction to specific legal developments. An obvious example is found in the 1972 "Patient's Bill of

Rights" of the American Hospital Association. This bill was passed in large part because of consumer pressures for better care and facilities, as well as for more appropriate standards of respect. This increased respect was made manifest through provisions calling for recognition of the need to obtain informed consents and honor refusals of treatment [13].

To recap, Faden and Beauchamp maintained that the current duty of medical professionals to obtain informed consent from eligible subjects had been the result of a successful democratic reaction of the patient-consumer against an increasingly technological, impersonal, self-interested, untrustworthy, and inadequate medical care, a specific reaction that took place in the wider context of a successful social reaction against individual oppression and social inequality.

This view is now regarded as the official history of informed consent.

2.11 Problems of Historiography

However reasonable it may seem, the official history of informed consent has several shortcomings.

First, it fails to acknowledge that the real transition was from a fiduciary order to a contractual one. True, the contractual order effectively hands over the authority to the patient, and in this sense we are indeed dealing with a power shift whose beneficiary seems to be the patient. Having said that, at least in one respect, the contractual order also incurs a loss to the patient. They lost the caring doctor. Now they must take private responsibility for their own choices. The official explanation ignores this point altogether.

Second, it lacks specificity: it fails to account specifically for the rise of informed consent. The same circumstances it lists could have equally explained a number of alternative historical outcomes. For example, they could have explained the continuation of the fiduciary order with some reinforcement of the fiduciary ethics. Alternatively, they could have explained the rise of a doctrine of assent, which does not impose private responsibility on the patient, instead of the doctrine of consent, which does.

Moreover, the official history also lacks specificity as regards time and place. It notes correctly that the rise of the medico-ethical doctrine took place in the context of a general social-ethical transformation, that of the "1960s". However, it does not explain the latter at all. It also fails to explain why informed consent rose first in the US, why it emerged in Europe only a decade later, and why it has since been globalized, also appearing in many countries that had not gone through the "1960s".

Third, it fails to account for the fact that the ethical shift actually targeted primarily the benevolent medical paternalist, not the malevolent one. Indeed, the new ethic does not tackle the problem of malevolence any better than the old one.

Fourth, it works on the potentially false presumption that in the fiduciary era doctors indeed held the power. This may have been the case when medicine had been a guild, that is, before the mid nineteenth century. Later, however, they primarily became subcontractors on behalf of the state. It was the latter, then, that held the power.

Fifth, it wrongly regards the rise of informed consent as a successful reaction against a number of injustices. As a matter of fact, under the contractual arrangement, the patient has done increasingly badly. The same, incidentally, goes for the doctor. The official account gives us the false impression that the patient has been fully emancipated. The worldwide collapse of the public healthcare system, which does not collide with informed consent, indicates that this is not the case.

Finally, the official history fails to explain the gap that exists between the criteria of autonomy and the tests that are to ensure that they have been met. To be more specific, the criteria demand a lot, whereas the tests demand very little. In other words, the latter potentially impose private responsibility on patients who are not really privately responsible for their choices. This point, as I will now argue, is the key to a new understanding of the ethical shift.

2.12 Informed Consent Revisited

A rigorous structural-contextual analysis of informed consent reveals some disturbing points about it, points that have so far been hidden from the eye.

Let us start the analysis by noting that *private responsibility presupposes private will*. Indeed, a private will, and only a private will, entails private responsibility. Put differently, if the patient's will had been not private (privately formed) but rather *collective* (collectively formed) or, worse, *induced* manipulatively by some third party, then the patient should not have been given private responsibility for their choices.

Let us note, for example, that the test of competence requires that the patient have values and goals (an abstract will), which are then to be translated into a concrete choice (a concrete will). It works on the assumption that both wills are privately formed. Indeed, it gives us the false impression that both the abstract will and the concrete will were formed under circumstances over which the patient had full control. It ignores the patient's socio-economic background, education, exposure to manipulative advertisements of various kinds, etc., all of which are shaping both wills in such a way that cannot justify imposing private responsibility on the patient.

Thus, the first question we, patients (and doctors) need to ask ourselves is why we embraced an ethical doctrine that falsely presupposes that our will is private and hence falsely imposes private responsibility on us. Let us leave this question open for now.

The second point pertains to the notion of *freedom of choice* implicit in the doctrine. As we have seen, the doctrine regards the patient's choice as a free one if (1) they have more than one option to choose from and (2) they are not coerced to choose any particular option.

This notion of freedom of choice may seem reasonable. However, I would like to draw attention to the fact that it is only a particular notion of freedom of choice, and that there is also one philosophical view that denies the possibility of freedom of choice altogether, and one alternative notion of freedom of choice.

Both views take their point of departure in the correct premise that people make their choices under circumstances on which they have no control. As Karl Marx observed,

> Men make their own history, but they do not make it as they please; they do not make it under self-selected circumstances, but under circumstances existing already, given and transmitted from the past [14].

This observation may lead to two radically different conclusions: either that the notion of freedom of choice makes no sense at all or that it makes sense only when the circumstances offer people *certain* options.

According to the latter view, the *nature* of the options available to the person, as opposed to the mere *existence* of several options to choose from, is crucial to whether the choice will be free or not.

We do not have to accept this view or another. However, we must ask ourselves why we embraced a doctrine with a limited notion of freedom of choice, a notion that focuses strictly on the *existence* of options to choose from.

The third point takes us to the fact that the tests assessing the ability to take private responsibility for one's choices have a low pass threshold. The typical justification for that goes as follows:

> Overprotection is a form of dehumanisation and lack of respect; for example, to classify persons as incompetent in order to protect them from their own judgment is the worst form of abuse [15].

We may agree about that. However, we must also remember that the same criticism applies to underprotection as well. True, tests with a low pass threshold would not entail underprotection if those who passed them could equally pass the highest threshold tests, such that ensured *absolute autonomy*, which is exactly what the criteria of informed consent presuppose (after all, less than absolute autonomy would not justify taking private responsibility for one's choices). But this is not the case: patients are often given private responsibility for their choices although they were far from absolutely autonomous [16–26]. In other words, the presumption that people who pass the tests of informed consent can indeed take private responsibility for their choices is a *legal fiction* [27].

For example, let us take a quick look at one issue pertaining to the prevailing notion of adequate disclosure. You may remember that according to this notion, the medical party to the contract is obliged to disclose any potential conflicts of interest (particularly such that involve financial interests). The doctrine of consent works on the assumptions that such disclosure covers all conceivable conflicts of interests and that it precludes the possibility that the interests that are in conflict with the duty of care will prevail. This is not necessarily the case. In this regard, such a disclosure turns the patient information sheet into a potentially manipulative disclaimer.

The suggestion that the professional legal representative in emergency research necessarily makes an independent pro-patient judgement is another example of the fictitious nature of consent.

In this light, we must ask ourselves why we embraced a doctrine that is strongly inclined to impose private responsibility on those who should not really take it.

The key to all these questions can be found where contractual relationships are the norm, that is to say, in the capitalist marketplace. Let us note that such relationships require a regulatory doctrine that presupposes the very possibility of private responsibility, even though there is no such thing, and imposes such a responsibility on players who pass ludicrous tests that seem to entail it. If the tests of eligibility to enter commercial contracts had a higher pass threshold, the capitalist economy could not survive for longer than five minutes.

Why is this point relevant to the understanding of the medico-ethical doctrine of informed consent? Because the doctrine did not rise only in the context of a wide social reaction against the old order, a reaction that — one must admit — has failed where it indeed tried to tackle its fundamentally capitalist essence, but also and perhaps above all in the context of a shift in the capitalist agenda. Indeed, the doctrine rose at a historical point in time wherein medicine in general and the doctor–patient relationship in particular (and many other social relationships as well, notably between parent and child, teacher and pupil, and state and citizen) moved from the capitalist sphere of *production*, where the labour force had to be repaired and put back to work, to the capitalist sphere of *exchange*, where commodities are bought and sold. This move, which features the decline of the welfare state and the rise of the parsimonious all-privatizing neoliberal state, was no longer compatible with fiduciary relationships regulated by fiduciary ethics. It required a contractual order with a contractual ethic, an ethic that speaks highly of respect for the patient's autonomy, patient-centred medicine, and freedom of choice, but all it does is turn the patient into an unwitting vulnerable agentless customer and the doctor into an unwitting subcontractor on behalf of preying sellers whose interests in human health are accidental at best.

References

[1] Edelstein L. *The Hippocratic Oath: Text, Translation and Interpretation.* Baltimore: Johns Hopkins University Press, 1943; p. 56.

[2] Percival T. *Medical Jurisprudence or a Code of Ethics and Institutes Adopted to the Professions of Physic and Surgery.* Manchester: privately circulated, 1794.

[3] Percival T. *Medical Ethics; or, a Code of Institutes and Precepts, Adapted to the Professional Conduct of Physicians and Surgeons.* London: J. Johnson, 1803.

[4] *Code of Medical Ethics of the American Medical Association.* Chicago: American Medical Association Press, May 1847.

[5] Caplan A.L. *If I Were a Rich Man Could I Buy a Pancreas? And Other Essays on the Ethics of Health Care.* Bloomington: Indiana University Press, 1992; p. 259.

[6] Beauchamp T.L. Informed consent: Its history, meaning and present challenges. *Cambridge Quarterly of Health Care Ethics* 2011; **20**(4): 515–523.

[7] Mental Capacity Act 2005: Chapter 9. http://www.legislation.gov.uk/ukpga/2005/9/pdfs/ukpga_20050009_en.pdf [accessed 4 March 2014].

[8] *Gillick* v *West Norfolk and Wisbech Area Health Authority* [1985] 3 All ER 402. http://www.bailii.org/uk/cases/UKHL/1985/7.html [accessed 4 March 2014].

[9] *WMA Declaration of Helsinki — Ethical Principles for Medical Research Involving Human Subjects,* Fortaleza, 2013. http://www.wma.net/en/30publications/10policies/b3/ [accessed 4 March 2014].

[10] *Bolam* v *Friern Hospital Management Committee* [1957] 1 WLR 582. http://oxcheps.new.ox.ac.uk/casebook/Resources/BOLAMV_1%20DOC.pdf [accessed 4 March 2014].

[11] The College of Emergency Medicine (UK). Acting as a Professional Legal Representative for Medical Research: Guidance from the FAEM Research Committee, 2005. www.collemergencymed.ac.uk/code/document.asp?ID=3172 [accessed 4 March 2014].

[12] Buchanan A.E. and Brock D.W. *Deciding for Others: The Ethics of Surrogate Decision Making.* Cambridge: Cambridge University Press, 1989; pp. 117–118.

[13] Faden R.R. and Beauchamp T.L. *A History and Theory of Informed Consent.* New York: Oxford University Press, 1986; p. 87.

[14] Marx K. *The Eighteenth Brumaire of Louis Bonaparte.* Rockville, MD: Serenity Publishers, 2009 [1852]; p. 9.

[15] Levine R.J. Informed consent. In Stephen G. Post (ed.) *Encyclopedia of Bioethics 3rd edition Vol. 3.* New York, NY: Thomson Gale, 1995; p. 1283.

[16] Fletcher J.C. Realities of patient consent to medical research. *Hastings Center Report* 1973; **1**: 39–49.

[17] Ingelfinger F.J. Informed (but uneducated) consent. *New England Journal of Medicine* 1972; **287**: 465–466.

[18] Palmer A.B. and Wohl J. Voluntary admission forms: Does the patient know what he's signing? *Hospital Community Psychiatry* 1972; **23**: 250–252.

[19] Meisel A. and Roth L.H. What we do and do not know about informed consent. *Journal of the American Medical Association* 1981; **246**: 2473–2477.

[20] Geller J.L. State hospital patients and their medication: do they know what they take? *American Journal of Psychiatry* 1982; **139**: 611–615.

[21] Byrne D.J., Napier A., and Cuschieri A. How informed is signed consent? *British Medical Journal* 1988; **296**: 839–840.

[22] Estey A., Wilkin G., and Dossetor J. Are research subjects able to retain the information they are given during the consent process? *Health Law Review* 1994; **3**: 37–41.

[23] Lawson S.L. and Adamson H.M. Informed consent readability: subject understanding of 15 common consent phrases. *IRB* 1995; **17**: 16–19.

[24] Fortney J.A. Assessing recall and understanding of informed consent in a contraceptive clinical trial. *Studies in Family Planning* 1999; **30**: 339–346.

[25] Leeb D., Bowers D.G. Jr, and Lynch J.B. Observations on the myth of informed consent. *Plastic & Reconstructive Surgery* 1976; **58**: 280–282.

[26] Cassileth B.R., Zupkis R.V., Sutton-Smith K., *et al.* Informed consent: why are its goals imperfectly realized? *New England Journal of Medicine* 1980; **302**: 896–900.

[27] Palmer A.B. & Wohl J. Voluntary admission forms: Does the patient know what he's signing? *Hospital Community Psychiatry* 1972; **23**: 250–252.

Additional Reading:

Brazier M. *Medicine, Patients and the Law. Third Edition.* London: Penguin Books, 2007; the chapter 'Agreeing to Treatment'.

Hope T., Savulescu J., and Hendrick J. *Medical Ethics and Law: The Core Curriculum.* Edinburgh: Churchill Livingstone, 2008; the chapter 'Consent'.

Jackson E. *Medical Law: Text, Cases and Materials.* Oxford: Oxford University Press, 2006; Chapters 4 and 5, pp. 180–313.

American Medical Association http://www.ama-assn.org/ama/pub/category/4608. html

BMJ website, a collection of articles on informed consent: http://bmj.bmjjournals. com/cgi/collection/informed_consent

Canadian Medical Association Journal http://www.cmaj.ca/cgi/collection/informed_ consent

General Medical Council: Seeking Patients' Consent — The Ethical Considerations. http://www.gmc-uk.org/standards/consent.htm, http://www.gmc-uk. org/standards/good.htm

Monash University (Australia) http://www.arts.monash.edu.au/bioethics/resources/
consent.html

University of Virginia (US) http://www.med-ed.virginia.edu/courses/rad/consent/

University of Washington School of Medicine http://depts.washington.edu/bio-
ethx/topics/consent.html, http://depts.washington.edu/bioethx/topics/infc.
html

A history of informed consent http://www.cnahealthpro.com/amt/consent_history.
html

3

Ethical Issues in Medical Confidentiality and Privacy

Philip Hébert

Maintaining confidentiality and respecting a patient's right to privacy are core duties or obligations of healthcare professionals. Long before modern law, Hippocrates cautioned that whatever one heard in the course of medical practice must "never be spread abroad" [1], the expectation being that doctors would not speak publicly about what they learned privately in attending to their patients. Such a prescription may be found in many cultures throughout the world. Islamic religious teaching and law have also long been protective of patient privacy [2]. Maintaining patient confidentiality is considered the "highest virtue of a Muslim physician" [3]. Buddhism similarly recognizes a patient's right to privacy and confidentiality [4].

But just what these notions entail for physicians and surgeons will vary from time to time and country to country. While professional medical practice acknowledges the obligations to respect these notions of confidentiality and privacy, subverting them under specific circumstances is also recommended or, at times, required. Determining when it is indeed appropriate to breach confidentiality and privacy can prove challenging for medical professionals. This chapter will outline some essential features of the "classical" concepts of confidentiality and privacy and then detail the exceptions to these principles. While the paper has an undeniable Anglo-American focus, many of the considerations apply to other countries as well.

In everyday practice, despite their avowed importance, informal breaches of confidentiality and privacy occur all the time: patients are discussed in halls and hospital elevators within earshot of visitors [5], a board with the names of the inpatients is easily seen by visitors approaching the nursing station of the neurosurgery ward, patients are discussed on internet chat sites, the surgical team on ward rounds talks to a patient about his post-operative bowel movements in full hearing range of the roommate on the other side of the curtain. The large number of people with access to the confidential information contained in the hospital chart — data clerks and hospital administration employees in addition to healthcare professionals — increases the risk that such information may be inappropriately accessed or misused.

More alarming breaches of confidentiality occur frequently as well. For example, an inquiry in the late 1970s into the confidentiality of health records in Canada revealed that confidential medical information was disclosed frequently and casually to the police by doctors and hospital employees without patient consent [6]. These circumstances are not unique to Canada [7]. The complexity and importance of medical information has resulted in information practices that seek to limit informal and serious breaches of medical privacy and confidentiality.

3.1 Confidentiality

3.1.1 *Definition*

"Confidentiality: the confiding of private or secret matters to another; the relation of intimacy between persons so confiding; confidential intimacy" [8].

Medical confidentiality, the duty of healthcare professionals to respect patient wishes regarding their private information, is considered essential for medical practice. It may be defined as "the obligations of individuals and institutions to use information under their control appropriately once it has been disclosed to them. One observes rules of confidentiality out of respect for, and to protect and preserve, the privacy of others" [9]. Confidentiality receives strong support from the two main schools in philosophy and law: consequentialism and deontology.

3.1.2 *Rationale for confidentiality*

Consequentialism judges the moral appropriateness of a duty, act, or practice by its outcome, its balance of harms versus its benefits. Utilitarianism is one type of consequentialism that looks to the balance of pleasure versus pain before deciding upon the moral status of an issue. By contrast, deontology privileges rules, obligation, and duties (such as the commandment, "Thou shall not kill") that ought to be followed no matter what the consequences. Neither theory is satisfactory as an account of ethics or law [10]. While consequentialism dissolves rules into preferences, deontology does not easily handle a clash of duties. Most accounts of privacy and confidentiality contain both kinds of rationale.

For example, a non-utilitarian rationale for medical confidentiality connected with the nature of the doctor–patient relationship is suggested in a Supreme Court ruling from Canada.

> Certain duties arise from the special relationship of trust and confidence [between doctor and patient]. These include the duties of the doctor to act with utmost good faith and loyalty, to hold information received from or about a patient in confidence, and to make proper disclosure of information to a patient … When a patient releases personal information in the confines of the doctor-patient relationship, he or she does so with the legitimate expectation that these duties will be respected [11].

Similarly, the European Convention on Human Rights protects confidentiality under Article 8, s. 1, stating: Everyone has the right to respect for his private and family life, his home and his correspondence [12].

In the case of *Z* v *Finland* the European Court of Justice (ECJ) explained,

> The protection of personal data, not the least medical data, is of fundamental importance to a person's enjoyment of his or her right to respect for private and family life as guaranteed by Article 8… [13].

In many countries such as France and Germany with strongly deontological ("deontic") criminal codes governing professional practice, the professional duty of protecting confidentiality is an uncompromising one and backed up by legal sanctions, such as fines or imprisonment [14].

The consequentialist rationale for these ideas also seems self-evident. Patients disclose to doctors intimate details of their lives they would never reveal to others, often from the very first meeting. Without the assumption of confidentiality on the part of healthcare professionals, it is argued that patients would conceal their symptoms, worries, and illnesses, resulting in illnesses being unreported and untreated. "[T]hose in need of medical assistance may be deterred from revealing such information of a personal and intimate nature as may be necessary in order to receive appropriate treatment..." [15].

3.1.3 *The doctor–patient relationship and confidentiality*

Circumstances may make these ideas more complicated in reality. The doctor's duty is inherently a contradictory one. For proper medical care to take place, a patient's informational, physical, or mental privacy must be "invaded". In the course of carrying out this complex duty, the physician may elicit information relevant to the health and safety of others and to the administration of justice. As such, there can be compelling grounds at times for doctors to break confidentiality. These circumstances will be discussed in greater detail later on in this chapter.

3.1.4 *Confidentiality and privilege*

It is sometimes held that doctors' communications with their patients are sacrosanct, "privileged" in the way that communications between lawyers and their clients are. But what exactly is "privileged"? According to one UK court, a

> witness is said to be privileged when he may validly claim not to answer
> a question or to supply information which would be relevant to the
> determination of an issue in judicial proceedings [16].

In other words, to be privileged means not having to provide the courts with information you possess that others would be obligated to divulge [17].

While medical confidentiality is protected by professional regulations and standards, in most jurisdictions doctor–patient communications are not "privileged" *per se* [17: Ch. 2]. There is no right to withhold information gained within the context of this "special relationship" between doctor and patient. At a minimum, in most countries and cultures, doctors must disclose information about a patient if properly requested to do so by the courts.

More protection has traditionally been given to psychiatrist–patient communications [18]. The more intimate nature of information shared with their therapists and the ill consequences that can accrue to patients if their psychiatric history is revealed make the professional requirement for confidentiality and privacy more exigent in this sphere of medicine. Nevertheless, psychiatrists and other mental health professionals can be compelled to give evidence in court. For example, in Quebec ("French Canada") which, like France, has a strict deontic code of justice ("No physician may be compelled to declare what has been revealed to him in his professional character" [19]), there are case precedents requiring disclosure of medical information to a court [20]. Presumably, the interests of justice may outweigh the benefits of privacy, even in the psychotherapeutic relationship.

3.1.5 *Confidentiality in court*

Information disclosures in a court of law are circumscribed and usually require legal documents such as a subpoena to appear and give witness. It is important for healthcare professionals to recognize, nonetheless, that a subpoena is not in itself a licence to reveal private patient confidences to lawyers and others. It is a simply a command to attend court. Legal advice around what is precisely required to be disclosed in court should always be sought.

Private medical information may receive more protection from legal scrutiny in the area of sexual assault charges. The fear of having one's personal, psychiatric, and medical information laid bare in a courtroom has traditionally made victims of sexual assault wary of laying charges. New legal trends in parts of North America are aimed at encouraging the reporting of such crimes by restricting access to medical, counseling, therapeutic, and other personal records of complainants [21].

The duty of confidentiality ought to prevent doctors and other health-care professionals from becoming an arm of the law — their main allegiance should be to the patient, not to third parties. The police, for example, may request that a physician perform a blood test on or release the toxicology report of a patient suspected of impaired driving. In various jurisdictions, the physician is not expected to collude with the police in most matters of inebriation [22]. Unless the patient has given consent or the police have a valid warrant (a document authorizing the release of certain information regarding a specific individual), informal requests to breach patient confidentiality ought to be acknowledged, but resisted — either deferred until proper documentation is obtained or referred to higher powers. Some jurisdictions, such as the UK, may allow forensic testing of unconscious patients in exceptional emergency circumstances [23].

3.2 Privacy

3.2.1 *Definition*

Privacy is "the state or condition of being left alone, undisturbed, or free from public attention, as a matter of choice or right; freedom from interference or intrusion" [24].

The right to privacy is also a fundamental tenet of modern medicine, although more vague in specification. Autonomy — the "respect for persons' principle" — is both the root and fruit of privacy and confidentiality. Autonomous persons establish a sphere of privacy and that sphere in turn protects and nourishes their individuality. In 1890, the American Supreme Court justices, Warren and Brandeis, defined *privacy* as "the right to be left alone" [25], in other words, the right to be free from physical intrusion or interference. Individuals should be allowed to define how far others may access their "private space". Most important would be not just a physical but also a mental and informational private space whereby individuals define and carve out their own decisions.

Privacy is thus a sword and a shield — a sword by which patients make their own choices and also a shield against unwanted interventions. In the context of health information, privacy means the "capacity to control when, how, and to what degree information about oneself is communicated to others" [26]. "The confiding of the information to the physician for medical purposes gives rise to an expectation that the patient's interest in and control of the information will continue" [27].

3.2.2 Health records

In many North American and UK jurisdictions, patients have access to, and some measure of control over, their personal health information [28–30]. As such, their permission is required for identifiable health information to be released, such as to a lawyer for a medico-legal report or an insurance company or to other physicians. The moral rationale is that patients should ultimately control what aspects of their information may be disclosed and to whom it may be disclosed.

The healthcare record can be considered a trust account for the patient. While the physical record belongs to the recording professional or his or her institution, the *contents* of the record, by Anglo-American jurisprudence, belong to the patient. Thus, if a patient asks the doctor for his or her medical record, the doctor is usually obliged to provide the patient with the entire record — even notes from consultants. Information may be withheld but only on the grounds that the patient or others might be harmed by it. This does not give a patient unlimited access to his or her records. Nor do most patients want such access. In over 20 years of practice this author has had only two requests from patients to examine and modify their record — in each case due to a loss of confidence by the patient in the trustworthiness of healthcare staff. Allowing them to amend the record healed the rift.

The right of access to one's own information helps ensure the well-being of the patient and the proper functioning of the doctor–patient relationship. Openness on the part of the patient must be mirrored by directness and transparency on the part of the healthcare professional. Such frankness not only respects patients but also improves, rather than undermines, the therapeutic relationship.

3.2.3 Privacy legislation

With the advent of computerized medical records and ease of electronic data collection, there is even more potential for unauthorized access to and use of a patient's private data [31]. Large-scale abuse and abuse from half a world away is now possible. Laptop computers make medical information readily portable now but increase the risk of sensitive patient data being lost or stolen. Surveillance societies have introduced patient identification cards that can link and reveal different realms of a patient's private life — efficient care, perhaps, but dangerous if not properly protected.

The ascendency of electronic medical records and the accumulation of data banks containing private information have resulted in the creation of "safe information practices" such as laws and new institutions whose function is to protect citizens from inappropriate intrusions into their private affairs. Privacy laws are to be had by the legion these days. National governments have them; provincial and state legislatures have theirs, too. Privacy-acknowledgement forms must be signed everywhere from dentists' offices to financial institutions. In medicine, privacy laws remind health professionals of the seriousness of protecting the private health information entrusted in them by patients. Health professionals and their institutions are now often called "health information custodians". Such language may be found in many jurisdictions. Information that is scrupulously collected for clinical purposes is to be accessed, used, disclosed, and disposed of but only under a specific set of "information practices".

Many fear an overemphasis on privacy will be bad for patients and bad for research. They argue that this might inhibit healthcare professionals from disclosing needed information to other clinicians in the patient's "circle of care" and that it might make research too unwieldy. These arguments are not without their merit but it should be remembered that when it comes to serious illness, few people will stay at home fretting about gaps in data protection.

Unfortunately, clinicians may cleave too closely to what they perceive as restrictive legislation and so inhibit their clinical instincts. In the UK in 2007 a journalist died when a number of clinicians — perhaps fearing legal repercussions — did not, or were unable to, access the patient's medical record and failed to recognize the seriousness of her condition [32]. Good clinical care — surgical, medical, rehabilitative — involves coordination with a large number of colleagues who also provide care to the patient [33]. Concerns over privacy should not cause physicians to shy away from entirely appropriate information-sharing with other healthcare professionals.

Consider an example. A surgeon is asked to see an elderly patient in the Emergency Department who has fractured her hip in a fall in her home. When he seeks her consent for the appropriate surgery, the patient adamantly refuses. Instead, she asks that her hip be fixed with a "surgical glue". She appears not to be in excessive pain, and can get up to a chair. She refuses to have anyone else notified and demands to be released to her home with a wheelchair. What should the surgeon do?

At first glance the patient's request, although certainly unusual, may seem a capable one. She understands what a hip fracture is and how it can be treated, although her reference to fixing it with "glue" is a little obscure. As well, the patient speaks coherently and scores perfectly on some simple cognitive testing.

What should, of course, concern the surgeon is the very prospect of allowing an isolated elderly patient to refuse routine surgery and to go home. He could inquire no further and abide by this woman's wish for "privacy". But a more thorough course of action would be to involve other professionals — especially psychiatry and geriatrics — to more fully explore whether this patient's treatment refusal is a competent one. If a more careful assessment finds her incapable due to a failure to appreciate her illness and her treatment options, a substitute decision maker should be found or appointed. Privacy concerns should not delay the surgeon in consulting with others in his care for this patient.

While there may be some concern that medicine by teams compromises patient autonomy and privacy, the compromises need not be excessive. Advanced information technologies offer the possibility of the "patient-centered medical home" which seeks to improve "all aspects of care simultaneously" [34]. Such models of coordinated and comprehensive care require the safe and trustworthy use of the new information technologies.

3.2.4 *Research and genes*

As for research, new privacy acts seem threatening if they allow access to patient records or patient data only with the patient's explicit consent. However, safe information practices — for example, requiring approval of any such research by a duly constituted research ethics board/institutional review board, only allowing the transfer of anonymized or de-identified subject data, obliging encryption of data on mobile devices [35] — are compatible with robust privacy laws and viable medical research.

The new genetic-oriented medicine, having had its biggest impact on testing for diseases or for inherited susceptibilities to diseases in oneself or one's offspring, produces novel ethical challenges as well.

The consequences of genetic testing for an individual may not be innocuous, of course. For example, Dr X is a transplantation surgeon looking after Ms A, a young woman who is being worked up for a possible kidney transplant from a family member. As part of the requisite histocompatibility testing, genetic testing of family members is done. The parents and two siblings in their late teens seem a happy and supportive family. To Dr X's dismay, the testing reveals Mr A is not the biological father. Should such results be disclosed to *all* unsuspecting family members? The answer is not black or white, all or nothing. The principle of respect due persons would argue that such information should be revealed to *someone* in the family in a sensitive and careful fashion. The principle of respect for the family suggests disclosure be done in a way conducive to not harming all members of the family. There is no need now for the siblings, or indeed for the patient, to be informed. This is clearly an issue for the parents — who to tell first would be a matter of discretion, but it would be most likely the mother. She will no doubt need support in the disclosure to her spouse.

The alternative would be to not disclose at all, paternalistically deciding the people involved cannot cope with such information. This, I think, is less acceptable in today's world, and not as well supported by moral reasoning or ethical considerations. The better alternative, of course, would have been to have warned those involved in advance of genetic testing what might be discovered and describe the professional parameters of the clinic as regards privacy and disclosure of test results.

The practice of using and linking biomarkers — such as fingerprints and DNA information — and storing them in national databanks for police investigation has been found in an ECJ ruling to run counter to the European Convention on Human Rights. As of 2009, 20 countries (including the UK) out of 47 members of the Council of Europe permit such practices [36]. While there is no doubt such use and retention is a breach of privacy, the UK argued this was necessary to prevent acts of terrorism. This may be so, but it is challenging for the police to use information, such as DNA from those before the courts, in circumscribed ways. Data are collected for one reason, are never deleted, and then used later for other compelling reasons such as state security or the investigation of crime. It is not, then, surprising to learn that of the over five million DNA samples in the UK data bank, a million have been obtained from people never convicted of a crime and half a million are from juveniles. Whether such information practices are accepted by the public will depend on how they are used and by whom.

Should everyone charged with or found guilty of an offence before the law be obligated to submit their DNA into a national "criminal data bank"? In a 2005 case before the Supreme Court of Canada (SCC) [37], the disposition of a DNA sample taken from a juvenile found guilty of assault was considered. As the juvenile had no criminal record, the SCC did not allow its inclusion in a national data bank. A judge for the majority held:

> [A]n individual's DNA contains the "highest level of personal and private information" (quoting from *R v SAB* [38]). Unlike a fingerprint, it is capable of revealing the most intimate details of a person's biological makeup. Without constraints on the type of information that can be extracted from bodily substances, the potential intrusiveness of DNA analysis is virtually infinite [37].

One commentator observed that this outcome was not surprising, but what *was* worrying was that so many judges, up to and including some on the Supreme Court, were prepared to have this youth's DNA included in the national data bank for a minor offence [39]. What was once unheard of has now become, so it seems, routine.

What should a surgeon do if, in the investigation of a crime, the police ask for the DNA from one of her patients? Unless the patient consents, the surgeon should not comply. She could point the police in the direction of the patient's waste-bin. Tissue from the patient discovered there is considered by the courts to have been discarded by the patient and may be used for forensic purposes.

3.2.5 *Information in the public domain*

Other complexities as regards the protection of personal health information arise. If some details of a patient's health history come into the public domain, does a duty of confidentiality by professionals still exist? If a patient has died, does confidentiality persist? Answers to both these questions morally must be "yes". Just because someone has been identified in the public domain does not mean he or she has no interest in preserving what privacy remains. A UK judge in 1814 stated,

> Though the defendant might not object to a small window looking into his yard, a larger one might be very inconvenient to him, disturbing his privacy and enabling people to come through to trespass upon his property [40].

As for the second question, the privacy and the respect due to persons does not end with death of the person [41]. Just as we treat his or her physical remains in a respectful and dignified way, so should we treat his or her "informational remains". This is common decency.

A contemporary case confirms this view. A war surgeon turned journalist returned from a war-zone, reporting in the public media on the brutal death by "friendly fire" of a fellow soldier he had witnessed. The soldier was identified by name. The consent of neither the deceased nor the family had been obtained. This is so clearly unprofessional it hardly needs comment. Suffice to say the surgeon-journalist was eventually found guilty of unprofessional conduct [42].

3.3 Secrets

In their day-to-day practices, healthcare providers are faced with more common invasions of privacy. They may be put in the difficult position of having to weigh patients' requests for privacy against their other professional responsibilities. In those instances where the patient's secretive information concerns only him- or herself, the patient is generally owed the duty of confidentiality. However, this may not necessarily be so. A relative may let a clinician know, for example, that a patient with a history of cirrhosis and alcohol abuse, and planned for hepatic transplantation, has again fallen off the wagon, or that a diabetic patient's poor glycemic control is due to failure to follow his or her diet, or that a seemingly "with-it" elderly patient hospitalized with a broken hip is not looking after himself properly at home because of a failing mind. In each of these cases the information supplied by others can be used to more thoroughly assess patient compliance and patient competence.

The challenge for the practitioner is in deciding what to do with such secretive information. At the very least, to avoid compromising his or her role as the patient's advocate, the wise clinician would try to convince the family to tell the patient that they have shared this information and explain why. Doctors should not participate in a family cover-up but encourage an open and supportive discussion within the family. (In some situations, such as the elderly vulnerable patient, the physician may have a statutory duty to report. This is discussed later in this chapter.)

Must all of a patient's secrets be protected by the practitioner? The short answer is no. It depends on the nature of the secret and the nature of the patient's relationship with the person who divulges the secret. In other words, some secrets are more worthy of respect because they derive from an altruistic impulse. By contrast, secrets that are self-serving are often not morally acceptable. For example, a 44-year-old male married patient admits to an affair and tests positive for a sexually transmitted disease. He wants his wife treated for the same infection without being told the reason why. Obviously, it would be unacceptable to treat the patient's wife for a venereal disease without her consent. The physician could offer to help the husband in his disclosure. Public Health authorities would have to be notified of his communicable disease and they would then pursue contact tracing. The patient would have to decide what would be preferable: that he, or a stranger, inform his wife about the infection.

3.3.1 *Failing to respect confidentiality*

It is possible, but uncommon, in North America at least, for patients to recover damages from a medical professional for breach of confidentiality [43]. Even rarer are criminal charges against physicians for breaking confidentiality. Most likely this is because successful prosecutions would require showing intent, on the professional's part, to willfully and improperly breach the duty of confidentiality. However, professionals must also live up to regulations set by their licensing bodies which tend to have a lower bar for discipline. Professional regulations bind professionals, as a matter of professional responsibility, to protect their patients' information from others. For example, one code for healthcare professionals states that professional misconduct includes

> …[G]iving information concerning a patient's condition or any professional services performed for a patient to any person other than the patient without the consent of the patient unless required to do so by law [44].

Regulated health professionals may be found guilty of professional misconduct, with resultant disciplinary proceedings, should they, without appropriate rationale (that is, without the patient's permission or unless required by law), disclose private information about a patient. In 1980 a well-known Canadian physician and newspaper columnist was found guilty of professional misconduct after disclosing information about a woman — she was named in the article! — in his column. This confidential material, somehow obtained from her record without her consent, contained information of which even she was unaware. Because she was not his patient, the doctor claimed he owed her no duty of confidentiality. Not surprisingly, the court was unimpressed by this argument [45].

An appropriate subversion of medical confidentiality was set in Canada in *Smith* v *Jones* [46]. In a case which went to the Supreme Court, a psychiatrist was retained by a defence attorney to examine his client who had been charged with aggravated assault on a prostitute. The attorney indicated to the accused that what he said during the psychiatric consultation would be privileged. During the interview, the accused described in some detail his plan to kidnap, rape, and kill prostitutes. The psychiatrist duly informed the defence attorney that he considered the accused to be dangerous and likely to commit future offences unless he received sufficient treatment. The accused subsequently entered a plea of guilty. When the psychiatrist later discovered his concerns about the client's dangerousness would not be addressed in the sentencing hearing, he commenced action for declaration allowing him to disclose such information in the interests of public safety. The trial judge ruled the psychiatrist should be mandated to breach confidentiality. When the case was subsequently brought up to the Court of Appeal, it was agreed disclosure was warranted in this case because the threat was clear, serious, imminent, and directed against an identifiable group of persons.

Strong reactions to physicians' breaches of confidentiality occur in countries with deontic codes. In France, confidentiality is protected by legal sanctions as well as by professional regulations. The ethical duty to maintain medical confidentiality is uncompromising. "The professional secret established in the interest of the patient is imposed on every physician according to the conditions stated by law" [47]. The circumstances that permit French physicians to subvert confidentiality are few, however. Physicians there can be imprisoned if found guilty under the criminal code for violating patient confidentiality — even in circumstances where the patient consents or where the public might be protected from harm. To avoid such charges, French physicians must be wary about reporting their findings in court. In one case, a physician treated and made his report on a young girl who had been the victim of a sexual assault. When it came to trial, however, he refused to give testimony, despite authorization by the girl's parents, citing the absolute nature of medical confidentiality [48: p. 69]. The French system, it seems, leaves a wide latitude for physician discretion to disclose confidential information in a court of law.

In another case of a woman accused of murdering her spouse, her consent to allow her physician to reveal confidential medical facts about her *own* history was not allowed by the courts in France.

> The consent of the accused cannot be seen as a justification taking away the criminal nature of a disclosure of confidential information... The principle [of] medical confidentiality is general and absolute [48: p. 70].

It has been noted by one commentator that courts in France may yet allow physicians to decide when disclosure might be appropriate, based upon the assumption that "the physician knows better than the patient what the patient's interests are" [48: p. 87]. This paternalistic assumption seems outmoded in modern democracies and would be unlikely to survive judicial scrutiny outside a strict deontic system of justice.

3.3.2 *Weighing of consequences*

In no society is man an island. Societies vary in the ways and degrees to which they "disturb" the right of their citizens to be left alone. All societies require doctors to comply with these disturbances to some degree. Of concern, some countries may in theory protect privacy in statute or in their constitution but fail to uphold it in their everyday practices. Clinicians in these jurisdictions face challenges in maintaining privacy and meeting the country's bureaucratic practices.

For example, some countries welcome foreign labourers so long as they are well. If a surgeon in one such country comes to know that a foreign labourer requires surgery for a large operable tumour, should he call the authorities, knowing the patient will be sent back to his impoverished country of origin and not receive proper treatment there? Or should he "forget" to call and go ahead with the surgery? What should he do if the surgery is an emergency and it is unsafe for the labourer to leave the hospital? The circumstances of and consequences for the surgeon will vary, so no firm ethical advice can be given to healthcare professionals in those countries. The "right" answer is: the patient's needs come first. Yet if to do so might cause the surgeon loss of licence or imprisonment, maintaining patient privacy can hardly be a duty. The morally superior course could also be considered reckless and vain. It cannot be the duty of physicians to save everyone — especially if one's own life is put at risk.

While the problem of privacy is not so seriously degraded elsewhere, no country is perfectly consistent in its information practices. Often, the best that can be expected of healthcare professionals is to recognize the dilemmas regarding confidentiality and privacy, struggle with them, and try to address them in an ethical way. For example, in the case cited above, if the surgeon is not allowed to operate, he could attempt to facilitate the labourer's treatment in his home country.

3.4 Limits to Confidentiality

While respecting privacy and maintaining confidentiality are important responsibilities of a healthcare professional, these are not the sole responsibilities. Their importance must be constantly weighed against the sometimes countervailing principles of beneficence and justice:

> [For example], there may be cases in which reasons connected with the safety of individuals or of the public, physical or moral, would be sufficiently cogent to supersede or qualify the obligations prima facie imposed by the confidential relation [49].

Based on this premise, there are a number of circumstances that permit and others that require confidentiality to be breached. The specific circumstances will vary from place to place. The exceptions to privacy and confidentiality are common in the Anglo-American world but cannot be extrapolated to the whole world. I will start with the most important exception — the danger to others — that countenances breaching secrecy and then review other common exceptions to privacy.

In many jurisdictions — in most democracies — there are no laws requiring citizens to report persons they believe may be dangerous. In the past, physicians were similarly not expected to report, particularly given the duty of confidentiality. This is now recognized as mistaken. Forty years ago a jurist sagely observed:

> No patient has the moral right to convince his psychiatrist that he is going to commit a crime and then expect him to do nothing because of the principle of confidentiality [50].

3.4.1 *Duty to warn, duty to protect*

It is, of course, not just any crime at issue, but serious crimes. For example, there is now a widely recognized "duty to warn" — set by the Tarasoff case from the 1970s in the US. In 1969, a university psychologist was informed by one of his patients of murderous intentions directed at a former acquaintance, Ms Tarasoff. Two months later, the patient, who did not return for therapy, murdered her. Because no one had warned the victim of her peril, the California Supreme Court later found the psychologist and university negligent [51]. Although the victim was not the therapist's patient, the court felt she was owed a duty of care because of his knowledge of the murderer. The special relationship between patient and therapist engenders an affirmative duty for the benefit of third parties who might be harmed if the patient is not properly detained or treated.

The court weighed the importance of protecting the patient's privacy but concluded that this must take second place to "the public interest in safety from violent assault ... The protective privilege ends where the public peril begins" [51].

According to this ruling, where there is a real hazard to an individual or a community and no other way of relieving this peril, the patient–physician confidentiality rule must yield to the interests of safety. The duty to warn will sometimes be the only way to protect the public from harm.

In a later US ruling on Tarasoff ("Tarasoff II") the court reaffirmed its view that medical professionals ought to err on the side of public safety when it comes to dangerous patients, despite the possible negative implications for privacy: "The risk that unnecessary warnings may be given is a reasonable price to pay for the lives of possible victims that may be saved" [52]. In the years since the Tarasoff case, virtually every US jurisdiction, other than Texas, that has ruled on the issue has found a Tarasoff-like duty to warn or protect [53]. The extent of this duty outside the US, however, varies considerably [54]. One author, commenting upon the evidence regarding the impact of this judicial trend in the US to allow breaches in privacy when public danger looms, concluded, "The widespread acceptance of an ethical duty to protect made the additional impact of the *Tarasoff* ruling on therapists' conduct minimal" [55].

The Tarasoff ruling does not legitimize wholesale infringements on confidentiality. Rather, breaching confidentiality by issuing a warning is justifiable only when there is no other way to protect third parties. However, the "minimal impact" seen by Appelbaum in the US depended on therapists anticipating and already acting on principles of public protection — in other words, they were doing it already. Surveys of the public showed they, too, knew that confidentiality was not absolute. In other jurisdictions, such as Europe, where this is not so — where there is no historical experience of professionals revealing patient confidences in ways protective of public welfare — the recognition of a duty to warn or protect would likely have a much bigger impact on physician practice and public expectations.

Sometimes, however, it takes only one high-profile case to change professional practice. A sea-change in Canada came about in part due to the conviction in 1993 of an individual for the first degree murder of his estranged wife. Although the man had informed his physician of his plan to murder his wife, his doctor took no action to warn his wife, following the code of strict confidentiality of the Canadian Medical Association at that time.

A consensus panel made recommendations in 1998 regarding the duty to warn for the Canadian medical profession.

> There should be a duty to inform when a patient reveals that he or she intends to do serious harm to another person or persons and it is more likely than not that the threat will be carried out ... Taking all the circumstances into account, physicians will want to consider very carefully whether they should report threats and will, if there is any doubt, err on the side of informing the police because of the potential seriousness of the consequences in the event that they decide not to inform [56].

The argument is compelling but has not led to clear precedents elsewhere. What remains uncertain is how grave and imminent the threat to public safety must be in order to trigger disclosure. This is a continuing issue — or should be — in every jurisdiction. Europe is vague as regards any "duty to warn." The UK has permitted non-consensual disclosure where there is an identifiable target group. Germany recognises such disclosure might be justified in an "emergency" threat to life, as a "defense of necessity". France has no legislative allowance for breaching confidentiality except in emergencies when the doctor might have to defend himself [48: pp. 320–321]. These are narrow grounds indeed for protecting the public.

3.5 Grounds for Mandatory or Allowable Disclosure

In most jurisdictions today, however, there are a number of circumstances in which it is mandatory or allowed by statute or law to divulge a patient's private medical information. Grounds for mandatory or permissible disclosure of private medical information include the areas of communicable disease, child abuse and neglect, elder abuse, driving or flying safety, fitness to work, knife and gunshot wounds, antiterrorism provisions, the administration of justice, and routine information disclosure.

1. Communicable disease. All North American jurisdictions, as well as the UK, Australia, and New Zealand, require notification in cases of contagious, communicable, and virulent diseases, such as HIV and TB. Healthcare practitioners need only form an "*opinion* that the person is or may be infected with an agent of a reportable disease [and] shall as soon as possible ... report thereof to the medical officer of health" [57]. Specialized forms, that attempt to preserve patient privacy, may be required to notify authorities of stigmatized diseases such as HIV or AIDS. Public health authorities in turn must meet strict confidentiality requirements [58].

2. Child maltreatment. In the majority of jurisdictions, medical practitioners are required to report information regarding the *possible* mistreatment of children [59]. The threshold for professional reporting should be forming an *opinion*, based on some reasonable grounds, that abuse *may* be taking place (rather than being *certain* of abuse, a higher threshold that would require the physician to be a detective). Children may be in need of protection because of neglect, failure to provide proper medical treatment, physical or sexual abuse, and/or failure to provide the necessities of life. Failure to report within a reasonable period of time can result in a fine, professional sanctions, or both. It is best to inform those responsible for the child's welfare that this reporting is taking place. However, if the child is at risk of further injury on account of such disclosure, reporting could take place without consent.

3. Elder abuse. At the present time, there are few mandates for healthcare professionals anywhere in the world to report elder abuse and neglect [60]. In some Canadian provinces, there is the provision for mandatory reporting of abuse of the elderly or "serious incidents" in long-term care institutions [61]. For community-dwelling elderly, except in the UK [62], there is unfortunately little official requirement to report in cases of suspected neglect, physical, financial, or emotional abuse.

4. Dangerous vehicle operation. Under highway traffic legislation, in most Canadian provinces and in many US states, physicians are

required to report the names of patients who, by virtue of disease, disability, or drugs, may be a danger to others if they drive. (In other jurisdictions, such as the UK, this reporting is allowed but not mandated [62: p. 193]. In some areas, as in Australia [29: pp. 391–392], it is up to the individual to self-report.) Where there is mandatory reporting, the physician must report the patient to the local transport authority, which may conduct an investigation and suspend the person's licence [63]. All that is required is the patient's name and a statement that he or she suffers from a medical condition making vehicle operation potentially unsafe [64]. The exact circumstances of the patient need not, and ought not, be routinely reported.

Physicians typically do not relish this responsibility. Reporting such patients can create great distress as driving may seem to be their last vestige of autonomy. Nonetheless, the principle of autonomy does not involve the right to run over others.

Physicians may be similarly required to report pilots and air traffic controllers if they have conditions that might affect flight safety [65]. Likewise, legislation may require physicians to report individuals in positions critical to railway safety who may be unable to perform their duties. Merchant seamen may also be required to undergo medical examinations by a physician.

5. Fitness to work. Physicians do not have consistent statutory duties to report work-related medical conditions of their patients. "Fitness-to-work" assessments are owed a duty of confidentiality, even if the assessment reveals that the employee has impaired functional capacities [66]. Because such an assessment may have important implications for the patient, a physician doing such assessments must ensure the patient knows who is requesting the assessment and why. Before doing this assessment, the physician should obtain the patient's informed consent to release the results of the assessment to those requesting it (such as an employer or insurance company) [29: pp. 389–390].

6. Evidence of serious crimes. In many jurisdictions, regulations require hospitals and the physicians who work there to promptly report knife and gunshot wounds of patients who present at their facilities [67,68]. This allows police to act as soon as possible to prevent further violence, injury, or death.

7. Antiterrorism laws. The apparent vulnerability of society to acts of terrorism has resulted in laws restricting medical confidentiality. In the UK, the Terrorism Act of 2000 requires doctors to divulge information about planned or actual acts of terrorism. Specifically, to avoid criminal charges, a doctor must report to the police any information regarding money or property used, or intending to be used, for terrorist purposes [69]. This is a rather unusual piece of legislation as this is hardly the type of information that doctors would obtain from their patients.

    American examples of more seriously intrusive legislative acts are the US Patriot Act authorizing new powers of government surveillance and the amended US Federal Health Privacy Act (HIPPA) that is meant to improve the efficiency of patient care. The first act permits the collection of personal data while the second allows the transfer of a patient's medical record — in each case without the consent of the patient. These laws are seen as a broadside assault on confidentiality and privacy [70].

8. Administration of justice. Prevention of the conviction of the innocent is an important social end. To achieve this, some jurisdictions allow physicians to report information they have about patients that may be relevant to preventing a miscarriage of justice. Whether such information would be disclosed would depend on a decision by the court [30: pp. 168–169].

9. Information disclosure is routinely required of physicians in their normal course of work. For example, physicians must disclose births, stillbirths, and deaths they attend or of which they are aware. Certain deaths also require prompt reports to the Coroner or the Medical Examiner. None of these would usually constitute a morally concerning breach of confidentiality.

A caveat. Not surprisingly these many exceptions to confidentiality would be unlikely to apply in France — it imposes upon its citizens, for example, a duty to report crimes or child abuse but exempts physicians from disclosing "professional secrets" [48: pp. 74–79]. Thus, "If the physician holds information regarding a crime that has already been committed, he/she has to maintain confidentiality" [48: p. 76]. The French system may not be as rigid as it seems on the surface. It does provide considerable discretion for the physician to disclose or to withhold information and not to be prosecuted on either account. The difficulty for the professional will be to identify when he/she may legitimately breach a patient's confidence. Courts have determined that if a physician's testimony "constitutes a breach of the duty of confidentiality, it must be disregarded" [48: p. 80]. While this system protects medical confidentiality to the extreme, uncertainty about its boundaries may leave the public and patients at risk of foreseeable harm.

3.5.1 *Impact of mandated disclosures*

How do mandated or permissible breaches of confidentiality affect the doctor–patient relationship? The common assumption that medicine, patients, and society would suffer were the duty of confidentiality subverted has not in fact been empirically supported. Indeed, the weight of evidence is to the contrary. One Canadian study found that being informed about scenarios requiring confidentiality to be broken did not prevent most patients from seeking treatment [71]. In addition, many therapists did not think patients avoided care on account of such possible breaches. Thus, while the issue of confidentiality may prevent some patients from seeking medical attention, it tends to take a back seat to the reasons the majority of patients seek medical care in the first place: they are unwell and suffering. Think of patients with a serious knife or gunshot wound. Despite concerns about privacy, they will generally seek medical attention because they are more worried about their health [72].

The minimal impact of exceptions to confidentiality may also be due to permissible breaches of confidentiality being sufficiently narrow so as to allow an atmosphere of trust to still prevail in medicine. The exceptions ought to be rare in frequency and limited in scope. One UK court noted:

> The judge will respect the confidences which each member of these honourable professions [the doctor or the clergyman or the banker] receives in the course of it and will not direct them to answer unless not only is it relevant but also it is a proper and indeed necessary question in the course of justice to be put and answered [73].

This seems a just and proportionate limit to the exceptions to confidentiality and privacy. These duties have not disappeared, but they have changed.

3.6 Conclusions

Confidentiality is far from a decrepit concept [74]. Along with privacy, it remains an enduring component of medical professionalism and is defended by the courts and the medical profession. Medical confidentiality and privacy are inconsistently applied throughout the world although there are promising attempts to devise a common code of ethical practice for all healthcare professionals [75].

References

[1]   Oath of Hippocrates. In W. Reich W (ed.) *Encyclopedia of Bioethics, revised edition Vol. 5*. Toronto: Simon & Shuster MacMillan, 1995: p. 2632.

[2]   Anon. *Islamic Charter of Medical and Health Ethics*. Ch. 3. <www.emro.who.int> [accessed 4 March 2014].

[3]   Hedayat K. and Pirzadeh R. Issues in Islamic biomedical ethics: A primer for the pediatrician. *Pediatrics* 2002; **108**: 965–971.

[4]   Keown D. *Buddhism and Medical Ethics: Principles and Practice*. Accessed at: http://www.buddhismuskunde.uni-hamburg.de/fileadmin/pdf/digitale_texte/Bd7-K03Keown.pdf

[5]   Ubel P., Zell M., Miller D., *et al.* Elevator talk: observational study of inappropriate comments in a public space. *American Journal of Medicine* 1995; **99**: 190–194.

[6]   Picard E. *Legal Liability of Doctors and Hospitals in Canada, 2nd ed.* Toronto: Carswell Legal Publications, 1984; p. 8.

[7]   Wacks R. *Privacy: A Very Short Introduction*. Oxford: Oxford University Press, 2010: pp. 72–79.

[8]   *OED*. CD-Rom 2nd ed, v. 3.0.

[9]   *R* v *Potvin* [1971] 16 C.R.N.S. 233 (Que. C.A.).

[10] Hebert P. *Doing Right: A Practical Guide to Ethics for Medical Trainees and Doctors, 3rd ed.* Toronto: Oxford University Press, 2014: Ch. 1.

[11] *McInerney* v *MacDonald* [1992] 2 S.C.R. 138.

[12] *European Convention on Human Rights* (ECHR). Quoted in Michalowski S. *Medical Confidentiality and Crime.* Aldershot: Ashgate Books, 2003; p. 34. The author reports that the ECHR has not been ratified in all European countries.

[13] *Z* v *Finland,* Judgment of 25 Feb 1997, [1998] 25, EHRR 371.

[14] Michalowski S. *Medical Confidentiality and Crime.* Aldershot: Ashgate Books, 2003; pp. 50–51.

[15] *Z v Finland.* Quoted in Michalowski S. *Medical Confidentiality and Crime.* Aldershot: Ashgate Books, 2003; p. 36.

[16] Tapper C. *Cross & Tapper on Evidence, 7th ed.* Oxford: Oxford University Press, 1990; p. 416.

[17] McHale J.V. *Medical Confidentiality and Legal Privilege.* London: Routledge, 1993.

[18] Sharpe G. Footnote 88. Quoted in Picard E. *Legal Liability of Doctors and Hospitals in Canada, 2nd ed.* Toronto: Carswell Legal Publications, 1984: p. 13. Psychiatrists may be "...a special breed of physician who require the certainty of confidentiality even if their brethren can exist without it."

[19] Quebec Medical Act (1973) RSQ Ch. M-9 Article 42 c.46 s.40.

[20] Picard E. and Robertson G. *Legal Liability of Doctors and Hospitals in Canada, 3rd ed.* Toronto: Carswell Thomson Canada Ltd, 1996: p. 21.

[21] Gibson E. Whither privacy of health information at the Supreme Court of Canada. In J. Downieand E. Gibson (eds) *Health Law at the Supreme Court of Canada.* Toronto: Irwin Law, 2007: pp. 331–335.

[22] Breen K., *et al. Good Medical Practice: Professionalism, Ethics and Law, 2nd ed.* Australia: Cambridge University Press, 2010: pp. 248–249.

[23] BMA Ethics Department. *Medical Ethics Today: The BMAs Handbook of Ethics and Law, 2nd ed.* London: BMJ Books, 2004: pp. 546–547.

[24] *OED.* CD-Rom 2nd ed, v. 3.0.

[25] Warren S.D. and Brandeis L.D. The right to privacy. *Harvard Law Review* 1890; **4**: 193–220.

[26] Gostin L., Turek-Brezina J., Powers M., Kozloff R., Faden R., and Steinauer D. Privacy and security of personal information in a new health care system. *Journal of the American Medical Association* 1993; **270**: 2487–2493.

[27] *McInerney* v *MacDonald* [1992] 2 S.C.R. 138.

[28] BMA Ethics Department. *Medical Ethics Today: The BMAs Handbook of Ethics and Law, 2nd ed.* London: BMJ Books, 2004: pp. 216–217.

[29] Breen K. *et al. Good Medical Practice: Professionalism, Ethics and Law, 2nd ed.* Australia: Cambridge University Press, 2010: pp. 93–95.

[30] Marshall M. and von Tigerstrom B. Confidentiality and disclosure of health information. In J. Downie and T. Caulfield (eds) *Canadian Health Policy and Law*. Toronto: Butterworths, 1999; pp. 152–154.

[31] Wacks, R. *Privacy: A Very Short Introduction*. Oxford: Oxford University Press, 2010: pp. 1–22.

[32] Out-of-hours GP failures led to patient's death. *The Guardian*, 26 May 2007. http://www.guardian.co.uk/society/2007/may/26/health.uknews [accessed 4 March 2014].

[33] Pham H., *et al.* Primary care physicians' links to other physicians through medicare patients. *Annals of Internal Medicine* 2009; **150**: 236–242.

[34] Reid R. and Wagner E. Strengthening primary care with better information transfer. *Canadian Medical Association Journal* 2008; **179**: 987–988.

[35] Wellcome Trust. Towards consensus for best practice: use of patient records from general practice for research. *British Medical Journal* 2009; **338**: b6641.

[36] Annas G. Protecting privacy and the public: Limits on police use of biomarkers in Europe. *New England Journal of Medicine* 2009; **361**: 196–201.

[37] *R* v *RC* [2005] 3 SCR 99 [RC].

[38] *R* v *SAB* [2003] 2 SCR 678 [SAB].

[39] Gibson E. Whither privacy of health information at the Supreme Court of Canada. In J. Downie and E. Gibson (eds) *Health Law at the Supreme Court of Canada*. Toronto: Irwin Law, 2007; 330.

[40] J. Cambell Rep. Cases King's Bench III. 81 [1814].

[41] BMA Ethics Department. *Medical Ethics Today: The BMAs Handbook of Ethics and Law, 2nd ed*. London: BMJ Books, 2004: p. 179.

[42] BC doctor censured for article on soldier's death. *Vancouver Sun*. 28 Jan 2009. http://www.canada.com/vancouversun/news/westcoastnews/story.html?id=8f664c67-01de-47d4-af53-e536520be26d [accessed 4 March 2010].

[43] Irvine J. The physician's other duties: Good faith, loyalty and confidentiality. In B. Sneiderman, J. Irvine, and P. Osborne *Canadian Medical Law: An Introduction for Physicians, Nurses and other Health Care Professionals, 3rd ed*. Toronto: Thomson Carswell, 2003; p. 212.

[44] Medicine Act, O. Reg. 856/93, s. 1(1)(10) [1991].

[45] *Shulman* v *CPSO* [1980] 29 O.R. (2d) 40 (Ont. Div. Ct.).

[46] *Smith* v *Jones* [1999] 1 S.C.R. 455.

[47] *The Code of Ethics* issued by the French medical profession. As quoted in Michalowski, S. *Medical Confidentiality and Crime*. Aldershot: Ashgate Books, 2003; p. 59.

[48] Michalowski, S. *Medical Confidentiality and Crime*. Aldershot: Ashgate Books, 2003.

[49] *Halls* v *Mitchell* [1928] SCR 125.

[50] Quoted in Mills M., Sullivan G., and Spencer E. Protecting third parties: a decade after Tarasoff. *American Journal of Psychiatry* 1987; **144**: 70.

[51] V. *Tarasoff* v *Regents of the University of California* [1976], 17 Cal. 3d 425, 551 P.2d 334, 131 California Reporter.

[52] V. *Tarasoff* v *Regents of University of California* [1976] 17 Cal. 3d, 131 California Reporter 26 (S.C.C.).

[53] Mills M., Sullivan G., and Spencer E. Protecting third parties: a decade after Tarasoff. *Am J Psychiatry* 1987; **144**: 68–74.

[54] BMA Ethics Department. *Medical Ethics Today: The BMAs Handbook of Ethics and Law, 2nd ed.* London: BMJ Books, 2004: pp. 190–194.

[55] Appelbaum, P. *Almost a Revolution: Mental Health Law and the Limits of Change.* New York: Oxford University Press, 1994; p. 88.

[56] Ferris L., Barkun H., Carlisle J., *et al.* Defining the physician's duty to warn: consensus statement of Ontario's Medical Expert Panel on Duty to Inform. *Canadian Medical Association Journal* 1998; **158**: 1473–1479.

[57] Health Protection and Promotion Act R.S.O. 1990, Chapter H.7.

[58] Lopez W., Freiden, T. Legal counsel to public health practitioners. In R. Goodman (ed.) *Law in Public Health Practice, 2nd ed.* Oxford: Oxford University Press, 2007; 212–214.

[59] See for example: *US State Laws on Mandatory Reporting of Suspected Child Abuse.* Accessed at: http://www.preventchildabusenj.org/documents/links_government/Child_Abuse_Reporting_Laws.pdf

[60] Lachs M. and Pillemer K. Abuse and neglect of elderly persons. *New England Journal of Medicine* 1995; **332**: 437–443.

[61] Canadian Network for the Prevention of Elder Abuse. *Mandatory reporting requirements across Canada for abuse and neglect in institutions.* 2005. Accessed at: http://www.cnpea.ca/mandatory_reporting.htm

[62] BMA Ethics Department. *Medical Ethics Today: The BMAs Handbook of Ethics and Law, 2nd ed.* London: BMJ Books, 2004: pp. 194–196.

[63] Redelmeier D., Venkatesh V., and Stanbrook M. Mandatory reporting by physicians of patients potentially unfit to drive. *Open Medicine* 2008; **2**(1): E8–17.

[64] *Toms* v *Foster* [1994] OJ No 1413 (CA).

[65] Canadian Medical Association. *The Physician and the Aeronautics Act: A Guide to Mandatory Reporting.* Ottawa: Canadian Medical Association, 1995.

[66] Canadian Medical Protective Association. Quoted in *Newsletter of the Section on Occupational and Environmental Health.* Ontario Medical Association. Nov 1994.

[67] *Mandatory Gunshot Wounds Reporting Act*, 2005, S.O. 2005, c.9

[68] Morris K. UK doctors begin reporting gun and knife crime. *Lancet* 2009; **374**: 2041–2042.

[69] Medical Defense Union. New antiterrorism measures means doctors must breach patient confidentiality. London, November 6, 2001.

[70] Program for Psychiatry and the Law at Harvard Medical School. Brief for *Amicus Curiae* before US Court of Appeals for the Third Circuit. Case No. 04-2550. Sept 1, 2004. Accessed at: http://www.pipatl.org/data/library/17158%20pdf%20Zalkin.pdf

[71] Shuman D.W., Weiner W.F., and Pinnard G.I. The Privilege Study. *International Journal of Law and Psychiatry* 1986; **393**.

[72] May J., Hemenway D., and Hall A. Do criminals go to the hospital when they are shot? *Injury Prevention* 2002; **8**: 236–238.

[73] Lord Denning. As quoted in McHale J.V. *Medical Confidentiality and Legal Privilege*. London: Routledge, 1993.

[74] Siegler M. Medical confidentiality — A decrepit concept. *New England Journal of Medicine* 1982; **307**: 1518.

[75] World Medical Association. *International Code of Medical Ethics*. 2006. Accessed at: http://www.wma.net/en/30publications/10policies/c8/index.html

4

Resource Allocation in Healthcare

Ariel Zosmer

4.1 Introduction

There can be no doubt that resources available for healthcare are scarce as there is, and always has been, a discrepancy between supply and demand. The assumption predating the establishment of public healthcare systems asserting that the provision of a comprehensive healthcare which is free at the point of delivery will become cheaper in time as the presumed finite ill-health in the population is eliminated turned up to be wrong [1]. For example, prescription charges were introduced in 1948 under the British National Health Service (NHS) Act of 1946, as it became clear that the costs would exceed the resources [2]. In 1956, the first committee of inquiry into the costs of the NHS conceded that,

> "The growth of medical knowledge adds continually to the number and expense of treatments and, by prolonging life, also increases the incidence of slow-killing diseases ... there is no reason at present to suppose that demands on the service as a whole will be reduced thereby so as to stabilise (still less reduce) its total cost in terms of finance and absorption of real resources" [3].

In 1979, the Royal Commission on the National Health Service said,

> Demand for health care is always likely to outstrip supply ... the capacity of health services to absorb resources is almost unlimited. Choices have

75

therefore to be made … The more pressure there is on resources, the more important it is to get the priorities clear [4].

Within 23 years, the uncertainty as to whether it may be possible to reach equilibrium between demand and supply turned into the certainty that it will not.

In 1949, the NHS expenditure was 3.5% of the gross domestic product rising to 6.4% in 2001 [5] and 9.4% in 2007 [6]. However, if we are to believe TV and newspaper reports, resources seem scarcer than ever as problems with neonatal beds, waiting lists for cardiac and hip replacement surgery, and drugs for cancer patients are constantly in the news.

The reasons for the discrepancy between demand and supply are multiple and complex. Modern social conditions, of which medicine is only one component, resulted in a significant increase in life expectancy. Thus, the prevalence of chronic diseases such as diabetes or hypertension increased, resulting in increased costs. Technological advances are expensive to develop, to run, and to maintain and add to the costs by enabling treatment for conditions that were previously untreatable. As such, medicine is a system that by its nature creates more and more need for its services. For example, better understanding of the genetic background of disease offers the possibility of reducing the genetic susceptibility to disease. Genetic modifications have the potential of reducing the costs of chronic conditions such as diabetes, heart disease, and cancer. They are also likely to be expensive. It has been said that "Every advance in medical science creates new needs that did not exist until the means of getting them came into existence" [7], and that

> It is endemic to a system in which an expanding medical establishment faced with a healthier population, is driven to medicalizing normal events like menopause, converting risks into diseases, and treating trivial complaints with fancy procedures. Doctors and "consumers" are becoming locked within a fantasy that everyone has something wrong with them, everyone and everything can be cured [8].

The perceived success of modern medicine generates huge expectations. Today, we expect the provision of healthcare services free at the point of delivery as a matter of right. Indeed, there is a widespread feeling that modern medicine should, as a matter of right, provide cure and remedy to every conceivable disease, disorder, or disability, if not today than at least in the very near future. In fact, it seems that, soon enough, people will expect to live forever, to be young forever, and avoid any suffering whatsoever as a matter of right. One manifestation of the public's expectations from the healthcare system is the massive increase in clinical negligence claims and, perhaps more significantly, the willingness of the judiciary to find for the plaintiffs and to award damages at levels that have come to represent a significant drain on the system's funds (in the NHS, estimated at £466 million in 2002) [9].

There is a conflict between the individual's needs, rights, and wishes and the interests of the public as to the best way to ration the resources available. Rationing in the healthcare system means that no matter how resources are allocated, at least some patients will be deprived of optimal treatment. As such decisions can have immeasurable impact on people's lives, it is important that the decision making process will be and appear to be one that inspires confidence. It is therefore vital that the decision making process is done in consultation with all parties concerned including public representatives, healthcare professionals, and patients. It is also important that the process allows for the consideration of all the relevant facts. The process has to be fair, unbiased, and consistent [2: p. 82]. In this way, it will enable the authorities that are in charge of making these difficult decisions to defend them. Most importantly, the process needs to be transparent so that the affected individuals will understand the process, the reasons for the decision that may have had a negative impact on their welfare, and be able to present their point of view or challenge the decisions.

Decisions regarding resource allocation are done mainly by public authorities that derive their power from statute and therefore can be challenged in court. However, the courts are reluctant to interfere with funding decisions as they acknowledge that resources are scarce, that decisions have to be made, that making these decisions is difficult, that the solution may not be clear-cut, and that the courts are not and cannot be in possession of all the facts (e.g., what other deserving patients there may be who are not represented in court). Therefore, in most cases, the courts restrict their involvement to the legality or to the rationality of the authorities' decisions. Thus, it is not surprising that the number of cases challenging resource allocation that come to court is small.

4.2 The Distribution of Healthcare Resources

The simple answer to the discrepancy between the demand and the supply of healthcare services and goods is to increase the recourses allocated. But this will not and cannot solve the problem. Indeed, it has been argued that providing everyone with the best possible medical care available will "... consume the entire gross domestic product" [10]. One study estimated the cost of all beneficial healthcare to each French citizen at five and a half France's gross national product [11].

Not everyone agrees that an increase in resources is the answer. There are those who argue that forcing people to pay for healthcare through taxation is illegitimate [12] and that justice will be served if everyone decides how much of their legitimately acquired wealth they would like to spend on their own health.

Donald Light suggests that rationing can be avoided by reducing or eliminating waste and inefficiency in the system by implementing evidence-based medicine — "So long as good outcomes are not measured ... everything will be a 'cost' without a benefit and wasteful practices will have equal weight with effective practices" [13].

On the other hand, it has also been suggested that it is the demand that needs to be reduced by educating the public to avoid unnecessary use of services and making health information available on the phone or internet (thus reducing unnecessary GP or hospital visits).

Moreover, not everyone agrees that the resources already allocated for healthcare in wealthy countries are necessary. Richard Nicholson argues that the expenditure of rich countries on healthcare is not justified [14]. He argues that childhood immunization that accounts for 0.1% of the NHS budget contributes about 1.5 years to life expectancy, while the other 99.9% of the budget contributes only 2 to 2.5 more years. Furthermore, there is no correlation between expenditure and life expectancy. In 2002, the expenditure in China was only 1% of that of the US ($45 v $4,500 per person), while life expectancy there was 92% of that in the US (70.8 v 76.8 years) [14: p. 17]. He suggests that

> What really matters in terms of life expectancy are of course social and economic factors. Greater wealth allows people to live in better, less crowded, housing and to buy more adequate food [14].

He argues that there is no or little evidence that health services reduce morbidity or improve the quality of life [14: pp. 17–18]. Nicholson remarks that "What has become clear ... is the extent to which healthcare provision is now driven by patient demand rather than by health needs" [14: p. 18], [15].

Indeed, the Bristol Enquiry remarked:

> Governments of the day have made claims for the NHS which were not capable of being met on the resources available. The public has been led to believe that the NHS could meet their legitimate needs, whereas it is patently clear that it could not. Health-care professionals, doctors, nurses, managers, and others, have been caught between the growing disillusion of the public on the one hand and the tendency of governments to point to them as a scapegoat for a failing service on the other ... The NHS was represented as a comprehensive service which met all the needs of the public. Patently it did not do so... [16]

and

> ...What governments can not do is to renew its commitment to a comprehensive accessible healthcare service for all and then fail to fund it to the level of the demand government makes of it [16: p. 308, para 17].

Apart from identifying at least one reason for the increased demand for healthcare services (i.e., expectations fuelled by government declarations), the Bristol Enquiry Report also identifies some of those who may be charged with making rationing decisions (i.e., government, doctors, managers, and others such as economists or the public).

A detailed analysis of the merits or otherwise of the level of resources allocated by the government is beyond the scope of this essay. This chapter is mainly concerned with the ethical and legal aspects of rationing decisions that are made at the intermediary level that is directly responsible for the delivery of services. At this level the macroeconomic decisions have already been made and the authorities received a budget. The scarcity of resources has now become an undisputed fact. The question is therefore, what are the relevant ethical and legal aspects that need to be considered by [the authority] in its decision making process —

> On what basis could a creature of the state adopt any principle of selection? Whoever is excluded can justifiably complain that he is thereby being disadvantaged by the very institution whose special duty is to extend equal protection to all persons [17].

4.3 Ethical Considerations of Resource Allocation

4.3.1 *The concept of justice in ethical theory*

Justice is the concept of rightness in action or attitude and is considered a key feature of society — "…it is remarkable that the morality of most cultures gives prominence to the central virtues of justice and benevolence" [18]. This may not be surprising in view of studies indicating that reactions to fairness are "wired" into the brain and that "Fairness is activating the same part of the brain that responds to food in rats … This is consistent with the notion that being treated fairly satisfies a basic need" [19]. Research conducted in 2003 at Emory University, Georgia, involving capuchin monkeys demonstrated that other cooperative animals also possess such a sense and that "inequality aversion may not be uniquely human" [20], indicating that ideas of fairness and justice may be instinctual in nature.

In Aristotle's ethical theory, justice is one of the basic virtues [18: p. 166]. John Rawls explains that —

> The more specific sense that Aristotle gives to justice … is that of refraining from *pleonexia*, that is, from gaining some advantage for oneself by seizing what belongs to another … or by denying a person that which is

due to him, the fulfillment of a promise, the repayment of a debt, the showing of proper respect… [21].

As far as Rawls is concerned, "Justice is the first virtue of social institutions, as truth is of systems of thought" [21: p. 3]. Expanding on the social contract argument, Rawls suggests that "…the principles of justice for the basic structure of society *are* [my emphasis] the object of the original agreement" [21: p. 11], stressing the fundamental social importance of justice. Rawls argues that justice, and in particular distributive justice, is a form of fairness — the impartial distributions of goods: starting from a hypothetical original position of equality, arguing that the concept of justice is universally accepted (even if the conceptions of justice differ), using the "veil of ignorance" scenario [21: p. 12], and applying the principle of efficiency [21: p. 67], the principle of fair equality of opportunity, and the difference principle [21: pp. 75–80], he formulates the two principles of justice (in that particular hierarchal order) that would be accepted in the original position: "First: each person is to have an equal right to the most extensive basic liberty compatible with a similar liberty for others" [21: p. 60] and

> Second: social and economic inequalities are to be arranged so that they are both (a) to the greatest benefit of the least advantaged and (b) attached to offices and positions open to all under conditions of fair equality of opportunity [21: p. 83].

Therefore, Rawls's theory distinguishes two kinds of goods: liberties — that are to be distributed equally, and social and economic goods — that are to be distributed equally unless inequality improves the position of the worst off.

Not everyone agrees that justice is so fundamental to ethical theory. Utilitarianism maintains that justice builds on a more basis standard — total happiness. According to Mill — "The utilitarian doctrine is that happiness is desirable, and the only thing desirable, as an end; all other things being desirable as means to that end" [22] and —

> The happiness which forms the utilitarian standard of what is right in conduct, is not the agent's own happiness, but that of all concerned. As

between his own happiness and that of others, utilitarianism requires him
to be as strictly impartial as a disinterested and benevolent spectator [23].

So, the proper principles of justice are those which tend to have the best consequences. Therefore, justice is important, if at all, only as being derived from the fundamental standard of maximizing happiness.

Rawls argues that rationally and under the "veil of ignorance" everyone will reject the utilitarian theory of justice that we should maximize happiness because of the risk that our own good will be sacrificed for the greater benefit of others. His point of view is that of the ignorant yet self-interested *individual*, while the utilitarian point of view is that of the knowledgeable yet disinterested spectator. Therefore, Rawls argues, "Utilitarianism does not take seriously the distinction between persons" [21: p. 27].

Similarly, one of the most serious arguments against utilitarianism is that it is incompatible with the ideal of justice. In McCloskey's imaginary scenario a utilitarian spectator may conclude that he has a duty to bear false witness in order to bring about the punishment of an innocent man, if he knows that this will stop the riots and killings [24]. This of course will violate Kant's Categorical Imperative — "Act so that you treat humanity, whether in your own person or in that of another, always as an end and never as a means only" [25]. By sacrificing the innocent, the utilitarian is treating him as a means only and is thus violating his autonomy.

How do those principles translate into the real world's healthcare resource allocation? Some concepts such as equality (e.g., of resources, of access to healthcare resources, or of opportunities), needs, or cost-effectiveness evolve from the abovementioned basic principles of justice.

4.3.2 *Equality in resource allocation*

Equal distribution of all healthcare resources among all members of the community seems a fair way to solve the problem. After all, if no one has neither more nor less than anyone else who can complain? However, a strictly egalitarian approach that does not take account of personal circumstances hardly seems to satisfy the conception of justice. Surely, we will want to take account of personal needs in order to satisfy Kant's

Categorical Imperative so that we will wish that such a system will become a universal law according to which people will be treated with dignity as autonomous entities. Nor will such an egalitarian system satisfy Rawls's second principle that requires that the worse off will benefit the most. Indeed, an equal distribution of resources will adversely affect the worse off who will usually need more resources than the average they will receive. On the other hand, those with minor problems will get more than they need, making the system extremely inefficient. Those who need more will suffer. Those who need less will waste resources. From a utilitarian point of view, this surely is not the best way to maximize happiness. Intuitively, there is no virtue in such a strict egalitarian approach.

Another way to apply the principle of equality is to consider equality of access. This means that

> ...every person who shares the same type and degree of health need must
> be given an equally effective chance of receiving appropriate treatment of
> equal quality so long as that treatment is available to anyone [26].

This system allows for inequality between two patients suffering from different problems in type or degree. Also, it does not guarantee the availability of any particular treatment nor the quality of any treatment on offer. Indeed, the lower the quality of care offered, the greater the equality achieved. It does not mean equal outcomes either, as the equality of access relates to the health problem only, while outcomes will be affected by a variety of other factors such as compliance and other personal characteristics. However, it limits the liberties of the rich by banning them from obtaining extra treatments that are not available to the poor. As such, it does not seem to benefit the worse off but clearly disadvantages those who are well off. Equality of access seems more just than strict egalitarian allocation of resources but again fails to address the problem of individual needs.

4.3.3 *Resource allocation according to needs*

Karl Marx said "From each according to his ability, to each according to his needs" [27] and more recently Tony Blair reiterated the second half — "if you are ill or injured there will be a National Health Service there to help; and access to it will be based on need and need alone" [28].

Resource allocation based on "need and need alone" seems a just way of distribution. It takes into account the individual circumstances thus treating individuals with dignity and respect. It benefits the worse off who usually have the biggest needs and are the less likely to be able to meet their needs by themselves. To help those in the greatest need first seems the virtuous thing to do. And, at least in some cases, it will maximize happiness as treating those with the greatest need will generate more happiness than treating those with lesser needs.

The first problem is in deciding what constitutes a "need". Apart from the differences in personal and cultural perceptions, "medical" needs are not fixed but change and expand mainly as a consequence of man-made economic and technological advances and environmental manipulations —

> Medical "need" is an infinitely expandable concept. We need what is available, and in a creative and inventive society such as our own, there is no end to what we can do to treat aging bodies [29].

The next and main problem is in deciding which need is greater. According to Norman Daniels a health need is greater when there is greater impairment to the "normal species functioning" resulting in greater negative impact on the "…normal opportunity range" [30]. Therefore, the greater need is in those situations where the opportunity range is most affected. There is, however, the problem of defining what constitutes "normal opportunity range". Is the "normal range" fixed or, for example, age related? It clearly depends on culture — life expectancy in the Western world rose in the last 100 years while in sub-Saharan Africa, where AIDS is endemic, the lack of medical resources contributes to the declining life expectancy. Thus, the prior availability of healthcare resources impacts on the decision as to whether resources should be made available in a way that favours the better off instead of the worse off.

Moreover, the "normal opportunity range" principle clashes with the utilitarian principle of maximizing happiness or its practical form — cost-effectiveness. According to this principle, the most ill have priority over those with minor problems. This may be counterproductive. It may take similar resources to prevent ten people from having kidney failure as to treat one patient with kidney failure. Treating the one "deserving" patient means that in time there will be no resources for anyone. On the other hand, many medical treatments that we value and are cost-effective are not intended to restore normal species function at all. Instead, they are designed to prevent potential reductions in normal function. Such interventions include contraception, abortion, antenatal care, and palliative care [2: p. 47]. And how should we classify fertility treatments where no disease is treated or prevented but life is created?

4.3.4 Cost-effectiveness

There can be no doubt that healthcare resources should be cost-effective. No conception of justice will be served by wasting scarce resources on treatments that provide no benefit. But while quantifying the cost is relatively simple, it is not simple to quantify the effect.

Quality Adjusted Life Years (QALYs) is an attempt to quantify the cost and benefit of treatments. In this way the relative cost-effectiveness of different treatments for similar or different conditions can be determined. Determinations of QALYs involve the determination of the quality of life (from 0 — death to 1 — full health). This quality of life score is multiplied by the life expectancy in years to give the number of QALYs. The difference between the QALY before and after the treatment is the QALY score. In this way the cost of 1 QALY can be compared for each treatment or condition. Such a calculation may show that a hip replacement is very cost-effective at £1,800/QALY while a neurosurgical intervention is cost-ineffective at £107,780/QALY [31].

There are many problems with QALYs. How should the quality of life be measured and by whom? Is it possible to "measure" the quality of someone's life at all? This is surely a subjective matter. The patient will be biased because of his condition. Others (doctors or the general public) have no intimate knowledge of actually having the condition. Judgements pertaining to life expectancy are also extremely inaccurate. Moreover, the end result, i.e., QALY score, has no real meaning. Which one is better — to live five years in a wheelchair or two years without one arm?

QALYs may be useful for a particular patient in deciding which option will suit him best. It may possibly also be of value for a particular condition in order to decide which treatment will be the most cost-effective [32]. However, QALYs should not be used in deciding which group of patients to treat or not to treat, or to which conditions to give priority in resource allocation. This is because, as John Harris says,

> What matters is that the person is not prepared to agree that his interest in continued life is of less value than that of anyone else, nor that that interest necessarily varies with the quality of his life nor with his life expectancy. In short, if a person wants continued existence, then ... his interest in continued existence is entitled to be treated as on par with that of anyone else. All people who want to go on living have an interest in continued existence, the value of which can only be determined by themselves [33].

QALYs ignore the fairness of distribution to the individual and concentrate on the total aggregate size of the (anonymous) health improvement (e.g., more health to the healthy may give more QALYs than health to the sick). But most people will probably want to treat a few sufferers of cancer and heart disease instead of many who suffer from flu or mild headache.

QALY discriminates against the elderly, the disabled, and the terminally ill in favour of children, for example, because of the shorter life expectancy of the former or their (low) pre-existing quality of life, or both. This is what John Harris calls "double jeopardy" [32: p. 120] — those (innocent) people who have been disadvantaged by the indifferent nature of other people are further disadvantaged by policy makers [34].

QALY discriminates between patients with equal needs by denying them equal access on the basis of cost —

> Thus systematic discrimination could result against, say, those from ethnic minority groups who require interpreters, those living in poorer housing who might require inpatient stays rather than day surgery ... suppose ... a condition, suffered by men and women, for which treatment gave equal health gain for both sexes but, for some biological reason, treatment for a woman costs more ... Would it be acceptable to follow the logic of QALY maximisation and give treatment of men higher priority...? [35]

4.3.5 *Meritocracy*

Jonathan Glover suggests that sometimes the benefit to third parties such as children or the society as a whole should be taken into account —

> But, while rejecting discrimination based on supposed social worth as a general policy, it would be wrong to rule out the possibility of exceptions in extreme cases. It seems doctrinaire to say that, if Winston Churchill in 1940 had been in a lifeboat situation, it would have been wrong to give him priority [36].

Tom Beauchamps and James Childress argue that

> ...in an outbreak of infectious disease, it is justifiable to inoculate physicians and nurses first to enable them to care for others. ...priority on ground of social utility ... we should limit judgements of comparative social value to the specific qualities and skills that are essential to the community's immediate protection without assessing the general social worth of persons. If we limit exceptions based on social utility to emergencies involving necessity, they do not threaten the ordinary moral universe or imply the general acceptability of social-utilitarian calculations in distributing health care [37].

However, John Harris disagrees on grounds that discriminating against childless or single people violates the principle that all lives have equal moral worth and fails to respect their intrinsic value [38].

If we accept that the benefit to children and dependents should be taken into account, where do we draw the line? We may prioritize in favour of people who work, therefore adults against children or pensioners, people in full-time against part-time employment, or high-skilled against low-skilled workers (based on their contribution to the wider society). Such criteria will favour the white middle class male. On the other hand, the benefit to others from treating alcoholics and drug users will be considerable. It may be legitimate to take this indirect benefit into consideration in the decision making process as the purpose of the system is not only to treat the individual but also to promote the welfare of the community as a whole. Taking into account indirect benefit may be legitimate at the macro level, as it does not discriminate against particular individuals [39].

4.3.6 *Age*

Treating older people costs more, as their recovery takes longer and they suffer from more complications, which makes their treatment less cost-effective. Their life expectancy is lower than younger people resulting in less QALYs. The aged have already had "fair innings" meaning that money should be directed so as to give younger people the opportunity to live a fulfilling life [40]. There are two ways to look at the "fair innings" argument: one is to consider everyone below a certain age as young and everyone above this age as old; the second way is to always give priority to the younger patient.

On the other hand, the perception that treatments in older patients have lower efficacy may be wrong due to their underrepresentation in research trials. In addition, the prognosis of patients is affected by many factors, and in many cases age may not even be the most important one. Many old people are fitter than younger ones. Although the severity of the condition is a much more accurate prognostic factor, we will not want to deny healthcare from the severely ill patients as a group. Thus, age discrimination is arbitrary and therefore unjust. Assessment should be made on an individual basis and not be based on age alone.

Finally, systematic disvaluing of the aged leads to undesirable social consequences —

> The society that accords lower priority ... to the old ... is saying, in effect, that their lives are less worth saving, in short, are less valuable. ... which would make, for example, the crime of murder inevitably less serious when the victims are old or terminally ill... [41].

4.3.7 *Individual responsibility*

How shall we treat patients who become ill or disabled as a consequence of their own behaviour, such as alcoholism, drug abuse, careless driving, or extreme sports? Should they bear the costs or be given a lower priority [42]? It will be very difficult to apply a policy of discrimination against smokers, drug abusers, etc. without invading their privacy. It should also be remembered that most of us behave irresponsibly at least occasionally. Some of this "unhealthy" behaviour is influenced by genetic, social, or environmental factors beyond the control of the individual.

4.3.8 *Ability to pay*

Rationing according to ability to pay is against the original principle of public healthcare that it should be free at the point of delivery. But, "[t]he concept of the NHS as a comprehensive service may have outlived its usefulness" [43]. Is it time to move to a free market?

Even the original British National Health Act of 1946 contained provisions which allowed patients to pay extra for what was known as an "amenity bed" [2: p. 64]. There is already a thriving private sector. In the British NHS, dental and optical care are no longer widely available. Fertility treatments are only partially funded. Also, the NHS interacts with the private sector on a regular basis and on different levels. The NHS offers private services (e.g. fertillity investigations and treatments for patients who are not eligible for NHS funding according to the criteria that were set by the NHS itself). Such services are delivered by NHS personnel on standard NHS contracts. In emergencies (not clearly defined) [44], but also in other circumstances (not defined)[45], NHS Consultants may attend to private patients during their contracted hours, thus subsidising the private sector. Patients seen privately for consultation or treatment (and therefore quickly) are put on NHS waiting lists as if they were seen for the consultation or had their treatment in the NHS (supposedly because and according to their needs) [46]. This disadvantages NHS patients with similar needs who may need to wait longer for their NHS consultation or treatment before being scheduled for the next stage of their management. This also creates a possible conflict of interest for the consultant who may also be the one who decides whose need is more urgent and who should be seen or treated first. The NHS purchases services from the private sector for its patients in order to meet government targets. Tens of thousands of NHS-funded operations are carried out in the private sector each year [6: p. 233]. The state pays private companies to build and maintain hospitals and provide clinical services (Private Finance Initiative (PFI)).

The free market system as practiced in the US is not necessarily better than the NHS. Even under the new legislation [47], most people will not be able to pay for their full health needs in an acute situation. Currently, many cannot even afford to buy any insurance coverage. Some health problems will not be insured at all. Treatment for these patients will come from the public purse. The providers are paid per procedure and therefore have an incentive to overinvestigate and to overtreat, which increases the costs and creates further expectations and demand from the public.

Surely, a free market health service will disadvantage many and will not necessarily be cheaper. The question is not whether healthcare should be provided entirely by the state or entirely as a free market. But what is the right balance between the two systems?

4.4 Legal Aspects of Resource Allocation, with Special Reference to the UK

Rationing means that patients will be denied treatment on the grounds that resources can be better spent on other patients. It is therefore important that the decision making process is fair and consistent, that all relevant considerations are taken into account, and that the authorities are prepared to justify their decisions [2: p. 82].

The decisions of any public body are judicially reviewable. Therefore, in the UK for example, the decisions taken by a health authority (HA) have to be lawful (i.e., within their statutory power) and rational (i.e., not unreasonable [48]). Claims for judicial review may be brought against statutory bodies under illegality, irrationality, or procedural impropriety [6: p. 178]. The court has no jurisdiction to take the decision on the authority's behalf and will refer the matter back to the statutory body concerned for consideration when appropriate. Claims can also be brought under the Human Rights Act 1998.

Claims in negligence against statutory bodies are assessed with reference to the principles of judicial review and must satisfy the tri-partite test laid down in the Caparo case [6: p. 179], [49].

4.5 Conclusion

Resource allocation in healthcare requires a fine balance between the needs and interests of the individual and those of the society as a whole. Maintaining public confidence that the decision making process for resource allocation is fair and just is probably the most important thing. In most cases, finding the just solution is obvious and intuitive. In the minority of cases, competing demands can seem both equally deserving so that it seems impossible to make a black-and-white decision. In those cases, turning the focus of attention to the individual patient will usually solve the problem. Thus, a decision making process that is flexible enough to accommodate ethical principles with different starting points probably has the best chance of maintaining public confidence. Utilitarian principles seem to be suitable for macro decisions while principles of autonomy and freedom are more adequate for dealing with the individual patient.

Because decisions have to be made even in the most difficult situations, it is extremely important that the decision makers are free to make these decisions according to their best possible judgement. Public scrutiny should concentrate not on the outcome of the decision but on the thought process through which the decision was made. When the process is informed, fair, transparent, and in good faith, the outcome will usually be acceptable by the public and understood by the affected individual. However, when the decision making process is arbitrary and/or self-interested, the law should be there to restore justice.

References

[1] Hunter D.J. *Desperately Seeking Solutions: Rationing Health Care*. London: Longman, 1997; p. 20.
[2] Jackson E. *Medical Law. Text, Cases, and Materials*. Oxford: Oxford University Press, 2006; p. 35.
[3] Report of the Committee of Enquiry into the Costs of the National Health Service. Cmnd. 9663, 1956; para 95.
[4] Royal Commission on the National Health Service. Cmnd. 7615, 1979; para 6.1.
[5] Yuen P. Compendium of Health Statistics. Office of Health Economics, 2002; para 1.1.

[6] Newdick C. *Who Should we Treat? Rights, Rationing, and Resources in the NHS, 2nd ed.* Oxford: Oxford University Press, 2005; p. 5.

[7] Powell E. *A New Look at Medicine.* London: Pitman Medical Publishing, 1966; p. 26.

[8] Porter R. *The Greatest Benefit to Mankind — A Medical History of Humanity from Antiquity to the Present.* London: Fontana Press, 1997; p. 718.

[9] Making Amends — A consultation paper setting out proposals for reforming the approach to clinical negligence in the NHS. Department of Health, 2003; para 35.

[10] Hall M.A. Rationing Health Care at the Bedside. 69 New York University Law Review, 1994, pp. 693, 694.

[11] Jackson E. *Medical Law. Text, Cases, and Materials.* Oxford: Oxford University Press, 2006; p. 37.[Cited in Lamm R.D. Rationing of Health Care: Inevitable and Desirable. 140 University of Pennsylvania Law Review, 1992, pp. 1511, 1512.]

[12] Nozick R. *Anarchy, State and Utopia.* Oxford: Blackwell, 1974.

[13] Light D.W. The real ethics of rationing. *British Medical Journal* 1997; **315**: 112–115.

[14] Nicholson R. Justice and sustainability in healthcare. *Bulletin of Medical Ethics*, March 2006; 15–28.

[15] For a comprehensive discussion on this subject see — Illich I. *Limits to Medicine.* Tel Aviv, Israel: Am Oved Publishers Ltd, 1978 (Hebrew translation from English).

[16] Bristol Royal Infirmary Enquiry. Learning from Bristol. DoH, Cm. 5207, 2001; p. 57, para 31.

[17] Lomasky L.E. Medical progress and National Health Care. *Philosophy and Public Affairs* 1980; **10**: 82.

[18] Benn P. Ethics. London and New York: Routledge, 2006; p. 26.

[19] UCLS (News room).

[20] Brosnan S.F. Monkeys reject unequal pay. *Nature*, 18 September 2003; **425**: 297–299.

[21] Rawls J.A. Theory of Justice. Oxford: Oxford University Press, 1971; p. 10.

[22] Mill J.S. *Utilitarianism.* (1861). [quoted in: J. Rachels (5th ed. by S. Rachels). *The Elements of Moral Philosophy.* New York: McGraw Hill, 2007; p. 100.]

[23] Mill J.S. *Utilitarianism.* Indianapolis, IN: Bobbs-Merrill, 1957; p. 22. [quoted in: J. Rachels (5th ed. by S. Rachels). *The Elements of Moral Philosophy.* New York: McGraw Hill, 2007; p. 100.

[24] McCloskey H.J. A non-utilitarian approach to punishment. *Inquiry* 1965; **8**: 239–255.

[25] Kant I. *Foundations of the Metaphysics of Morals*. Translated by L.W. Beck. Indianapolis, IN: Bobbs-Merrill, 1959; p. 47. [quoted in: J. Rachels (5th ed. by S. Rachels). *The Elements of Moral Philosophy*. New York: McGraw Hill, 2007; p. 131.]

[26] Gutmann A. For and Against Equal Access to Health Care. Milbank Memorial Fund Quarterly/Health and Society 59(4) (1981). In G. Pence (ed.) *Classic Works in Medical Ethics*. Boston: McGraw Hill, 1998; pp. 367–381.

[27] Marx K. Critique of the Gotha Program. In D. McLellan (ed.) *Karl Marx: Selected writings*. Oxford: Oxford University Press, 1977; p. 569.

[28] The New NHS — Modern, Dependable (21997, Cm. 3807), para 1.5.

[29] Lamm R.D. Rationing of Health Care: Inevitable and Desirable. *University of Pennsylvania Law Review* 1992; **140**: 1511, 1512.

[30] Daniels N. HealthCare Needs and Distributive Justice. *Philosophy and Public Affairs* 1981; **10**: 154.

[31] Maynard A.M. Developing the health care market. *The Economic Journal* 1991; **101**: 1277–1286.

[32] Harris J. QALYfying the value of life. *Journal of Medical Ethics* 1987; **13**: 117–123.

[33] Harris J. Double jeopardy and the veil of ignorance — a reply. *Journal of Medical Ethics* 1995; **21**: 151–157.

[34] Harris J. More and Better Justice. In J.M. Bell and S. Mendus (eds), *Philosophy and medical welfare*. Cambridge: Cambridge University Press, 1988; 75–96, p. 80.

[35] Mullen P. and Spurgeon P. *Priority setting and the public*. Abingdon: Radcliffe Medical Press, 2000; p. 42.

[36] Glover J. *Causing death and saving lives*. London: Penguin, 1977; pp. 222–223.

[37] Beauchamps T. and Childress J. *Principles of Biomedical Ethics, 5th ed.* Oxford: Oxford University Press, 2001; p. 271.

[38] Harris J. *The Value of Life*. London: Routledge, 1985; pp. 104–106.

[39] Brock D. Separate spheres and indirect benefits. (2003) Cost effectiveness and resource allocation ¼. http://www.resource-allocation.com/content/1/1/4 [accessed 5 March 2014].

[40] Harris J. *The Value of Life*. London: Routledge, 1985; p. 93.

[41] Harris J. The age-indifference principle and equality. *Cambridge Quarterly of Healthcare Ethics* 2005; **14**: 93–9.

[42] Blank R. *Rationing Medicine*. New York: Columbia University Press, 1988; pp. 199–200.

[43] British Medical Association Health Funding Review. BMA review of UK
      health care funding. http://web.bma.org.uk/pressrel.nsf/wall/812F34951AC
      06752802568F500543209?OpenDocument [accessed 5 March 2014].
[44] A code of conduct for private practice. DoH 2004; 2.6, p. 3
[45] A code of conduct for private practice. DoH 2004; 2.8, p. 3.
[46] A code of conduct for private practice. DoH 2004; 2.13, p. 4.
[47] Public Law 111–148. 111th United States Congress. Washington, D.C.:
      United States Government Printing Office. March 23, 2010.
[48] *Wednesbury Corporation* v *Minister of Housing and Local Government* [1966]
      2 QB 275.
[49] *Caparo Industries plc* v *Dickman* [1990] 1 All ER 568.

5

Ethical and Legal Issues in Clinical Research

Andrew J. T. George

5.1 Introduction

At the Yad Vashem (Holocaust Memorial) in Jerusalem there is a statue that shows two halves of a sphere that have been slightly separated, and one half is sliced into sections and distorted. It is the memorial to those that were victims of Mengele's research projects that took place in the Nazi death camps — in which he had a particular interest in twins and used to separate them, experimenting on one and using the other for comparison. It is the terrible crimes of Mengele and other doctors, and the international realisation of the terrible things that were done in the name of science, that has led to much of the development of the ethical and legal frameworks that control clinical research.

The research that the Nazis conducted was often barbaric and had little connection with any real scientific purpose or methodology. It is therefore tempting to dismiss all they did as a form of sadistic torture justified by a supposed pseudo-scientific purpose — and indeed for many of their actions this is so and what they did was neither ethical nor research. However, some of the research that they did may well have produced data that is useful (for example in understanding hypothermia). This work was answering important scientific questions, and, in a very narrow sense, was well conducted (if it is possible to describe totally unethical research as well conducted). It shows that doctors and scientists are capable of doing terrible things for science. This cannot and must not be taken as justification for their actions. We also need to think about what we should now do with that data; is it acceptable to use data that was obtained in an unethical and reprehensible manner?

There is a risk that we see what happened during the Nazi period as something that was confined to a particular time and place — that there was something about Nazi Germany that made a group of people act in an evil way. This belief insulates us from any danger or association; there is no need for us to learn the lessons of what happened because it cannot happen here, in the UK in the twenty-first century. We assume that no scientist or doctor would ever behave like that here. However, to believe that is to ignore other events in history — events that show that doctors or scientists in the UK or the US or any number of other countries can do things that society sees as totally unacceptable. One of the more notorious cases is the Tuskegee Syphilis trial when 399 black males in Alabama with syphilis were left untreated (even when penicillin had been demonstrated to be effective) so that US Public Health Service researchers could follow the natural history of the disease. The participants were also subject to invasive procedures, such as spinal taps, that were described as "special treatment". This trial was not terminated until 1972, and among the "victims" of the study are not only the men that died of syphilis but their wives and children that had been infected.

In the UK there have been scandals associated with clinical research, perhaps the most damaging being the Alder Hey retained organ scandal. In this, organs from children who died at Alder Hey's children's hospital from 1988 to 1995 were removed and retained at *post mortem* without permission from the parents. This uncovered a massive difference between what was common practice in the NHS (retention of organs *post mortem* without permission) and what the public saw as acceptable behaviour. The resulting furore led ultimately to the Human Tissue Act, which regulates all research in the UK that involves human tissue and is seen by some as being overly restrictive for research.

There are two main lessons to draw from this history. The first is that doctors and scientists can do the wrong thing but with good motives. The doctors involved in the Tuskegee study wanted to improve the treatment of syphilis. They did not set out to be cruel or to harm their participants.

However, they got blinded by the importance of their science, and presumably ceased to see the individuals who were the participants (possibly made easier by the participants being illiterate black sharecroppers). The second lesson is that public opinion can diverge from opinion within a professional body, to an extent that they cease to make contact and there is a total breakdown in trust. This is what happened in Alder Hey (and in other hospitals); the pathologists acted in a way that they thought was reasonable (and indeed in a way that they believed was in the best interest of relatives who would be spared the distress of consenting for organ retention, and would supply material that would help develop new treatments), but failed to realise that public opinion had moved on. The result was a breakdown in trust.

These considerations have all led to the establishment and development of processes by which research is reviewed by independent bodies. In the rest of this chapter I will discuss five things; why we need research ethics committees (RECs), the history and mechanism of UK RECs, what ethical issues RECs look at, what tools they use, and finally a discussion about whether this process ensures that research is carried out in an ethical manner.

5.2 Why Do We Need RECs?

Much of the answer to this question will be apparent from the introduction. Scientists and doctors can do things in the name of science that are not acceptable. They may do this because they are "blinded" by their scientific quest and they see obtaining the answer to the question as being more important than what they do to their research participants. This may be for "honourable" reasons (the desire to develop a new cure for a disease) or "less honourable" (the need for promotion or payment). They may do this because they have developed particular values or beliefs that do not agree with those of the public or the participants (as in the Alder Hey example). They may be habituated to certain things being acceptable by virtue of their job. Or they may simply be incompetent or bad, though this is probably a tiny minority.

For these reasons it is important that an ethical review of research involving patients should be performed as it gives an outside body the chance to look at the research. The presence of lay people on any review panel can provide a check that what is being done is reasonable. It therefore serves to protect the research participant from unreasonable behaviour by the doctor (though note that it does not serve to protect the participant from harm occurring as a result of the study — this will be discussed later).

An allied reason for the need for ethical review is that it promotes and encourages public confidence in the research (and clinical) process. This is important if research is to continue, as researchers are dependent to a large extent on the public for funding their research (either through charitable giving or taxation). In addition, if public confidence is lacking then there is more pressure for an increase in regulation of research. A clear example would be the Human Tissue Act that arose as a consequence of public distrust of the medical/scientific world following the events at Alder Hey and other "scandals". There can also be more knock-on consequences; it has been suggested that the Tuskegee Syphilis trial helped damage the trust of the black community in medical care, public health, and medical research, and may even be responsible in large part for the suspicion that HIV is a man-made virus created by the US government to kill black people. Ethical scrutiny of research can preserve public confidence either by identifying and preventing bad research, or by assuring the public that there is adequate oversight of clinical research (though it is an open question as to whether the public know enough about the research ethics system for such assurance to be effective).

A more prosaic reason for needing an ethical review of research is that it is a requirement, in many cases a legal requirement and increasingly a requirement of journals, grant giving bodies, higher degree exam boards, professional bodies, and others. It could be argued that this is not only a hurdle that researchers have to climb over, but that it also affords protection to researchers (and to the organisations that employ them, fund them, or publish their results) if something were to go wrong.

Finally the process of ethical review can improve research. Often research is devised solely from the point of view of the researcher and answering a research question. Ethical review considers the participant's point of view, and will often seek to reduce the burden to the subject. This, together with improving the information provided, can motivate the participant and improve compliance while reducing drop-out rates.

5.3 What is the Mechanism for Ethical Review?

In this section I will concentrate on the system in the UK. Every jurisdiction has its own systems for ethical review, and it is not the place here to do an exhaustive survey. There have been interesting comparisons of the ethical review process across the European Union [1]. It is also not my intention to give an exhaustive description of the detailed processes and regulations for ethical review. These are subject to change, and are described in detail in the Governance Arrangements for NHS Research Ethics Committees (commonly termed GAfREC) [2] and the standard operating procedures for Research Ethics Committees (RECs) which are available on the Health Research Authority website [3].

It is, however, worth considering what the situation used to be like in the UK. Prior to the formal establishment of RECs many institutions had their own committees that provided ethical review for studies that took place in those hospitals and universities. These were officially established in 1991 by the Department of Health who issued guidance that indicated broad precepts of what the committees should do. However, there were no common operating procedures, and no cross-recognition of decisions by different RECs. Therefore a researcher who wanted to carry out research in more than one hospital had to apply to each REC individually, which would necessitate filling in separate forms and following different procedures. There were no agreed standards of operation, so while some RECs were efficient others would take a long time to make a decision. The understandable frustration of researchers led, in 1997, to the formation of Multi-centre Research Ethics Committees who could look at research that was carried out in multiple sites. There was then the establishment in 2000 of the Central Office of Research Ethics Committees (COREC), the gradual evolution towards common practice ith the publication of GAfREC in 2001, the institution of a single UK-wide ethical opinion in 2004, and the implementation of the European Union Clinical Trials Directive in 2004. These changes were taking place in parallel with other modifications in research governance within the UK (for example the publication of the Research Governance Framework for Health and Social Care [4]). Researchers welcomed the single opinion, and the use of a single form. However, there were concerns that the process was still too cumbersome and bureaucratic, resulting in an inquiry in 2005 (the "Warner Report";

Report of the Ad Hoc Advisory Group on the Operation of NHS Research Ethics Committees [5] which made a number of recommendations. To a large extent COREC was already working towards streamlining the REC system, and the formation in 2007 of the National Research Ethics Service (NRES) which includes all RECs in England (and works closely with RECs in Scotland, Wales, and Northern Ireland) marked the move to a more responsive REC service. In 2009 the National Research Ethics Advisors' Panel was set up, to provide NRES (including RECs) with strategic oversight and advice on general ethical issues.

Changes have continued since 2010 after concerns about the obstacles that inhibited clinical research led to the publication in 2011 by the Academy of Medical Sciences of a report (commissioned by the government) that reviewed the entire governance structure for research [6]. The report indicated that NRES had made considerable progress in streamlining its processes. However, it did made important recommendations in improving processes for regulating research, and as a result the Health Research Authority (HRA), which incorporated NRES and other functions, was established to oversee and promote clinical research [3].

These changes have not been without difficulties. Some REC members and chairs have felt that the centralisation of the organisation has restricted their independence, and have therefore resisted the changes. It should be noted that while the organisation has dictated operational procedures the ethical decision is independent and solely within the domain of the REC. There has also been a move away from RECs that are associated with an institution (and often named after that hospital). This has clear advantages in terms of public perception (and indeed institutional perception) of independence. It also reflects more closely the real situation where one REC gives their opinion for the whole of the UK, and where researchers are more willing to seek ethical approval from RECs that are not geographically local to them but either have appropriate expertise or can review an application rapidly. However, there has been some loss of local help to researchers and a less flexible support than was historically available. The changes have also led to fewer applications to RECs (in large part because of the single UK-wide opinion and other increases in efficiency). This has led to closures of RECs that have meant that some volunteers and staff who have worked loyally for the REC system are no longer needed.

However, it is clear that HRA operates in a way that is immeasurably more efficient, consistent, and coherent than prior to the changes.

A researcher who is seeking REC approval will now use a common application form. All RECs follow the same procedures, and as only one REC has to approve the study they can apply to a REC anywhere in the country — not just the one closest to them. While there is no hierarchy of RECs, with some being superior to others, there is differentiation of function between RECs. Thus Clinical Trials of Investigative Medicinal Products (CTIMPs) have to be seen by RECs with the appropriate expertise and membership. The same is true for other forms of research, including phase I studies, gene therapy studies, research on participants unable to give consent (falling under the Mental Capacity Act), and others. A Social Care Research Ethics Committee has been set up to look at social research [7]. The situation is therefore that while all RECs follow common procedures, have common standards, and will see a broad range of applications, there is a degree of specialisation and expertise within individual committees. Work is currently underway to improve the sharing of that expertise.

Once the application has been made then the REC has a transparent process, with strict time lines, for consideration of the application. Thus a decision on all applications has to be made within 60 days of receipt of the application (though in general the average time to final decision is 35–40 days). The REC is allowed to ask the researcher one set of questions (while the researchers respond the "clock stops"). For full details of the process see the HRA website [3].

RECs have up to 18 members, of which a third are lay. This is an important factor to consider when making an application; a common problem is that the application is written in a language more suitable for a grant application which is often incomprehensible to lay people (and indeed to experts outside the narrow field!). At present applications are seen in full meetings of the REC, though pilot schemes are underway to test new mechanisms of proportionate review where projects that raise no substantial ethical issues are handled more rapidly by a small group of reviewers. The researcher will always be invited to attend the meeting and will be asked questions. Normally this does not involve a formal presentation of the proposal but offers opportunity for clarification and dialogue.

The REC can make a number of decisions on the proposal: favourable opinion, provisional opinion, and unfavourable opinion. When giving a favourable opinion the REC can insist on certain conditions, in general a requirement to make specified alterations (e.g., minor corrections in the information sheet). A provisional opinion essentially means that the researcher has to make minor modifications and/or clarifications to the proposal.

It is important that researchers see the process of ethical review as a dialogue. RECs are capable of making mistakes. In some cases this will be because they do not understand some aspect of the research, or that they do not fully appreciate the circumstances of a particular patient group or research setting (what is obvious to a clinician who has spent their career in a speciality may not be evident to people who have read a single application). The REC may also make a suggestion to overcome a problem, but the researcher may have a better idea. It is important in these settings to enter into a dialogue with the REC, either through the coordinator, the Chair, or an individual delegated to liaise with the researcher (an increasingly common practice). The REC should be able to listen to the researcher and, if they agree, modify their opinion. Equally researchers need to listen to the concerns of the REC members. If at the end of any process the researcher fundamentally disagrees with the REC opinion then there is an appeal process that can be initiated.

It is important to remember that ethical review is only part of the regulatory framework that researchers need to follow to undertake clinical research. Governance of clinical research is a collaboration between a number of regulatory bodies, each of which has a distinct role. In addition to the researcher and the ethics committee another key group is the sponsor. The sponsor, who is distinct from the funder of the research, is normally the NHS Trust, the university, or a pharmaceutical or commercial company. They take responsibility for much of the conduct of the research and for ensuring the research is appropriately carried out. Then there are other regulatory bodies: for trials involving drugs or devices then MHRA approval is needed, for trials involving radiation ARSAC must be approached. The researcher will normally need approval from their Research and Development Office. This can be bewildering and put off researchers from initiating projects. There are moves to make the system simpler and more streamlined — and the introduction of Integrated Research Application System (IRAS) a single form, which can be used to seek approval from the REC, MHRA, and R&D Office, is a major and welcome step in this direction. It is also likely that sponsors of research, including trusts and universities, are going to have to take a more proactive role in helping their employees obtain the necessary approvals. In many cases it is straightforward, but it can be very daunting for someone who does it infrequently.

5.4 What are the Ethical Factors that RECs Look at?

Three main things that RECs look at when considering the ethical aspects of a proposal are:

- Validity of the research.
- The welfare of the research participant.
- The dignity of the research participant.

The validity of the research covers questions around the importance of the research question and whether the proposed research can answer that question. The main consideration here is that all research will impose a burden or risk of harm on the research participant, however minor (see below for discussion of burden and harms). Therefore the research question has to be sufficiently important as to justify the risk or burden on a research participant. In addition the research methodology has to be such that it will (or at least is likely to) answer the research question — the argument being that it would unethical to subject participants to research if there is no chance of the research producing any useful data.

It is this aspect of the ethical review that can result in complaints from researchers. In a large part this is because there is a danger that RECs can take upon themselves the role of a scientific review panel. In general RECs are not constituted to be able to carry out a detailed scientific review of a complex research project in a narrow field, and often will make themselves look stupid if they suggest modifications to a project that has been proposed by an eminent expert in the field. This has led to the ruling that RECs should not consider the science of a project, and that they should rely on the sponsor and external peer review of a project to determine whether the research methodology is valid or not. However, it also has to be said that RECs do end up considering a lot of projects that are badly designed and put together, and that there is often considerable expertise within a REC on statistics and trial design that may not be available to the researcher. In addition the level of peer review provided by researchers can be limited. The committee also need to be able to understand the science well enough to come to a judgement as to the importance of the research. RECs need to be aware of this tension, and ensure that they do not slip into becoming a scientific review panel (which is often the comfort zone of the expert members). They need to make sure that all their comments about scientific aspects of the research do impact on the ethics of the study. If they do have scientific suggestions that do not concern the ethics (and it would be surprising if discussion of a project by 18 intelligent people did not occasionally result in such suggestions) then they should feel free to feed these back to the researcher making it absolutely clear that these are suggestions and do not form part of the ethical approval process.

The other problem with this aspect of review can be student research. When a student does a project for a BSc, MSc, or equivalent it may well not be answering a really important question, and it may not be capable of answering that question properly (for example, student projects are often statistically underpowered due to constraints of time). It can therefore be argued that student projects are unethical. An alternative view is that student projects are worthwhile, because they train future researchers and clinicians, and that RECs should consider this benefit when weighing up the ethics of the proposal. This is reasonable, and so long as the risks and burdens of the research are low and the potential participants are informed that the main aim of the project is educational, then that should be acceptable. It is worth asking whether supervisors could improve the design of student projects so that they were scientifically more valid — but that is outside the remit of this chapter!

The second aspect that the REC considers is the welfare of the research participant. Here the committee is addressing what the research will involve for the patients and what the risks and burdens of the research are likely to be. They then come to a decision as to whether these are acceptable or not. What is meant by a burden is the inconvenience and hardship that the participant will undergo — how many hospital visits and for how long? Will they need to eat a special diet? Will they need to keep a diary? These are not things that put the participants at risk of harm, but they do impose an inconvenience. The risks of harm consider the risks of the participant being damaged in some way (as well as the consequences of such damage). In some cases the risks will be well known (the risk of a particular invasive procedure); in other cases the risks will be unknown (in a phase I study of a new drug). The REC will try to ensure that the risks and burdens of a project are as low as can be achieved, and that these risks and burdens are commensurate with the importance of the research. They will also want to be assured that the consequences of any harm are minimised as far as possible (for example, ensuring appropriate facilities are in place to resuscitate a participant, use of the minimal radiation dose compatible with obtaining the necessary results). It is important to note that the REC cannot ensure that there is no risk to a research project, nor that the research participant will not be harmed by the project.

Most procedures done on patients will involve both a risk and a burden. If a patient has a colonoscopy then there is a considerable burden — they have to be pre-treated with enemas and it can only be described as an unpleasant experience. There is also a small risk, that there may be bowel perforation.

It is necessary to consider how much risk is acceptable. One area where this is quite well worked out is in studies involving ionising radiation. In these the dose of radioactivity that is "allowed" depends on a balance of the risk of that radiation causing damage (cancer) to the participant and the risk to that individual due to other causes. Therefore, the amount of radiation that is permissible in young people is less than that permissible in the elderly — the elderly have a higher risk of death and disease due to their age and so the relative extra risk due to the higher radiation dose is reduced. Similarly, in patients who have a disease that is likely to kill them in the near future the added risk of radiation due to a study is insignificant, and so it is normally acceptable to allow for higher doses of radiation. This can be a difficult area and involves complex judgement calls, and also the risk of inappropriately using certain patient groups for relatively high-risk research simply because they have a terminal diagnosis.

The final area of consideration is the dignity of the research subject. This is a clumsy term, but encapsulates concerns around treating the participant appropriately, as an autonomous individual able to make decisions and with rights. This area covers ensuring that the participant's confidentiality is ensured and, perhaps most importantly, that their consent is sought for taking part in the research.

The consent process is probably the area that takes up the most time for a REC. A whole chapter could be taken up describing the consent process, and it is an area that I am not convinced we are doing correctly. In this section I will briefly touch on what I see as the major issues. I will not address any specialist issues, such as paediatric consent or what to do in cases where individuals cannot consent for themselves.

The importance of consent is outlined in the Helsinki declaration, where quite detailed guidance is given as to what information the patients should be given. The researcher is then told to ensure that the patient has understood the information, before obtaining their informed consent.

For informed consent to be valid it should be voluntary, it should be informed, and the person giving it should be competent to give it. It has to be given before any part of the study starts (including randomisation). The REC will want to ensure that wherever possible participants are given plenty of time to decide whether to take part in the study and consult with other people if at all possible. They will also want to know that they are capable of taking in all the information and giving informed consent.

In the vast majority of projects the information process involves a Patient Information Sheet that contains the relevant information about the study. This needs to contain a description of the research and an account of what the study entails (including any risks). There is also a lot of additional information that is required — the easiest way to approach this is to use the template that HRA offer which contains all the necessary headings. The information sheet needs to be written in a manner that the participants can understand — and researchers need to remember that 16% of adults in the UK have a reading age of 11 or less [8]. It has been suggested that the Patient Information Sheet should be written at the level of *The Sun* newspaper. It can be difficult to imagine describing research at the level of *The Sun*, but it is achievable. Indeed, the science section of that newspaper put across complicated concepts in a clear and intelligible (and accurate) way. The really great scientists are able to communicate their science clearly, and they can do that because they can identify what is important and what is extraneous material that is not germane to what is being discussed. There can be a danger that the researcher sees the information sheet as an opportunity to educate the participant in their field of science, however this is not the moment to correct any deficiencies in the education system. It is important to avoid jargon or medical terminology ("double blind randomised placebo controlled trial" means little to most people). It is important not to be coercive or to play on the natural gratitude that a patient might have for the clinical team treating them.

There are some difficult aspects of information sheets. One of these is the portrayal of risk. If someone says that a particular procedure is low risk — what does that mean? Individuals will disagree on their definition of what low risk is (1/1,000 or 1/1,000,000?) and also will not really understand what these figures mean (few people are aware of what their risk of death is over the next 24 hours, or what the risk of crossing a road or flying in a plane is). We need to work on better ways of communicating risk.

While the information sheet is important, and is a major part of what a REC considers, it must be admitted that there are problems with our current approach to consent. It is clear that in spite of the best efforts of researchers and RECs, information sheets remain difficult to understand. In part this is because of their length — many patients are not able or willing to read seven- to ten-page typed documents. Jargon still creeps in, including legal jargon around clauses to do with indemnity. There remains a lot of information in the information sheet that is not central to the potential participant's decision making process.

Another problem with the information sheet is that it focuses the attention on one point in time, the point at which the researcher "obtains consent". This is treated as though it is a single event, which only needs to be done once. In some cases this might be correct (for example collecting a blood sample), but many studies go on for months or years, and the researchers (and RECs) need to consider how to keep the patient informed over that time and how to maintain their consent (or allow them to withdraw it).

It could also be argued that the process spends too much of its time considering how to give potential participants the information and not enough time in checking that they have understood the information.

Anecdotally it would seem that participants obtain much of the information they need to make the decision verbally from the researcher. However, the REC has no control over this. It may be more useful to agree minimum information that the participants need to understand in order to take part in the trial, and then agree a method of checking that they understand and can recall this minimum information.

As discussed above, there are three major ethical questions that the REC considers. There are of course special or complex cases in which other things need to be considered. It is also true that the three questions are not isolated from each other, but need to be considered in conjunction. For example, any consideration of risks and burdens impinges on the validity of the research (the risks and burdens must be commensurate with the importance of the research), on the welfare of the research subject (the risks and burdens should be minimised and reasonable), and on the dignity of the research subject (the potential participant must be adequately informed of the risks and burdens).

5.5 What "Tools" Do RECs Use in Considering Ethical Issues?

While there can be people with expertise in academic ethics on RECs, there is no requirement for any "expert" in ethics to sit on such committees. The emphasis is rather on common sense, with the view of the lay members being central to deciding if something is acceptable or not. That being said there are certain ways of reasoning that are often used by individuals on the committee.

One that is commonly used is a utilitarian argument; at its simplest one weighs up the potential harm that can result from an action and the potential benefit. If the harm exceeds the benefit then the action is ethical. Clearly this is a simplistic way of presenting a utilitarian argument and raises a number of issues (can we agree on how we weight benefits and harms? What can we do when the benefits and harms are unknown?). However, it is of use especially when considering the validity of the research question.

A second way of reasoning is to posit that the researcher has duties to the research participant, and that if these duties are disregarded then the research is not ethical. These duties can be framed in phrases such as "You should not knowingly harm your patient." "You should not lie to your patient." This method of codifying ethics has a long history, the Hippocratic oath being an early example, but the practice has continued with countless declarations and statements by international organisations and professional bodies that have sought to outline the duties of doctors, other healthcare professionals, and scientists.

The final approach is the rights-based approach, which states that individuals have rights and that it is important not to transgress those rights. Thus in our society an individual has the right for self-determination, to privacy, to access to healthcare (among others). A REC will want to know that these rights are not contravened by the study. As in many cases an individual is free to set aside their rights, this approach is central when thinking about the informed consent process. In many cases if the participant gives fully informed consent then their rights are being respected; I may have a right not to be assaulted, but I can give permission for a doctor to take an extra biopsy.

It should be noted that any one of these approaches to ethical reasoning would normally be incomplete or insufficient in themselves. For example, it is possible using a strictly utilitarian approach to argue that research can be done that harms an individual if it is of benefit to society. This might be used to support the Tuskegee trial, the Alder Hey organ retention, and even some of the Nazi experiments. Similarly the rights-based approach has its limitations; there are rights that society limits (I can give permission to be assaulted, for example in a boxing ring or by a surgeon, but society does not accept that I can give permission to be murdered). In the duties-based approach it is worth noting that different professions will see themselves as having different duties to research participants; nurses and doctors have a different view as to their duties. There are also big differences between (for example) research by the medical professionals and that by social scientists, which can lead to clashes. Some social scientists consider NHS ethics committees as being unreasonably obstructive for imposing duties on the researcher that spring from a medical paradigm of ethical behaviour. For example, anthropologists often use covert observation as part of their research — a research technique that the medical profession often find problematic, in part because it threatens the trust between doctors and patients. No doubt similar tensions would be seen if medical research was sent to an ethics committee that operated within a more social science paradigm! This does raise the issue that the authority for deciding what duties are important is not always clear (though there may be general acceptance of "core duties"), and may simply be a codification of behaviour that is accepted within a profession and has little validity or authority outside that profession (or indeed with the research participants). Similar considerations arise for rights-based reasoning — we may all agree on some central rights, but we are unlikely to agree on them all!

It is also important to realise that, over time, what are regarded as important rights and duties will change. This does mean that what is considered to be ethically acceptable will also change with time. The obvious example is organ retention in the UK. In the fairly recent past both society and the medical profession would have seen it as acceptable for pathologists to retain small amounts of tissue following a *post mortem* examination for research purposes (though it might be suggested that society's acceptance was in part the result of ignorance of the procedure). However, over time the public understanding of doctors' duties and patients' (or relatives') rights evolved. The Alder Hey scandal was in part because the medical and research profession had not kept pace with this evolution, due in large measure to a lack of communication between all those involved and a widespread ignorance of what was happening. It is probably not fair to say that in the past researchers were "wrong" to retain tissue, because that was acceptable behaviour within the ethical framework that was current. Where they made a mistake was not to keep in touch with general opinion and modify their behaviour (or seek to modify general opinion by education) accordingly.

The duties- and rights-based approaches also cause issues with some forms of research. Research on human subjects can be considered either therapeutic (a project that is testing a treatment for a disease, and so there might be potential benefits) or non-therapeutic (in which there is no potential benefit for the research subject). If it is assumed that researchers have a duty of care for the research participant not to harm that individual, then it can be difficult to justify non-therapeutic research. One can argue that, whatever the research project, there is a small risk of harm and/or a burden on the research participant. As there is no benefit then one has a duty not to inflict the research on the potential participant. However, in general there is an acceptance that so long as the risk and burden is sufficiently small that, so long as the individual consents to take part in the study (in full knowledge that there is no benefit to them), it is reasonable to conduct the research. The participant's permission allows the researcher to set aside their duty not to harm the participant. This is more problematic in settings where the participant is unable to consent to research — if they are incompetent to give consent for whatever reason. This is an area where the Mental Capacity Act has given a framework for researchers to operate in.

For therapeutic research the situation is clearer. The potential benefit to the patient means that the researcher can maintain their duty not to harm the patient and still carry out the research. For therapeutic research one important principle is equipoise — that before the study the researcher does not know that they are giving any of the participants in the study sub-optimal treatment. Once the study is complete the researchers may well know that they have, in retrospect, given some of the participants substandard treatment. To take the example of a randomised control trial of a new drug; it is common to randomise patients to receive either the new agent or current treatment. If the researcher knows that one of the treatments is better then it is probably unethical to conduct the research (though naturally the researcher may well hope/believe that their new treatment is better, they do not know that it is). Similarly if the researcher denies the control arm standard current best therapy then it is probably also unethical — so the control arm should not be given placebo alone if is there is an effective treatment, nor should they be given an out-of-date treatment that is no longer in standard use.

5.6 Does REC Scrutiny Ensure Ethical Research?

It is reasonable to ask whether the REC review system ensures that research is carried out in an ethical manner. Most of the REC process is focussed on the application. The REC has little control over how the research is conducted, once it has issued a favourable opinion. Therefore while there is little opportunity to ensure that researchers are being ethical when they discuss the projects with potential participants, there is plenty of opportunity for coercion.

However, while this might seem to indicate that the REC are impotent at ensuring research is ethical, it has to be remembered that there are several partners in the regulation and conduct of research. Not least amongst these is the researcher (and their team), who have a duty to conduct any research ethically. In addition the sponsor of the research has duties in ensuring the proper conduct of research. Other bodies (MHRA, ARSAC, Human Tissue Authority, etc.) all have roles to play. The REC is only a part of the process.

The scrutiny of the REC (and the other regulatory bodies, in particular the MHRA that has a key role to play in safety) also cannot ensure that research is safe. The trial of TGN1412, a monoclonal anti-CD28 antibody developed by TeGenero, in which six healthy volunteers underwent a severe "cytokine storm" after being treated with the antibody, is a case in point. There are lessons to be learnt from that study, which will improve the scrutiny of future trials of similar agents. However, there can be no guarantee that any new study will be safe. All research carries risks to the participants, and in some cases these risks are not known. The REC can help ensure that the risks are reasonable, and minimised as far as possible, are fully explained to the participant, and that suitable procedures are put into place to look after the patient if something does happen.

There is also a danger that there are negative consequences to the ethical scrutiny of research. The main danger is probably the "opportunity cost" that would be the consequence if good and useful research did not happen (or was slowed down) by the existence of the REC review. To take an extreme example, over a million people a year die of malaria worldwide. If the REC review were therefore to delay the development of an effective vaccine by just one day then more than 2,800 people, mostly children, would die as a result. This is of course an unfair example; REC approval will be one of the most insignificant reasons for delay in the development and implementation of an effective vaccine. But it does convey a serious point, that unnecessary delay of good research is unethical. The REC process has considerably improved, and is much more efficient and streamlined than a decade ago. The REC process continues to adapt and improve, and other regulatory hurdles are now more problematic for the researcher. However, REC members need to be aware that there is a risk that they will contribute to developing a culture that inhibits research, and that they should seek to be proportionate and facilitate ethical research, while maintaining their duty to protect the research participant.

5.7 Conclusions

Researchers can sometimes perceive the ethical review process as unnecessarily burdensome and intrusive. It is reasonable to consider that aspects of the process in the UK could be improved to make it more proportionate (especially for low risk studies) — and there are improvements to the process that are currently underway that should go a long way into answering these concerns. However, most researchers want to do the right thing and acknowledge that good research is ethical research.

Acknowledgements

I would like to thank all the members of the Hammersmith, Queen Charlotte's and Chelsea Research Ethics Committee (now West London 1 REC), and its coordinator Clive Collett with whom I had the honour and joy of working for many years. The opinions in this article are my own and may not reflect that of any organisation to which I belong.

References

[1] European Forum of Good Clinical Practice, 2006. http://www.efgcp.be/EFGCPReports.asp?L1=5&L2=1 [accessed 28 June 2010].
[2] Department of Health, 2012. Governance Arrangements for Research Ethics Committees. https://www.gov.uk/government/publications/health-research-ethics-committees-governance-arrangements [accessed 27 July 2014].
[3] Health Research Authority, 2014. http://www.hra.nhs.uk/ [accessed 27 July 2014].
[4] Department of Health, 2005. Research Governance Framework for Health and Social Care. http://www.dh.gov.uk/en/Publicationsandstatistics/Publications/PublicationsPolicyAndGuidance/DH_4008777 [accessed 28 June 2010].
[5] The "Warner Report", 2005. Report of the Ad Hoc Advisory Group on the Operation of NHS Research Ethics Committees. http://www.dh.gov.uk/en/Publicationsandstatistics/Publications/PublicationsPolicyAndGuidance/DH_4112416 [accessed 28 June 2010].

[6] Academy of Medical Sciences. *A New Pathway for the Regulation and Governance of Health Research.* 2011. http://www.acmedsci.ac.uk/policy-projects/ [accessed 27 July 2014].

[7] Social Care Institute for Excellence. Social Care Research Ethics Committee. http://www.screc.org.uk/ [accessed 28 June 2010].

[8] National Literacy Trust. http://www.literacytrust.org.uk/about/faqs#q284 [accessed 28 June 2010].

6

Medical Negligence and Malpractice

Bernard M. Dickens

6.1 Introduction

The Shorter Oxford English Dictionary defines "malpractice" as "Improper treatment or culpable neglect of a patient by a physician or of a client by a lawyer." This confirms a popular understanding that negligence is the main if not the only feature of professional malpractice, particularly in disciplinary proceedings and litigation. In medical law, however, negligence and malpractice are distinguishable.

Negligence implies a lack of necessary or reasonable care, but there are legal wrongs ("torts" or "delicts") that constitute malpractice that may be committed without carelessness. Surgery that is undertaken with due care but without the patient's consent or other lawful source of consent will be a battery, for which compensation may have to be paid, and may also amount to a punishable criminal assault. It may also or alternatively depart from terms contractually agreed between surgeon and patient, and so be breach of contract. For instance, if a cosmetic surgeon promises that a given effect will be achieved, or an effect will be achieved within a given time, and that effect proves impossible to achieve even with the most carefully undertaken procedure, legal liability will arise for that breach of contract. Impossibility of performance is not a defence for failure to keep a contractual undertaking.

Some legal systems hold the doctor–patient relationship to be a fiduciary relationship, binding the doctor to act in good faith in the patient's best interests. If doctors place their own interests or comfort above patients', for instance, in not disclosing treatment options lawfully available to patients because the doctors object to such options on grounds of conscience, such as their religious conscience opposing abortion, they are liable to be found not only negligent but also in breach of their fiduciary duty. Their legal duty is to disclose all options, and to refer patients to other practitioners for procedures they decline to perform. If they communicate honestly held, reasonable but incorrect and stigmatizing information about patients, or colleagues, to others who have no legal interest to receive it, such as a doctor communicating a diagnosis of the discreditable origin of a patient's condition to a family member, they may be liable for defamation.

Defamation is either slander, for spoken or transitory communications, or libel, for communications in a more permanent or widespread form, such as in writing. However, professional (qualified) privilege may protect sharing of incorrect information with a colleague involved in a patient's care, if no negligence or malice are involved. Defamation is wrongful communication of an injurious falsehood. Communication of an injurious truth to someone with no legally recognized interest to receive it may be regarded as breach of privacy in legal systems that recognize a right of privacy. Breach of professional confidentiality will usually raise issues of negligence, and possibly also breach of contract.

Additional sources of legal liability include performance of surgical procedures prohibited by local law, such as female genital cutting or circumcision, sometimes described as mutilation, and non-criminal wrongs, such as improperly preventing a patient from leaving a confined area, which is described as false imprisonment. Accordingly, there are several potential sources of legal liability that constitute medical malpractice lying outside the scope of negligence law. Nevertheless, the bulk of medical law is negligence-based.

6.2 The Law of Negligence

Negligence is usually identified by the party who alleges it, the plaintiff in litigation, proving, on a balance of probability, that:

a) The defendant physician owed the plaintiff a legal duty of care.
b) The physician breached that duty of care.

c) The plaintiff suffered legally recognized damage.
d) The defendant caused that damage by breach of the duty of care.

6.2.1 *Duty of care*

6.2.1.1 *Duty to patients*

As independent practitioners and in many other settings, physicians are free to decide whether or not to accept applicants for their care as patients. They may face liability under anti-discrimination laws if they reject applicants on the basis of race or another prohibited ground of discrimination, but if they reject applicants on such grounds as incapacity to accept additional patients, or to treat the applicant's presenting condition, they do not owe the applicant any medical duty of care, and are not required to refer the applicant to another practitioner.

Physicians may accept people as their patients by explicitly saying that they do, by implication, such as from initiating their treatment or, for instance, by working in a hospital, clinic, insurance, or other systems that assign people to them as their patients. Questioning people, for instance about their symptoms or past medical care, may not by itself be sufficient to create a doctor–patient relationship, since the physician may only, for instance, be establishing capacity to provide treatment for the person's needs and goals. Some legal systems have mandatory "Good Samaritan" laws under which physicians and others are obliged to offer such assistance as they reasonably can to others, including strangers, who are clearly in peril. Physicians are therefore required to treat, for instance, victims of traffic or industrial accidents, as best they can in the circumstances, including by medical care. They may then be liable for negligence if they act unreasonably, but usually only for "gross" negligence, meaning extreme negligence exceeding any excusable by the pressure of circumstances, rather than ordinary negligence.

Physicians other than, or in addition to, surgeons may owe a patient a duty of care. For instance, a family practitioner who fails to detect or chart a patient's allergy or susceptibility to a routine drug or treatment, so that a surgeon remains unaware that it is contraindicated, may bear sole or principal liability for the patient's resulting injury. Similarly, an anesthesiologist bears a patient a legal duty of care that is independent of the surgeon's duty, and may become liable for injuries due to inattention or other negligence when the surgeon was not at fault.

Laws differ on independent duties of care owed by nurses. Nurse-practitioners, nurse-midwives, and nurses allowed to undertake independent practice, such as in South Africa where legislation empowers nurses to terminate first trimester pregnancies, bear direct duties of care to their patients. Where nurses are engaged by hospitals, clinics, or comparable employers, however, they may in law be "servants" whose employers are vicariously (that is, indirectly) liable for their negligence. When nurses are appointed by their employers to assist in surgery, the surgeon may be liable for their negligence under the doctrine that nurses are "transferred servants" of the surgeons they assist. However, a surgeon held liable due to a nurse's negligence may be able to claim an indemnity from the hospital that employed the nurse or from the nurse (usually meaning the nurse's insurer).

An important aspect of medical professionalism is knowing the limits of one's skills. Accordingly, a physician may bear a patient a duty of care not to undertake treatment of the patient's condition that the physician knows, or should know, exceed the physician's skill or capacity, but to refer the patient to another practitioner who is capable of performing the treatment indicated for the patient's care. Practitioners who undertake procedures that exceed their skills will be liable to be found in breach of their duty of care, except in cases of emergency when it is necessary that they intervene. Surgeons may be similarly liable for placing their patients under the care of students or others whose training they supervise, when they entrust such personnel with the conduct of procedures for which they are not ready.

A physician's acceptance of an individual as a patient for whose care the physician will be responsible may be undertaken relatively informally, by implication rather than by a formal acknowledgement, but the physician's termination of that relationship, in order to be released from the legal duty of care, may require some attention. Patients cannot be abandoned, since abandonment is a form of negligence. If termination is anticipated, due for instance to the physician's retirement or distant relocation, advance notice must be given, and all reasonable efforts made to recommend the patient's transfer of care to another reasonably accessible appropriate practitioner.

If the termination of the relationship is sudden, compelled, for instance, by the patient's hostile or refractory conduct or request that the physician should undertake a non-emergency procedure to which the physician has a conscientious objection, the physician should disclose and explain the intention to terminate the professional relationship at the end of a specified time that allows the patient to obtain services elsewhere, and maintain appropriate healthcare services until that time expires. If the request the physician finds objectionable is for care that, in the patient's health interest, requires prompt attention, a fiduciary obligation may arise to refer the patient to an appropriate physician who does not object to it, or to, for instance, a medical association or support group that can facilitate the patient's access to a suitable physician.

6.2.1.2 *Duty to non-patients*

In treating a patient negligently, a surgeon may incur legal liability not only to the patient but also to others foreseeably at risk of suffering material and/or emotional injury, such as a spouse or children, especially young dependent children. The governing test is reasonable foreseeability of a person other than the patient being injured by the negligent act. In a Canadian case, for instance, a surgeon who negligently removed a patient's only healthy kidney was held liable to her father who then donated one of his kidneys for transplantation to aid her survival. The court found it foreseeable that a parent, as opposed to a stranger, would donate in these circumstances.

Legal systems differ on the liability of physicians whose negligent treatment of pregnant women, or women of usual reproductive age, injures their fetuses or subsequently born children. Most systems follow the "born alive" rule, by which no claims are recognized unless and until a fetus is born alive, when claims may be based on prenatal injuries. Some US state courts are exceptional, however, in recognizing claims from fetal viability *in utero*. The concept of a "fetal patient" is otherwise a benign fiction, serving protective or cautionary purposes. It allows women to provide children they intend to deliver with care they consider appropriate. Physicians are not entitled to subordinate patients' interests to those of their fetuses without patients' consent [1].

There is no negligence if a physician anticipates the risk of injury to a fetus or child subsequently born alive, and so advises the woman patient.

Her agreement to take that risk immunizes the physician from liability, because she is legally entitled to determine her own medical care once informed of its possible implications for herself and others. Negligent failure reasonably to foresee such a risk, or to inform the woman of it, may, however, provide her with a successful claim, if she suffers consequent injury, such as birth of an avoidably handicapped child or loss of an opportunity to lawful abortion. It may also base a claim by a subsequently born child, if its injuries could have been prevented by the mother's informed decision. Few courts will recognize a child's claim that it was injured because its mother was denied the chance not to conceive or to abort it; the so-called "wrongful life" action is usually disallowed.

Judicial approaches to these issues do not support claims that fetuses as such have legal rights, although account may be taken of their future interests that arise following live birth [2], because the same principles may be applied before conception. If, for instance, abdominal surgery negligently damaged a patient's uterus so that any subsequently conceived fetus would be harmed by gestation in constricted or otherwise compromised space, the child on live birth may receive compensation. If the negligence doomed any fetus to impaired gestation and life following birth, the child's rights to normality would have been harmed, and the parents might succeed in claiming the additional costs of accommodating the child's disability. Remoteness in time would be of no consequence to liability, analogously to a negligently designed or built structure standing for twenty years before collapsing onto a child. The patient, on being informed of the surgical negligence, however, might decide to forgo childbearing and succeed in a claim for losing that opportunity, because that decision is reasonably foreseeable.

6.2.2 Breach of duty

6.2.2.1 The standard of care

The law does not require perfection, but only a standard of professional competence in discharge of the legal duty of care, usually measured by reference to acceptable practice among peers. Compliance with that standard of performance will satisfy legal requirements of meeting the standard of care. The law will assess that standard, however, since, if a profession can unilaterally set its own standard of care, failure to satisfy which constitutes negligence, it has a self-serving or self-protective incentive to pitch the standard at a lower level than serves the public interest. If the professionally maintained standard of performance bears obvious risks, the profession itself may become open to legal liability, and so gain an incentive to raise its standards. This occurred when courts heard claims arising from injuries due to sponges or instruments being left in patients. If they found that there was no sponge or instrument count before surgery was concluded and patients were taken to recovery, courts would be strongly disposed to find negligence. Responsibility was vested in surgeons themselves, and could not be delegated to nurses, even if nurses monitored or conducted the counts. This reinforced the practice to order and supervise counts before patients received post-operative suturing.

By this test of applying a reasonable degree of skill, knowledge, and care, general surgeons are held to the standard of general surgeons, and those who profess to be specialists are held to the higher standards that prevail within their specialty. Newly qualified practitioners and experienced practitioners are held to the same standard of performance, and may be interchangeable. That is, surgical consent agreements with patients, often but not necessarily written, may provide that surgery will be conducted by a named surgeon, or by another appointed by that surgeon. Patients may insist, of course, that only specified surgeons may conduct procedures, and, when informed of the health effects of delay, be willing to await such surgeons' availability. Surgeons are not required to inform patients that the surgery will be the first occasions on which they will conduct the procedures without supervision, unless patients take the initiative to ask. The law considers it not in the public interest that surgeons be required to volunteer such information, since it would be liable to delay and even prevent any surgeon's first unsupervised experience.

There may be more than a single standard of care. Legal systems often apply the so-called "learned minority" rule, in which the practice of a minority of practitioners will be found acceptable. For instance, recently qualified practitioners may be familiar with newer techniques, equipment, or materials than the mainstream of practitioners. Similarly, veteran practitioners may prefer to conduct procedures by traditional, time-tested techniques rather than in the "modern" way. The newer, mainstream, and older traditional standards may each be legally satisfactory, although eccentric, experimental, or unproven practices, and older, discredited practices, will not be.

Legal systems differ on whether professional standards are those of a particular practitioner's locality, or those of the whole jurisdiction. This may depend on a jurisdiction's geographical range, and its variety, for instance of urban, suburban, rural, and remote or inaccessible areas. It may also depend on funding of governmental health services, their scope, and interaction with private health insurance. A population liable to the same level or system of taxation to support health services would expect them to be equally available, and delivered at the same standard. While a common basic or minimum universal standard might be expected, university-based centres of medical excellence or leadership might be justified or required for advancement. This unavoidably raises the Orwellian spectre among equals that some are "more equal than others", by enjoying greater advantage. Courts may accept, however, that practitioners be held to different standards of practice, depending on the resources reasonably available to them. For instance, some would be expected to refer their patients to accessible well-equipped facilities, or to refer them to specialists, while others would be required to do no more than their best with the limited resources and choices available to them.

Physicians are not found negligent for failure to employ resources that are not practicably available to them. Where resources are accessible, however, physicians are required to use them in their individual patients' best interests, not to deny them to their patients in order to serve goals of overall economy. That is, as advocates for their patients, they cannot sacrifice their individual patients' well-being in order to serve interests of the general healthcare system, or to meet institutional or governmental goals. The potential harm to a patient from forgoing indicated and available treatment usually greatly exceeds the harm to the healthcare budget or system of one more patient's care. The aggregate burden to the budget or system of different practitioners' loyalty to their individual patients falls on health service administrators and budget directors, not on practitioners bound to provide their patients with the legally required standard of care.

6.2.2.2 *The duty of disclosure*

Most national and comparative studies of medical law include one or more lengthy chapters on consent [3], so the discussion here is necessarily a brief outline, with a focus on surgical negligence.

A patient's consent protects a surgeon who has conducted a procedure from civil (that is, non-criminal) liability for battery, and guilt of criminal assault. Influential legal systems have accepted, however, that if the patient's consent was not based on adequate information, because insufficient disclosures were made of the nature and implications of the treatment, and that, had such disclosures been made, it is more likely than not that the patient would not have consented to that treatment, the patient may have a claim under the law of negligence. That means that not only must surgery be conducted without negligence, but that the duty of care requires that information be disclosed to the patient before consent to surgery is given that meets the required standard of care.

Legal systems agree that responsibility to ensure the adequacy of disclosure rests with surgeons who propose interventions, whether or not they personally conduct discussions to make their patients adequately informed. Medical and related literature often refers to patients' "fully informed consent", but the test of "fullness" is not medical or scientific fullness, but full to the legal requirement, which is that patients are offered adequate available information that is material to the choices they have to make. "Informed choice" is a preferable term to "informed consent", since the purpose of disclosure is not to induce consent, but to facilitate choice. Even if the physician considers that there is only one treatment of choice, the patient still has an option to decline it.

A difference in legal systems is their required focus of disclosure, meaning the level at which disclosure is pitched. Historically, physicians were required to meet a professionally oriented standard. They had to tell patients what their professional peers would tell them. The duty of disclosure was approached simply as an aspect of the general standard of care, assessed by reference to the professional knowledge, competence, skill, and conscientiousness of other comparable practitioners. As seen above, general practitioners were held to the standard of disclosure of other general practitioners, and specialists to the standard of comparable specialists.

There are legal jurisdictions in which courts continue to judge disclosure by reference to such professionally oriented standards. From the early 1970s, however, another test arose in the US that several other jurisdictions have found appropriate. This rejects the concept that if physicians want to know what to say to patients they must consider what other physicians would say, and adopts the principle that they must instead consider what their patients, as intelligent, prudent, responsible people, need to know.

This patient-oriented standard is directed to disclosure of information that might be material to the patient's decision, disclosure being modeled on patients in the apparent circumstances of their lives. Its application is illustrated in the leading Canadian case adopting the patient-oriented standard of disclosure. A surgeon advised a patient that surgery on his carotid artery was advisable to forestall the patient suffering a potentially fatal or severely disabling stroke. The surgeon indicated the eventual risk to the patient of forgoing the surgery, and the irreducible minimum risks of the surgery itself, although without quantifying them. The surgeon presented the option to the patient of either accepting or not accepting surgery, and the patient consented to the operation. Unfortunately, the patient suffered a severely disabling stroke, which was an inherent risk of the surgery. He sued the surgeon alleging lack of adequately informed consent, in that he was denied the option of postponing the operation for 18 months. The surgery would not have been safer after that time, and the patient would not have been at greater risk of suffering a stroke during that time. The 18-month postponement was of no significance to the surgeon. It was, however, of critical significance to the patient, because he had disability insurance protection of his employment income, at an 80% level, but was 18 months short of the 100% protection he needed to support his family, and provide his children with the educational opportunities he wanted them to have.

The Supreme Court of Canada [4] held that reasonable, prudent patients would want to know about the possible effects of having and not having surgery, including effects on their family life. The surgeon was not held to a purely subjective standard of disclosure, in order to satisfy the particular needs of the individual patient, but to a so-called "modified objective" standard, based on reasonable assessment of information material to patients in the individual patient's general circumstances. For instance, risk of surgery to fertility and childbearing will be material to a young woman, who may value the opportunity to have a family, but not to a woman of post-menopausal age. The ability to play sports may matter to young, athletic patients but less to others. The ability of working parents to maintain the level of economic support they provide to their families is a reasonably foreseeable concern on which they require adequate information and discussion.

Attention must be paid to what patients disclose about themselves, especially if their disclosures show them to differ from what may reasonably be understood about patients in comparable circumstances. Active tennis-playing octogenarians, for instance, may be expected to explain their lifestyle priorities. Surgeons uncertain about their individual patients' priorities should ask them appropriate questions. In the Canadian case, the patient was asked whether his house mortgage had been repaid, but not whether his employment income was fully insured in case of disability, although the surgeon knew that, even without surgical negligence, there was a calculable risk of the operation causing disability.

By this patient-oriented standard of disclosure, surgeons must know not only medical factors relevant to the surgery they conduct, but also information about the sorts of people who may become their patients, about their lifestyles, and their reasonably predictable priorities. This standard may require an expansion of awareness and empathy when surgeons and patients are from different cultural, ethnic, or socio-economic backgrounds. In deciding what questions surgeons should ask, and how to interpret the answers they receive, judgement will often have to be exercised, with the risk of the interpretation proving erroneous.

6.2.2.3 *Error of judgement*

Making decisions, for instance about appropriate surgical techniques or approaches, or about what people mean by what they say, often requires judgement, which bears inherent risks of being erroneous. The law does not require that correct decisions be made, but that they be made correctly. That is, all relevant factors should be taken into account, and irrelevant considerations should be excluded. It was seen above, for instance, that deciding whether or not to use an available scarce resource in a patient's care should be decided by a conscientious assessment of that patient's best interests, not by feeling a need of compliance with a hospital administrator's or governmental health official's urging of economy. Economy may be achieved by administrators or officials making a resource unavailable, rather than by pressuring physicians to compromise or prejudice their judgement in employing resources that are available to best serve their patients.

Errors do not necessarily indicate negligence, although if they are errors that normally competent, attentive practitioners would not make, they may be so held. For instance, when a patient fails to respond to treatment indicated by the diagnosis, there may be a legal duty to reconsider that diagnosis [5]. In 1981, an authoritative judicial ruling came from the highest court in England. The case involved a senior hospital registrar who took charge of a delivery after the mother's prolonged labour. The consultant in charge of the maternity unit had identified the pregnancy as likely to be difficult, and that a trial of forceps delivery would have to be undertaken before proceeding to delivery by cesarean section. The registrar examined the mother, read the consultant's notes, and embarked on a tentative trial of forceps delivery. Attaching forceps to the baby's head, he pulled six times coincident with the mother's contractions. When there was no movement on the fifth and confirming sixth pulls, he decided, some 25 minutes after attaching the forceps, to undertake a cesarean section. He quickly and competently delivered the baby, which was soon found to have sustained severe brain damage due to asphyxia.

The subsequent negligence action claimed that the defendant, the registrar, had pulled too long and strongly, thereby causing the baby's head to become wedged, resulting in brain damage from asphyxia. At trial, expert medical witnesses established that the force to be properly applied in a trial of forceps is a matter of clinical judgement, but that no attempt should be made to pull a fetus past a bony obstruction. The trial judge accepted the expert conclusion that if the baby's head had become so stuck as to cause asphyxia, excessive force must have been used, and found negligence.

Two of the three Court of Appeal judges found differently, and the case went to the highest court of England, the House of Lords. The five judges there each upheld the Court of Appeal's finding of non-negligent error. They noted that clinical judgement had been legitimately applied to the circumstances, including that the patient was only 4 feet 10.5 inches in height, the fetus was "fair sized", and that the patient had refused a lateral x-ray, so that the registrar lacked accurate measurements of the pelvis and of the ischial spines. No evidence was found that the pulling on the baby's head was due to the registrar wedging the head or attempting to pull it past a bony obstruction. In drawing the contrast between legal negligence and legitimate though regrettable error, Lord Fraser observed, in the gendered language of the time, that:

an error of judgement may, or may not, be negligent; it depends on the nature of the error. If it is one that would not have been made by a reasonably competent professional man professing to have the standard and type of skill that the defendant [registrar] held himself out as having, and acting with ordinary care, then it is negligent. If, on the other hand, it is an error that a man, acting with ordinary care, might have made, then it is not negligence [6].

In any given case, what a "reasonably competent" physician would and would not do, and what would be "ordinary care", are matters of expert evidence, legal advocacy, and judgement. The fact that the trial judge was reversed in his finding by the appeal judges shows that judges too can make legitimate errors.

Although making an error may not be negligent, its repetition may be. Failure to expose, study, and learn from an error may violate the duty of care owed to a subsequent patient, because the standard of care requires that errors not be dismissed as inevitable or bad luck, but that they serve as a stimulus to investigation and attempted improvement. Suppression or denial of error, perhaps for fear of litigation, falls below standards of transparency and professional responsibility. That is, "reasonably competent" physicians exercising "ordinary care" are expected to acknowledge their own errors, treat them as opportunities for learning and prevention, and to approach colleagues' errors in the same way without applying concepts of fault, blame, negligence, or condemnation. Learning and prevention should also be undertaken by medical facility administrators, since the root cause or conditioning environment of surgical errors may be, for example, excessive working hours required, encouraged, or allowed of surgeons or surgical team members, appointment to surgical duty of under-qualified staff, inadequate or delayed information-sharing, and comparable systemic defects in institutional management.

The duty of care owed to a patient is to disclose the occurrence of significant error in the patient's care. A test of significance is whether the error affects the patient's health or subsequent treatment. For instance, dropping a surgical instrument that must then be autoclaved before further use, prolonging the operation by a short time, need not be disclosed. Similarly, finding, on double-checking, that a drug or dosage was erroneously selected, so preventing the initial mistake from causing harm, need not be revealed. At the other extreme, operating on the wrong organ or limb, or on the wrong patient, obviously must be revealed. Courts have also required patients to be informed when an error, negligent or not, exposed the patient to the potential harms of prolonged anesthesia, or requires repeated or additional surgery. Even when it is correctly explained that no negligence occurred, this may influence the patient to have the subsequent procedure conducted by a different surgeon. Non-disclosure may lead to legal proceedings for negligence, and/or proceedings based on deceit.

6.2.3 *Damage*

Unlike the tort or delict of battery, which is actionable *per se* (i.e., in itself), negligence is actionable only when plaintiffs can show that they suffered injury or damage. In most cases, the injury is obvious, such as organ or tissue damage, pain and inconvenience, for example repeated or additional surgery, or lost employment income or business opportunities. Courts will also recognize future losses, such as rehabilitation expenses, and quantify anticipated pain, suffering, and loss of earnings from a career that can no longer be maintained. Losses to non-patients can also be recognized, such as lost support children would enjoy, including guidance, home comforts and indulgencies, and lost educational opportunities. However, the more remote and speculative the claimed loss, the more conservative judicial estimates will be, and courts will reject claims of losses that were not reasonably foreseeable consequences of the breach of duty of care. A spouse's or long-time partner's lost emotional support and companionship, or *solatium*, will often be recognized, but not lost opportunities of friendship or collegiality.

In some cases there is doubt whether a claim of injury can be recognized. Lost economic opportunities may be considered too speculative, not least in times of economic volatility or downturn, and in the past, courts were often skeptical about mental or psychological suffering not consequent upon physical injury. This was because of reservations about the credibility of psychiatric or psychological injury, and because claimed symptoms could be simulated for self-serving purposes of litigation. With the growing prestige of psychiatry, however, and growing acceptance that mental health impairments are real, courts are becoming more responsive to compensating claims of, for instance, depression due to causes such as negligent misdiagnosis of an ominous ailment, affecting a patient or a spouse.

A long-standing rule, however, has been that, if negligent or if other wrongs have been committed, perpetrators take their victims as they find them, and are accountable to compensate their idiosyncratic characteristics, such as emotional frailty. The "eggshell skull" rule is that one person striking another's head bears responsibility for unexpected injuries due to the victim's unusually thin skull. Accordingly, if treatment to remedy surgical negligence requires, for instance, a patient's regular travel to a major population centre for outpatient care, compensation will cover added stress due to agoraphobia. However, if the need for travel was due not to negligence, but, for instance, to non-negligent error, the patient's additional stress from this condition does not render the treatment or error negligent.

Cultural challenges have arisen from legal claims due to negligence in gynecological surgery and vasectomy [7]. Courts may remain ambivalent over compensation for negligent sterilization procedures resulting in unplanned births of healthy children their parents love. Courts will often accept that individuals have rights to reject uninvited benefits, but have aesthetic inhibitions, sometimes reinforced by religious sentiments, about classifying such a child's birth as a species of legal damage. Courts may compensate the costs and inconvenience of repeating the surgery, and, if a child is born with serious disabilities, the additional costs of rearing a disabled child above the ordinary expenses of child rearing.

However, although more senior appeal courts may introduce some standardization of approach, records show that trial judges span the full spectrum of responses. Some treat the healthy child as an unmitigated blessing beyond compensation, while, at the other extreme, others have ordered payment of full costs of the child's maintenance and upbringing to the point of adult self-reliance. A middle ground is to acknowledge the injury to parents, but to off-set the benefits of the child's eventual contribution to the parents' well-being, which reduces and may even extinguish the parents' compensation for their injury.

Legal systems may allow "wrongful pregnancy" claims when negligent sterilization or prenatal diagnosis resulted in pregnancies terminated by spontaneous or induced abortion, and, when lawful abortion was an option that became foreclosed due to negligence, allow "wrongful birth" actions. An action of this nature cannot be defended by arguing that the patient should have had such an abortion. Courts will not usually reduce damage awards in order to penalize women who decline abortion choices, and defendants who negligently perform sterilization or prenatal diagnostic procedures cannot seek relief because their patients are people who reject abortion and adoption choices, because of the "eggshell skull" principle of taking the victims of one's negligence as the individuals they happen to be. Where laws allow abortion only for severe fetal handicap, negligent failure of timely prenatal diagnosis that causes a lost opportunity of abortion may justify full compensation of the costs of supporting and caring for a handicapped child until adulthood and beyond. Such awards are often the largest that courts award in medical negligence claims.

With very few exceptions, courts have been relatively uniform in disallowing claims by, or on behalf of, even seriously handicapped children that, but for defendants' negligence, they would not have been conceived or born, and that they have thereby been compelled to endure a "wrongful life." A visceral rejection of the claim that human life is a legal injury is often rationalized by the explanation that awards of legal damages are intended to place injured parties in the positions they would have been in had the wrongs not occurred. A court can measure in money the difference in being negligently impaired when, without the negligence, one would have been unimpaired, but cannot measure the difference between being impaired and the void of non-existence. However, courts often engage in providing damage awards for incommensurable injuries, so this basis of rationalizing rejection of "wrongful life" claims is decreasingly convincing. Courts are becoming more sympathetic to children's claims if they suffer gross afflictions, on the argument of public policy that negligence causing such injuries should not be immune from payment of compensation simply because it results in live human birth.

Some courts resist approaching claims for negligent sterilization, such as by tubal ligation or vasectomy, by reference to principles of public policy, and take a pragmatic approach to the reason why such a procedure was requested. If it was to prevent future pregnancy and the inconvenience of contraception, and a healthy child is born that the family can afford to support, damage awards will tend to be modest, covering the costs and inconvenience of repeating the procedure. If the child is disabled, additional childcare costs due to the disability will usually be awarded. If the reason to seek the procedure was to prevent conception and birth of a child that, due perhaps to unavoidable genetic inheritance, would predictably suffer disability, parental costs of coping with the disability will be awarded and perhaps an award for loss of the lifestyle the parents intended to have, such as for restricted social, recreational, and travel activities. If the procedure was requested because the parents cannot afford to bring up a child or another child, the damage award will cover the full costs of child support up to adulthood, whether the child is handicapped or healthy.

Injured plaintiffs are usually legally required to mitigate, meaning minimize, the damage they suffer. If, for instance, negligent injuries prevent their continuation of highly skilled, highly paid occupations, they must pursue lesser paid occupations. Their damage awards for lost income will be the difference between what they were earning and could reasonably anticipate earning in their former occupations, and what they earn in the type of occupations to which they were reduced, or which they reasonably should have pursued, taking account of reduced future prospects. However, it has been seen that mitigation is not required of pregnancy and childbirth due to negligent sterilization, by abortion or adoption.

Further, defendants cannot claim liability to pay reduced damages because plaintiffs had, or should have had, insurance protection against financial implications of the injuries they suffered. Insurance companies have legal rights of subrogation, under which, having become liable to pay compensation under plaintiffs' insurance policies with them, they can require the plaintiffs to take legal action against defendants or to give their names to such legal action maintained by the insurance companies, to recover the costs the companies have incurred. Even governmental health insurance plans may enforce subrogation rights, analogously to private commercial plans. Much medical litigation is driven by insurance interests.

6.2.4 *Causation*

Following proof of damage, plaintiffs must show that it was suffered not simply subsequently to negligence, but consequently on that negligence. Judges are wary of *post hoc ergo propter hoc* ("after this, therefore because of this") arguments, and, in jurisdictions that have trial by jury, they warn juries against this type of reasoning. In the US there is a constitutional right to jury trial, and lawyers for both sides know how to appeal to jurors' sometimes irrational sympathies. In other systems that have juries, however, juries are often considered unsuitable when the link between negligence and damage turns on complex medical, physiological, or biological evidence, presented by expert witnesses placed in conflict.

Although medical evidence on causation may be complex and fiercely contested, the purpose is usually to satisfy a simple test, often expressed as the "but for" test. The plaintiff has to show, on a balance of probability that, but for the defendant's negligence, the injury would not have occurred. For instance, if surgery was conducted negligently and the patient died, the plaintiff has to show that but for the surgical negligence the patient would not have died. If the patient was very ill, and the surgery was undertaken in a desperate bid to prolong life, it may be difficult to show that the patient would have survived but for the surgical misconduct.

Similarly, there may be an intervening act that breaks the chain of causation between the proven negligent act or omission and the patient's death, such as a nurse's failure to monitor the patient during postoperative recovery and raise an alarm when the patient's vital signs faltered. The defendant could claim that, but for the nursing oversight, it is as likely as not (that is, at least 50% likely) that the patient would have survived. This argument might prevent the plaintiff showing at least a 51% likelihood that the surgical negligence caused the death.

Scientific causation may be different from legal causation. The scientific evidence may relate to whether, for instance, a surgical act or omission in violation of the surgeon's standard of care resulted in physiological effects in the patient that accumulated or cascaded to culminate in the patient's death. In law, a defendant can be found to have caused a result that the defendant had an obligation to act reasonably to prevent. For instance, when a tubal ligation or vasectomy is conducted negligently and, through the patient's sexual intercourse a pregnancy results, the negligent surgeon is considered in law to be responsible for the pregnancy, that is, to have caused it.

The same "but for" test applies to alleged negligence due to non-disclosure of material information relevant to informed choice. Even if a patient suffers the irreducible minimum risks of a procedure conducted without surgical negligence or error, the patient may claim that, but for the omission or misrepresentation of material information about the procedure, the patient would have chosen not to agree to the procedure, and therefore would not have been exposed to its inherent risks. The claim is that the failure of information caused exposure to the risk of the injury suffered. The fact that a choice to forgo any procedure, or to agree to a different procedure, would have exposed the patient to different risks of injury does not affect the defendant's liability, but may be relevant only to the amount of damages awarded. If the defendant can show it as likely as not that, had the patient received the correct information, the patient would have made the same choice, then the patient's claim will fail.

A claim of causation available in principle but exceptionally difficult to apply in practice is that the causative link between negligence and injury is self-evident and "speaks for itself" (*res ipsa loquitur*), meaning that occurrence of the accident necessarily in itself implies negligence. The claim succeeded in a historical English case when a pedestrian walking on a street outside a warehouse was injured when an item fell on him from an upper opening. The warehouse occupier was found to have no defence. It may appear comparable if, for instance, a surgeon were to remove a patient's healthy kidney and leave in place the diseased kidney. The surgeon's negligence might not be axiomatic or self-evident, however, if, reasonably relying on information provided by a colleague who read an x-ray plate the wrong way round, or if the plate was installed on a screen the wrong way, or if the sides of the plate were incorrectly marked in reverse. The plaintiff would have to conduct detailed enquiries into hospital procedures and personnel to determine who might be sued successfully, and whether to join the hospital as a defendant, for instance on an allegation of its vicarious liability for negligence by its employee.

6.3 Defences

The legal burden of proving each of the four elements of negligence falls on the plaintiff, so a common means of defence is to deny that the plaintiff has satisfied that burden on one or more of the elements. When the plaintiff is a patient of the defendant surgeon, the existence of a legal duty of care may be difficult or unconvincing to deny, but it may be contended that there was no breach of the duty, because treatment satisfied the required standard of care. It may also be denied that there was any damage, and/or that any damage was caused by any breach of the duty or standard of care. It is common in legal argument, by both the plaintiff and particularly the defendant, to raise mutually inconsistent claims, or to argue in the alternative, in the form that "the defendant violated the plaintiff's right to A, and/or B, and/or C." The defendant similarly denies violating the plaintiff's right to A, and/or B, and/or C. That is, that right A was not violated, but if it was, B was not, and if B was, C was not.

While a scientific standard of proof may approach 100%, the legal standard in a civil (that is, non-criminal) action is 51%, the "more likely than not" standard. Existence of a legal duty of care has to be proven, or denied, as a matter of law, not evidence, but whether discharge of a legal duty of care satisfied or breached the legally required standard of care is a matter of evidence. Similarly, what constitutes compensable damage is a matter of law, but whether damage the law recognizes was caused by the defendant's act or omission is a matter of evidence. The defendant may contest the plaintiff's claims of both law and evidence. The terms "proof" and "evidence" are often interchangeable, in that proof is evidence that a court accepts meaning evidence that proves a claim. A contest of the plaintiff's evidence is to try to show that the defendant's claim is at least as likely as not to be convincing, that is, at least 50% likely, so that the plaintiff's claim fails to meet the required minimum 51% standard of proof.

Beyond challenging the plaintiff's arguments of law and the credibility of the plaintiff's evidence, defendants may raise the procedural objection that a legislated limit to the time within which a claim may be initiated was exceeded. The proposition that "the law aids the vigilant, not the indolent" is applicable to support enactment and application of laws to let potential defendants "close their books" on their potential liabilities, because claims were brought out of time. The concept arose with capitalism and the use of resources, mainly money, to promote business and prosperity. Legislation was enacted, often called Limitation Acts, to allow businesses and individuals that prudently set aside money to meet prospective liabilities, often described in their books of account as contingency funds, to release those funds for ordinary business application and investment after a specified time. That is, they can close their books on such potential liabilities.

Limitation laws differ in their details among jurisdictions. Some set the beginning of the time within which proceedings must be initiated at the time of the incident alleged to found the claim, others when the medical treatment was concluded, and yet others at the time when the plaintiff actually knew or reasonably, as a vigilant person, should have known of the claim. In all cases, the running of the limitation period will be suspended if the defendant deliberately concealed facts that would found a claim. The limitation period would almost invariably be suspended during the plaintiff's incapacity to bring the claim, due to infancy or being below adult age, or mental impairment.

Some laws set both a relative and absolute limit, for instance allowing a person time, such as two or three years, within which to initiate proceedings after knowing that a cause of legal action has arisen, but disallowing any proceedings after, say, 12 or 15 years even if a person remained unaware of an incident on which a claim might be based, unless the defendant had deliberately concealed means to know. This extension of potential liability for non-disclosure of material information supports the wisdom, as well as the legal requirement, of informing patients of errors in their treatment that may affect their health or other interests, even if the errors are believed to have been non-negligent.

Limitation periods, despite their purpose to allow potential liability to be finite and books closed, can be quite lengthy. For instance in claims arising from birth trauma, a child's claim may be suspended for 18 years of minority age before a two-, three-, and sometimes six-year limitation period begins to run. Further, negligence in a patient's care that impairs reproductive capacity may not become suspected until the patient proposes reproduction, perhaps a decade or more after surgery. A justification of absolute time limits on rights to sue, in the absence of deliberate concealment, is that medical records and evidence based on personal recollection fade or become inaccessible with the passing of time, as does availability of witnesses. For this reason, legal systems usually allow infants' guardians, such as parents or others with no conflict of interest, to initiate proceedings on behalf of children, with comparable accommodation of claims on behalf of incapable adults.

A defence that may reduce rather than eliminate a negligent defendant's liability is that the plaintiff's own negligence contributed to the injury. This is called the (partial) defence of contributory, or comparative, negligence. For instance, a defendant may claim that, as an alternative to being found liable to compensate the plaintiff for the full injury suffered, the defendant's liability should be proportionately reduced because the plaintiff failed to follow pre-operative or post-operative advice, and thereby increased the extent of the injury suffered.

Another claim may be that the plaintiff failed to mention a history of adverse reaction to an ordinarily prescribed medication, or of significant use of drugs, lawful or illicit, or of tobacco or alcohol use liable to affect recovery from surgery. Failure to make or keep a follow-up appointment that would have identified a curable post-operative condition may reduce liability to a high degree, and even satisfy the "but for" test of causation, showing the failure to be the actual cause of injury, breaking the chain of causation between a surgeon's negligence and the patient's injury. Patients who drive vehicles or use machinery soon after treatment or medication, when appropriately warned not to, are liable to be found at least contributorily negligent when claiming their treatment resulted in accidents, and courts may find that, but for their own acts, the accidents would not have occurred; that is, their claims of the defendants' causation of their injuries fail.

6.4 Cross-Border Jurisdiction

The emergence of telemedicine and robotic surgery has raised new issues in surgery that fit within one of the most ancient bodies of law, and one of the most intellectually complex. Cross-jurisdictional law is sometimes described as Private International Law, but is better known as Conflict of Laws. If a surgeon licensed only in jurisdiction A effects robotic surgery on a patient in jurisdiction B, does this violate B's laws against unlicensed practice? Further, if the surgery is negligent, is the surgeon liable under the law of A, or B, or both? If the treatment is lawful in A but not B, or vice versa, such as abortion or sterilization of a mentally impaired patient, has an offence been committed? These are the types of legal issues raised by cross-border surgery [8].

A historical approach has been found in the principle that a tort or wrong is done where its effects are felt. Accordingly, although a surgeon licensed in jurisdiction A may not violate B's laws by effecting surgery there, a patient in B claiming injury due to negligence may sue in B's courts. The court system in B will have to decide if the surgeon in A is required to respond to proceedings in B, and whether any award can be enforced against the defendant's assets in A, for instance by agreements on reciprocal enforcement of judgements. If a plaintiff resident in B can sue in A, where the defendant has assets, the courts there will have to decide whether A is the more convenient trial jurisdiction, if evidence of the injury and witnesses to its effects are in B. Under the *forum non conveniens* (not the more/most convenient court) principle, a court has discretion to decline jurisdiction if finding a case is better litigated in another court system.

Patients with an option to sue in a US jurisdiction may prefer to do so, because lawyers there may be able to act on contingent fee systems ("no win, no fee payment"), lawyers may be more experienced in medical claim cases, there is a right to jury trial, damage assessments may be high, and juries may award punitive or exemplary damages far exceeding material losses incurred. Courts in US states uncertain that they are the more convenient to try the claims of foreign plaintiffs may not want to deny them justice when US-based defendants have no obligation to defer to the jurisdiction of a more convenient foreign court. They may therefore decide that they will hear the claims, unless the defendants voluntarily agree to submit to foreign courts more convenient to try the claims.

The scope of this chapter does not allow fuller consideration of legal complexities arising from surgery effected across jurisdictional boundaries [9]. Surgeons may want to consult lawyers before undertaking cross-border practice, however, and also consult their insurers or medical defence associations to determine whether they have coverage for such practice. Some European and other insurers and associations may not cover claims brought, for instance, in US states. An advantage of private law is that individuals can often agree in advance, such as in contracts, by what legal systems their arrangements will be governed. Surgeons may accordingly agree with patients in advance that any claims for compensation arising from treatment be litigated under jurisdictions of the surgeons' choice.

6.5 Medical Malpractice

6.5.1 *Battery*

Battery is now understood as touching another person without consent. This usually means the patient's own consent, but legally effective consent may be provided by others legally capable of approving another's medical care, such as a young child's parent, the adult child of an incapable parent, a judge following a legal application, or, for instance, a legally empowered public guardian. Battery claims differ from surgical negligence claims, in which plaintiffs bear the burden of proof, in that plaintiffs need show only the fact of being touched and the surgeon has the burden of proving the defence of legally effective consent. In ordinary circumstances, people often assume the risk of being innocently touched, such as by entering crowded vehicles, but surgical touching is different. Consent may be implied from conduct, however, such as when a patient presents a limb for a physician to examine or inject, and under the legal recognition of necessity to save life or prevent risk of seriously health-endangering injury.

A legal proposition is that peril invites rescue. If a person is taken unconscious into a hospital emergency department, suffering for instance from head trauma in an industrial or traffic accident, the person's consent to medically indicated care, including surgery, may be implied. This may allow surgery that, in the absence of medical necessity, would count as maiming the person (or "mayhem"). Even in cases of apparent attempted suicide, life-saving surgery may be lawful, under the common view that the attempt indicates mental disorder. If patients are conscious and refuse intervention, however, imposition of treatment may be unlawful. For instance, adult Jehovah's Witnesses can decline life-saving blood transfusions and use of blood products, and many legal systems allow mature minors of this faith the same right, although not necessarily when their lives are at serious risk. If unconscious adults and some minors carry indications of the medical care they will not accept, even in emergency, such as a Jehovah's Witness card, imposition of such care will usually be found a battery.

6.5.2 *Breach of contract*

The doctor–patient relationship is frequently contractual, and often unwritten, although consent for significant surgery may involve information in writing and a signed consent by or on behalf of the patient. Where physicians are paid on a fee-for-service basis, contracts will exist with patients in principle even when payments are made on the patient's behalf, at rates set by the funding insurers or governmental health insurance plans. When physicians are salaried by hospitals or health services, however, or paid on a capitation basis, meaning by the number of persons enrolled on their patient panels, there may not be contractual relationships with patients. Particular plans may therefore exclude contractual relationships, such as is generally (although not universally) accepted where physicians are employed and paid on a capitation basis within the UK National Health Service or a NHS Trust hospital [10]. Contracts, even when partly written, may have terms that are implied. A common term or provision is that the physician will exercise reasonable care in treating the patient. If a patient sues a doctor, it is common practice to claim for breach of the contractual term and for a separate wrong of negligence. In most cases, suing for both contractual and negligent wrongs will have no effect on the outcome of the case, since evidence to support each case will largely be the same.

In relatively rare cases, however, the contractual claim may succeed when the claim in negligence fails. The duty to observe the required standard of care in negligence law is based on reasonableness, with no requirement of perfection. Similarly, physicians are not generally held to guarantee the success, or the safety, of procedures they conduct. However, if a contract clearly guarantees a particular outcome of surgery, there will be breach of contract even if the guaranteed outcome proved impossible to achieve. For instance, if a cosmetic surgeon promises full recovery from a procedure in time for an event, such as a wedding, liability will arise even if an unforeseeable non-negligent medical obstacle renders recovery impossible by that time.

A patient's claim for fraudulent misrepresentation in inducing a contract may succeed if the surgeon failed to disclose that repetition of surgery was necessary due to negligence or error in conduct of an initial procedure. The same liability may arise when a surgeon accepts general care of a patient, or employment at a hospital or comparable healthcare facility, without prior disclosure that there are procedures within the range of reasonably expected duties, such as those of a gynecological surgeon, that the surgeon will refuse to undertake on grounds of conscientious objection.

6.5.3 *Breach of fiduciary duty*

Legal systems incorporate ethical values in different ways. Those based on religious sources or texts derive them from that inspiration, and the systems derived from the French or Napoleonic Civil Law tradition have ethical principles in their provisions. These include, for instance, the requirement of reasonable rescue, meaning a duty to come to the aid of strangers in peril by taking reasonable measures. This may require physicians, for example, to render aid to those injured in motor vehicle accidents they encounter. The Anglo-Saxon Common Law system introduces ethical or moral precepts not through the Common Law itself, but through the notion of fiduciary duties, developed historically through the ancient Court of Chancery and the surviving rules of equity.

The Court of Chancery, presided over by the Lord Chancellor, who was historically a senior ecclesiastic as well as a political officer, was the "Court of Conscience." The focus of its rules of equity was and remains on an individual's virtue and their duty to act fairly. Those seeking equitable justice must do justice. For instance, those seeking protection of their rights of conscience are required to be respectful of the rights of conscience of others. Where the physician–patient relationship is held to be of a fiduciary nature, as it is for instance in North America, physicians invoking conscientious objection to justify withholding service options from their patients cannot deny them information of such options, and must refer them to means of access to those options.

Judicial decisions have involved physicians taking sexual advantage of patients, for instance requiring sexual favours in exchange for additional prescriptions of drugs to which their patients are addicted. Advantage can also be taken by physicians favouring their own interests over their patients' possible interests in access to lawful services the physicians object to provide on grounds of their religious convictions, such as by withholding advance information of reasonably expected services the physicians intend not to provide, disclosing refusal only if patients request them.

The good faith that the fiduciary duty requires to be observed includes disclosure of all information relevant to a patient's options for care, and, for instance, disclosure of errors. Patients should be informed of their own medical condition and prognosis. The law of informed consent requires this disclosure, whether or not the doctor–patient relationship is fiduciary, but legal doctrine often includes the physician's "therapeutic privilege" of non-disclosure or generalization, meaning not being explicit about factors that may be harmfully distressing for patients to learn. The so-called privilege reflects historical paternalism, and modern doctrine is to minimize its scope, since it may subvert the general requirement of disclosure of material information. It is uncertain whether the fiduciary duty of care can justify withholding or generalizing information on the ground that providing it may prejudice a patient's treatment, such as by inducing countertherapeutic tenseness.

6.5.4 *Additional malpractice*

Beyond the non-negligent potential wrongs addressed above, surgeons may incur legal liability for the full spectrum of legal wrongs, both civil and criminal. Surgeons are not more vulnerable than other physicians to incur liability, for instance, for defamation, breach of privacy, false imprisonment, or breach of trust. They may come under greater scrutiny than other physicians, however, under aspects of criminal law. This is clearly so regarding procedures prohibited by several countries' laws, such as unlawful abortion and female genital cutting, and they may be more liable to charges of manslaughter or criminal negligence causing death or serious bodily harm, due to the seriousness of such consequences of negligence. In several instances, anesthesiologists have incurred prosecution and conviction.

Many legal systems pay respect to medical professional codes of conduct and ethical guidelines, and courts do not casually disregard standards of professional and personal conduct that the medical and other professions set for their members. Courts do not defer entirely to the standards of even self-regulating professions, however, since courts are guardians and illuminators of the law within the rules of which all professions, including, for instance, the medical and legal professions, guide and govern their members. It is necessary that courts and legal systems understand the principles within which surgeons and other healthcare professionals act, and equally that such professionals understand the key principles within which courts and legal systems assess their conduct. Courts determine whether medical conduct is lawful, but all citizens judge whether the laws under which they live and work are just. The process of law reform requires dialogue between those who declare and apply the law, and those whom the law claims moral authority to guide and govern.

References

[1] Dickens B.M. and Cook R.J. Ethical and legal approaches to "The Fetal Patient". *Intl. J. Gynecol. Obstet.* 2003; **83**: 85–91.

[2] Steinbock B. *Life Before Birth: The Moral and Legal Status of Embryos and Fetuses.* New York: Oxford University Press, 1992.

[3] Grubb A. (ed.) *Principles of Medical Law, 2nd ed.* Oxford: Oxford University Press, 2004; pp. 131–310.

[4] *Reibl* v *Hughes* [1980] 114 Dominion Law Reports (3rd) 1 (Supreme Court of Canada).

[5] Merry A. and McCall Smith R.A. *Errors, Medicine and the Law.* Cambridge: Cambridge University Press, 2001.

[6] *Whitehouse* v *Jordan* [1981] 1 All England Reports 267, 281.

[7] Mason J.K. *The Troubled Pregnancy: Legal Wrongs and Rights in Reproduction.* Cambridge: Cambridge University Press, 2007.

[8] Dickens B.M. and Cook R.J. Legal and Ethical Issues in Telemedicine and Robotics. *Intl. J. Gynecol. Obstet.* 2006; **94**: 73–78.

[9] Briggs A. *The Conflict of Laws.* Oxford: Oxford University Press, 2002.

[10] Grubb A. (ed.) *Principles of Medical Law, 2nd ed.* Oxford: Oxford University Press, 2004; pp. 315–318.

7

Surgical Training

S. R. Patel, P. Chadha and N. Hakim

7.1 Introduction

Hippocrates, in his timeless relic from 400 BC entitled "The Oath", wrote the following: "I will not cut, and certainly not those suffering from stone, but I will cede this to men who are practitioners of this activity".

With this statement, the founding father of ethics himself seems to be prohibiting doctors from undertaking surgery in our efforts to cure. This sidelining of surgical intervention is fortunately omitted from modern interpretations. Therefore surgeons, now considered partners to physicians and no longer supplementary "practitioners", are not exempt from rigorous ethical inquisitions into their practice.

The previous chapters have beautifully highlighted ethical and legal issues specific to the various individual specialties within the wider surgical arena. However one issue, thus far left untouched and that is common to all, is that of surgical training, a constantly evolving and controversial aspect of surgery. The approach we adopt in training future surgical experts requires thorough ethical evaluation and legal clarification, a process that is unfortunately complicated by both practical and political pressures, not only at a local level, but also internationally.

Traditionally, surgical training followed an "apprenticeship" model, whereby learning was expected to occur in response to first watching and listening. With observational experience being gained over time, the first practical forays into surgery occurred directly on anaesthetised patients. Supervision terminated early and out-of-hours work in particular was often delegated to junior surgeons. There have been numerous recent influences in surgical practice that have shifted focus from such "apprenticeship" models onto "studentship" models [1]. The focus is now on quality as opposed to quantity.

This paradigm shift, in the UK in particular, has been forced by three principal pieces of legislation that have shaped modern surgical training. They are the "Calman Training" scheme of 1996 [2], the "New Deal" of 2000 [3], and the "European Working Time Directive" (EWTD) of 2004 [4]. Together, and with the introduction of shift work patterns as well as guidelines set forth by The National Confidential Enquiry into Perioperative Deaths (NCEPOD), they have reduced out-of-hours operative opportunities for current and future surgical trainees. The ultimate influence for all these changes has undoubtedly been an increased emphasis on "clinical governance" and an appreciation for the importance of patient safety.

The aforementioned multiple changes in training paths have also impacted upon career progression, in that now there is a move to merge all trainees onto one common path. This integration has complicated competition for jobs and deranged hierarchies within the field. The current "Modernising Medical Careers" (MMC) model for higher training as well as opportunities for integration from the old system can be seen in Figure 7.1. There has been a move to introduce a separate academic training pathway in an attempt to encourage research and teaching, thus ensuring innovation and advancement of the field. While at first glance this seems a noble aim, ethical analysis is crucial to justify the decision to reduce operative time for surgeons even further.

This chapter will explore these and other "ethico-legal" issues that have dominated surgical training over the last decade and will undoubtedly continue to do so in the foreseeable future.

7.2 Learning through Operating

"One cannot learn to play the piano by going to concerts, even if they are given by Horowitz, Rachmaninoff, or Van Cliburn [5]."

This quotation by F.D. Moore in 1978 exemplifies the almost unanimous view in surgery that learning must be through practical experience.

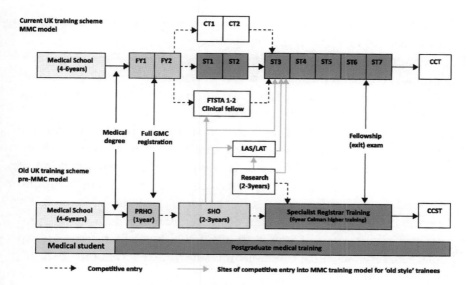

Figure 7.1. Current and former training pathways for surgical training and points of potential integration.

Whether this can be achieved without being to the detriment of our patients is the ultimate surgical training enigma. The issue is encapsulated by two conflicting, yet inextricably linked, themes. The first is the duty to maximally train future generations of surgeons and the other is the moral duty to ensure the patient has the most experienced surgeon operating on them, in the interest of patient safety [5].

It is interesting to note that this conundrum is only generally considered in the setting of an operative procedure. One openly accepts that juniors are able to perform ward duties, speak to the families of sick patients, and prescribe potentially dangerous drugs independently. After all, these and many other tasks can also be performed by more experienced doctors. The one justification to this would be that of risk and it is reasonable to assume that the risk of operative intervention exceeds that of these relatively simpler tasks.

So, should trainees be allowed to operate? This is dependent on many factors but is undeniably an essential part of their learning, without which they will be unable to progress. We must consider the influences that the patient has on the decision made, if any, and the duty of doctors to openly explain the implications of a trainee surgeon operating under supervision. At the heart of this issue is informed consent.

Stemming from the horrors of Nazi Germany and the subsequent Nuremberg Trial enquiries, informed consent is now a pre-requisite for all medical interventions that carry significant risk. It respects autonomy, a "pillar" of modern biomedical ethics that empowers individuals with the right to make decisions regarding their own body. This remains the cornerstone of our practice in which we act in the best interests of our patients. For a patient to make a decision regarding their provision of care, however, they must be fully informed of the circumstances around this, and in the setting of surgery, the identity of the surgeon surely requires clarification. Nomination of the surgeon in the consenting process is a requirement, if one is to avoid the unacceptable scenario of "ghost surgery", in which the surgeon is substituted without the patient's knowledge [6].

Thus, to openly inform patients about trainee involvement respects autonomy and the expectations of fiduciary responsibility that are deeply engrained in the practice of medicine. If they then refuse to permit trainee participation, this on an ethical and legal level must be respected. Of interest, it has been suggested that once informed of trainee involvement, patients are often eager to participate in the education of trainees [7]. This should serve to dispel any fears or misconceptions that consultants hold with regards to patients refusing the request of trainee surgeons to operate.

Nonetheless, patients are not obliged in any way, morally or otherwise, to contribute to the training of surgeons. And so, if surgeons feel it unnecessary to request permission for trainee involvement, they must at the very least inform the patients of the realities of theatre dynamics and that trainees will play some role in their care. This discussion should take place well in advance of the operating day, which in reality often does not occur. It would allow time for consideration on the part of the patient, enabling them to make an informed and valid decision. Never should trainee involvement be mentioned "in passing" or on the actual day of the surgery, when the patient is at risk of making unconsidered decisions in a vulnerable state [8].

A further ethical consideration is the concept of justice, particularly in the setting of limited resources. This dictates the unconditional fair and equal treatment of all individuals to whom we provide a service. In reality, it is very difficult to achieve with demand outstripping supply probably in every health system worldwide. Admittedly, with resources rather more extensive in the UK than other countries, we should strive to provide consultant-based surgery at all times. In developing countries, however, the question is not so much "Who will do my surgery?", but rather "Will I have my surgery?" In this case, to question the identity of the surgeon is purely academic and trainee involvement should be actively encouraged for the benefit of patients.

In legal terms, it has been suggested that if a patient is operated on by a surgeon other than the one who gained consent, then they may be a victim of "battery" [6]. This is of more concern to teams of surgeons, where different consultants share patient lists, but the principles may be extrapolated to consider trainees operating as opposed to the consultant. Interestingly, no harm would need to befall the patient for it to become a legal issue of "battery". In cases where harm has befallen the patient, however, courts have ruled in favour of the medical team in situations when consent was given for trainee surgeons to operate [9]. Therefore, it seems that to ensure legal security, identity of the operating surgeons should be specified, whether trainee or not.

It is difficult to balance the best possible care given to our patients whilst ensuring progression of the field through training competent future surgeons. One must appreciate the necessity of maximising observational experience before allowing practical involvement. Shortening the learning curve for trainees can be safely achieved by innovative new techniques such as simulation. These technologies are increasingly being incorporated in surgical training and may be successful in enhancing the technical potential of trainees before they begin operating. Ultimately, patient safety and duty of care must be prioritised over surgical training. However, in the modern day, with the resources available to us in the UK, there is no reason why both cannot be achieved.

7.3 The European Working Time Directive (EWTD)

The EWTD introduced a 48-hour working week that has been in practice in European countries, by law, since 1998. It was initiated in response to the assumption that long working hours and severe sleep deprivation impair the performance of doctors and reduce patient safety.

Initially, a phased approach to implementation was adopted and the week began as 58 hours in 2004, was subsequently reduced to 56 in 2007, and then to 48 in 2009. Despite over ten years' notice for the changes to the working week, the latest reduction from 56 to 48 hours appears to have been the most difficult to manage. The legislation was launched as a "Protection of the clinical personnel against overwork for the benefit of Patients" [10]. Medical and surgical trainees have the opportunity to "opt out" to a voluntary 54-hour working week, however rotas cannot be constructed on this assumption.

The context of the EWTD must be appreciated before assumptions or consequences are drawn. The transition to the current working week has been implemented at a time when other societal, organisational, and political changes are taking place. These include increased competition for surgical training positions, curriculum changes, and changes to length of training.

In order to ensure patient safety and maintain all services, a considerable amount of overtime work occurs, which is unpaid and undocumented. In a study undertaken in Ireland, 70% of trainees felt that they could not comply with the working week because it did not enable them to achieve and deliver a continuity of care [10].

The reduction in working hours and working days per year has had inevitable consequences for both trainee surgeons and patients. A graphical representation of a questionnaire study (see Figure 7.2) undertaken in 2010, illustrates the opinion of 25 surgical senior house officers (SHOs) with regards to the effect of the EWTD compliant roster and the quality of their training [10]. Studies have been published to highlight UK opinion on the impact of the EWTD on training. One such study reports that 100% of cardiothoracic trainees believe that the EWTD has had a negative effect on their training and only 30% were satisfied with their training [11]. Another study concludes that 68% of surgical trainees reported a reduction in the quality of their training due to EWTD rotas, with 71% claiming that reduced working hours do not improve their quality of life [12].

It has been shown that approximately only 50% of medical institutions meet the legal requirements that satisfy the conditions of the EWTD [13]. A considerable amount of overtime work is undertaken

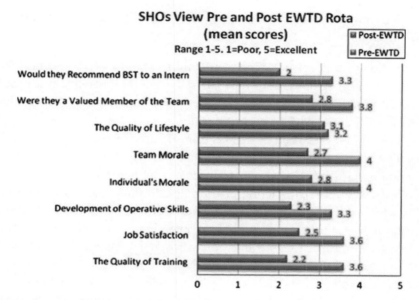

Figure 7.2. SHOs' opinions with regards to the implementation of the EWTD and the quality of training [10].

despite the abolishment of payment for this. This "voluntary" work occurs in an attempt to ensure that patient care and services are maintained. Furthermore, it is an opportunity for the trainee surgeon to gain exposure to surgical procedures that occur outside traditional working hours. Thus, with the introduction of the EWTD, a grey area of legality has developed, as the overtime work remains undocumented.

Trainees are aware of the rumour that they will not be indemnified if they were to be involved in a clinical incident when working beyond their contracted hours. The unsure nature of this issue creates ethico-legal dilemmas. Doctors working within the NHS are covered for indemnity by clinical negligence schemes for their trust, administered by the NHS Litigation Authority [14]. In 2007, the authority released a circular entitled "CNST indemnity for clinicians working in excess of EWTD limits". In this, a statement concluded:

> Any activity carried out by a clinician which would be the subject of an indemnity if carried out during 'allotted' hours will be treated no

differently under out schemes because that work was being done outside those hours [15].

Although trainees are clearly indemnified by the NHS beyond their contracted hours, they are strongly advised to act responsibly, ensure good medical practice, and put patients' safety first. It is made very clear that indemnity will not cover a neglect of duty.

The EWTD has resulted in the trainee surgeon seeing considerably fewer patients during his/her training, with participation in 30–40% fewer operations [16]. This results in trainees having had far less exposure to surgical cases upon completion of training and thus consultant-led practice, which should be the gold standard, will not be as comprehensive. Additionally, trainees are also unable to "experience" the full extent of care, from a full clinical history at admission to hospital discharge. Consequently, the rate and diversity of competency is reduced, which may result in a decreased quality of medical care. Additionally, the lack of exposure to surgical patients may diminish the confidence of trainees, as they have simply not acquired the skills through repetition and practice.

General discontinuity of care, accompanied by frequent handovers and complex rotas, have serious implications for patient safety by increasing the occurrence of adverse events. Additionally, care delivered to patients is very impersonal, which can be confusing and unsettling. It seems ethically unjust to potentially reduce patient safety and good medical practice as a consequence of the altered working week.

As a result of the EWTD, trainees are now allocated to various trainers at random, depending on daily availability. This has meant that the rotations with a specific trainer (the tandem model) and achievements of certain training goals during such rotations are no longer possible. Not only is continuity therefore lost between patients and trainee surgeons but also between trainee surgeons and their mentors.

It has been suggested that some of the repercussions of the EWTD can be combatted by formal lectures, courses, and training systems. Although this may be suitable for medical specialties, they are not suitable models for surgical specialties where hands-on practical experience and training is required in addition to direct observation. To overcome this downfall, surgical simulation again plays an essential role in providing basic exposure for all trainees and is an ever-increasing part of the current training process.

The creation of 10–15% more posts for trainees and consultants has been calculated as necessary to meet requirements of the EWTD [13]. However, this would increase overall costs. Also, it would serve to burden mentors' time and dilute the number of patients and variety of surgeries available per trainee.

Similarly, a prolongation of training time has been suggested to ensure adequate surgical experience and competency. This would have implications elsewhere such as increased costs and age of doctors. It also has the potential to decrease motivation to enter a specialist training programme when there may be other, more appealing and better paid professions.

Not only does the EWTD appear to have many practical creases that require ironing out, but also mentors and senior surgeons generally do not support it. This makes it very difficult for trainees to establish working relationships. Consultants, who have previously trained under longer and more challenging working hours, do not understand or appreciate why the current cohort of surgical trainees cannot do the same. Surgery is a form of apprenticeship that follows the old trusted motto of "see one, do one, teach one" that has stood the test of time and thus many do not support the change that forces it to be abolished.

7.4 Academic Surgery

Historically, the concept of academic surgery may have been considered oxymoronic. It is now accepted that those on the front line, i.e., surgeons themselves, should lead progress in the field, through research. The translation of research from "bench to bedside" has always proved difficult and the academic pathway is one effective method to ensure a smoother transition. It encourages innovation and progress of the field as well as promoting teaching. It is undeniably a commendable venture.

Yet, when put in the context of current surgical training, the academic pathway has the potential to further impair clinical experience for surgeons. Having already discussed the unfortunate impact that the EWTD is having on training, there needs to be logical reasoning behind the decision

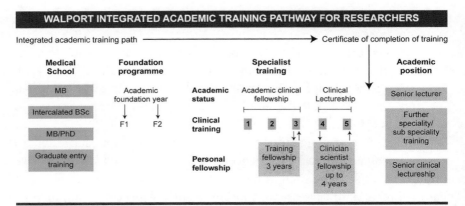

Figure 7.3. The Walport integrated academic training pathway for researchers.

to permit surgeons to devote a significant proportion of their paid working time to non-operative pursuits.

The Walport report in 2005 documented shortages of academics in medicine and recommended the creation of new training pathways to resolve the problem [17] (see Figure 7.3). The pathway can begin upon the completion of medical school, with entrance into an academic foundation programme. Increasing levels of academic commitment accompany progression along the integrated academic training path, whist maintaining clinical excellence. However, it has been suggested that the time spent out of clinical training may lead to "rustiness at the higher end of clinical decision-making" and that extra guidance and support during this time can offset these difficulties [18]. With non-academic trainees struggling for operative time themselves for aforementioned reasons, extra clinical support for academics may strain our already stretched resources.

The ethical justification for academic pursuit in our current resource- and experience-starved arena would centre on the intrinsic deontological value of research and progression of the field. If we believe in the necessity of research and academia for the greater good of the field and, more importantly, our patients on a moral level, then the associated limitations may be dismissed. The modern-day safety and success profile of surgery is as a consequence of academic progress, translation to the clinical arena and teaching. Formalising academic surgery as a career path will only serve to hasten further breakthroughs and refinement of practice. Additionally, dedicating extra clinical support to academics should not be seen as a hindrance or strain as described earlier, but rather as a necessity to ensure continued development.

7.5 Surgical Training Abroad

Many motivations underlie a surgical trainee's decision to practice abroad. The lack of hands-on experience resulting from a gradual reduction in working hours is one of the major contributing factors. Often, there is no set position in the surgical training pathway that people choose to undertake an international elective and thus it varies from trainee to trainee. Of course, there are some natural breaks in the pathway in which the majority of trainees choose to leave the UK and train abroad.

Commonly, after the completion of basic surgical training, most surgical SHOs will have obtained their membership examinations, undertaken audits, and perhaps published and presented original research work. A few of these doctors will be successful in obtaining a specialist registrar position but many unfortunately will not. For those that do not, there is the option of training abroad in the hope of improving and maintaining their surgical skills and further completing their log books.

International electives seem to be an excellent opportunity for trainees as they see large volumes of patients, a wide variety of pathology, and at the same time provide benefit to the local population. In addition, trainees are often given the opportunity to operate and assist in surgical procedures that their seniors may undertake, in preference to them, here in the UK. Furthermore, if the international institution that is chosen has a reciprocal relationship with the UK, then often the training and experience gained abroad can contribute to the training years upon return, provided it has been pre-approved by the deanery and the General Medical Council (GMC).

Hospitals that receive surgical trainees vary with regards to the resources that they have at their disposal, their acceptance protocol, the curricula that they provide, and the supervision that they offer. It is important for international institutions to assess and develop the surgical competence in their foreign trainees [19]. Often, different techniques are used in international countries, especially in developing countries, compared to the UK and these need to be taught to trainees with the appropriate supervision. Additionally, trainees should keep up-to-date with regards to current practice abroad and this should be done through the attendance of conferences, formal teaching, and mentoring.

Trainees who choose to practice abroad have an ethical obligation to act in the best interests of their patients [20]. As with training in the UK, there is a concern about the quality of care delivered when trainees are learning surgery. This concern is heightened when trainees choose to train internationally, as local surgeons are already overwhelmed with patients and therefore may not be able to dedicate adequate clinical supervision.

Lack of resources in developing countries has previously been cited as encouragement for medical students and trainees to operate abroad. This is justified under the principle that some surgery is better than no surgery, however expert. This argument is counteracted by Raja and Levin who explain that a lack of resources in developing countries makes a greater imperative for getting surgery done right the first time [20]. Poor surgical outcomes burden health systems with increased iatrogenic morbidity and it is essential for surgical trainees to provide services at an appropriate level and standard of care [19].

A concern of many is that training abroad may foster a poor sense of professionalism. As international electives provide ample opportunity for trainees to learn to operate, it may falsely be perceived that patients from other cultures and countries are more appropriate for surgical training. This incorrectly promotes the idea that some patients are more valuable than others [21]. Furthermore, it unfairly distributes the risk of trainees to developing countries, which in turn, contributes to the ethos of global health inequality.

On the contrary, many have supported the concept of international training having a positive impact on the professionalism of trainees [22]. By training abroad, junior surgeons have the opportunity to experience global health inequalities. These experiences help to teach Western surgeons to become better advocates for the poor around the world. Many surveys have also suggested that those surgeons who go on international electives are more likely to volunteer in the future [22, 23]. Trainees may also serve to lighten the workload and volume of patients seen in international institutions.

An experienced trainee surgeon, operating independently, may increase the surgical output and increase the institution's efficiency.

In general, surgical training years abroad are viewed as a valuable educational opportunity. However, this view is only adopted under the premise of two conditions. First, the trainee must have a minimum degree of competency with regards to his/her surgical skills and they must have acquired a sufficient amount of experience such that they will practice in accordance with current guidelines whilst optimising patient safety. Second, trainees are recommended to choose an appropriate time in their career to undertake international work. Work abroad does not necessarily contribute to the surgical training pathway in the UK and thus careful selection of timing is advised. All trainees are recommended to gain pre-approval from the deanery and the GMC in addition to securing a training post on their return.

7.6 Conclusions

The age-old adage "see one, do one, teach one" has been made less possible to achieve as a result of numerous changes to surgical training. There is a risk of threatening patient safety by introducing such drastic changes that have not been ethically or practically evaluated. Justification for these and future changes must centre around our duty to optimise care delivered to patients.

The EWTD has undoubtedly been a major contributor to this transition. Reduced working hours, the introduction of shift work, and financial restrictions have all decreased experience for current and future trainees. Training abroad may substitute valuable experience that can be difficult to acquire in our current climate. However, we must ensure that respect is given to all patients worldwide and that the value attributed to human life is not inconsistent. We should encourage our trainees to take such opportunities abroad and welcome them back upon their return, as they may bring with them enhanced and competent surgical skills.

We must endeavour to allow continued operative experience for trainees whilst maintaining the integrity of our doctor–patient relationships through honesty and informed consent. Simulation and other revolutionising technologies may serve to shorten the learning curve of trainees whist ensuring competent levels of technical skill. This may help to relieve the current pressures exerted by legal working hour restrictions.

The future of surgery will be dependent on continued innovation, research, and teaching. The academic training path has been designed to this end.

When taking all of this into consideration, alteration of the age-old adage seems appropriate; for modern-day trainees, the aim will be to, "see one, simulate many, do one competently, and teach everyone" [24].

References

[1] Blencowe N.S., Parsons B.A., and Hollowood A.D. Effects of changing work patterns on general surgical training over the last decade. *Postgraduate Journal of Medicine* December 2011; **87**(1034): 795–799.

[2] Department of Health and Sir Kenneth Charles Calman (Chairman). Hospital Doctors: Training for the Future: The Report on the Working Group for Specialist Medical Training. London: Department of Health, 1993.

[3] NHS Management Executive. Junior Doctors, The New Deal. London: NHS Management Executive, 1991.

[4] Parliament. Guidance on the Working Time (Amendment) Regulations (Statutory Instrument 2003 No 1684). London: The Stationery Office Ltd, 2003.

[5] Moore F.D. The surgical internship and residency. *Bulletin of the New York Academy of Medicine* July–August 1978; **54**(7): 648–656.

[6] Kocher M.S. Ghost surgery: the ethical and legal implications of who does the operations. *Journal of Bone and Joint Surgery, American Volume* 2002; **84**(1): 148–150.

[7] Richardson P.H., Curzen P., and Fonagy P. Patients' attitudes to student doctors. *Medical Education* July 1986; **20**(4) :314–317.

[8] Raja A.J. and Levin A.V. Challenges of teaching surgery: ethical framework. *World Journal of Surgery* 2003; **27**: 948–951.

[9] *Monturi* v *Englewood Hospital* [1991] 246 N.J. Super. 547, 588 A.2d 408.

[10] Kelly B.D., Curtin P.D., and Corcoran M. The effects of the European Working Time Directive on surgical training: The basic surgical trainees perspective. *Irish Journal of Medical Sciences* June 2011; **180**(2): 435–437.

[11] West D., Codispoti M., and Graham T. The European Working Time Directive and training in cardiothoracic surgery in the United Kingdom. *Surgeon* 2007; **5**(2): 81–85 (quiz 85, 121).

[12] Optimising working hours to provide quality in training and patient safety. The Association of Surgeons in Training at The Royal College of Surgeons of England. 2009.

[13] Benes V. The European Working Time Directive and the effects on train-ing of surgical specialists (doctors in training): a position paper of the surgi-cal disciplines of the countries of the EU. *Acta neurochirurgica* 2006; **148:** 1227–1233.

[14] NHS Litigation Authority, 2013. http://www.nhsla.com/Pages/Home.aspx [accessed 4 January 2012].

[15] NHS Confederation, 2009. www.healthcareworkforce.nhs.uk/bulletins/ wtd/2009/chiefexecutivesummary/indemnity [accessed 4 January 2012].

[16] Reulen H.J. The European Working Time Directive and the effects on training of surgical specialists (doctors in training). A position paper of the surgical di-ciplines of the countries of the EU. *Acta Neurochirurgica* 2006; 148: 1227–1233.

[17] Academic Careers Sub-Committee of Modernising Medical Careers and the UK Clinical Research Collaboration. Medically- and dentally-qualified aca-demic staff: recommendations for training the researchers and educators of the future. London: MMC, 2005.

[18] Mukherjee R. *Careers In... Academic Surgery*. Publication Date: 21 January 2009. BMJ Careers http://careers.bmj.com/careers/advice/view-article.html?id= 20000004 [accessed 11 January 2012].

[19] Bernstein M. Ethical dilemmas encountered while operating and teaching in a developing country. *Canadian Journal of Surgery* 2004; **47**(3): 170–172.

[20] Raja A.J. and Levin A.V. Challenges of teaching surgery: ethical framework. *World Journal of Surgery* 2003; **27**(8): 948–951.

[21] Huijer M. Treating despite discomfort and self-doubt. In: T.K. Kushner and D.C. Thomasma (eds) *Ward Ethics: Dilemmas for Medical Students and Doctors in Training.* Cambridge: Cambridge University Press, 2001; pp. 33–37.

[22] Gupta A.R., Wells C.K., Horwitz R.I., *et al.* The international health program: the fifteen-year experience with Yale University's internal medi-cine residency program. *The American Journal of Tropical Medicine and Hygeine* 1999; **61**(6): 1019–1023.

[23] Miller W.C., Corey G.R., Lallinger G.J., *et al.* International health and inter-nal medicine residency training: the Duke University experience. *American Journal of Medicine* 1995; **99**(3): 291–297.

[24] Vozenilek J., Huff J.S., Reznek M., and Gordon J.A. See one, do one, teach one: advanced technology in medical education. *Academy of Emergency Medicine* 2004; **11**: 1149–1154.

8

Great Expectations: Towards a Greater Understanding of Ethics in Policing by Exploring Practices in the Medical Profession

Allyson MacVean

While it may appear on first impression that the practices of medicine and policing have little in common, this perception is wholly deceptive; they are both inextricably linked by a number of professional obligations and responsibilities. These include:

- Both professions are service-oriented — that is they offer a valuable public service.
- They are both first responders in emergencies and other crises.
- Doctors and police officers have to make fast time decisions in challenging and rapidly changing situations.
- Policing and medicine have points of reference towards the satisfaction of fundamental needs in health and justice.
- Practitioners deal with matters and make decisions of significant importance to the welfare of individuals which may have great benefits or cause severe harm.
- Medicine and policing have specialist knowledge and expertise that enables them to fulfil their role in ways that untrained members of the public cannot. Therefore the public seek the services of medicine and

policing to intervene and assist them in situations that they have neither the knowledge or expertise to be able to do so for themselves.
- The professions are characterised by a high degree of autonomy and
  discretion.

The fact that medicine and policing have a wide latitude of discretion
and autonomy, and make decisions that can bring significant benefit or
harm to individuals, families and communities makes both practices an
immensely ethical matter. The medical professionals have considered ethics an integral element since its inception, and physicians are educated and
socialised about professional ethics during their initial training as well as
ongoing education and professional development [1]. Almost 50 years ago,
multidisciplinary hospital ethics committees were established in hospitals
to support medical practitioners and inform their decision making in situations involving ethical dilemmas. These ethics committees fulfil three
broad functions: education about ethics and ethical decision making;
ethics consultation, advice, or oversight of the consultation process; and
the development and review of ethics policy. This chapter considers how
ethics committees, using the medical paradigm, can be developed and
implemented into the police service in England. In doing so, it deliberates
on some of the key characteristics of policing that influence and affect how
ethics is conceptualised by both police officers and the organisation.

Whereas medicine has long been recognised as a profession, it has only
been recently that there has been debate as to whether the police service is
ready to transform itself into a profession or remain an occupation.
Traditionally, policing was considered a blue-collared occupation; it
recruited from the white working class community, was viewed exclusively
as a job for men and had its own unique "cop" culture [2,3]. However, the
police service is undergoing a significant paradigm shift: this change is
characterised by a set of features that emphasise community engagement,
proactive rather than reactive tactics focusing on prevention, evidence-
based strategies, greater partnership working, and an integrated approach
to criminal justice [4,5]. The transformation has facilitated the process for
the police towards fulfilling the requirements necessary to be recognised a
profession. For an occupation to transform itself into a profession it has to
fulfil a number of key requirements. It has to be underpinned by vocational

practice and develop its own body of knowledge that informs policy and procedure; it has to have its own professional association that has the power to regulate entry into the profession; that association has to define and establish professional autonomy, discretion, and self-regulation; and it has to have a code of ethics [6, 7].

A code of ethics is a set of statements that represent the collective moral values and beliefs of the profession. It therefore provides a framework of professional behaviour, responsibility, accountability, and compliance. The code presents a set of principles that allow members to consider their conduct, behaviour, and actions in discharging their duties. In addition, a code of ethics may also increase public confidence in an organisation as it demonstrates that members are committed to working within an ethical framework [5]. The police service does have a number of statements and principles in relation to behaviour and conduct for police officers. These include the Oath of Office, Statement of Common Purpose and Values, Code of Conduct, and the ethical decision making model [5,8,9]. The Association of the Chief Police Officers widely circulated a draft code of ethics, Principles of Policing, in 1992 but this code was not taken up or introduced as police protocol, although the Police Service of Northern Ireland (PSNI) implemented a code of ethics which was defined in Section 52 of the Police (Northern Ireland) Act 2000. This code of ethics also acts as a disciplinary code for police officers in the PSNI for behaviour both on and off duty. Compliance with the code is compulsory as officers are legislatively bound by its provision and it is linked to the police officers' annual performance reviews [10].

Compared to the medical profession, police ethics is significantly undeveloped. Until recently, the concept of ethics has been associated and coalesced with professional standards; all police forces have their own professional standard departments and these are responsible for overseeing complaints and allegations of misconduct. The disciplinary arrangements of the police originally mirrored the paramilitary philosophy on which modern policing was founded. Disciplinary rules and regulations focused on what police officers were prohibited from doing, creating a destructive and adverse approach to dealing with unacceptable and corrupt behaviour. The process was overly bureaucratic, legalistic, and lengthy. This system was to change when the Home Secretary commissioned a review into the arrangements for dealing with police misconduct and unsatisfactory performance in 2004. This review also sought to consider the extent to which the Code of Conduct was fit for purpose and the development of a code of ethics for the police service. The review, known as the Taylor Report [11], heralded a shift from blame and sanction to development and improvement encapsulating commercial employment law even though police officers are not "employees" in the traditional sense, but "Servants of the Crown" and therefore not subject to the normal sanctions of employment law [12]. However, while the review introduced a new single code of conduct it did not provide a distinct police code of ethics. With the notion of ethics being associated with professional standards, there was a lack of knowledge and clear understanding of what constitutes police ethics as an issue within its own right, separate and independent of professional standards.

In addition to the merging of the concept of ethics with professional standards, the paramilitary structure of policing meant that orders despatched through the ranks by the chain of command could not challenged or questioned. Orders were assigned to officers by supervisors and the orders had to be carried out as instructed as it was considered a disciplinary offence to question such orders. As Pagon observes "there is not much need for moral deliberations. The basic virtue of police officers within this framework is obedience" [4: p. 5].

The fact that ethics, given it is a key component of policing, has remained relatively undeveloped is quite remarkable. Pollock has argued that the study of ethics is essential for criminal justice practitioners in general and for the police in particular as they are empowered with significant discretion to make decisions that can affect the life, liberty, and property of members of the public [13: p. 3]. In carrying out their duties police officers are conferred by the state with a considerable array of powers as the agents to enforce the law: they are empowered to use force in certain situations including lethal force as well as the use of intrusive, covert, and deceptive methods to detect and investigate crime. As public servants bestowed with these authorities, officers have to demonstrate the highest standards of integrity and ethical behaviour. However, the challenge here for policing is that police officers are required to uphold and enforce the law regardless of the moral consideration or content. For example, the Criminal Procedure and Investigations Act 1996 sets out that the role of the police is to investigate and present all relevant evidence, both inculpatory and exculpatory, and not just to present the evidence that a police officer has deemed relevant on the basis of what they consider morally right or wrong. If police officers were to enforce the law equally and without discretion, and apply the law according to the law there would be no need for consideration of ethics [5]. But policing comprises of more than law enforcement, it includes protecting the rights of members of the community as well as being the gatekeepers of citizenship and respectability [13]. Policing therefore embraces a range of social justice issues rather than just criminal justice matters. The police cannot discharge all operational duties by merely applying the law according to the law; they take into account context and circumstances of the situation and in doing so use discretion and autonomy. The wide latitude of discretion accorded to police officers is essential to the practice of policing. As noted by Lord Scarman [14]:

> the exercise of discretion lies at the heart of the policing function. It is undeniable that there is only one law for all: and it is right that this should be so. But it is equally recognised that successful policing depends on the exercise of discretion on how the law is enforced. ... *Discretion is the art of suiting action to particular circumstances* [author's own emphasis].

Thus given the nature and function of police work, ethics should be an integral part of policing. While the development of a code of ethics would be laudable and provide a statement of organisational ideals, aspirations, principles, and requirements for its employees, this alone is not enough. What also are required are models of applied ethics that are embedded into the organisation's policy and practice. Research has demonstrated that in professions that are empowered with great autonomy, good people may do bad things if they are placed in an environment that does not value morals and ethical practice [15].

Therefore, the police service has to think beyond the introduction of philosophical ethics and move towards the development of normative applied models of ethics. Pagon remarks:

> the link between "theory" and "practice" is what makes applied ethics different from philosophical ethics. Applied ethics is the field that holds ethical theory accountable to practice and professional practice to

theory. Therefore, the philosophers should not dictate to professionals the norms that are supposed to govern their professional practice, without a very thorough knowledge of that practice. On the other hand the professionals have to understand that their experience and intuition are insufficient for defensible judgment [4: p. 2].

The idea of developing applied ethics through police ethics committees, drawing on the clinical ethics committee model, is a highly novel approach. The introduction of ethics committees affords the police organisation the opportunity to develop a body of knowledge of what constitutes ethics and ethical dilemmas in policing. It allows the Service to contemplate the ethical issues that officers and the organisation encounter as well as the relationship between ethical behaviour and professional standards in developing an ethical culture. Lebeer has argued that from a sociological perspective ethical committees appear to be "capable of launching a deep seated transformation of the decision making process" [16: p. 4] and therefore able to facilitate cultural change.

In addition, it allows police officers the possibility to reflect about the extensive and subtle ethical issues of policing and assist them in clarifying complex or difficult situations and take morally acceptable decisions (individually and collectively). Ethics committees offer the prospect of submitting ethical dilemmas to wider collective discussions that are advisory and informative; they do not have authority or ownership over the ethical issue. In that sense the committee is postulated in Habermas's sense of collective critique of principles and rules of action in that ethics is not a body of specific knowledge that can be mastered but a process that presents wider points of deliberation [17].

To conclude, the current interest and scrutiny in police ethics and professional standards (for example, the Leveson Report (2012), the Hillsborough Review (2012) [18], and the case of Mark Kennedy the undercover operative) together with the significant changes taking place in British policing signifies that ethics is to come to the forefront as being one of the most important components of policing. As Gargan notes "it is no longer enough to have the luxury of occasional interest in professional standards and ethics. This needs to be an area of unrelenting focus, constant reflection and innovation supported by a determined operational commitment to maintaining standards" [19: p. xvii]. The introduction of ethics committees, bringing in the learning and wisdom from medical ethics committees, will signal a radical new approach to a better understanding of police ethics in practice.

References

[1] Gaudine, A., Lamb, M., LeFort, S., and Thorne, L. *The Functioning of Hospital Ethics: A Multiple-Case Study of Four Canadian Committees.* Healthcare Ethics Committee Forum: An Interprofessional Journal on Healthcare Institutions' Ethical and Legal Issues 2011; **23**(3): 225–238.

[2] Reiner, R. Police Research in the United Kingdom: A critical review. In M. Tonry and N. Morris (eds.) *Modern Policing.* Chicago, IL: University of Chicago, 1992.

[3] Loftus, B. *Police Culture in a Changing World.* Oxford: Oxford University Press, 2009.

[4] Pagon, M. *Police Ethics and Integrity.* Maribor: University of Maribor, 2003.

[5] MacVean, A. and Neyroud, P. *Police Ethics and Values.* London: Sage, 2012.

[6] Boone, T. *Constructing a Profession.* An International Electronic Journal for Exercise Physiologists. 4(5) May. ISSN 1099–5862.

[7] Bullock, A. and Trombley, S. *The New Fontana Dictionary of Modern Thought.* London: Harper Collins, 1999.

[8] ACPO (Association of Chief Police Officers) 1993.

[9] ACPO (Association of Chief Police Officers). *Statement of Missions and Values.* Presented at the Higher Education Forum for Police Learning and Development, University of Northampton, 6 September 2011.

[10] SQA (Scottish Qualifications Authority) *PDA Diploma in Police Service Leadership and Management: Professional Ethics in Policing.* Glasgow: SQA, 2007; CB3740.

[11] Taylor, W. *The Review of Police Disciplinary Arrangements Report.* London: HMSO, 2005.

[12] Taylor, W. *The Taylor Review.* In A. MacVean, P. Spindler, and C. Solf (eds) *Handbook of Policing, Ethics and Professional Standards.* Oxford: Routledge, 2012.

[13] Pollock, J. *Ethics in Crime and Justice.* Belmont, CA: Wadsworth, 1998.

[14] Scarman, Lord *A Report into the Brixton Disturbances of 11/12 April 1998.* London: Home Office, 1981.

[15] Ethics Resource Center, USA.

[16] LeBeer, G. *Ethical Function in Hospital Ethics Committees*. Amsterdam: IOS, 2002.

[17] Calhoun, C., Mendieta, E., and Vanantwerpen, J. *Habermas and Religion*. Cambridge: Polity Press, 2012.

[18] Hillsborough: The Report of the Hillsborough Independent Panel. London: The Stationery Office, 2012.

[19] Gargan, N. Foreword. In A. MacVean, P. Spindler, and C. Solf (eds) *Handbook of Policing, Ethics and Professional Standards*. Oxford: Routledge, 2012.

Part 2
Specialist Practice

9

Ethical and Legal Issues in Anaesthetics

Jeremy Campbell and Felicity Plaat

9.1 Consent for Anaesthesia

Beauchamp and Childress [1] assert that there are four guiding ethical principles in medical practice: respect for autonomy (the patient's right to be involved in decisions that affect them), beneficence (do good), non-maleficence (do not harm), and justice (fair distribution of resources). Of these, the principle of respect for autonomy now takes precedence over the other three principles, reflecting the gradual replacement of medical paternalism with a situation in which doctors and patients are partners in health.

Respect for patients' autonomy is reflected in the requirement for clinicians to obtain consent for treatment [2]. Failure to obtain consent before performing a procedure may lead to a claim of battery — the unlawful touching of another person [3]. In practice this is rarely an issue in claims against doctors. Far more likely is a claim of negligence after a complication, on the basis that had the patient been told of the risk, he or she would not have undergone the procedure and the complication would not have occurred.

For consent to be valid, it must be given voluntarily by a patient who has been appropriately informed and who has the capacity (competence) to make a choice [4]. Adults have the legal capacity to consent to a medical procedure if they are able to understand the information given to them,

169

remember that information, use that information in order to decide whether or not to undergo the treatment proposed, and communicate that decision [5]. Adults are presumed to be competent to give consent unless there is evidence to the contrary. The practitioner treating the patient is the person who must decide whether the patient is competent or not. If the patient is deemed to lack capacity, they should be treated in their best interests.

In current medical practice, patients who have consented to surgery are considered to have implied consent to anaesthesia. However, anaesthesia is associated with its own risks that are quite separate from those associated with surgery. Anaesthetists must therefore always seek consent from patients for anaesthesia [6].

The process of consent for anaesthesia should begin before the anaesthetist and patient meet. The patient should be provided with an information leaflet about their anaesthetic at the time of their pre-operative assessment. The anaesthetist should meet the patient face to face before their operation so that further discussions can take place. Under some circumstances it may be acceptable for a suitably trained healthcare practitioner who is not an anaesthetist to discuss anaesthetic aspects of management, but the opportunity to speak directly to an anaesthetist should be available to all patients. The anaesthetic room however is an inappropriate place to provide patients with new information, other than in exceptional circumstances [7].

Patients whose first language is not English are entitled to an explanation of their anaesthetic in their own language. Hospitals which treat a large number of patients from ethnic minorities should ensure that independent, professional interpreters are available at all times. The use of relatives or friends as interpreters is inappropriate because it may filter or distort the passage of crucial information between the patient and their anaesthetist. (However members of the local community specifically trained to be "patient advocates" have been successfully used for obstetric patients.)

The Association of Anaesthetists of Great Britain and Ireland (AAGBI) has given specific advice about the nature of information that anaesthetists should provide to patients [7].

- The anaesthetist should explain what will happen to the patient before and after anaesthesia. This includes the need to fast, administration and effects of pre-medication, cannula insertion, non-invasive monitoring, induction of general anaesthesia/regional anaesthetic technique, monitoring throughout surgery, and transfer to the recovery area. Post-operative analgesia, anti-emesis, and fluid therapy should also be described.
- Where appropriate, alternative anaesthetic techniques should be discussed.
- Commonly occurring side-effects (e.g., nausea and vomiting, post-dural puncture headache) should be explained.
- Rare but serious complications (e.g., awareness, nerve injury) should be provided in written information, as should the very small risk of death.
- Specific risks or complications that may be of increased significance to the patient (e.g., the risk of vocal-cord damage from tracheal intubation if the patient is a professional singer) should be explained.
- Increased risk from anaesthesia and surgery due to the patient's medical history, nature of surgery, and/or urgency of the procedure should be explained.
- If a local or regional technique is to be used alone, the risk of intra-operative pain should be discussed, as should the need to convert to general anaesthesia.
- The benefits and risks of associated procedures (e.g., insertion of a central venous line) should be explained.
- Procedures of a sensitive nature, such as the insertion of an analgesic suppository, should be explained.

The AAGBI is of the view that a formal signed consent form is not necessary for anaesthesia since most procedures carried out by anaesthetists are done either to facilitate another treatment (e.g., anaesthesia for surgery) or as part of a larger process (e.g., epidural analgesia for labour) [7]. If, however, the anaesthetic procedure is the primary therapeutic intervention (e.g., an anaesthetic intervention for a patient with chronic pain), it is wise to ask the patient to sign a consent form.

9.2 Special Circumstances

9.2.1 *Obstetrics*

The principles of consent in obstetric anaesthesia are no different from those described above, although they may be more difficult to apply in the often stressful circumstances on the delivery suite.

It is inappropriate to burden patients with excessive information when they are in the full throes of labour. Obstetric units should therefore provide women with information about epidural analgesia beforehand (e.g., in the antenatal clinic). However, since up to half of primigravidae who end up with an epidural did not want one antenatally [8], it is essential that the anaesthetist also provides the patient with information at the time of the procedure, and this discussion should be documented.

The adult parturient is presumed to have capacity, although when she is in labour this may be compromised by fatigue, pain, anxiety, and/or the effects of powerful analgesic drugs (but this should not be assumed). The anaesthetist must decide whether or not she has the capacity to understand what treatment is being proposed: if she is deemed to be competent, she may consent to (or refuse) treatment as in any other situation; if not, then the anaesthetist is obliged to treat her in her best interests. The woman's partner is a useful source of information as to what the woman's best interests might be if she lacks capacity to give consent [9].

A particular problem arises when a woman has written an antenatal birth plan in which she steadfastly refuses an epidural even if she requests one in labour (the so-called Ulysses directive), and then presents in labour screaming for pain relief. In this situation the anaesthetist must first decide whether she has capacity or not. If she does, her request must be respected and it is appropriate to proceed with an epidural, although it may be wise to ask her to give written consent for the procedure. If she is considered to lack capacity, then the birth plan should be treated as an advance decision, and any documented refusal of therapy must be respected. In such circumstances, it is wise to make sure that a witness (usually the midwife) is present and that everyone agrees on what has been decided. It is essential that the anaesthetist then records these discussions in the patient's medical records. Trainee anaesthetists faced with such a situation should consult with senior staff [9].

The presence of the fetus does not affect a competent woman's right to make an autonomous decision about her own care, even if this puts the unborn child at risk of harm or death [7]. Respect for the autonomy of pregnant women is now supported in common law where the rights of competent women to refuse consent, even in the extreme situation of refusing to undergo caesarean section, were upheld [10].

9.2.2 Children

Anaesthesia and surgery are stressful experiences for children and it is therefore not uncommon for children to be uncooperative in the anaesthetic room. When faced with an uncooperative child, the anaesthetist should use their own judgement when deciding how much restraint is acceptable in order to achieve induction of anaesthesia, even if the parents appear willing to have their child restrained. If the child is uncontrollable, the anaesthetist should consider not proceeding with anaesthesia. In such circumstances, the parents should be given an explanation and future management should be arranged [7].

9.2.3 Critical care

Many patients in the intensive care unit (ICU) lack competence either due to their disease or because of their treatment (e.g., sedation). However, patients should not be assumed to lack competence merely because they are seriously ill, are receiving sedative drugs, and/or are unable to communicate orally [11]. The Mental Capacity Act 2005 states that all practicable steps should be taken to help a temporarily incapacitated individual in making an informed decision [12]. This will often be impossible because the patient is unconscious; in such settings doctors may treat patients in their best interests. There should be clear documentation that capacity could not be achieved despite best efforts.

After the event, it is good practice to explain to previously incapacitated patients what interventions were performed during their stay on ICU [7].

9.3 Maternal Fetal Conflicts and the Role of the Anaesthetist

9.3.1 *Participation in termination of pregnancy*

Section 4 of the Abortion Act (1967) [13] allows individuals to refuse to participate in terminations of pregnancy if they have a conscientious objection. Difficulties may arise when an anaesthetist who does not normally anaesthetise for terminations is asked to add one to the end of their elective gynaecology list as an extra case. In such circumstances, his or her conscientious objection should be respected. However, Section 4 also stipulates that conscientious objection does not extend to a refusal to participate in care that is necessary to save a woman's life or prevent grave permanent injury to her physical or mental health. The professional consequences of refusing to participate under these circumstances are potentially serious.

9.3.2 *Tensions between anaesthetists and obstetricians*

In obstetric practice, the anaesthetist's first duty of care is to the mother [14]. The presence of a fetus influences how an anaesthetic is conducted, but the anaesthetist's duty of care to the fetus must not override a consideration of maternal safety.

Obstetricians may not have been able to consider the risk of anaesthesia to a woman when they are preoccupied with the urgent delivery of a baby. Consequently, they may urge the anaesthetist to have a patient ready for an emergency caesarean section so quickly that it puts the woman's life in danger. These circumstances are most likely to arise out of hours, where relatively inexperienced obstetricians are working with trainee anaesthetists. It is the anaesthetist's responsibility to protect the mother by proceeding at a pace where consideration of maternal safety takes precedence over fetal well-being [15].

9.4 Anaesthesia for Jehovah's Witness Patients

Jehovah's Witnesses are members of the Watch Tower Bible and Tract Society, a religious denomination founded in the US in 1872. It is estimated that there are nearly 6.5 million Jehovah's Witnesses worldwide, of whom 145,000 live in the UK [16].

Jehovah's Witnesses do not accept transfusion of blood or its major components. They believe that to be transfused with blood is equivalent to eating it, and they consider this to be prohibited by scripture (Genesis 9: 3,4; Leviticus 17: 11,12; Acts 15: 28,29) [16]. The prohibition of blood transfusion is a deeply held core value, and they are prepared to die rather than compromise this refusal.

There are no absolute rules regarding acceptability of blood and blood products, but treatments generally regarded as unacceptable by Jehovah's Witnesses include [17]:

- Transfusion of whole blood, packed red cells, white cells, plasma (FFP), and platelets.
- Pre-operative autologous blood collection and storage for later reinfusion.

Treatments that Jehovah's Witnesses consider as being of personal choice are:

- Blood salvage.
- Cardiac bypass (provided the pump is primed with non-blood fluids and blood is not stored in the process).
- "Fractions" of plasma (e.g., albumin, clotting factors).
- Transplantation, including solid organ, bone, tissue, etc.
- Epidural blood patch.

The AAGBI strongly recommends that at the pre-operative visit, the views held by each Jehovah's Witness patient should be ascertained to determine which treatments are acceptable and which are not. The patient should be made fully aware of the risks of refusal of blood and blood products. The AAGBI also recommends that, if possible, this discussion should take place without the presence of relatives or members of the local community who may influence the patient. Agreed and unacceptable treatments should be documented in the patient's medical notes. Most hospitals provide specific Jehovah's Witness consent forms which should be completed.

Many practising Jehovah's Winesses carry an advance decision document which also details their wishes, and copies are usually lodged with their GP, family, and friends.

The absolute refusal of blood transfusion by a Jehovah's Witness may be at odds with a doctor's personal beliefs and desire to preserve life. However, a competent individual has a right to refuse consent for medical treatment for any reason, even if this may lead to his or her death [11]. Consequently, to proceed with the administration of blood to a patient who has competently refused to accept it, either by the provision of an advance decision or by its exclusion in a consent form, is ethically unacceptable and unlawful. It may also lead to referral to the General Medical Council [17].

A more difficult situation arises when suddenly faced with an unconscious patient whose status as a Jehovah's Witness may be unknown and who is at immediate risk of dying from bleeding. In their guidelines, the AAGBI advises that "the doctor caring for the patient will be expected to perform to the best of his ability, and this may include the administration of blood transfusion" [17]. If relatives or associates suggest that the patient is a Jehovah's Witness who would not accept a blood transfusion even if that resulted in his or her death, they should be asked to provide documentary evidence such as an advance decision. Without this, blood should not be withheld in life-threatening circumstances. Every trust should formulate local guidelines for such emergencies with the help of the trust's solicitors.

The guidelines published by the AAGBI also provide useful advice for the transfusion of children of Jehovah's Witnesses below the age of 16 years. For elective procedures, there should be a full and frank discussion between the surgeon, anaesthetist, parents, and child (if they are old enough to understand). Most parents accept that whilst every attempt will be made to avoid blood, a doctor will not allow a child to die for lack of transfusion. If the parents refuse to give permission for blood transfusion, the trust can apply to the High Court for a "Specific Issue Order" in order legally to administer the blood. In such cases, two consultants should document in the patient's medical record that blood transfusion is essential, or likely to become so, to save the child's life or prevent serious permanent harm. In an emergency situation where the child of a Jehovah's

Witness is likely to die without immediate administration of blood, application to the courts will be too time-consuming and blood should therefore be transfused without consulting the court [17].

The AAGBI states that anaesthetists may refuse to anaesthetise a Jehovah's Witness in an elective situation, but should refer the case to a colleague who is prepared to undertake it. In an emergency, the anaesthetist is obliged to provide care and must respect the patient's competently expressed wishes [17].

The use of extra resources to satisfy the religious beliefs of Jehovah's Witness patients may result in a lack of resources being available to other patients. Examples include the use of erythropoietin to optimise haemoglobin levels before surgery, the additional theatre time necessary to achieve bloodless surgery, the use of blood salvage equipment, and the possible requirement of prolonged periods of high dependency or intensive care post-operatively.

9.5 Anaesthesia for Patients with "Do Not Attempt Resuscitation" Decisions

If an individual suffers a cardiac or respiratory arrest, cardiopulmonary resuscitation (CPR) may be undertaken in an attempt to restart the breathing and circulation. Interventions in CPR include external chest compressions, attempted defibrillation, ventilation of the lungs, and the use of large doses of vasoactive medication [18].

In some cases (e.g., terminal illness), cardiac and/or respiratory arrest will be an expected part of the dying process and CPR will not be successful. In such circumstances an advance decision may be made not to attempt CPR, in order to help ensure that the patient dies in a peaceful and dignified manner. These management plans are called "Do Not Attempt Resuscitation" (DNAR) decisions [18].

Once a DNAR decision is in place, the situation may then arise when the patient requires anaesthesia for an operative intervention. Procedures that would be considered appropriate in these circumstances include surgery to relieve pain (e.g., repair of a fractured neck or femur) and surgery for a condition related to the underlying problem but not a terminal event (e.g., bowel obstruction). However, the provision of anaesthesia for a patient with a pre-existing DNAR decision places the patient and anaesthetist on the horns of a dilemma. Many of the routine interventions used when giving an anaesthetic may be considered as "resuscitation". These include the insertion of an intravenous cannula, administration of intravenous fluids, delivery of oxygen, and insertion of an artificial airway. Furthermore, the administration of an anaesthetic is likely to result in cardiovascular instability and respiratory depression that will require support. If the anaesthetist were to proceed with anaesthesia but also obey the DNAR decision, he or she would be initiating cardiorespiratory compromise and yet be unable to treat this once it had occurred. If the anaesthetist insisted that the DNAR order be suspended in order to allow anaesthesia and surgery to take place, and then instituted resuscitative measures against the patient's wishes, this would constitute assault and may be in breach of Article 3 of the Human Rights Act (prohibition of torture or of inhuman or degrading treatment) [19].

The AAGBI has published guidelines which recommend that all DNAR decisions should be reviewed by the anaesthetist and surgeon with the patient (as well as other relevant decision makers, if indicated) before proceeding with anaesthesia and surgery [20]. There are three options for managing the DNAR decision:

Option 1: The DNAR decision is to be discontinued. Anaesthesia and surgery are to proceed, with CPR to be used if cardiopulmonary arrest occurs.

Option 2: The DNAR decision is to be modified to permit the use of drugs and techniques commensurate with the provision of anaesthesia. This option is used most commonly.

Option 3: No changes are to be made to the DNAR decision. Under most circumstances this option is not compatible with the provision of general anaesthesia.

Once the DNAR management option has been agreed, it should be documented in the patient's medical notes. The DNAR management option should apply for the duration of the patient's stay in the theatre environment including the recovery area. The prior DNAR decision should be reinstated when the patient is handed over to the nursing staff from the ward [20].

References

[1] Beauchamp T.L. and Childress J.F. *Principles of Biomedical Ethics, 6th ed.* Oxford: Oxford University Press, 2009.

[2] Young R. Informed consent and patient autonomy. In H. Kuhse and P. Singer (eds) *A Companion to Bioethics.* Massachusetts: Blackwell, 1998; p. 441.

[3] Body D.I. Civil and criminal actions against anaesthetists. *British Journal of Anaesthesia* 1994; **73**: 83–92.

[4] White S.M. and Baldwin T.J. Consent for anaesthesia. *Anaesthesia* 2003; **58**: 882–888.

[5] *Re MB (an adult: medical treatment)* [1997] 2 FLR 426 (CA).

[6] White S.M. Consent for anaesthesia. *Journal of Medical Ethics* 2004; **30**: 286–290.

[7] Association of Anaesthetists of Great Britain and Ireland. Consent for Anaesthesia. London: AAGBI, 2006.

[8] Broaddus B.M. and Chandrasekhar M.D. Informed consent in obstetric anesthesia. *Anesthesia and Analgesia* 2011; **112**: 912–915.

[9] Yentis S. and Malhotra S. *Analgesia, anaesthesia and pregnancy: a practical guide, 3rd ed.* Cambridge: Cambridge University Press, 2013.

[10] *St George's Healthcare NHS Trust* v *S; R* v *Collins and others, ex parte S* [1998] 3 All ER 673.

[11] General Medical Council. Consent: Patients and doctors making decisions together. London: GMC, 2008.

[12] Mental Capacity Act 2005 (c.9). London: HMSO.

[13] Abortion Act 1967. London: HMSO.

[14] Knapp R.M. Medicolegal aspects of obstetric anesthesia. In G.W. Ostheimer (ed.) *Manual of Obstetric Anesthesia, 2nd ed.* Philadelphia: Churchill Livingstone, 1992.

[15] Scott W. Maternal foetal conflicts and the anaesthetist's role. In H. Draper and W. Scott (eds) *Ethics in Anaesthesia and Intensive Care.* Edinburgh: Butterworth-Heinemann, 2003.

[16] Marsh J.C.W. and Bevan D.H. Haematological care of the Jehovah's Witness patient. *British Journal of Haematology* 2002; **119**: 25–37.

[17] Association of Anaesthetists of Great Britain and Ireland. Management of anaesthesia for Jehovah's Witnesses, 2nd edition. London: AAGBI, 2005.

[18] General Medical Council. Treatment and care towards the end of life: good practice in decision making. London: GMC, 2010.

[19] McBrien M.E. and Heyburn G. 'Do not attempt resuscitation' orders in the peri-operative period. *Anaesthesia* 2006; **61**: 625–627.

[20] Association of Anaesthetists of Great Britain and Ireland. Do Not Attempt Resuscitation (DNAR) Decisions in the Perioperative Period. London: AAGBI, 2009.

10

Neurosurgery: Ethical and Legal Issues

Howard Morgan, Louis Whitworth, Christopher Madden
and Duke Samson

The traditional practice of neurosurgery is fraught with questions and issues that have ethical and legal implications, for example, is it appropriate to withdraw life-sustaining treatment from a patient who has sustained a severe irreversible head injury leading to brain death or persistent vegetative state? Who should be the decision-maker for the patient? Should the ventilator be removed from a quadriplegic patient who has sustained a high cervical spinal cord injury, has no chance of significant recovery, and asks to die? Because a central nervous system disease may alter the decision-making capacity of those afflicted, who makes the decision for the incapacitated patient and how? Those issues, often involving neurosurgical patients, were discussed, debated, and written about during the latter part of the twentieth century in the medical ethics literature, by court decisions and by institutional ethics committees. Although still sometimes contentious, those questions are not as unique as they once were and society seems to have come to terms with an approach for most. Because surgery on the nervous system is inherently a risky business, neurosurgeons are frequently the subject of medical-legal action as defendants in medical malpractice actions or as expert witnesses in court opining on standard of care in malpractice litigation. Neurosurgical societies have crafted codes of ethics as guidelines for their members who testify in medical malpractice cases, for example, the American Association of Neurological Surgeons [1] and the World Federation of Neurosurgical Societies together with the European Association of Neurosurgical Societies [2]. Future advances in technology and disease understanding will likely lead to unforeseen treatments for neurological maladies. Lipsman and Bernstein predict the ethical challenges in the field of neurosurgery of the future: "As technology continues to advance, the onus will be on the practicing neurosurgeon to justify the application of novel technology to new and evolving patient populations" [3]. These "new and evolving patient populations" will likely include those with movement disorders, some with neuropsychiatric conditions (for example, obsessive compulsive disorder, depression, alcoholism, drug addiction, and severe obesity), those with chronic pain, possibly those who are "normal" but seek neuroenhancement through surgical means, those who are paralyzed and seek to walk, and the blind who seek to see via brain-machine interface implants.

10.1 Ethics and the Neurosurgeon

During the late decades of the twentieth century and the first decade of the twenty-first century, the field of medical ethics — also known as biomedical ethics and bioethics — seemed to spring up and grow rapidly. Medical ethics is now routinely taught in medical schools, and institutes (both secular and religious) have been formed and journals published regarding ethical issues in healthcare delivery. Actually, throughout medical history (for example, consider works of Hippocrates in ancient Greece and Maimonides in the twelfth century CE) the practice of medicine has been known to be filled with ethical questions and challenges. The development of artificial life support techniques as well as modern diagnostic imaging in the second half of the twentieth century seemed to engender more ethical questions than answers when it came to the evaluation and care of patients with serious neurological disorders. We as neurosurgeons need to stay active in the discussions of the ethical aspects of our field — if we do not, philosophers, clergymen, lawyers, nurses, and "neuroscientists" with an interest will likely overtake us, and consequently we may have little say about the ethical application of the new and emerging technologies and the ethical standards for management of our patients. The purpose of this chapter is to introduce ethical and legal issues that are important and/ or particular to the practice of neurosurgery currently or likely to occur in the future.

10.1.1 *Severe neurological injury*

Ethical issues are commonly encountered by the clinician caring for patients who are severely injured neurologically. Decisions about prognosis, withdrawal of care, decision making for the incompetent patient, and futility of care are often necessary and involve ethical dilemmas that may also become legal issues.

10.1.1.1 *Coma*

A patient with a devastating intracranial injury will usually present in coma, a term which describes the impaired consciousness in the acute setting. The pathophysiology of that condition was extensively reviewed by Plum and Posner [4]. It is a state in which there is no ability to interact with the surrounding environment even after stimulation. Clinically the patient is noted to have no eye opening, speech, ability to follow commands, purposeful movement, or ability to localize noxious stimuli. During coma there is no EEG evidence of sleep/wake cycles and responses are only reflexive. Coma rarely lasts longer than two to four weeks, however, and the patient who does not regain consciousness will then be classified as in a vegetative state [4, 5].

A patient in coma obviously is not able to consent to treatment decisions regarding care. In keeping with the idea of respect for patient autonomy, decisions in this situation are usually either made in accordance with a patient's previously expressed wishes (either through a living will or as expressed to family or close friends) or are delegated to surrogate decision makers (proxies). Advance directives can be of two general types. A living will delineates the treatments that a patient would consider acceptable or unacceptable in the event that they are no longer capable of making an active decision. A durable power of attorney delegates the task of decision making to a specific person who presumably knows that patient well and who will make decisions in accordance with that patient's wishes and beliefs. Advance directives may include both a living will and a delegation of power of attorney. In the absence of an advance directive, the clinician needs to seek surrogate decision makers. These will usually be family members who presumably know the patient well and can represent the patient's preferences and interests. It is best to seek some consensus if possible from family members regarding treatment decisions but if there is disagreement among the family, many legal jurisdictions prioritize relations in order of being able to speak for the patient (e.g., spouse, children, or parents).

A patient who has suffered a devastating neurological injury but does not meet the formal definition of brain death requires that the physician prognosticate as to the potential for recovery. What a family invariably will want to know is whether their injured family member will be able to live through the injury, and if the individual does survive, will he or she be able to return to some sort of normal life? In a patient who has had a severe neurological injury (e.g., from stroke, trauma, or anoxic encephalopathy), the clinician must make an assessment as to whether a meaningful neurological recovery is likely. Many individuals in today's society would prefer not to be kept alive nor keep a family member alive if the stricken person were to suffer with permanent, severe neurological deficit, especially if that deficit were to include loss of conscious interaction with the world.

Studies which document factors associated with poor outcome, combined with clinical experience, may serve as a guide to judgment. Glasgow Coma Scale (GCS) score in the setting of traumatic brain injury has been correlated with chances of survival and subsequent disability. Other factors (e.g., age, blood pressure, pupillary light response, and CT scan findings) taken together with the GCS score may improve the ability to predict the patient's prognosis [6, 7]. Somatosensory-evoked potentials can predict a poor prognosis for recovery of consciousness after trauma if there are negative bilateral cortical responses [8]. In non-traumatic coma (e.g., spontaneous hemorrhage or ischemic injury after cardiac arrest), Hamel et al. identified five factors associated with poor survival: abnormal brainstem response, absent verbal response, absent withdrawal to painful stimuli, creatinine level greater than or equal to 1.5 mg/dL, and age greater than 70 [9]. If four of these five factors were present, mortality at two months was 97%. Abnormal brainstem reflexes and an absent motor response to pain were the most accurate predictors and if either was present, the rate of death or severe disability at two months was 96%. In patients who are comatose after cardiopulmonary resuscitation, pupillary light response, corneal reflexes, motor responses to pain, myoclonus status epilepticus, serum neuron-specific enolase levels, and somatosensory-evoked potential studies are all reliable tests to assist in determining patients who will do poorly [10]. To predict recovery or lack thereof in children is more difficult, and studies identifying prognostic factors in adults may not be applicable in the pediatric age group. It is also true that evidence must always be interpreted with regard to the individual patient's case.

10.1.1.2 *Vegetative state*

If the severely neurologically injured patient survives coma and does not regain normal consciousness, he or she enters into what is termed a vegetative state. Unlike coma, the eyes are open and patients are usually able to breathe without a ventilator. EEG evidence of a sleep cycle returns and the patient will have periods of wakefulness. The patient exhibits no conscious recognition of the self or the environment and no interaction with the environment. Specifically, there will be no evidence of language (comprehension or expression) and no non-reflexive response to stimuli. Incontinence is also present. Vegetative patients invariably require extensive nursing care and some form of nutrition and hydration to stay alive — for example, a gastrostomy feeding tube [5]. The term "persistent" or "permanent vegetative state" has been used in those cases that have remained in the state for greater than a year [11]. Rare cases of emergence from a vegetative state after a prolonged period of time have led to the suggestion that vegetative state be classified according to etiology and period of time spent vegetative as both these carry important prognostic information rather than labeling it as permanent [12–15].

10.1.1.3 *Minimally conscious state*

In the last few decades, there has been increasing awareness of the entity known as minimally conscious state. The minimally conscious patient will exhibit some level of interaction with the environment and will do so in a reproducible way. Obviously speech or the expression of understanding of speech through a verbal or non-verbal response is sufficient for the diagnosis. Emotional response, visual tracking, and appropriate handling of an object can all signify some level of consciousness [12]. Careful neurological examination repeated a number of times over an extended period may be particularly helpful in diagnosing the patient who is minimally conscious since many signs of consciousness may be subtle. Imaging modalities such as positron emission tomography (PET) and functional magnetic resonance imaging (fMRI) may also be useful in recognizing that a patient has more than vegetative functions [16, 17]. Like the patients in a vegetative state, minimally conscious patients require intensive nursing care to stay alive.

In recent years, case reports have brought attention to the fact that some patients in a prolonged minimally conscious state can emerge to fuller consciousness. Some of these patients' stories have received attention in the broader press [18–20]. Family members may be more reluctant to withdraw therapy if they feel there remains a chance that their relative may wake up at some time later like the story of the fellow in the news. Medical interventions to facilitate this recovery such as thalamic stimulation or pharmacological inducement have been reported though confirmation of the efficacy of these treatments awaits further studies [21, 22].

Cases such as that of Terri Schiavo in the US can quickly bring into focus many of the ethical issues at stake in the care of the patient in a vegetative or minimally conscious state. A decision must be made in such cases as to whether the patient is in a vegetative state or is in a minimally conscious state. Who will speak for the patient? Is it acceptable to withhold treatment such as hydration and nutrition? Most ethicists are in agreement that it is reasonable to withhold heroic measures but whether nutrition via a gastrostomy tube qualifies as heroic engenders disagreement [5].

10.1.1.4 Brain death

The most severe neurologically injured patients will progress to brain death. In some respects, this makes it easier for the physician and the family as pronouncement of brain death has become generally accepted in the Western world by both physicians and the public as a definition of death. Details of the procedures for ascertaining brain death are well documented [23, 24]. The original impetus to define brain death came as a consequence of the desire to make more organs available for transplantation. Recently, "donation after cardiac death" has attempted to again expand the numbers of patients who would potentially be available to donate. In the controlled setting, a patient who has been determined to have a severe neurological injury but who is not brain dead will be allowed to die (care withdrawn and heart stops). After a period of some minutes has passed and it is felt that the brain has undergone anoxic "death," the organs are harvested. Many ethical issues have been raised about the process. The responsible team must keep the interests of the patient foremost. An accurate and realistic assessment of the prospects for survival will also be requested from the treating physician. What is the appropriate length of time before organs may be harvested? Once the determination that organ harvest will be made, is it acceptable to give drugs which may harm the patient (e.g., anticoagulants) but which will help the donor? Who is to consent for the withdrawal and donation? These issues are still being discussed and are not fully resolved.

10.2 Neurosurgeons and the Law

Neurosurgeons most commonly interact with the law in four types of situations: as defendants in medical malpractice litigation, as expert witnesses in malpractice cases for either the defendant or plaintiff, as "external reviewers" for hospitals or other health care entities as a part of case review to identify possible liability or quality of care issues, or to give testimony regarding a certain party's injury or illness in criminal or civil matters. Unfortunately in the US, appearing in medical malpractice litigation as a defendant is relatively common for neurosurgeons in many jurisdictions. This likely has to do primarily with the fragile nature of the structures with which neurosurgeons deal and the inherent risk to the nervous system for disease and surgical manipulation. Expert witnesses for both the defendant and the plaintiff give testimony in medical malpractice (professional liability) matters and are hired by the respective law firms. Only in the US are medical malpractice lawsuits tried before a jury of lay persons. Medical expertise is utilized by a court of law in civil and criminal cases when there are questions about medical issues beyond the ordinary knowledge base of the average citizen. Medical experts within the field under question may be asked by the court or by parties in litigation to explain the medical aspects of an injury or a disease process, to comment on forensic evidence, to render an opinion on the prognosis for a certain clinical entity or for a particular patient, or to render an opinion on the standard of care in medical liability cases. Standard of care is defined as the "measurement of assessment applied to a defendant's conduct for liability determination comparing what an ordinary, reasonable and prudent" physician or surgeon of the same or similar specialty would have done under the same or similar circumstances [25]. That definition has varied little since first articulated by a Connecticut court in 1832 (*Landon* v *Humphrey* [26]).

During the past few decades, there has been a perception by physicians in the US, particularly surgeons including neurosurgeons, that the high cost of medical professional liability insurance, the increasing frequency of medical malpractice suits, and the high monetary awards in some cases are caused by greedy patients and/or their families, unscrupulous plaintiff attorneys, and expert witnesses for the plaintiffs who will testify to anything for a fee, all working together against the defendant doctor. Because contemporary medical and surgical evaluation and treatment is highly technical and the scientific background required for understanding such "raw" information offered in court is beyond that of the average citizen hearing the testimony as a jury member or the judge who may have little scientific or medical background, an expert witness is called to "assist the trier of fact" (judge and/or jury) to help the court understand an issue and render an opinion on standard of care and possible deviations. In some countries (for example, the UK), independent experts are called to testify by the court itself. Decisions are rendered by judges or magistrates

> not because they are experts in medicine — but because they are experts in law, controlling the legal process as they attempt to dispense justice while drawing on testimony from a pool of medical experts selected and maintained by the court [27].

In the US with a common law adversarial justice system, expert witnesses are hired by the defendants and plaintiffs separately and often "duel it out" in court in front of the judge and jury attempting to persuade the court to follow their side of the story. Ordinary witnesses in most court cases testify only to facts — who, how, what, when, where — and are not allowed to render opinions about matters such as standard of care. However, an expert witness, because of his or her expertise beyond that of the ordinary citizen, is allowed to do so. Occasionally, a hospital or some other healthcare entity may ask for expert review of a case as a part of its quality assurance/ risk management process before any suit is filed (e.g., Case No. 5 below).

10.2.1 *Medical expert witness testimony*

In the latter decades of the twentieth century in the US, the medical malpractice insurance liability crisis and the questionable practices of some expert witnesses led many medical societies to fashion guidelines for their members who testify in court as expert witnesses in professional liability cases — for example, the American Association of Neurological Surgeons [1] and the American College of Surgeons [28]. When a member is thought to have deviated from the guidelines, a complaint may be filed against the member with the organization, usually only by another member, and an informal investigation is launched by the professional conduct committee (or a similarly named committee) of the organization. After informal investigation, a formal hearing is commonly held by the committee members, usually assisted by legal staff. During the hearing, testimony is rendered by the accused physician and by committee members who investigated the case as well as by whoever filed the complaint. The hearing body decides whether to recommend expelling or censuring the member or to render some other form of rebuke/punishment or to dismiss the complaint. To avoid future legal entanglements, due process is best observed during such investigation and hearing. The final disposition may come before a meeting of the entire society. The legality of this type of action on the part of a medical society was challenged in *Donald C. Austin* v *American Association of Neurological Surgeons* [29] and decided in 2001 in favor of the AANS. That ruling encouraged other medical societies to closer scrutinize their members who testify in court. Plaintiff attorneys have complained that the process is unfair because it disciplines only expert witnesses who testify for plaintiffs.

A question raised in the past about expert witness testimony involves whether or not such testimony is a part of the practice of medicine. If it is, then there seem to be valid reasons for medical societies and governing boards that grant medical licenses to be involved in the performance of their members when they are engaged in expert witness work in medically related matters. If expert witness testimony is not a part of the practice of medicine, then medical societies and licensing boards have no business in such affairs. The American Medical Association through its Committee on Ethical and Judicial Affairs has opined that the physician or surgeon's expert witness medically related testimony in court or at deposition is considered a part of the practice of medicine and therefore subject to peer review [30].

In the US federal court system, expert witness testimony admissibility is governed by the Federal Rules of Evidence 702 to 706 [31]. Many state courts, where the majority of professional liability cases are actually tried, have adopted similar rules. For 70 years starting in 1923, US federal courts utilized the Frye test to determine admissibility of expert witness testimony which generally stated that the testimony was to be admitted if it had "general acceptance within the relevant scientific field" (*US* v *Frye*, 1923 [32]). In the 1970s and 1980s, perceptions grew and newspaper articles and books were written claiming that "junk science" too often was being admitted in the courtroom. The US Supreme Court ruled on such a case in 1993 (*Daubert* v *Merrell Dow* [33]) and held that the admissibility of trial testimony was to be determined by the trial judge under the FRE and outlined four criteria the judge could use in making the determination: 1) peer review and publication of the theory or evidence under question, 2) empirical testing with the possibility of falsifiability, 3) the known or potential error rate if the testimony involves a test or process, and 4) acceptance of the explanation or theory within the relevant scientific field. Many state jurisdictions in the US have adopted the Daubert test themselves, but some still follow the Frye test.

10.2.1.1 *Ethical rules for expert witness testimony*

A few simple ethical rules may help the neurosurgeon who reviews cases in malpractice actions or other medical-legal proceedings for either the defense or the plaintiff or when court-appointed. While the rules are intended for an adversarial justice system and apply particularly to giving sworn testimony in a deposition or in a courtroom, the rules also apply to a non-adversarial justice system. The witness in any court testimony, especially during cross examination, might do well to remember that while testifying on the stand or at deposition he or she is all alone — no one else is available for immediate consultation or coaching. As James J. Walker, aka Jimmy Walker or Beau James and a mayor of New York City in the Jazz Age, said, "There are three things in life you must do alone: be born, die, and testify" [34].

10.2.1.1.1 Tell the truth

The expert witness should be truthful and not lie which means not using intentionally deceptive messages when communicating with others [35]. Note that the expert witness usually takes an oath to tell the truth before giving testimony. However, the attorneys questioning the witness do not. Perhaps that is how opposing attorneys justify making up outrageous counter-scenarios to attempt to discredit the expert. Recognize the difference between resolving intellectual questions in law as opposed to science. In science including medicine, we primarily use the scientific method involving experimentation, observation, and/or empirical testing followed by analysis of the results to come to a conclusion as opposed to the method in law involving collecting testimony, constructing opposing stories, and then voting on the best story [36].

10.2.1.1.2 Do not become an advocate

The expert witness should not become an advocate for either party. The attorneys are advocates for their clients. The expert witness is not. While the expert witness should advocate for his or her account of the facts and the conclusions reached, the expert witness should remain as independent as possible from the parties when reviewing the material and rendering opinions.

10.2.1.1.3 Stay within your field of expertise

The expert witness who ventures beyond his/her field of expertise risks being discredited and made to appear a fool (for example, see the first case example mentioned below). Although the attorney who hires the expert witness in an adversarial justice system should have access to the witness for case discussion and preparation for forthcoming testimony at deposition or in court, no one else should be allowed to write the expert's report or put words in his/her mouth.

10.2.1.1.4 Be respectful of all parties

When opposing attorneys argue during trial or deposition, the expert witness should stay out of the fray. Even if provoked by insult, the expert witness should be even-tempered. An opposing attorney may try to unsettle and/or anger the expert during cross examination. If that tactic is successful, the expert risks losing credibility with the jury. A simple "yes" or "no" answer to an attorney's question is usually best whenever possible, especially during cross examination. Legal terms have specific definitions. A term used by an attorney during questioning may sound similar to a non-legal term, but as a legal term, it may carry a different connotation. If the expert is uncertain about a term, he/she should politely ask for a definition.

10.2.1.1.5 Apply the golden rule

The expert witness should consider the impact his/her testimony might have on the lives of others — for example, on the career of a colleague falsely accused of medical malpractice or on the life of a plaintiff or his/her family who may have been the recipient of substandard medical care.

10.2.1.1.6 Be fair

The expert witness should ask for reasonable compensation and charge for time spent on the case and not for giving testimony of a specified nature. Contingency fee arrangements make being a non-advocate impossible. The expert witness should remember that medical-legal case review is retrospective and subject to hindsight bias.

10.2.1.1.7 Look for and avoid conflicts of interest

For example, the expert witness should not engage in discussion with the opposing party's attorney or representatives without the knowledge and permission of the side that hires him or her. That is termed *ex parte* contact. It may appear harmless but should be strictly avoided unless approved by the hiring lawyer. The expert witness should consider excusing himself or herself due to conflict of interest if he or she has had any therapeutic or financial relationship with any of the parties.

A conflict of interest situation can occur if a subsequent treating neurosurgeon is asked to render an opinion about the surgical treatment of a previous treating neurosurgeon even if he/she considers the earlier treatment to have been clearly substandard. Since the subsequent treating neurosurgeon is an advocate for his/her patient as any doctor should be and the expert witness should be a non-advocate when reviewing cases and giving testimony regarding standard of care, confusion may be encountered if the expert witness is asked to wear two hats — to go from being an advocate to being a non-advocate and vice versa. For a more thorough discussion of this issue and a case example, see "A Conflict of Roles" [37]. Besides, the subsequent treating neurosurgeon can render testimony as a fact witness if called to do so without becoming an expert witness — in other words testify about the facts of the case (such as what was found and what was done) but not about the standard of care.

10.2.1.1.8 Carefully review the case material

The expert witness should thoroughly review the pertinent medical records and imaging studies as well as the applicable scientific literature before forming his/her opinion. Imaging studies a neurosurgeon ordinarily relies on for patient care and reads himself/herself (such as CT scans, MRI scans, and skull and spine x-rays) should be actually seen by the reviewer.

10.2.1.1.9 As much as possible, use an evidence-based approach

When forming and stating opinions, especially regarding standard of care, the expert witness should be able to back up his/her opinions and remember that personal opinions and anecdotes do not equal standard of care. If the expert witness gives testimony that is a personal opinion only, he/she should state that fact.

10.2.1.1.10 Have the necessary credentials to testify on the matter in question

The expert witness should be an active, licensed, and trained practitioner (or perhaps recently retired) in the specialty of the defendant (or a closely related field) and have experience with management of the type of malady in question. For an example of a testimony in a closely related field, see Case No. 3 below.

10.2.1.2 *Case examples of problematic expert witness testimony*

10.2.1.2.1 Case no. 1

An example of dubious expert witness testimony occurred during the deposition of the plaintiff's expert in the case of a 40-year-old business-man who underwent anterior cervical fusion at C6-7 for a left-sided C7 radiculopathy and awoke from surgery with blurred vision which did not resolve. Ophthalmologic and neurologic evaluation disclosed bilateral partial cortical blindness. Post-operative MRI of the brain showed scat-tered bilateral occipital infarcts. Recovery of vision was incomplete after several years. The patient sued the neurosurgeon who performed the pro-cedure. Although the plaintiff's testifying neurologist was well-qualified to comment on the issues of stroke, he was not a surgeon and had never performed or even assisted on the operative procedure in question. During his deposition and after testifying about the cerebrovascular issues of the case, the neurologist went on to state that the surgeon was negligent for operating on the wrong side of the patient's neck. Since the patient's radiculopathy symptoms were on the left side, the surgeon was in error, claimed the neurologist, for making the incision for the exposure on the right side. Of course, any first-year neurosurgery resident knows that the side of the approach for anterior cervical spine surgery has more to do with the surgeon's training, personal preference, and handedness and usu-ally little to do with the laterality of the pathology itself since from either side the tissues overlying the anterior spine are retracted contralaterally and the approach is actually more from a straight on anterior direction no matter which side is chosen for the incision or on which side the pathology is located. The neurologist in this case did not stay within his field of

expertise and his unqualified comments on surgical technique were fool-
ish, thus possibly tainting his entire testimony had the case gone to trial,
but fortunately for the plaintiff, the case was settled beforehand.

10.2.1.2.2 Case no. 2

Although the medical profession is understandably primarily concerned
with faulty expert witness testimony for plaintiffs against physicians and
surgeons, questionable testimony may come from the defense side, too.
Consider the case of a 35-year-old office worker who had a three-day history of progressively severe generalized headache with nausea and vomiting.
He was taken to a local hospital and on CT scan of the head and paranasal
sinuses appeared to have a large sphenoid sinus mucocele without intracranial abnormality or extension. An otorhinolaryngologist (ENT surgeon)
was consulted, and the following day surgery was undertaken to drain the
mucocele. No intraoperative imaging was used. During a transnasal tran-
sethmoidal endoscopic approach to the sphenoid sinus, brisk arterial
bleeding was encountered following biopsy of suspicious tissue. The
biopsy proved to be brain, and the hemorrhage ceased after packing with
between 250 to 500 ml of blood loss (the former estimate by the surgeon
and the latter by the anesthesiologist). The mucocele was drained successfully transseptally. The post-operative CT scan showed transgression of the
roof of the ethmoid sinus/skull base and blood and surgical packing material as well as air in the base of the right frontal fossa. There was
subarachnoid hemorrhage appearing similar to that which might be seen
following rupture of an aneurysm originating from the anterior communicating artery complex. In addition, bone fragments were identified
within the intracranial cavity not seen on the pre-operative CT scan.
Emergency angiography showed occlusion of both A1 anterior cerebral
arteries. The patient underwent craniotomy several days later for successful
repair of the skull base and debridement of the traumatized brain.

Before the onset of symptoms from the sphenoid sinus mucocele, the
patient had been in excellent health until a few months earlier when he
was treated for nephrotic syndrome secondary to minimal change disease
(a renal tubular disorder frequently causing nephrotic syndrome in children and occasionally in adults). His renal malady was responsive to

steroid therapy, and at the time of the hospitalization for the sphenoid sinus mucocele, he was on a tapering dose of prednisone every other day. Although at first barely responsive after sinus surgery, the patient slowly awoke during an extended hospital and rehabilitation stay. Three years later the patient was alert but apathetic, had mild spastic paraparesis but could walk unaided, answered most simple questions simply and concretely, and had a low normal score (25 of 30) on mini mental status exam [38]. His CT scan at that time showed extensive bilateral anterior cerebral artery territory infarcts. The patient, through his wife as guardian, filed suit against the ENT surgeon.

The plaintiff's expert neurosurgeon testified that the bone fragments seen on the post-operative CT scan and their likely trajectories from the disrupted skull base were in the vicinity of the anterior cerebral artery complex and concluded that the fragments were driven into the brain by the surgical instrument used to penetrate the skull base and thus displayed at least in part the extent of the intracranial penetration and trajectory. The infarction, said the plaintiff's expert, was most likely a consequence of direct arterial trauma and thrombosis, subarachnoid hemorrhage, and possibly vasospasm. The defense neurosurgical expert witness initially ignored and later discounted the skull base trauma, arterial injury, and subarachnoid hemorrhage as well as the in-driven bone fragments and concluded in his initial report that the cause of the anterior cerebral artery occlusion was the chronic exposure of the anterior cerebral arteries to the effects of the infected mucocele contents due to erosion of the skull base in the vicinity of the anterior cerebral arteries intracranially (for which there was no imaging study evidence). Later he changed his opinion and stated that the cause of the anterior cerebral artery occlusion and stroke was a combination of vasoconstriction from hyperventilation during surgery (end title pCO_2 varying from 30.6 to 26.3 mmHg intraoperatively) and hypercoagulability from the nephrotic syndrome. While that scenario is conceivable (hypocarbic vasoconstriction and hypercoagulability from nephrotic syndrome) as a factor in arterial thrombosis, it is unlikely and weak as the sole or proximate cause (a legal term meaning an outcome would not have occurred but for the action in question, and given the action in question, the outcome was foreseeable [39]) compared to the likelihood of causation by direct anterior cerebral artery trauma for which there was imaging study evidence. The latter scenario was the opinion of the plaintiff's expert witness. The jury found for the plaintiff. Of note is that neither neurosurgical expert witness for either side in this case was qualified to comment on the standard of care for the ENT surgeon (unless, of course, the neurosurgeon had training in both specialties). In other words, the neurosurgical experts were qualified to comment on the issues surrounding the skull base and intracranial trauma and stroke causation and associated brain/neurological damages but not on issues of the performance of the ENT surgical procedure itself. Standard of care opinions regarding performance of a procedure in a certain field (ENT in this case) are appropriately rendered only by experts (specialists) in that field. Occasionally, different specialties may treat the same malady similarly — for example, orthopedic surgeons and neurosurgeons when dealing with lumbar disc surgery (see Case No. 3 below). In such cases, the court usually permits testimony from either specialty.

10.2.1.2.3 Case no. 3

An example of effective defense expert witness testimony occurred in the case of a 48-year-old female cafeteria worker who hurt herself at work and complained of severe right leg pain but little back pain. She failed non-surgical treatment. She had signs and symptoms of a herniated disc at L5-S1 with S1 radiculopathy, and MRI showed a large extruded disc fragment at L5-S1 on the same side as her pain. She was referred to a neurosurgeon who recommended and soon undertook a microsurgical lumbar laminotomy and discectomy. The procedure went smoothly until the neurosurgeon prepared to close the wound when the patient suddenly became hypotensive and tachycardic. Fluid resuscitation was begun immediately, blood was ordered, and a vascular surgeon was summoned. The patient was flipped supine after clamping the wound shut and applying an adhesive sterile drape. The belly was promptly explored by the vascular surgeon with findings of a retroperitoneal hematoma and laceration of the iliac artery. After repair of the vascular injury, the abdomen was closed, the patient was turned prone again, and the lumbar wound was closed. Recovery from both surgeries was uneventful. Post-operatively, the patient was relieved of her radicular and low back pain but sued the surgeon alleging negligence for causing the arterial injury and subjecting her to an unexpected surgical procedure.

The plaintiff's expert witness, an experienced orthopedic spine surgeon, seemed to speak down to the attorneys who questioned him during his deposition. He stated that a retroperitoneal vascular injury during lumbar disc surgery could only come about as a consequence of negligence on the part of the surgeon; it was a case of *res ipsa loquitur* (meaning the thing speaks for itself), he said. On questioning, he claimed to be familiar with the pertinent orthopedic and neurosurgical literature on the subject of vascular injuries during lumbar disc surgery which, he said, helped to cement his conclusion. However, when pressed to cite the literature he reviewed to support that opinion, he could remember none specifically, only "textbooks and journals."

The expert witness for the defendant, a neurosurgeon, listed references and testified that the vascular injury which the patient suffered was an unfortunate but well-known complication of the surgical procedure the plaintiff underwent and noted the near-universal opinion in the spinal surgery literature that vascular injury during lumbar disc surgery cannot always be avoided, even in careful, experienced hands [40–48]. Besides, the expert witness testified that the defendant's management of the complication, once it occurred, was exemplary. The plaintiff soon dismissed the suit.

Note that the plaintiff's expert could not cite the literature he referred to and seemed to consider himself above the other people attending the deposition. Those actions and attitudes likely would not sit well with the judge and jury had the case gone to trial. The plaintiff's expert was not from the same field (orthopedic surgery versus neurosurgery), but he cared for and did surgery for lumbar radiculopathy secondary to lumbar disc herniation in a similar manner as the defendant; therefore, he was allowed to testify as an expert. The defendant was humble and not over-confident and knew the medical literature concerning the complication. The expert witness for the defendant was likewise knowledgeable and tried to "connect" with those in attendance at the deposition by making eye contact. If the case had gone to trial, he would have attempted to do the same with the jury and the judge. These are usable bits of advice for anyone involved in giving court or deposition testimony, no matter on which side. For further discussion of courtroom decorum of the expert witness toward those in the courtroom and an example with humor, see Fager's *Stop Talking to the Jury* [49].

10.2.1.2.4 Case no. 4

Occasionally, reviewing a case of alleged medical malpractice does not lead to contentious deposition or courtroom drama because one of the parties cannot find a qualified witness to support their client — unfortunately, more often an attorney for either side can find an expert witness willing to say almost anything, no matter how outrageous. For example, a 54-year-old male laborer had low back and left leg pain following a work injury that progressed over several years and was not responsive to physiotherapy, various medications, nor a series of lumbar epidural steroid injections. He was unable to work, he claimed. Physical examination showed marked limitation of range of motion of the low back and equivocal positive straight leg raising. He was intact neurologically. MRI showed a degenerative disc signal change at L4-5 with mild central bulging but no definite herniation or stenosis. Plain spine x-rays were unremarkable including flexion and extension lateral views except for modest reduction of the L4-5 disc space height. Surgery at L4-5 was recommended by a neurosurgeon who saw the patient in consultation to include bilateral decompressive laminectomy, discectomy, instrumentation using pedicle screws and rods, and posterior intervertebral body fusion. Surgery was undertaken, and during the procedure toward the end of the discectomy, the patient's blood pressure suddenly fell. No bleeding was appreciated in the wound. The neurosurgeon began closing the wound, and the patient was given two liters of normal saline. The patient was only partially responsive — the blood pressure rose but the urine output did not; the patient was pale and cool. A vascular surgeon was called, the patient was turned to the supine position and the abdomen explored. The vascular surgeon evacuated a large retroperitoneal hematoma and repaired lacerations of the left iliac vein and artery. The patient was given blood, the abdomen was closed and then he was turned prone again. The neurosurgeon re-opened the lumbar wound and instrumented the spine bilaterally with pedicle screws and rods at L4 and L5. He also placed an intervertebral bone graft at that level, and while doing so, arterial blood began to well up in the disc space cavity as the blood pressure fell once more. The lumbar wound was rapidly closed and the vascular surgeon was called again. After turning the patient supine once more, the blood pressure was difficult to detect even with maximal efforts at blood and fluid replacement. This time a defect in the arterial wall adjacent to the first arterial injury site was repaired and a large hematoma was evacuated. The patient was taken to the ICU where resuscitation for shock continued, but he never awoke and was withdrawn from life support on the fifth post-operative day. The patient's family sued.

After reviewing the pertinent material, the neurosurgery expert witness for the plaintiff was not critical of the defendant for causing the complication itself (see discussion in previous case). However, she opined that the treating neurosurgeon was negligent for continuing with the lumbar surgery after the first vascular repair and for not immediately taking the patient to the ICU after the belly was closed the first time to promptly assess and more thoroughly evaluate and treat the shock (himself or consulting a critical care specialist). Moreover, the reviewer stated that there was no compelling reason to continue with the instrumentation and fusion after the first vascular repair. The procedure was purely elective. Doing so placed the patient needlessly at risk, she testified, and had it been necessary to instrument and fuse the spine, the "stabilizing" portion of the surgical treatment could have been staged and done later when the patient had recovered from shock. Some spinal surgeons would argue whether or not the instrumentation and fusion were indicated in the first place or even if the patient was a candidate for any surgery at all with or without fusion and instrumentation. Assuming the patient was a reasonable surgical candidate, continuing on with an elective procedure in the face of intraoperative shock encountered earlier in the procedure in a surgery that could have been staged was considered a breach of the standard of care. The defense attorney could find no qualified expert witness willing to testify in support of the defendant neurosurgeon, and the case was settled without trial through mediation with a significant monetary award going to the plaintiff's estate.

10.2.1.2.5 Case no. 5

From time to time, a medical expert may be asked to review a case by a hospital or other healthcare entity before any court action has been initiated as a part of the institution's quality assurance/risk management program, particularly when there is concern for possible liability. While conducting this type of review, the reviewing neurosurgeon may come upon unexpected findings that are significant for the patient and/or the institution. Such a case involves a nine-year-old female who began to complain of headache and refused to attend school. The child was seen by her pediatrician, and neurological and general physical examination was normal. She was treated symptomatically and improved transiently. The child returned to her usual activities for ten days before the onset of an excruciating, nocturnal, suboccipital headache. She was taken to the local hospital emergency department where her neurological and physical examinations were normal except for nuchal rigidity. Cervical spine x-rays were normal for age. Since CT scanning was not available, the child was transferred to another hospital where a non-contrast CT scan of the head was interpreted as normal. After an overnight stay and non-narcotic analgesics, the child was discharged to be followed by her pediatrician. Ten days later, she developed a severe headache and was admitted once more to the second hospital through the emergency department. Imaging studies showed that the child had suffered an extensive subarachnoid and intraparenchymal hemorrhage from a complex cervico-medullary arterio-venous fistula having a large intra-medullary aneurysmal varix. The lesion was embolized several times with ultimate disappearance of the abnormal vessels. The child was markedly quadriparetic after the initial hemorrhage and improved little over the course of one year. The hospital asked for an independent review of all the records prior to any legal action being filed. Benefiting from knowledge of the ultimate radiological diagnosis, the reviewer identified the apex of the intaspinal varix on the most caudal axial slice of the first CT scan of the head that had been read as showing no abnormality when the child was initially seen in the emergency department — in other words, ten days before the devastating hemorrhage. The lesion had simply been missed. By bringing this oversight to the attention of the hospital administration and their legal staff, measures were initiated with the child's family to resolve the matter before more costly and contentious court action.

Note: Cases No. 1–4 are based on summaries and simplifications of finalized cases from the files of HM, and Case No. 5 was supplied by DS.

10.2.1.2.6 Differing opinions

While some expert witnesses may present questionably truthful verbal or written statements in or to the court, just because two opposing expert witnesses in a medical-legal dispute have differing opinions does not necessarily mean that one side or the other is lying. After all, that is the essence of the concept of differential diagnosis — considering all the <u>reasonable</u> possibilities. In the practice of medicine, explanation for and treatment of a certain malady is not always certain or uniform; there may be more than one way to evaluate and/or treat a certain disorder. Consider the case of a patient with cervical radiculopathy caused by laterally herniated soft cervical disc. While many if not most neurosurgeons in this day and time would approach the problem anteriorly if surgery were deemed necessary, another group would approach the pathology posteriorly with equally good results — in other words, from exactly opposite directions or 180° apart. While there may be arguments for one or the other surgical approach in certain situations, often either approach produces the desired effect — decompression of the nerve root. The decision rests with the patient and the surgeon and both approaches are within the standard of care given a patient with a soft laterally herniated disc causing radiculopathy. In medical-legal cases, it is up to the court (judge and jury) to decide which testimony bears the stronger weight and ferret out faulty testimony. Unfortunately, expertise to do so may be lacking.

10.2.2 *What to do if you are sued*

Being a defendant in a professional liability (medical malpractice) case is not uncommon for neurosurgeons in many states in the US and is becoming more frequent in some other countries. When a neurosurgeon learns of a claim of medical malpractice (professional liability) or the possibility of a claim by way of a letter from the plaintiff's attorney or by some other means, the neurosurgeon should notify his/her professional liability insurance carrier and safeguard the patient/plaintiff's medical records. The medical record should be stored in a safe and secure place and not altered in any way. If an addendum is necessary, the date and time of the entry should be clearly noted. In the case of electronic medical records, processes are usually in place to secure and "freeze" the record should litigation come about, but all the complex issues that are likely to be encountered with the electronic medical record (EMR) have not yet been decided by the courts. The defendant should strive to work with the defense attorney (usually hired by the insurance company) and take the attorney's advice in defending the suit, especially in matters of legal procedure. The defendant can help his or her case by explaining medical/surgical issues of the case to the defense attorney and possibly identifying experts for the defense attorney to contact and request review. The defendant should not be the one to contact possible defense witnesses. Suits usually travel slowly through the court system. Depositions (sworn testimony concerning the case given before a court reporter and the attorneys for each side prior to the case actually being heard in court) are taken and various motions filed by both sides. All this takes time — months or even years. Most cases are settled or dismissed before going to court, but the process may be lengthy. Medical malpractice litigation is usually difficult for the defending neurosurgeon and impacts him or her professionally and personally. Sanbar and Firestone term the phenomenon the "medical malpractice stress syndrome" with primary psychological manifestations and secondary physical symptoms; there are similarities to the post-traumatic stress syndrome [50]. For the young neurosurgeon experiencing his or her first lawsuit as a defendant, the situation can be particularly stressful, especially if there is no senior partner or associate to give guidance or advice and serve as a listener.

10.3 Stereotactic and Functional Neurosurgery

According to The Society of Neurological Surgeons, stereotactic and functional neurosurgery (SFNS) is defined as a

> subspecialty of neurosurgery which is concerned with stereotactic and physiological techniques, including framed and frameless stereotactic systems, stereotactic radiosurgery, electrical recording, and electrical stimulation for localization and treatment of target structures in the central and peripheral nervous system (Stereotactic neurosurgery) and the surgical alteration of the nervous system (either by ablation or augmentation) to treat neurological diseases such as movement disorders, epilepsy, chronic pain, degenerative diseases, neurological injuries, and psychiatric disorders (Functional neurosurgery) [51].

The modern era of stereotactic and functional neurosurgery has been greatly influenced by technological advances and changes in treatment modalities. Prior to the 1960s, all functional procedures had in common the goal of creating a destructive lesion within the nervous system. The earliest surgeries involved cortical or subcortical resections of brain parenchyma. This was followed by procedures aimed at sectioning select white matter tracts within the brain. Eventually, with the aid of stereotactic techniques, the operations focused on the creation of discrete thermal or chemical lesions within the nervous system. As the field of functional neurosurgery evolved, new techniques provided for safer and less invasive surgeries; however, they did not fundamentally differ in the way the underlying disease was addressed — through selective destruction of neural tissue. The modern era would see a paradigm shift away from these neuro-destructive procedures and toward neuro-augmentative techniques.

10.3.1 *Contemporary SFNS*

The use of subcortical or deep brain stimulation (DBS) is the most recent advancement in the treatment of Parkinson's disease and other movement disorders. Because of the risk of irreversible neurologic injury and the complications associated with performing bilateral thalamic lesions, neurosurgeons had been searching for alternative techniques to treat tremor. Since the introduction of stereotactic surgery, electrical stimulation has frequently been performed to improve target localization before creating a lesion in the thalamus for the treatment of tremor. It had been noted that, while low frequency stimulation would actually worsen symptoms, high frequency stimulation would actually suppress tremor. With technological advances in fully implantable stimulators and armed with the above knowledge, Benabid *et al.* [52] carried out the first large-scale series of thalamic DBS for tremor. The safety and efficacy of this technique fueled interest in applying DBS to other targets such as the globus pallidus and subthalamic nucleus for the treatment of various movement disorders.

The use of electrical stimulation was not confined to the treatment of movement disorders; similar techniques were being applied to psychiatric illnesses as well. As early as 1977, Heath reported a series of 11 patients in which he used cerebellar stimulation to treat schizophrenia, neurosis, and violent aggression [53]. Based on the successful use of DBS in regions that were previously the targets for ablation in Parkinson's disease, it was not long before stimulation was attempted in areas previously targeted for ablation in psychiatric illness. In 2003, Nuttin *et al.* described six patients treated with capsular stimulation for obsessive-compulsive disorder [54]. This was soon followed by its use in the treatment of depression, with Mayberg *et al.* reporting on six patients treated with DBS in the subgenual cingulate gyrus [55].

The surgical techniques developed over the last 100 years have minimized the risks associated with SFNS and allowed its application to an ever growing list of conditions. Deep brain stimulation is now being explored as a potential treatment for epilepsy, Tourette's syndrome, obesity, cluster headaches, Alzheimer's disease, mild cognitive impairment, drug addiction, and even aggressive behavior. However, as we can see from the preceding list, the applications are going beyond what might classically be defined as "disease." At some point we must define what is pathological disease versus what is normal human variation. Is the loss of cognitive function a natural part of aging and should surgery play a role in its reversal? Is having poor memory a disease state and should we attempt to correct it? Is anti-social behavior a disease and do physicians have the right to treat it? Should the goal of treatment be to restore "normal" function, and where do we draw the line between normal and enhanced performance? Should systems be put in place to ensure that these techniques are not used for pure human enhancement? Many of these questions have been asked in regards to medications that boost physical performance; however, they have well known and serious side effects, making the answers somewhat easier. What happens when SFNS techniques can safely and reliably be applied to enhance physical and mental abilities? Do we need a closer examination of the philosophical concepts of disease, illness, and sickness beyond those articulated by Jennings in 1986 [56]?

10.4 The Neuro-Revolution: The New Neuro-Disciplines and Neurosurgery

10.4.1 *Neuroscience*

On many college campuses, neuroscience has become a popular major for undergraduate and graduate study. Neuroscience is usually an interdisciplinary field incorporating aspects of zoology, molecular biology, genetics, biochemistry, neuroanatomy, philosophy, psychology, computer science, and possibly others to achieve a better understanding of brain function, human behavior, and the higher order cognitive processes we refer to as mind. Neuroscience centers have been formed by some hospitals and medical institutions usually consisting of specialists in neurology, neuro-surgery, neuro-otology, neuroradiology (interventional and diagnostic), neuro-ophthalmology, and perhaps other fields.

10.4.2 *Neurophilosophy*

Neurophilosophy is a field that came about largely as the result of a book of the same name published in 1986 by Patricia Smith Churchland [57], in which she argues for a "re-alignment" in philosophy reversing the anti-scientific bias of linguistic analysis, countering the idea that philosophical questions admit to *a priori* solutions, and using the tools of analytical philosophy and empirical science to understand the mind-brain problem.

10.4.3 *Neurolaw*

Neurolaw as a specific field goes back to 1991 when J. Sherrod Taylor, Esq., an attorney working with brain-injured individuals, coined the term and used it as a title for his newsletter aimed at attorneys and healthcare professionals involved in brain-injury litigation [58, 59]. In 2007 for a project titled "Integrating Law and Neuroscience," the MacArthur Foundation awarded a multimillion dollar three-year grant to a consortium of legal scholars from various law schools to "bridge law and neuroscience" and help "address difficult legal and ethical questions that are arising as advances in neuroscience deepen our understanding of human behavior" [60]. "Although the law still generally holds individuals personally responsible for their actions, various accommodations have been made in the past" for those "who offer explanations for misconduct." [61]. For example, justification for killing another may be excused as self-defense, and verdicts may be rendered as "not guilty" by one who commits a crime "by reason of insanity" [61]. The law "considers mitigating factors (e.g., extreme provocation, mental incapacity) in determining sentencing; it uses medical treatments that are made conditions of parole (e.g., chemical castration for pedophiles)" [61]. One can imagine how "similar kinds of accommodations and adjustments might be granted for brain-based explanations should these be forthcoming from neuroscience" [61]. But brain-based evidence may also go to convicting an accused. Consider the case from Pune, Maharashtra, India, of a guilty verdict in a murder case arrived at largely on the basis of a controversial BEOS (Brain Electrical Oscillations Signature) test, a special type of computerized EEG, relied on by the court [62]. The concern by some that neuroscience, especially neuroimaging, might radically transform criminal law seems ill-founded because "legal responsibility also requires a normative judgment" [63]. Neuroimaging and neuroscience

> can offer us only descriptive models of brain organization and function; ascriptions of responsibility, on the other hand, are unequivocally prescriptive. This is the reason why to explain, by itself, is not to excuse [63].

The issues of neurolaw and neurosurgery may intersect particularly in the future in the field of stereotactic and functional neurosurgery where surgical treatments "could be a future option in the treatment arsenal of addiction" [64].

10.4.4 *Neuroethics*

Neuroethics is a relatively new but burgeoning field within bioethics. Various definitions have been proffered. The late William Safire of the *New York Times* is often incorrectly credited with coining the term "neuroethics" in 2002 [65] and defining it as "the field of philosophy that discusses the rights and wrongs of the treatment of or the enhancement of the human brain" [66, 67]. But Safire's definition is not adequate for what has developed in the field during the past few years. Actually, the term first appeared in hyphenated form ("neuro-ethics") in 1973 in an article by Anneliese Pontius concerning "walking" in the newborn [68]. Roskies seems to best capture the basic idea when she wrote that neuroethics involves how we "reconcile our burgeoning knowledge of brain functioning and our increasing technical expertise" in neuroscience "with our more general deliberations about how we should live" [69].

Although there is no consensus on its scope, neuroethics is generally considered to be a sub-domain of bioethics and neurophilosophy. There are two separately identifiable but interdependent branches. First is the ethics of neuroscience dealing with the moral principles associated with evaluating and treating patients with brain diseases, the ethical principles involved with brain research, and the study of the effects that the advances in our understanding of brain functions will have on our social, religious, and philosophical views. The second branch, the neuroscience of ethics, has to do with understanding morality — exploring the brain systems associated with moral behavior and moral decision-making [69].

10.4.5 *Interactions*

The interactions of neuroscience, neuroethics, and neurolaw with neuro-surgery and related clinical fields in the twenty-first century will likely include the following aspects.

10.4.5.1 *Lie-detection*

Research into and the application of "lie-detection" testing include fMRI studies used to determine whether or not an individual being tested is lying. Should such test results be used in a court of law? Who has access to the information? Can these techniques be used by a government for national security purposes — for example, to interrogate suspected terrorists? The implied certainty and authority of science as well as the use of pictures instead of words can be prejudicial to juries. Does an individual have a legal right to privacy of thought and cognitive liberty [70–73]?

10.4.5.2 *Asymptomatic lesions*

Since most basic research into brain functioning with fMRI is done outside the medical setting with normal, healthy, paid "volunteers," how should a researcher manage the problem of a presumably normal subject found to have an asymptomatic but potentially serious brain abnormality such as a brain tumor or a vascular malformation [74–76]? Who should "read" the scans of healthy subjects, especially in those facilities not tied to medical institutions, or should the studies be read at all for possible pathological conditions? What is the liability of a missed lesion?

10.4.5.3 *Personal "brain characteristics"*

Brain imaging studies potentially may reveal rudimentary information about personality traits, suitability for employment, mental illness or a predisposition to mental illness and neurodegenerative disease, sexual preference, racial prejudice, and predisposition to lying and to drug addiction/recidivism [77]. Do we go there? Might we risk punishing people for their thoughts and not for their actions?

10.4.5.4 *Neuroethics and changes in the law*

According to Greene and Cohen, neuroethics will change the law, not by undermining the law's current assumptions, but by transforming our moral intuitions about free will and responsibility. As a result, they say, we will move away from a retributive approach to criminal justice to a consequential approach, i.e., one aimed at promoting future welfare rather than meting out just deserts [78]. How far in the future is that?

10.4.5.5 *EMR and imaging studies*

As medical records and imaging studies become more and more produced and stored electronically (EMR; also known as HIT or Health Information Technology), new ethical and legal issues will likely arise. Many physicians and surgeons do not realize the vast amount of material stored in the EMR beyond that of the easily-viewed progress notes, imaging studies, radiological and laboratory results, and orders he or she enters. For example, each time a patient's imaging studies are viewed, an electronic record is made that identifies the name of the one who is logging in, the studies called up, and the time the imaging study is displayed. This data about data is called metadata. Metadata likely will be used increasingly in the years to come by plaintiff attorneys, hospital administrations, third-party payors, and healthcare regulatory bodies to examine the doctors' practice patterns and rein in and discredit physicians and surgeons who fall below standards. For an introduction to EMR and metadata, see McLean *et al.* [79].

In the US, the vendors who sell electronic medical record technology products to healthcare practices and institutions presently enjoy a contractual and legal position that holds them virtually liability-free should a flaw in their product result in harm to a patient [80]. This is through a legal doctrine known as the *learned intermediary* which shifts the blame from the manufacturer and seller to the user via way of a *hold harmless clause* in the purchasing contract. Originally intended for the pharmaceutical industry, the doctrine protects drug manufacturers when ample warnings are issued to the physician prescribing the medication even if the patient is not warned directly by the manufacturer. Another troublesome feature of EMR contracts is the "keep defects secret" clause which prevents a user who discovers a serious flaw in the EMR from warning other users [80]. We agree with Koppel and Kreda that such contracts involving EMR are unethical, and hopefully the courts will soon rule them not legally binding. As a note of caution, Black and colleagues from the UK in early 2011 reported their systematic review of systematic reviews of eHealth technology literature including the EMR (electronic health record (EHR)) and concluded "there is a large gap between the postulated and empirically demonstrated benefits of eHealth technologies" [81].

Contemporary neurosurgical practice is highly dependent on good quality imaging studies. The transmission of patient imaging files is increasingly being accomplished by means of compact discs (CDs). The data files on the CD "are extremely vulnerable to alteration, and alterations are not detectable without detailed analysis of file structure" [82]. Should we be wary when a patient with a serious brain or spinal malady has imaging studies conveyed only by CD from an outside source and imprinted on the CD are statements such as "provided for reference purposes only" and "should not be used for diagnostic purposes"? What is the liability for the neurosurgeon who consults with a patient but is unable to open the accompanying CD from an outside imaging facility containing the patient's imaging studies because the program is absolutely "foreign" to the doctor and no one else nearby knows how to view the study? What if the insurance company refuses to pay for another scan and the patient cannot afford to pay out of pocket?

10.4.5.6 *Brain-machine and brain-computer interfacing*

Research into brain-machine or brain-computer interfacing could benefit paralyzed and blinded members of our society, particularly wounded veterans. In the US, much of that research is funded through the Department of Defense. Is that problematic?

10.4.5.7 *Neuro-enhancement*

What is the difference between treatment of neurological disorders and neuro-enhancement of normal functioning? Should such therapy be open to anyone asking for enhancing drugs or surgery and willing to pay? The American Academy of Neurology seems to respond in the affirmative by stating "[i]t is ethically permissible for neurologists to prescribe such therapies, provided that they adhere to well-known bioethical principles of respect for autonomy, beneficence, and nonmaleficence" [83].

10.4.5.8 *Neuroimaging and chronic pain*

Every neurosurgeon trained during or before the mid 1970s realizes the profound difference our modern imaging studies make in our practice and on the lives of our patients. In particular, MR and CT imaging have opened avenues for accurately and vividly studying, following, and treating disease that we previously often guessed at. fMRI differentiates brain region activation patterns in patients with chronic pain (a difficult disorder to treat) from patients with an acute pain problem (much more likely to respond to treatment) and suggests that chronic pain has similarities to degenerative processes of the CNS [84]. On the other hand, real-time functional magnetic imaging (rtfMRI) may benefit those afflicted with chronic pain to control "activities in brain regions involved with pain processing with corresponding changes in experienced pain" [85] — perhaps better termed a "new age biofeedback."

10.5 Conclusion

Because our patients are often seriously afflicted by their disease processes in terms of everyday functioning and neurologically hampered in their decision making processes, neurosurgical practice will continue to confront ethical and legal issues concerning treatment options, withholding treatment, and decision making by or for the patient. Seemingly novel dilemmas will likely arise as new technology becomes available or existing technology is applied to a new patient population. Unless radical tort reform is enacted in the US, which seems unlikely, neurosurgeons there will continue to interact with the justice system as defendants and expert witnesses in a hostile medical malpractice litigation atmosphere. Outside the US, neurosurgeons will continue to be asked to give testimony, render opinions, and supply records in a less contentious environment.

References

[1] American Association of Neurological Surgeons (AANS). *AANS Code of Ethics* 2007. http://www.aans.org/about/aanscodeofethics.pdf [accessed 14 Nov 2009].

[2] World Federation of Neurosurgical Societies, European Association of Neurosurgical Societies. Good practice: a guide for neurosurgeons. *British Journal of Neurosurgery* 2000; **14**: 400–406.

[3] Lipsman N. and Bernstein M. Future Ethical Challenges in Neurosurgery. In A.M. Lozano, P.L. Gildenberg, and R.R. Tasker (eds) *Textbook of Stereotactic and Functional Neurosurgery.* Berlin: Springer, 2009; 3229–3237.

[4] Plum F. and Posner J. *The Diagnosis of Stupor and Coma.* Philadelphia: F.A. Davis, 1982.

[5] Giacino J. and Whyte J. The vegetative and minimally conscious states: current knowledge and remaining questions. *Journal of Head Trauma Rehabilitation* 2005; **20**: 30–50.

[6] Jennett B., Snoek J., Bond M.R. *et al.* Disability after severe head injury: observations on the use of the Glasgow Outcome Scale. *Journal of Neurology, Neurosurgery and Psychiatry* 1981; **44**: 285–293.

[7] Born J.D, Albert A., Hans P. *et al.* Relative prognostic value of best motor response and brain stem reflexes in patients with severe head injury. *Neurosurgery* 1985; **16**: 595–600.

[8] Judson J., Cant B. and Shaw N. Early prediction of outcome from cerebral trauma by somatosensory evoked potentials. *Critical Care Medicine* 1990; **18**: 363–368.

[9] Hamel M.B., Goldman L., Teno J. *et al.* Identification of comatose patients at high risk for death or severe disability. SUPPORT Investigators. Understand

Prognoses and Preferences for Outcomes and Risks of Treatments. *Journal of American Medical Association* 1995; **273**: 1842–1848.

[10] Wijdicks E., Hijdra A., Young G.B. *et al.* Practice parameter: prediction of outcome in comatose survivors after cardiopulmonary resuscitation (an evidence-based review): report of the Quality Standards Subcommittee of the American Academy of Neurology. *Neurology* 2006; **67**: 203–210.

[11] Medical aspects of the persistent vegetative state (1). The Multi-Society Task Force on PVS, *New England Journal of Medicine* 1994; **330**: 1499–1508.

[12] Giacino J., Ashwal S, Childs N. *et al.* The minimally conscious state: definition and diagnostic criteria. *Neurology* 2002; **58**: 349–353.

[13] Arts W., van Dongen HR, van Hof-van Duin J. *et al.* Unexpected improvement after prolonged posttraumatic vegetative state. *Journal of Neurology, Neurosurgery and Psychiatry* 1985; **48**: 1300–1303.

[14] Childs N. and Mercer W. Brief report: late improvement in consciousness after post-traumatic vegetative state. *New England Journal of Medicine* 1996; **334**: 24–25.

[15] Haig A. and Ruess J. Recovery from vegetative state of six months' duration associated with Sinemet (levodopa/carbidopa). *Archives of Physical Medicine and Rehabilitation* 1990; **71**: 1081–1083.

[16] Kremer S., Nicolas-Ong C., Schunck T. *et al.* Usefulness of functional MRI associated with PET scan and evoked potentials in the evaluation of brain functions after severe brain injury: preliminary results. *Journal of Neuroradiology* 2010; **37**: 159–166.

[17] Owen A., Schiff N. and Laureys S. A new era of coma and consciousness science. *Progress in Brain Research* 2009; **177**: 399–411.

[18] Wikipedia. http://en.wikipedia.org/wiki/Terry_Wallis [accessed 1 December 2009].

[19] *The Guardian.* Trapped in his own body for 23 years — the coma victim who screamed unheard. 23 November 2009. http://www.theguardian.com/world/2009/nov/23/man-trapped-coma-23-years [accessed 1 December 2009].

[20] CNN. After decade in coma, just 10 months awake: Brain-injured firefighter dies of pneumonia. 22 February 2006. http://edition.cnn.com/2006/US/02/21/coma.death/index.html?section=cnn_us [accessed 1 December 2009].

[21] Whyte J. and Myers M. Incidence of clinically significant responses to zolpidem among patients with disorders of consciousness: a preliminary placebo controlled trial. *American Journal of Physical Medicine and Rehabilitation* 2009; **88**: 410–418.

[22] Schiff N.D., Giacino J.T. and Fins J.J. Deep brain stimulation, neuroethics, and the minimally conscious state: moving beyond proof of principle. *Archives of Neurology* 2009; **66**: 697–702.

[23] Practice parameters for determining brain death in adults (summary state-ment). The Quality Standards Subcommittee of the American Academy of Neurology. *Neurology* 1995; **45**: 1012–1014.

[24] Wijdicks E. The diagnosis of brain death. *New England Journal of Medicine* 2001; **344**: 1215–1221.

[25] American College of Legal Medicine (ACLM) *Legal Medicine.* St. Louis: Mosby, 2001; p. 616.

[26] *Landon* v *Humphrey* [1832] 9 Conn 209.

[27] Ward N.O. The essential and ethical expert: serving as a medical expert witness in the 21st century. *Otolaryngology, Head and Neck Surgery* 2007; **136**: 4–7.

[28] American College of Surgeons (ACS). Patient Safety and Professional Li-ability Committee, Statement on the physician acting as an expert witness (approved by Board of Regents, February 2004). *Bulletin of the American College of Surgeons* 2004; **89**: 3.

[29] *Donald C. Austin, MD,* v *American Association of Neurological Surgeons* [2001] 253 F.3d 967, 972-3 (7th Cir.).

[30] American Medical Association (AMA). Health and ethics policies of the AMA House of Delegates. H-265.993 Peer review of medical expert witness testimony. *AMA Policy Finder A-09.* Accessed 5 October 2009.

[31] Federal Rules of Evidence (FRE). Article VII. Rules 702–706. http://www.law.cornell.edu/rules/fre/ [accessed 1 November 2009].

[32] *US* v *Frye* [1923] 293 F. 1013 (D.C. Cir.).

[33] *Daubert* v *Merrell Dow Pharmaceuticals* [1993] 509 U.S. 579.

[34] Rees R. and Whelan W. Professional liability in dermatology. *Archives of Dermatology.* 1962; **86**: 788–799.

[35] Bok S. *Lying. Moral Choice in Public and Private Life.* New York: Random House, 1979; pp. 16–17.

[36] Jones J.W., McCullough L.B., and Richman B.W. Ethics of serving as a plaintiff's expert medical witness. *Surgery* 2004; **136**: 100–102.

[37] Morgan H. A Conflict of Roles: Expert Witness or Treating Physician? *SpineLine* 2006; **7**(4): 30–32.

[38] Folstein M.F., Folstein S.E., and McHugh P.R. Mini-mental state. A practical method for grading the cognitive state of patients for the clinicians. *Journal of Psychiatric Research* 1975; **13**: 189–198.

[39] Sanbar S.S. Etiology of Malpractice. In S.S. Sanbar (ed.) *The Medical Malpractice Survival Handbook.* Philadelphia: Mosby, 2007; pp. 122–123.

[40] Goodkin R. and Laska L.L. Vascular and visceral injuries associated with lumbar disc surgery: medicolegal implications. *Surgical Neurology* 1998; **49**: 358–372.

[41] Raptis S., Quigley F., and Barker S. Vascular complications of elective lower lumbar disc surgery. *Australian and New Zealand Journal of Surgery* 1994; **64**: 216–219.

[42] Brewster D.C., May A.R., Darling, R.C. *et al.* Variable manifestations of vascular injury during lumbar disk surgery. *Archives of Surgery* 1979; **114**: 1026–1030.

[43] Montorsi W. and Ghiringhelli C. Genesis, diagnosis and treatment of vascular complications after intervertebral disk surgery. *International Surgery* 1973; **58**: 233–235.

[44] Papadoulas S., Konstantinou D., Kourea H.P. *et al.* Vascular injury complicating lumbar disc surgery. A systematic review. *European Journal of Vascular and Endovascular Surgery* 2002; **24**: 189–195.

[45] Holscher E.C. Vascular and visceral injuries during lumbar-disc surgery. *Journal of Bone and Joint Surgery* 1968; **50-A**: 383–393.

[46] Solonen K.A. Arteriovenous fistula as a complication of operation for prolapsed disc. *Acta Orthopaedica Scandinavica* 1964; **34**: 159–166.

[47] DeSaussure R.L. Vascular injury coincident to disc surgery. *Journal of Neurosurgery* 1959; **16**: 222–229.

[48] Fortune C. Arterio-venous fistula of the left common iliac artery and vein. *Medical Journal of Australia* 1956; **1**: 660–661.

[49] Fager C.A. *Stop talking to the jury: Stories of a medical witness.* New York: Jay Street Pub, 1997.

[50] Sanbar S.S. and Firestone M.H. Medical Malpractice Stress Syndrome. In S.S. Sanbar (ed.) *The Medical Malpractice Survival Handbook.* Philadelphia: Mosby, 2007; pp. 9–15.

[51] The Society of Neurological Surgeons. Program Requirements for Fellowship Education in Stereotactic and Functional Neurosurgery. http://www.societyns.org/fellowships/requirements-stereotactic_functional.html [accessed 1 December 2009].

[52] Benabid A.L. Pollak P., Louveau A. *et al.* Combined (thalamotomy and stimulation) stereotactic surgery of the VIM thalamic nucleus for bilateral Parkinson disease. *Applied Neurophysiology* 1987; **50**: 344–347.

[53] Heath R.G. Modulation of emotion with a brain pacemamer. Treatment for intractable psychiatric illness. *The Journal of Mental and Nervous Disease* 1977; **165**: 300–317.

[54] Nuttin B.J., Gabriëls L.A., Cosyns P.R. *et al.* Long-term electrical capsular stimulation in patients with obsessive-compulsive disorder. *Neurosurgery* 2003; **52**: 1263–1274.

[55] Mayberg H.S., Lozano A.M., Voon V. *et al.* Deep brain stimulation for treatment-resistant depression. *Neuron* 2005; **45**: 651–660.

[56] Jennings D. The confusion between disease and illness in clinical medicine. *Journal of the Canadian Medical Asscoiation* 1986; **135**: 865–870.

[57] Churchland P.S. *Neurophilosophy. Toward a Unified Science of the Mind/ Brain.* Cambridge, MA: MIT, 1986; pp. 1–10.

[58] Taylor J.S. Neurolaw: towards a new medical jurisprudence. *Brain Injury* 1995; **9**: 745–751.

[59] Taylor J.S. (ed.) The Neurolaw Letter. http://www.braininjurybooks.com/ legal.html [accessed 10 October 2009].

[60] Stanford Law School to advance "neurolaw" as a part of $10 million grant. http://www.law.stanford.edu/news/pr/72/Stanford%20Law%20School%20 to%20Advance%20%22Neurolaw%22%20as%20Part%20of%20$10%20 Million%20Grant/ [accessed 14 July 2009].

[61] The President's Council on Bioethics. *An overview of the impact of neuroscience evidence in criminal law.* 2004. http://www.bioethics.gov/background/ neuroscience_evidence.html [accessed 16 July 2009].

[62] *State of Maharashtra* v *Sharma and Khandelwal* (India, 2008). http://anand. giridharadas.googlepages.com/BEOSruling.pdf [accessed 14 July 2009].

[63] Aharoni E., Funk C., Sinnott-Armstrong W. *et al.* Can neurological evidence help courts assess criminal responsibility? Lessons from law and neuroscience. *Annals of the New York Academy of Sciences* 2008; **1124**: 145–160.

[64] Stelten B.M.L., Noblesse L.H.M., Ackermans L. *et al.* The neurosurgical treatment of addiction. *Neurosurgical Focus* 2008; **25**: E1–5. http://thejns. org/doi/pdf/10.3171/FOC/2008/25/7/E5 [accessed 28 November 2009].

[65] Levy N. *Neuroethics. Challenges for the 21st Century.* New York: Cambridge, 2007; pp. 1–2.

[66] Blakemore C. Foreword. In J. Illes (ed.) *Neuroethics. Defining the Issues in Theory, Practice and Policy.* New York: Oxford, 2006; pp. v–vi.

[67] Hall Z.W. Mapping the Future. In *Neuroethics. Mapping the Field. Conference Proceedings, May 13–14, 2002, San Francisco, California.* New York: Dana Press, 2002; pp. 1–2.

[68] Pontius A.A. Neuro-ethics of "walking" in the newborn. *Perception and Motor Skills* 1973; **37**: 235–245.

[69] Roskies A. A case study in neuroethics: the nature of moral judgment. In J. Illes (ed.) *Neuroethics. Defining the Issues in Theory, Practice and Policy.* New York: Oxford, 2006; 17–32.

[70] NYC Bar, The Committee on Science and Law. *Are your thoughts your own? "Neuroprivacy" and the legal implications of brain imaging.* http:www.abcny. org/pdf/report/neuroprivacy-revisions/pdf [accessed 3 July 2006].

[71] Wolpe P.R., Foster K.R., and Langleben D.D. Emerging neurotechnologies for lie-detection: promises and perils. *American Journal of Bioethics* 2005; **5**: 39–49.

[72] Fins J.J. The Orwellian threat to emerging neurodiagnostic technologies. *American Journal of Bioethics* 2005; **5**: 58–60.

[73] Glenn L.M. Keeping an open mind: what legal safeguards are needed? *American Journal of Bioethics* 2005; **5**: 60–61.

[74] Illes J., Rosen A.C., Huang L. *et al.* Ethical consideration of incidental findings on adult brain MRI in research. *Neurology* 2004; **62**: 888–890.

[75] Kim B.S., Illes J., Kaplan R.T. *et al.* Incidental findings on pediatric MR images of the brain. *American Journal of Neuroradiology* 2002; **23**: 1674–1677.

[76] Grossman R.I. and Bernat J.L. Incidental research imaging findings: Pandora's costly box. *Neurology* 2004; **62**: 1932–1934.

[77] Canli T. When genes and brains unite: ethical implications of genomic neuroimaging. In J. Illes (ed.) *Neuroethics. Defining the Issues in Theory, Practice and Policy.* New York: Oxford, 2006; 169–183.

[78] Greene J. and Cohen J. For the law, neuroscience changes nothing and everything. *Philosophical Transactions of the Royal Society* 2004; **359**: 1775–1785.

[79] McLean T.R., Burton L., Haller C.C. *et al.* Electronic medical record metadata: uses and liability. *Journal of the American College of Surgeons* 2008; **206**: 405–411.

[80] Koppel R. and Kreda D. Health care information technology vendors' "hold harmless" clause: implications for patients and clinicians. *Journal of the American Medical Association* 2009; **301**: 1276–1278.

[81] Black A.D., Car J., Pagliari C. *et al.* The Impact of eHealth on the Quality and Safety of Health Care: A Systematic Overview *PLoS Medicine* 2011; **8**: 1–16. Available online at http://www.plosmedicine.org/article/info%3Adoi%2F10.1371%2Fjournal.pmed.1000387 [accessed 23 January 2011].

[82] McEvoy F.J. and Svalastoga E. Security of patient and study data associated with DICOM images when transferred using compact disc media. *Journal of Digital Imaging* 2007; **22**: 65–70.

[83] Larriviere D., Williams M.A., Rizzo M. *et al.* Responding to requests from adult patients for neuroenhancements: guidance of the Ethics, Law and Humanities Committee. *Neurology* 2009; **73**: 1406–1412.

[84] Borsook D., Moulton E.A., Schmidt K.F. *et al.* Neuroimaging revolutionizes therapeutic approaches to chronic pain. *Molecular Pain* 2007; **3**: 25–33.

[85] deCharms R.C. Applications of real-time fMRI. *Nature Reviews. Neuroscience* 2008; **9**: 720–729.

Ethical and Legal Issues in Modern Cardiothoracic Surgery

Kamran Baig and Jon Anderson

11.1 Historical Perspective

Cardiothoracic surgery is a relatively new discipline that has seen tremendous advancements over the past 50 years. Around the turn of the twentieth century there was much fear and trepidation regarding operating on the chest. Famously, Christian Billroth was quoted as saying: "Any surgeon who operates on the heart loses the respect of his colleagues" and "surgery of the heart has probably reached the limits set by nature to all surgery; no new method and no new discovery can overcome the natural difficulties that attend to a wound of the heart"[1]. Early attempts to bypass the heart's circulation using an adult donor were performed by Dr C. Walton Lillehei at Mayo Clinic in 1954 [2]. This technique was known as cross-circulation and involved connecting the healthy adult donor to the patient via the femoral vessels and the donor acted as the patient's oxygenator. At the time, there must have been serious ethical concerns regarding the use of healthy adults but there were no alternatives available to help save the lives of children dying with congenital heart disease. In the current era, one wonders whether such a technique would have ever been able to be performed. The technique was a success but was replaced by the discovery of the cardiopulmonary bypass machine by John Gibbon in 1953 and the bubble oxygenator in 1955. One of the next challenges in the evolution of cardiac surgery was the development of safe means to stop the heart. An interesting example of the climate in which the early pioneering heart operations were conducted was the first case of cardioplegic arrest performed at our institution, Hammersmith Hospital, in 1957 by Dennis Melrose [3]. It is reported that during the operation, there was great uncertainty and anxiety about whether this new technique would work and if the patient's heart would restart. Therefore, a priest and coroner were both present in the operating theatre and fortunately the operation went well and the patient survived.

An interesting development in the ethics of development of surgical procedures is exemplified by the early experiences of internal mammary artery ligation to treat angina. In the 1950s, ligation of the internal mammary artery was widely adopted as a standard surgical treatment to treat angina [4]. In order to evaluate the effectiveness of the technique, two sham controlled trials were conducted and both reported that ligation of the internal mammary artery was no better than a sham procedure involving just a skin incision under local anaesthetic [5, 6].

As a result of the publication of these trials findings, internal mammary ligation as a treatment for angina was abandoned, but ironically ligation of the internal mammary artery distally and its use as a conduit for revascularization was later to become the gold standard procedure in the treatment of ischaemic heart disease. These studies demonstrated the utility of sham controlled trials in determining the true effectiveness of a surgical intervention. However, there were serious ethical failings, especially with regard to informed consent. Patients were not informed that they might end up receiving a sham operation as opposed to the full operation that they were originally intended to undergo.

Perhaps the most significant event to influence cardiothoracic surgery in the UK was what became infamously known as the "Bristol Affair". In 1998, the General Medical Council (GMC) of the UK concluded its longest running case. Three doctors, two paediatric cardiac surgeons, and a medical director were found guilty of serious misconduct in relation to 29 deaths in 53 paediatric cardiac operations performed at the Bristol Royal Infirmary between 1988 and 1995. The central charges were that the surgeons had performed operations on children knowing that the risks of death were much higher than the national average and the surgeons failed to correctly inform the parents of the risks of surgery in their hands. The subsequent Bristol Inquiry, finally reported in 2001, cost millions of pounds and heard hundreds of witnesses. The inquiry identified many failings at personal, professional, and political levels. It set out 198 recommendations covering areas such as leadership within the health service; respect and honesty; competency of health professionals; safety and standards of care; public involvement; and care of children, especially those with cardiac conditions [7]. Two of these recommendations stated that patients must be able to obtain information on the relative performance of the trust and of consultant units within the trust. This resulted in an increasing belief that the interests of the public and patients would be best served by publication of individuals' surgical performance based upon mortality rates. Richard Smith, the then editor of the BMJ, prophesized this in a 1998 editorial entitled "All changed, utterly." The Bristol affair did transform British medical practice [8]. It ushered in a new era of clinical governance and risk management that have profound and far reaching effects on the current practice of medicine.

11.2 Coverage of Ethical Issues in Cardiothoracic Surgery in Literature

In 1995 Paola *et al.* published a study which compared the medical and surgical literature with respect to articles written about bioethics. They reported that 2.7% of articles in the medical journals and only 0.6% of articles in the surgical journals discussed ethical issues [9]. This finding stimulates the obvious question as to why surgeons consider ethical issues less frequently than other physicians in their publications. Some have countered that this "ethics gap" between physicians and surgeons may be explained by the fact that surgeons are more active in practising ethics, whereas physicians merely prefer to talk and more relevantly write about the subject [10].

However, there is evidence that the ethics gap is narrowing and in recent times, especially in cardiothoracic surgery, there has been an increasing interest in discussing ethical issues in the cardiothoracic surgical literature and international meetings. These efforts were best represented by the establishment of the Ethics Forum in 1999. This forum consists of members from the Society of Thoracic Surgeons (STS) Standards and

Ethics Committee and members of The American Association for Thoracic Surgery (AATS) Ethics Committee. Both the STS and the AATS have issued Ethical Codes of Practice for cardiothoracic surgeons [11, 12]. Members of the Ethics Forum published 113 articles on ethical topics in surgery literature between 2000 and 2005 and a special edition of Thoracic Surgery Clinics was dedicated to Ethical Issues in Thoracic Surgery [13].

A great majority of the literature on ethical issues in cardiothoracic surgery relates specifically to cardiac surgery, with a severe lack of articles related to issues in thoracic surgery.

The increasing discussion of ethical issues pertaining to cardiothoracic surgery is a very welcome development. However, there is a serious lack of teaching of ethical issues to those training in the speciality. For instance the core curriculum for cardiothoracic surgery training in the US has only one lecture relating to ethics amongst many hundreds covering the rest of the mainstream curriculum. In the UK, there is no specific mention of ethics in the curriculum, nor a counterpart of the US Ethics Forum nor code of ethics.

11.3 Principles of Ethics

In a recent article provocatively entitled "Do cardiologists and cardiac surgeons need ethics?" Bromage *et al.* present the predominant ethical theories and describe a valuable model that can be used to translate these theories into solving complex ethical issues such as in the case of an intravenous drug addict with infective endocarditis [14].

They present the Four-Principles Approach consisting of the following:

Beneficence	Acting in the patient's best interests, and above all providing a benefit and balancing this against risk and cost.
Non-maleficence (*non nocere*)	Minimising the causation of harm and seeking to prevent harm from happening.
Autonomy	Respecting and accepting the decision making capacity of the autonomous individual.
Justice	Treating all patients fairly without discrimination as well as fairly distributing benefits, risks, and costs.

The Four-Principles Approach provides a useful and widely accepted practical framework with which to start discussing complex ethical issues. The principles are founded upon the more classical ethical/moral theories of utilitarianism, rights based, duty based, and virtue ethics. The authors also present a modified version of Stirrat's five stage approach to address and resolve ethical issues [15].

In essence the five stages are defining the problem, identifying the objectives, considering the four principles in turn, considering any relevant ethical theories, and finally determining whether the patient is competent to give informed consent.

11.4 Informed Consent

Informed consent forms the central ethical pillar of surgical practice. Its foundation can be traced back to a landmark opinion which legally defined simple consent and changed the history of medical ethics. In 1914 in the case *Schloendorff* v *The Society of New York Hospital* a physician who believed he was acting in the best interests of the patient and removed a malignant tumour against the wishes of his patient was found guilty of battery. Judge Benjamin Cardozo wrote that,

> every human being of adult years and sound mind has a right to determine what shall be done with his body; and surgeon who performs an operation without his patient's consent commits an assault, for which he is liable in damages, ... except in cases of emergency, where the patient is unconscious, and where it is necessary to operate before consent can be obtained [16].

The patient's autonomy was seen as equally important as the physician's actions. Respect for autonomy obligated the physician to seek for the patient the greater balance of goods over harms, as those goods and harms are understood and balanced from the patient's perspective. The surgeon no longer possessed authority to act unilaterally on clinical judgements.

Further court decisions followed which effectively ushered in a new era of how surgeons would need to reconceptualise the patient–physician relationship. In the UK the GMC, the Medical Defence Union, and the government through the Department of Health have established guidelines for consent procedure.

Informed consent is of prime importance in cardiothoracic surgery, particularly because the surgical interventions are associated with significant mortality and morbidity. The physical as well as psychological impact of having an operation on one's vital organs like the heart and lungs is immense. For many patients, cardiothoracic surgery represents the most significant operation that they are ever likely to undergo and hence they naturally have many anxieties and concerns regarding the procedure itself as well as the potential complications and outcomes.

As well as constituting a medico-legal requirement, the process of obtaining informed consent is an important component of developing a healthy physician–patient relationship. The process of informed consent usually begins in the outpatient setting when the patient is seen at the request of the referring physicians, be they cardiologists or respiratory physicians. It is normally at this stage that the patient is offered surgery for their underlying condition and the benefits and risks of the operation discussed. If the patient is willing to proceed with surgery they are then placed onto the elective waiting list and admitted in due course. The process of informed consent is an integral aspect of the patient education process prior to surgery, enabling the patients to become well-informed, responsible, and willing members of the team. Studies have shown that a well-informed patient copes more effectively with surgery resulting in earlier discharge and decreased incidence of psychological problems [17]. An audit of 100 medico-legal cases in the West Midlands by Hawkins *et al.* in 1987 demonstrated that inability to obtain informed consent results from a failure of communication in 27% of cases [18]. One of the most significant fallouts from the Bristol Inquiry was the finding that the consent process for surgery in the UK was deficient since the Bristol parents seemed not to have been fully informed of the benefits and risks of the operations to which they consented. The inquiry recommended that there needed to be more transparency in the process of consent and the GMC subsequently published a landmark paper in 1998 entitled "Seeking patients' consent: The ethical considerations" which laid down guidelines for informed consent [19]. The GMC updated these guidelines in 2008 with the publication "Consent: patients and doctors making decisions together" [20]. The Department of Health produced standardised consent forms to be used in all NHS hospitals [21].

Serious deficiencies in informed consent were also highlighted in 1998 when a consultant paediatric cardiologist was found guilty of serious professional misconduct and suspended for six months by the GMC for performing a balloon dilatation catheterization on a patient, who tragically died the following day, without her parents' consent [22]. The parents had consented only to a diagnostic catheterization and gave evidence that they had specifically stated they did not want their daughter, who had previously had two open heart operations, to undergo an intervention procedure because they regarded it as risky.

Several studies have investigated the issues of informed consent in cardiac surgery following the Bristol Inquiry. In a survey by Vohra *et al.* conducted in Walsgrave Hospital, Coventry a questionnaire was developed to determine the extent to which informed patient consent for cardiac surgery corresponds with standard guidelines and to assess patient satisfaction with the consent process [23]. The questionnaire was administered to 82 patients the night before elective cardiac surgery after they had been consented by a doctor. In this study a substantial proportion (41%, n = 32) of patients asked questions, highlighting several unresolved issues such as what the surgical procedure itself involved (n = 11), future lifestyle (n = 10), and consequences of no surgery (n = 6). Overall, patients were pleased with the information provided but a small, yet significant, proportion of patients (19%, n = 15) felt that there was need to improve the consent process with suggestions including more use of booklets and videos, less technical detail, more information concerning alternative treatments, side effects of medicines, travel details, earlier bed availability, prompt cancellation information, and introduction to staff.

A similar study examining patient perceptions and recollections following surgical consent in 100 adult patients undergoing cardiac surgery in a London teaching hospital was published by Howlader *et al.* in 2004 [24]. In contrast to the previous study by Vohra cited above, the questionnaires were given to patients a day before their discharge from the hospital. The vast majority (89%) of patients stated that they were satisfied with information provided at the time of consent. However, a significant number of patients (43%) had forgotten the figure for risk of death quoted to them prior to the operation. In terms of the influence of media and publicity, 19 patients declared that the media had influenced their expectations of the consent process and 59 would have liked to see hospital league tables, while 26 would have liked to know the mortality figures for their surgeon prior to giving consent. This particular study was limited by recall bias since it was conducted just prior to the patients' discharge. Furthermore, the patients that did not survive surgery were not included. Several areas for further improvement were identified including the use of booklets, audiotapes, videotapes, defining optimum timing of consent, varying information depending upon patients needs and understanding, communicating risks and probabilities, and the inclusion of surgeons' previous results and hospital standing compared to other hospitals.

Murday's group in Glasgow developed a questionnaire to measure how informed patients are when giving consent for elective coronary artery bypass grafting [25]. It has been shown that patients are most informed and information recall is best immediately after signing the consent form and therefore patients were interviewed within two hours of signing the consent form. This study identified areas of informed consent where the minimal level of knowledge was below that recommended in the GMC's "Seeking patient's consent. The ethical considerations" 1998 guideline [19]. The areas where patients' knowledge and understanding were found to be lacking related to risks and complications of surgery, alternative options and their success rates, names of medical staff, awareness of the right to seek a second opinion, and post-operative management of pain.

One of the most contentious and variable aspects of informed consent is the level of risk disclosure. It may be argued that withholding or providing insufficient information about pre- and post-operative risk is a result of paternalism. Shinebourne and Bush claim that this is a form of paternalism when a doctor makes a decision for the patient or does not give full information on the grounds that it is better for the patient not to know [26]. Some researchers have argued that a fully informed consent can be needlessly cruel [27]. Importantly, patients also differ widely in their opinion about how much information they want about risks involved in surgery. Beresford *et al.* conducted structured interviews in 50 patients undergoing cardiac surgery at the Royal Brompton Hospital [28]. They found that

42% of patients wanted no information at all about the risks associated with cardiac surgery, 50% wanted no information about the risk of death, and 54% wanted no information on the risk of permanent stroke. They identified three groups of patients: those requiring little or no risk information, those requiring information about major risks, and those requiring full risk disclosure.

In contrast, Ivarsson *et al.* from Sweden demonstrated that extended written pre-operative information about complications following cardiac surgery did not cause increased anxiety or depression [29]. In this study patients were very positive about detailed pre-operative information provided. A large majority of patients (72%) waiting for cardiac surgery preferred to receive information about the risks. Post-operatively patients who had received detailed pre-operative information were significantly more satisfied compared to a control group.

11.5 Coronary Revascularization: Evidence-based Practice versus Informed Consent

An example of where the issue of informed consent has recently become the centre of much discussion and controversy is in the optimal treatment of coronary artery disease. In an era where evidence-based medicine has become a central tenet of best practice, the debate between cardiologists and cardiac surgeons over percutaneous coronary intervention (PCI) versus surgical revascularization in the form of coronary artery bypass grafting (CABG) has been hotly contested.

CABG represents one of the most extensively investigated surgical procedures, with follow-up data extending over 20 years [30]. It is highly effective in providing symptomatic relief and improving life expectancy in patients with left main stem disease, three-vessel disease, and especially those with impaired left ventricular function [31]. With advances in medical, anaesthetic, and surgical management, the procedure has become very safe with the average hospital mortality remaining around 2% over the past decade despite the treatment being used in older and sicker patients.

The main limitation of simple angioplasty was restenosis, affecting up to 40% of procedures, which was halved by bare metal stents. The advent of drug eluting stents claimed to effectively eliminate restenosis and there-fore reduce the number of reinterventions. Hlatky *et al.* recently performed a detailed analysis of ten randomized trials comparing PCI and CABG in patients with multivessel coronary artery disease [32]. Overall, there was a consensus that survival was similar with both interventions but that sur-gery greatly reduced the need for further intervention (from 20% with PCI to 5% with CABG). There was a significant survival advantage with CABG in diabetic patients and those over 65 years of age. However, a key flaw in these trials was that up to 80% of the participants had single or double vessel disease and normal ventricular function, a population already known not to benefit prognostically from surgery and the follow-up was only limited. Hence, through excluding patients with severe three-vessel coronary artery disease, who in reality make up the bulk of the population having surgery, these trials were, in effect, inherently biased against the prognostic benefit of surgery.

A landmark study, the SYNTAX (Synergy between PCI with Taxus and Cardiac Surgery) trial was recently published in the New England Journal of Medicine [33]. This multi-centre prospective randomized trial includ-ing 1,800 patients with three-vessel disease or left main stem disease concluded that CABG, as compared with PCI using drug eluting stents, is associated with a lower rate of major adverse cardiac or cerebrovascular events at one year among patients with three-vessel or left main coronary artery disease (or both) and should therefore remain the standard of care for such patients.

However, despite the overwhelming burden of evidence in favour of surgery over PCI in the treatment of coronary artery disease, PCI has been increasingly used to treat multivessel coronary disease, without the patients being fully informed about the risks of PCI and the benefits of the alternative treatment. In order for the patients to provide informed con-sent they must be given all the evidence to enable an informed choice about treatment. In reality though, the cardiologist often tells the anxious patient lying on the catheterization table following a diagnostic procedure that they could have their chest cracked open and have a bypass operation or alternatively undergo a quick percutaneous procedure and have a few stents put in and go home the same day. This approach does not fulfill the required standard of informed consent and therefore a multidisciplinary approach has been advocated in order to ensure that the best treatment is offered to the patients. There has been a move to ensure that all cases requiring intervention are discussed between the cardiologist and surgeon before deciding what is the optimal treatment for the patient.

Larobina *et al.* published a paper entitled "Is informed consent for PCI v CABG possible?" in which they assessed the understanding of the risks of interventions in patients undergoing CABG and PCI [34]. Patients at a tertiary hospital were interviewed with questionnaires focusing on the consent process, the patient's understanding of CABG or PCI, and associated risks and understanding of medical concepts. In addition, medical staff were questioned on the process of obtaining consent and understanding of medico-legal concepts. Fifty CABG patients, 40 PCI patients, and 40 medical staff were interviewed over a six-month period. No patient identified any of the explained risks as a reason to reconsider having CABG or PCI, but 80% of patients wanted to be informed of all risks of surgery. Eighty percent of patients considered doctors obligated to discuss all risks of surgery. One patient (2%) expressed concern at the prospect of a trainee surgeon carrying out the operation. Stroke (40%) rather than mortality (10%) were the important concerns in patients undergoing CABG and PCI. The purpose of interventions was only partially understood by both groups; PCI patients clearly underestimated the subsequent need for repeat PCI or CABG. Knowledge of medical concepts was poor in both groups: less than 50% of patients understood the cause or consequence of a heart attack or stroke and less than 20% of patients correctly identified the ratio equal to 0.5%. In conclusion, patients undergoing both CABG and PCI were found to have a poor understanding of their disease, their intervention, and its complications making the attaining of true informed consent difficult, despite their desire to be informed of all risks. PCI patients particularly were unduly highly optimistic regarding the need for reintervention over time, which indicated a specific failure to disclose realistic information regarding the limitations of PCI during the consent process.

11.6 Ethics of Innovation in Cardiothoracic Surgery

Cardiothoracic surgery is a relatively young speciality and within a short period of time many surgical procedures have been developed and evolved.

Due to the very nature of the underlying conditions and the surgery itself there can be significant risks of mortality and morbidity associated. Therefore, innovation in cardiothoracic surgery has been fraught with dangers and raised ethical concerns. Surgical innovation has resulted in remarkable advances from the invention of the heart-lung machine, development of heart and lung transplantation, and ventricular assist device therapy to coronary artery bypass and valve surgery.

In 1984 Shinebourne *et al.* published an editorial in the BMJ entitled "Ethics of innovative cardiac surgery" in which they addressed ethical concerns with the development of the new procedures in cardiac surgery [35]. One of the most critical aspects of pioneering new surgical procedures, especially in cardiac surgery where the margins of error are so small, is the learning curve. Early attempts of the operation may be technically more challenging due to difficulties not previously encountered. As the experience of the surgeons improves the technical difficulties can be overcome and the technique refined, resulting in improved outcomes. The learning curve places the first patient having the new procedure at a higher risk than those that follow. Although it may be claimed that this is a necessary path in order to successfully develop a new procedure it can be countered by arguing that no patient, especially a child, should be operated upon and subjected to higher risks, primarily for the benefit of future patients rather than for themselves. The ethical concerns may be addressed and resolved by ensuring safeguards are in place in order to protect the patients. Shinebourne proposed that it was unethical to introduce a new operation haphazardly without comparing the new treatment with existing treatments and recommended carefully selecting patients in order to minimize risks. The patients must be fully informed of the risks and benefits of the procedure as well as the alternatives available.

Shinebourne went on to specifically discuss the case of the artificial heart and the arterial switch operation for transposition of the great arteries. The implantation of the first artificial heart probably underwent more scrutiny and review than any previous innovation in surgery. The review process took over two years, mainly due to the need to analyse the many ethical issues raised by the new treatment and also to ensure that the right patients were selected for the artificial heart and that they were fully informed of the risks, benefits, and alternatives [36].

Over two decades later, the AbioCor artificial heart trial continued to raise many ethical and legal concerns which are very well analysed by Morreim [37]. The most clear distinction between trials involving implanted artificial hearts and other clinical studies is that it is often impossible for the patient to withdraw from the trial once the device has been implanted.

Shinebourne, a paediatric cardiologist, contrasted the extensive ethical analysis related to the artificial heart with the stark lack of ethical debate in the evolution of the arterial switch procedure for complete transposition of the great arteries. The standard surgical procedure for transposition had been the Senning or Mustard procedure which had been widely used for more than ten years with a hospital mortality reported at less than 10%. In 1976 Jatene introduced the arterial switch or anatomical repair of transposition of the great arteries [38]. This procedure consisted of reconnecting the great arteries to the appropriate ventricle and the coronary arteries are implanted into the new aorta. This procedure, unlike the preceding physiological repairs, had to be performed in the neonatal period and therefore consisted of a more technically challenging operation in younger patients. Yacoub and Ross soon afterwards published reports of their experiences of performing the arterial switch procedure [39, 40]. Interestingly, an accompanying editorial in the British Medical Journal applauded the surgical expertise but made no mention of the ethical considerations nor the selection of patients. The procedure was adopted in many units around the world but early results were associated with high mortality. At the time, the arterial switch operation, despite being associated with higher mortality, was justified on the hope that it would produce a better long-term survival than the previous established procedures. This hypothetical, anticipated to improve long-term outcome came at the expense of increased mortality in the early cases, but as the learning curve was overcome the mortality rates became lower than the previous procedures and the anticipated improved long-term outcomes were eventually realized.

De Laval elegantly documents his own experience in the changeover from the Senning procedure to the arterial switch [41]. They identified three separate components of the learning curve: the specialist community, the institution, and the individual surgeon performing the new technique.

The sharing of information and experiences within the international specialist community helps provide a global overview of the learning curve. For instance the early experience of Jatene was reported in 1979 and 54 deaths were reported in 89 patients undergoing the arterial switch procedure. Within an institution the specialist team also experiences considerable learning, with the cardiologists, anaesthetists, and intensivists all making important contributions towards successful outcomes. The greatest focus of the learning curves is upon the individual surgeon. The art of surgery has traditionally been acquired through the path of apprenticeship. However, when faced with a new operation that one has not performed before, there should be frameworks in place that limit the risk to the patients. Therefore, it is recommended that help is sought from more experienced surgeons in order to minimize the learning curve; best highlighted by the paediatric cardiac surgeon Arif Hasan when he was attempting to undertake the Ross procedure [42]. It is interesting to study the adoption of the arterial switch operation, especially considering that its devastating results by one surgeon were at the heart of the Bristol Affair, with 9 out of 13 patients dying and one sustaining serious brain damage. At the same time, in Birmingham only one death had occurred in 200 patients. The subsequent Bristol Inquiry highlighted the need for closer regulation, accountability, and responsibility.

The adoption of new surgical procedures requires appropriate scientific, logistical, and ethical frameworks aimed at maximizing benefits to patients whilst minimizing the risks. The main ethical issues are related to the decision to offer a new treatment and informed consent in accepting to undergo a new treatment with uncertain outcomes and risks. Clinical ethics committees play an important role in sanctioning the treatments and protecting the patient's best interests. There also needs to be a system in place to monitor outcomes and intervening to halt the trial if the outcomes are deemed to be poor.

11.7 The Ethics of Publication of Cardiothoracic Surgical Outcomes

The outcomes of cardiothoracic surgery were first publicized in 1990 when the New York state officials released hospital-specific data on raw as well as risk-adjusted mortality rates for patients who underwent CABG. This was followed up in 1992 with the publication of surgeon-specific mortality rates and the same approach was soon afterwards adopted by neighboring state Pennsylvania. The principle behind public reporting of cardiothoracic surgery outcome data is the belief that the publication of data on individual surgeons and hospitals into the public arena is useful to individual patients for choosing hospitals and surgeons, surgeons for improving their own outcomes and hospitals for quality improvement, and governmental bodies for developing health related legislation and policies. It is proposed that public access to such data would provide patients a higher level of knowledge regarding outcomes of their proposed intervention by the individual and hence strengthen the informed consent process. Jacobs *et al.* provided a comprehensive overview of the subject entitled "The ethics of transparency"[43].

However, there has been criticism of the policy related to complexity adjustment, incomplete or inaccurate data, reduced access to cardiac surgery by the sickest patients, statistical weaknesses that do not account for limited sample size and are based on flawed administrative databases, and insufficiently trained journalists. There is evidence that contemporary reporting of outcomes data is based on flawed methodologies that potentially mislead and deceive. Such ensuing deceptions may harm patients, surgeons, and hospitals in various ways, and could ultimately undermine quality of surgical care and patients' access to it.

One of the main difficulties in analysing the data is adjusting for the differences in case mix and risk profile, which is termed complexity adjustment or risk stratification. The data must be correctly adjusted to reflect the complexity of the case and the risk profile of the patient. Failure to correctly represent the data in this way may result in some surgeons' mortality figures appearing excessively high and in an effort to avoid such results surgeons may adopt risk-averse behaviour and turn down high-risk patients' cardiac surgery. Reliable and accurate methods of risk stratification could eliminate perverse incentives for surgeons to avoid taking on the highest-risk patients — who paradoxically represent those who might need surgery the most and who might benefit the most from the procedure.

Various models of risk-stratification and case-mix adjustment have been developed, with the STS Database (comprising General Thoracic,

Adult Cardiac, and STS Congenital Heart Surgery Databases) having been validated in several studies [44–47]. However, no risk-adjusted model can take into account all of the complexities of individual patients and there is room for misrepresentation of a surgeon's or institution's results which may affect subsequent practice.

Another, methodological, problem is that the limited sample size of any individual surgeon's or hospital's experience could lead to wide fluctuations in outcomes from year to year and also errors due to random variations rather than true statistical differences. For instance, without correct adjustments for sample size and random variations, a shift of one or two deaths a year in a small sample size can lead to alarming changes in mortality. Without adequate adjustment for sample size and random variation the data could prove deceptive and misleading.

An essential pre-requisite for valid data analysis is ensuring that the data collected is accurate and complete. Therefore much effort has been made to make sure that the data in the STS Database is a reliable and complete source of data. The data are verified for completeness and accuracy through an intrinsic verification process designed to rectify inconsistencies of data and missing elements of data, and an on-site audit programme that verifies data at its primary source. In addition, data in the STS Adult Cardiac Surgery Database and the STS Congenital Heart Surgery Database are randomly audited as part of a formal on-site audit programme conducted by an independent medical audit firm.

One of the criticisms of allowing the lay press to report cardiothoracic surgery outcomes is that the average healthcare reporter does not have the training and background to appreciate the science behind the analysis of medical and surgical outcomes. Therefore it is advocated that cardiothoracic surgeons play a substantial role in the process of media reporting of outcomes.

The benefits of public reporting of outcomes, when performed properly, can be significant not only to patients but also surgeons, hospitals, and governments. Public reporting, it is argued, can lead to improvements in the quality of care and reduction in cost by identifying the best providers so that we can learn from them, and by identifying low performing centres that can benefit from quality improvement initiatives.

Public reporting also promotes surgical professionalism by encouraging the honest, accurate, and complete collection of data which facilitates self-regulation and ultimately improves the standards of surgical practice. There is a desire for transparency demanded from patients, the media, and government. Cardiothoracic surgeons are ethically committed to serve the best interests of patients and to optimize access to appropriate healthcare. In order to serve the best interests of patients, efforts must be made to provide patients with all available information that would help them in deciding which surgeon they would want to perform their operation. Such provision of information empowers patients when making informed consent decisions about their care in terms of surgeons and institutions outcomes.

Following the highly publicized Bristol Inquiry, there was a call for wider transparency and one of the key recommendations made was that it would be in the best interests of the public and patients to publish surgeon-specific mortality data. The secretary of state for health, Alan Milburn, announced in 2002 that hospital and surgeon performance would be disclosed to the public. The Society of Cardiothoracic Surgeons have already been proactive for several years in collecting surgeon-specific and hospital-specific performance data as part of its quality assurance programme for several index procedures, which were isolated first-time coronary surgery, lobectomy for lung cancer, correction of aortic coarctation, and isolated ventricular septal defect. The performance marker chosen was in-hospital mortality since it was understandable, easy to measure, could be validated, and included all patients who died in hospital (not just those within a certain time frame). In addition, all public reporting systems in the US had also used this outcome marker. In 2005 The Guardian newspaper published surgeon-specific CABG mortality rates (not all of them risk-adjusted), which the newspaper had obtained through the Freedom of Information Act. This was soon followed by the announcement in March 2005 by the then secretary of state, John Reid, that fully risk-adjusted CABG mortality rates for every cardiac surgeon working in the National Health Service (NHS) would be available on a publicly accessible website by September 2005. The website was a joint collaboration between the Healthcare Commission, the independent regulator of healthcare in England, and the Society of Cardiothoracic Surgeons. The website provides patients with a "practice profile" of each surgeon, which includes the total number of surgical procedures undertaken in the past three years together with the proportion of isolated CABGs, isolated aortic valve replacements, and combined and other procedures performed. Two survival rates are given for each surgeon: one for CABG alone and one for all surgical procedures combined. These two percentages are each accompanied by the range of expected survival rates for patients treated at the surgeon's hospital. The expected outcomes are calculated using the logistic regression version of the European System for Cardiac Operative Risk Evaluation (EUROSCORE). All units and surgeons who have so far contributed their data have results that are within or better than the expected range.

The lessons learned from the experiences of public reporting in New York State have been heeded in the publication of data in the UK and overall the results have been excellent. This is best demonstrated by a 40% reduction in risk-adjusted mortality between 2000 and 2005 in the UK for cardiac surgery, despite an increasing risk profile of the patient population [48].

11.8 Withdrawing Life-sustaining Treatments

In cardiothoracic surgery, the outcomes from most procedures are generally excellent despite an increasingly elderly population and sicker patients. However, due to the very nature of the underlying conditions and surgery itself, a very small proportion of patients will not survive despite the best of efforts and maximal therapy. In some patients, prolonging treatment when the prospects of recovery are extremely bleak can seem futile and can be very distressing for the patient's family. In cardiothoracic surgery, examples of such patients would be those with multi-organ failure, extensive neurological injury, or those with advanced malignancies such as lung cancer or mesothelioma. A high proportion of deaths in intensive care occur after withdrawal or withholding of life support. A US study showed a large increase in the proportion of deaths in intensive care that were preceded by a decision to withhold or withdraw life support, from 50% in 1987 to over 90% in 1992 [49, 50].

The ethical challenges are deciding how much longer to continue with maximal therapy and when to consider withdrawing life-support treatment to allow the patient to die in a dignified manner. The effectiveness of medical technology in extending life makes it difficult to determine when it is appropriate to accept that a patient is dying, cease further aggressive treatment, and strengthen palliative support. Many factors contribute to the difficulty of withdrawing life-supporting treatments: the distinction between withholding and withdrawing treatment, religious and cultural considerations, the technologic imperative, prognostic uncertainty, variability in practice, and caregiver discomfort with death. Through understanding the limits of treatment, expertise in palliation of symptoms, skillful communication, and careful orchestration of controllable events the withdrawal of life-supporting treatments can be managed in a dignified and respectful fashion.

The GMC issued a directive in 2002 entitled "Withholding and withdrawing life-prolonging treatments: Good practice in decision-making" which sets out the standards of practice expected of doctors when they consider whether to withhold or withdraw life-prolonging treatments [51].

In understanding this issue, one of the most difficult challenges is differentiating between withholding and withdrawing treatment. In ethical and legal terms there is no distinction between withholding or withdrawing treatment. For instance, the act of withdrawing is ethically equivalent to an omission (withholding) when the physician has the same intention of relieving suffering and the end result of dignified death is the same. However, withdrawing life-sustaining treatment is not the same as withholding therapy. The act of withdrawing life-sustaining therapy involves an active process, which can be disturbing for the physician responsible who must take action and disconnect the ventilator or turn off the inotropic medications supporting blood pressure. These actions may lead to immediate death and can be associated with a feeling of responsibility and culpability for the death, despite theoretical distinctions, professional endorsements, and legal precedents. To withdraw life support is to recognize that the underlying disease process cannot be reversed. Withholding or withdrawing of care should not be considered killing (euthanasia) or assisted suicide because it is the medical condition rather than the act of withholding or withdrawing that is the cause of death. The intention is not to kill, although death certainly ensues. The intention is to acknowledge the limits of medicine. The death that follows, even if immediate, indicates the severity of the disease state and uncovers the inability of the patient's body to survive.

Another important practical consideration in withdrawing treatment is that many critically ill patients are unable to communicate for themselves when such decisions are made. One study demonstrated that physicians and families are responsible for the majority of the decisions about life support in intensive care units, because fewer than 5% of patients are able to communicate with clinicians at the time the decision is made [49]. In a small proportion of cases (10–20%), patients may have written an advance directive which is a document in which a competent adult sets forth direction about medical treatment in the event that he or she becomes incapacitated in the future. This can help identify certain desires and values that a patient may have around issues of death and dying (i.e., attitudes toward long-term ventilator management, wishes to avoid persistent vegetative state, etc.).

In such cases where an advance directive has not been written, the surrogate decision makers (healthcare proxies, family members, and so on) may play a vital role in the end-of-life decision making process. The difficulties arise when there is a difference of opinion between the surgeon and the proxy or surrogate. For instance, there may be situations where the surgeon wishes to continue treating the patient whereas the proxy or surrogate requests stopping on the basis that the patient would have chosen to stop treatment. Ethically and legally, such proxy or surrogate decisions should be based upon answering the question "What would the patient have wanted?" Without a written advance directive that specifies what the patient would want for themselves in a life-threatening situation, the acceptability of the proxy or surrogate depends on the extent to which the decision of the surrogate or proxy accurately reflects the patient's wishes. In both ethics and law, surrogate decision makers have essentially the same authority as the patient would have, if capable. When the patient is incapable of making a decision, the proxy or surrogate's choice is decisive *if* it accurately reflects what the patient would have wanted.

11.9 Ethical Issues in Heart and Lung Transplantation

The first heart transplant in man was performed in 1967 by a South African surgeon, Dr Christiaan Barnard in Cape Town. Dr Barnard's surgical team removed the heart of a 25-year-old woman who had died following a car accident and placed it in the chest of Louis Washkansky, a 55-year-old man. The patient unfortunately died 18 days later of pneumonia but this was a monumental breakthrough ushering in a new and exciting era for transplantation. In spite of rapid advances in the science and surgical techniques of heart and lung transplantation the field has always been surrounded by much ethical discourse. One of the earliest contributions on the subject was first presented by Robert Reeves, the chaplain of the Presbyterian Hospital, New York at the Symposium on the Surgical, Immunological and Ethical Considerations of Cardiac Transplantation in Man held at the Twentieth Annual Meeting of the New York Society for Cardiovascular Surgery, at The New York Academy of Medicine, 10 May 10 1968 [52].

11.9.1 *Ethical issues in organ distribution*

Heart and lung transplantation have revolutionized treatment for end stage organ failure over the past few decades. However, the demand for organs has far outstripped supply and many patients die every year on the waiting list for transplantation. Therefore, there has been much scrutiny over policies of the distribution of organs and several key ethical questions have been highlighted.

In considering ethical issues surrounding transplantation it is useful to apply the ethical principles of equity, justice, beneficence, and utility.

Equity consists of a sense of fairness or impartiality and ensures that there is no discrimination in the selection of an organ recipient for transplantation. Therefore, race, skin colour, nor religion should play a role in determining organ distribution. However, when it comes to age, matters are not so clearly defined. The International Society for Heart and Lung Transplantation (ISHLT) guidelines for heart transplantation state that patients should be considered for transplantation if they are less than or equal to 70 years old [53]. However, the guidelines also add that carefully selected patients greater than 70 years of age may be considered for cardiac transplantation but this may involve alternative algorithms and the use of older donors. In a study of 15 patients less than or equal to 70 years of age, the actuarial survival rates at one year and four years were not statistically different between older and younger patients (one-year survival: 93.3% v 88.3%; four-year survival: 73.5% v 69.1%). In addition, some data suggest that older patients have less donor organ rejection, which most likely represents immunosenescence in this older population [54–56]. Therefore, an increasing tendency to perform transplantation in older patients has been observed in recent years. For lung transplantation the ISHLT guidelines stipulate age older than 65 years to be a relative contraindication since older patients have less optimal survival, likely due to comorbidities [57].

The ethical principle of justice advocates providing individuals with what they deserve. Therefore, should a patient who contributed to their underlying heart and lung condition through lifestyle choices such as smoking and obesity be given the right to a transplant over an individual who developed end-organ failure through genetics? Beneficence dictates that there should be a greater benefit over harm for the patient by performing the transplant. Utility is based upon the classic ethical principle of utilitarianism, which advocates making best use of the scarce resource for the greatest good.

In deciding the distribution of organs one of the most fundamental questions is whether organs should go to the sickest patients or those who have waited the longest on the transplant list. Conventionally, the system of medical triage prioritizes patients who receive treatment first based upon clinical need and urgency. The ethical dilemma posed is whether to transplant the patient who has waited the longest or the patient who cannot wait any longer. The human imperative to save life would override any regulations of waiting time.

The effects of outcome also play a role in determining organ distribution. Those patients at higher risk of adverse outcome following transplantation such as those requiring a retransplantation for primary or chronic graft failure pose a difficult ethical quandary. Cardiac retransplantation is the gold standard therapy in these patients. According to data from the registry for the ISHLT, retransplantation accounts for about 2% of adult cardiac transplant procedures and 3% of pediatric heart transplant [58]. Previous studies reported lower post-transplantation survival rates in retransplantation patients compared with primary transplantation. Cardiac retransplantation for acute rejection has the worst survival rate (32% and 8% at one and five years, respectively) followed by retransplantation for early graft failure (50% and 39% at one and five years, respectively) [59]. Primary graft failure is the most common cause for retransplantation. Many valid and powerful ethical arguments have been put forward in discussing the merits of cardiac retransplantation. Patients who are offered second and third heart transplants may deprive a significant number of patients who have not had their first chance at transplantation. The results of cardiac retransplantation for acute cardiac rejection and early graft failure are poor enough to suggest that this option is not advisable. Retransplantation for allograft vasculopathy, however, is currently associated with reasonable results and an improvement in survival and is an appropriate indication for retransplantation. Collins *et al.* propose, based on justice, fairness, medical suitability, respect for anatomy, and principle of justice, that cardiac transplantation be a one-time treatment option and have strongly argued that retransplantation should not be allowed [60]. It may be advocated that our moral duty is to direct life-saving treatment and resources to those patients who are more likely to benefit from the intervention and thus a primary cardiac transplant candidate should receive priority over a retransplantation candidate because mortality after transplant is lower. Some groups propose that the allocation system needs to be revised to reflect this opinion and to give a primary cardiac transplant a better chance to receive a transplant than a retransplant patient. However, the overwhelming sense of duty and urgency to save the life of a critically ill patient whose first transplant has failed often overrides the ethical issues of justice in terms of bumping those patients who have been on the waiting list longest and also the principle of utility whereby the organs are used in the cause of greatest good and likely benefit.

The issue of active tobacco smoking also raises ethical concerns in relation to heart and lung transplantation. Emphysema and ischaemic cardiomyopathy are the primary indications for lung and heart transplantation respectively and both of these conditions are associated with smoking tobacco. The key ethical question, in the context of shortage of organs available for transplantation is whether organs should be allocated to individuals who choose to continue to smoke over those individuals afflicted by genetic diseases such as cystic fibrosis or cardiomyopathy through no fault of their own. The effects of continuing to smoke following transplantation is also a significant factor to take into consideration as smoking can contribute to accelerated atherosclerosis in the transplanted heart and also cause small airway injury in the transplanted lungs [61]. Therefore, based upon the principle of utility the ISHLT guidelines currently consider active tobacco smoking as a relative contraindication to heart and lung transplantation and stipulate that patients must abstain at least six months prior to transplantation [53, 62]. Unfortunately studies have shown that approximately 24% of heart transplant recipients return to tobacco abuse after transplantation [63]. Even the issue of whether patients afflicted with smoking related diseases such as chronic obstructive pulmonary disease (COPD) should be offered lung transplantation at all has been the subject of many lively debates.

11.9.2 Ethics of living donor lung transplantation

With the diminishing number of cadaveric donations, there has been increasing interest in living donor lung donation. However, the ethics of living donor organ donation are amongst the most contentious and debated issues in current practice. The ethics of living organ donation have been debated since the earliest recognition of the potential advantages of a living donor's organ for transplantation, and the likelihood that living donation could become the preferred approach [64].

In 1993, Starnes and colleagues performed the first bilateral living donor lobar lung transplantation at the University of Southern California (USC) for a patient with cystic fibrosis [65]. Since two living donors were required for the procedure many ethical concerns were raised and after extensive discussions guidelines were established for the pre-transplant assessment of recipients and donors. Living lung transplantation poses many ethical challenges. From the outset, the act of donating a lobe of lung from a living volunteer violates the fundamental Hippocratic pillar of medical ethics whereby the physician should first do no harm (*primum non nocere*). Beauchamp and Childress have applied the four basic principles of medical ethics approach in dealing with the complex issues surrounding living organ donation. The ethical principles involved in decision making for living organ donors were extensively analysed by a multidisciplinary group from the transplant community, which included physicians, nurses, psychologists, attorneys, social workers, transplant donors, recipients, and several ethicists. The resulting Consensus Statement on the Live Organ Donor was published in 2000 [66]. It provides a template for the structure of an ethically sound clinical programme. Emphasis is placed on ensuring both medical and psychosocial suitability of the potential donor and an optimal informed consent.

Respect for autonomy is one of the fundamental ethical principles and dictates that individuals have the right to decide what they want to do for themselves. However, a patient's autonomy must always be counterbalanced by the physician's medical judgement which is based upon the ethical principle of beneficence, which weighs up the risks against benefits to provide what is best for the patient.

In considering the risks against benefits, the ethical principle of non-maleficence towards the donor is given special weighting but ultimately the potential benefits towards the recipient are the most decisive motivation towards performing the procedure. One of the most significant advantages of living lung donation is that a lobe of lung from a living donor may be of superior quality than a cadaveric donor due to shorter ischemic time and the absence of the sequelae of brain death on various organ systems. In addition, a practical advantage of living lung transplant is that it may be performed at relatively short notice, especially in the case of a patient whose condition has deteriorated rapidly and would not survive on the waiting list for transplant. One of the most difficult predicaments faced is defining when a patient is too sick to justify placing two healthy donors at risk of lobectomy. However, it is in this very high risk category of patients that the potential to save lives could be greatest. In considering the donor, as well as the obvious risks of mortality and significant morbidity associated with lobectomy one should not underestimate the psychological, emotional, and spiritual benefits in addition to matters of self-esteem. A key part of the evaluation of a potential donor's suitability for the living lung donation is a comprehensive psychosocial assessment. The ultimate aims of this assessment are to determine that the donor is competent to make an informed decision by ruling out major uncontrolled psychiatric illness or significant developmental delay and also establishing that the primary motivation for the living donor is altruism, and that there has been absolutely no evidence of coercion. In obtaining informed consent there must be full disclosure of adverse effects and potential benefits. The disclosure process must also include an honest and realistic explanation of the expected outcomes for the recipient since most potential living donors are not aware that five-year survival after lung transplant is in the range of 50% [67].

The source of donation has also become a major focus of ethical scrutiny. In the early experiences of living lung donation, donors were always (genetically) related to the recipient since it was felt that the ties of kinship would be close enough to motivate individuals to donate organs altruistically and also accept the potential risks of lobectomy. With increasing experience and publication of outcomes of the benefits of living related transplantation the requirement for living donors to be related to the donors has been dropped.

The remuneration of donors in order to stimulate an increase in organ donation has been extensively discussed by physicians, politicians, economists, and ethicists. In Western countries there is a consensus that organs should not be sold for financial gain and be subject to market forces. However, in many other countries such as Iran there is a government-sanctioned commercial system of organ distribution that has enabled thousands of kidney transplants to be performed that may otherwise never have occurred [68]. Arguments used in favour of allowing commerce for organ donation begin with the principle of autonomy. It can be argued that the freedom of self-determination should not be denied if an individual chooses to sell a part of themselves. In support of the sanctioning of commerce for organs is the utilitarian viewpoint that proposes that since the present system of voluntary altruistic donation is not providing enough organs, allowing individuals to be financially rewarded for donation would provide the greatest good for both donors and recipients by providing more organs.

One of the most compelling cases against the commercialization of organs for transplantation is the potential for exploitation of the poor, which is rampant in many countries such as India and Iran [69].

11.9.3 *Ethics of xenotransplantation*

As the demand for organs continues to greatly outstrip supply, there has been growing interest in turning to alternative sources of donation such as animals as well as stem cells. Xenotransplantation is defined as the transplantation, implantation, or infusion into a human of live cells, organs, or tissues from a non-human animal source. Recent scientific advances in understanding the human and animal immune systems, development of new anti-rejection therapies, and production of transgenic animals has opened up new possibilities for xenotransplantation. However, despite the significant scientific breakthroughs the most important barrier remains the ethical and legal concerns associated with xenotransplantation [70]. Perhaps the most notorious venture into xenotransplantation was the transplant of a baboon heart into an infant "Baby Fae" in 1984. Baby Fae was born prematurely on 26 October 1984 with an underdeveloped left heart, known as hypoplastic left heart syndrome. Leonard Bailey was the surgeon at Loma Linda Medical Center in California who attempted to save Baby Fae by transplanting a baboon's heart into the infant twelve days after her birth. It was hypothesized that the infant's immature immune system would prevent Baby Fae from rejecting the baboon heart. The new heart initially worked very well but Baby Fae succumbed 20 days later from organ failure resulting from an aggressive immunological response. This case made spectacular headlines around the world and highlighted many ethical and legal concerns regarding the appropriateness of xenotransplantation that continue to be fiercely debated to this day.

One of the most prominent arguments against xenotransplantation is that the transfer of organs or tissues from animals to humans is a violation of what is deemed "natural". The difficulty with this concern is the definition of what is "natural" and what is "unnatural".

It may be argued that all actions performed by humans are "unnatural" in that they interfere with the non-human natural status quo and therefore all "unnatural" actions such as xenotransplantation cannot be deemed to be wrong in themselves and unethical. From an alternative perspective, all human actions could be seen as natural since humans themselves are considered part of nature. Hence, nothing humans do can be deemed "unnatural". Herein lies the difficultly in distinguishing natural and unnatural and defining what is ethical and unethical.

Most religions sanction the use of animals for the good of man. Islam and Judaism which both forbid the eating of pork nonetheless approve of xenotransplantation as long as the animal is treated humanely. Undoubtedly the strongest opposition against xenotransplantation comes from animal rights activists. They argue that the suffering endured by animals involved in xenotransplantation experimentation is unacceptable. It has also been claimed that much of the interest in xenotransplantation is commercially driven by private companies aiming to make lucrative profits.

The most striking controversy that was highlighted by the tragic Baby Fae case was the concept of informed consent. As discussed extensively in an earlier section, informed consent requires full disclosure of significant risks and benefits of the procedure as well as alternative treatments. In the Baby Fae case there were serious concerns regarding the quality and extent of information provided to the parents when attaining informed consent for the transplant of a baboon heart into their child. Some observers suggested that the parents were not fully informed about the already well-established procedure available to correct hypoplastic left hearts, known as the Norwood Procedure. Furthermore, at the time the scientific evidence available on xenotransplantation indicated that the success rate would have been very low and that the Norwood Procedure would have provided greater chances of survival. The NIH subsequently launched a committee which investigated the issue of informed consent in the Baby Fae case and found significant failings in the procedure, including an overestimation of the infant's chances for long-term survival.

One of the scientific barriers to xenotransplantation is the risk of transmission of infectious disease from animals to humans. Perhaps the most devastating example of such zoonoses (diseases transmitted between animals and humans under natural conditions) is the human immunodeficiency virus (HIV), which is thought to have been transmitted into human populations by a mutation of a related simian immunodeficiency virus acquired from wild primates in Africa. In the case of xenotransplantation, the most promising candidate species is the pig which possesses very close anatomical and physiological correlation with human organs, especially the heart and lungs. However, there has been much focus on the risk of cross-species infection since the recent discovery of porcine endogenous retroviruses which have been shown to be able to infect human cells *in vitro* [71].

More topically the recent H1N1 swine flu pandemic has caused worldwide alarm and may hamper the cause of using swine as sources for xenotransplantation.

Since xenotransplantation involves the direct insertion of animal cells, tissues, or organs into humans there is a real potential danger of transmitting infectious diseases from animals to humans, some of which may not have even been discovered yet. The more serious consequence could be the potential transmission of disease from the xenotransplantation recipient to their family, healthcare professions, and possibly the wider population. The hazards of transmitting diseases has serious implications for informed consent. The risks of xenotransplantation are currently high and unpredictable which would make attaining informed consent very difficult. Moreover, due to the potential of infecting contacts such as healthcare professionals and family, consent may have to be attained from these third parties also. In seeking consent from such potential contacts of a xenotransplantation recipient, disclosure of confidential information about the recipient would have to occur, which could only take place with the recipient's permission.

Another major legal requirement, related to the risk of spreading new infectious diseases, would be the need for new public safety monitoring measures and public health legislation to protect the individual and wider society from the risks.

Xenotransplantation is an exciting and promising technique that has the potential to help solve the desperate problem of donor organ shortages in cardiothoracic transplantation but it remains shrouded by a complexity of controversial scientific, ethical, and legal issues. Even if and when the scientific barriers to xenotransplantation are overcome, the critical decision to proceed with the application of this technique in humans will require the establishment of ethical, regulatory, and legal frameworks by consensus of physicians, scientists, ethicists, and politicians.

11.10 Stem Cell and Cloning Research

Another promising strategy being explored in the face of the critical organ shortage is stem cell-derived organ and tissue regeneration. However, akin to xenotransplantation, stem cell and cloning research has generated much intense ethical and legal debate that has limited its advancement.

The central ethical issue at the heart of the use of embryonic stems cells for research is the destruction of early human embryos. Those against stem cell research believe that the embryo is a human being with full rights from the moment of conception. Conversely, those supporting stem cell research take a developmental approach and believe that the embryo gradually becomes a person and therefore the early embryo is not entitled to the same moral protection as at a later developmental stage when it would be considered a fully formed human being. This exposes the limitation of science in defining the moral status of the very early embryo.

There have also been significant legal restrictions on the use of stem cells for research, most notably the announcement of the Human Embryonic Stem Cell Policy under President Bush in August 2001. However, on 9 March 2009 incumbent president Barack Obama issued an executive order entitled "Removing barriers to responsible scientific research involving human stem cells" which revoked the previous order and paved the way for advancement in stem cell research in the US [72].

The use of therapeutic cloning to provide stem cells for cardiothoracic research and treatment was excellently debated at the 2005 AATS annual meeting ethics forum [73].

11.11 Conclusions

Cardiothoracic surgery is a young, rapidly advancing speciality that can make significant beneficial impact to patients' lives. In an age of improving technology, greater public awareness and expectations, and increasing strain on healthcare resources, many ethical and legal challenges lie ahead. Issues related to informed consent will become more relevant as patients become better informed through wider availability of information resources such as the media and internet. As the population ages, more and more elderly patients will be subjected to cardiothoracic surgery and there will continue to be intense scrutiny placed upon analysing outcomes. Withdrawal of treatment issues may become more frequent with the increasing elderly population, as well as due to resource limitation and rationing. In times of economic uncertainty the allocation of resources will come under greater pressures and the cost-effectiveness of treatments such as transplantation and devices such as artificial heart and ventricular assist devices will need to be demonstrated. Cardiothoracic surgeons need to continue to lead the way with evidence-based medicine and ensure that the patient receives scientifically proven effective treatments that are in their best interests, such as surgical revascularization or valve replacements. Promising therapies such as xenotransplantation and stem cell therapy will only be able to be applied clinically in humans once the ethical and legal concerns have been resolved. At a juncture where the speciality of cardiothoracic surgery is facing threats over its future survival from interventional cardiologists and radiologists, innovation needs to be stimulated, but requires the establishment of ethical, legal, and scientific frameworks in order to minimize the hazards of the learning curve and protect patients from risks of the new procedure. With such exciting and challenging times ahead the importance and relevance of ethics to the speciality of cardiothoracic surgery could not be greater. Hence, there is a pressing need to increase the awareness of these issues and educate the current as well as future generations of surgeons of the role of ethics in modern cardiothoracic surgical practice. It is hoped that this effort is able to make a small contribution towards that goal.

Cardiothoracic surgeons are uniquely privileged to serve some of the sickest patients and have immense opportunities to do good but also may inadvertently do serious harm due to the hazardous nature of the speciality. However, they must always strive to "Above all, do more good than harm" and this is why moral responsibility and ethics is at the very heart our profession.

References

[1] Westaby S. *Landmarks in Cardiac Surgery*. Oxford: Oxford University Press, 1998.
[2] Gott V.L. and Shumway N.E. Cross-circulation: a milestone in cardiac surgery. *Journal of Thoracic and Cardiovascular Surgery* 2004; **127**(3): 617.
[3] Melrose D.G., Dreyer B., Bental H.H. *et al.* Elective cardiac arrest. *Lancet* 1955; **269**(6879): 21–22.
[4] Beecher H.K. Surgery as placebo. A quantitative study of bias. *The Journal of the American Medical Association* 1961; **176**: 1102–1107.
[5] Cobb L.A., *et al.* An evaluation of internal-mammary-artery ligation by a double-blind technic. *New England Journal of Medicine* 1959; **260**(22): 1115–1118.

[6]   Dimond E.G., Kittle, C.F., and Crockett, J.E. Comparison of internal mammary artery ligation and sham operation for angina pectoris. *The American Journal of Cardiology* 1960; **5**: 483–486.

[7]   Learning from Bristol: the report of the public inquiry into children's heart surgery at the Bristol Royal Infirmary 1984–1995. 2001. http://www. bristol-inquiry.org.uk/index.htm [accessed 30 July 2001].

[8]   Smith R. All changed, changed utterly. British medicine will be transformed by the Bristol case. *British Medical Journal* 1998; **316**(7149): 1917–1918.

[9]   Paola F. and Barten S.S. An 'ethics gap' in writing about bioethics: a quantitative comparison of the medical and the surgical literature. *Journal of Medical Ethics* 1995; **21**(2): 84–88.

[10] Sade R.M., Williams T.H., Perlman D.J. *et al.* Ethics gap in surgery. *The Annals of Thoracic Surgery* 2000; **69**(2): 326–329.

[11] *The Society of Thoracic Surgeons Code of Ethics.* www.sts.org/sections/ aboutthesociety/policies/code%20of%20ethics/ [accessed 25 April 2014].

[12] *The American Association of Thoracic Surgery Code of Ethics.* http://aats.org/ association/policies/Code_of_Ethics.cgi [accessed 25 April 2014].

[13] Sade R. Ethical issues in thoracic surgery. *Thoracic Surgery Clinics* 2005; **15**(4): xi–xiii. http://www.thoracic.theclinics.com/article/S1547-4127(05)00091-5/ fulltext [accessed 25 April 2014).

[14] Bromage D.I., McLauchlan D.J., and Nightingale A.K. Do cardiologists and cardiac surgeons need ethics? Achieving happiness for a drug user with endocarditis. *Heart* 2009; **95**(11): 885–887.

[15] Stirrat G.M. Education in ethics. *Clinical Perinatology* 2003; **30**(1): 1–15.

[16] *Schloendorff* v *Society of New York Hospital* [1914].

[17] Johnson J. *Psychological interventions and coping with surgery.* In *Handbook of Psychology and Health,* 1984; pp. 167–188.

[18] Hawkins C. and Paterson I. Medicolegal audit in the West Midlands region: analysis of 100 cases. *British Medical Journal (Clin Res Ed)* 1987; **295**(6612): 1533–1536.

[19] GMC (ed.) *Seeking Patient's Consent. The Ethical Considerations.* London: GMC, 1998.

[20] GMC (ed.) *Consent: Patients and Doctors Making Decisions Together.* London: GMC, 2008.

[21] Dept. of Health (ed.) *Reference Guide to Consent for Examination or Treatment.* London: Dept. of Health, 2001.

[22] Dyer C. Consultant suspended for not getting consent for cardiac procedure. *British Medical Journal* 1998; **316**(7136): 955.

[23] Vohra H.A., Ledsham J, Vohra H. *et al.* Issues concerning consent in patients undergoing cardiac surgery-the need for patient-directed improvements: a UK perspective. *Cardiovascular Surgery* 2003; **11**(1): 64–69.

[24] Howlader M.H., Dhanji A.R., Uppal R. *et al.* Patients' views of the consent process for adult cardiac surgery: questionnaire survey. *Scandinavian Cardiovascular Journal* 2004; **38**(6): 363–368.

[25] Mishra P.K., Ozalp F., Gardner R.S. *et al.* Informed consent in cardiac surgery: is it truly informed? *Journal of Cardiovascular Medicine (Hagerstown)* 2006; **7**(9): 675–681.

[26] Shinebourne E. For paternalism in the doctor–patient relationship. In R. Gillon (ed.) *Principles of Health Care Ethics*. Chichester: John Wiley and Sons, 1994.

[27] Tobias J.S. and Souhami R.L. Fully informed consent can be needlessly cruel. *British Medical Journal* 1993; **307**(6913): 1199–1201.

[28] Beresford N., Seymour L., Vincent C. *et al.* Risks of elective cardiac surgery: what do patients want to know? *Heart* 2001; **86**(6): 626–631.

[29] Ivarsson B., Larsson S., Lührs C. *et al.* Extended written pre-operative information about possible complications at cardiac surgery — do the patients want to know? *European Journal of Cardiothoracic Surgery* 2005; **28**(3): 407–414.

[30] Scott R., Blackstone E.H., McCarthy P.M. *et al.* Isolated bypass grafting of the left internal thoracic artery to the left anterior descending coronary artery: late consequences of incomplete revascularization. *Journal of Thoracic and Cardiovascular Surgery* 2000; **120**(1): 173–184.

[31] Yusuf S., Zucker D., Peduzzi P. *et al.* Effect of coronary artery bypass graft surgery on survival: overview of 10-year results from randomised trials by the Coronary Artery Bypass Graft Surgery Trialists Collaboration. *Lancet* 1994; **344**(8922): 563–570.

[32] Hlatky M.A., Boothroyd D.B., Bravata D.M. *et al.* Coronary artery bypass surgery compared with percutaneous coronary interventions for multi-vessel disease: a collaborative analysis of individual patient data from ten randomised trials. *Lancet* 2009; **373**(9670): 1190–1197.

[33] Serruys P.W., Morice M.C., Kappetein A.P. *et al.* Percutaneous coronary intervention versus coronary-artery bypass grafting for severe coronary artery disease. *New England Journal of Medicine* 2009; **360**(10): 961–972.

[34] Larobina M.E., Merry C.J., Negri J.C. *et al.* Is informed consent in cardiac surgery and percutaneous coronary intervention achievable? *ANZ Journal of Surgery* 2007; **77**(7): 530–534.

[35] Shinebourne E.A. Ethics of innovative cardiac surgery. *British Heart Journal* 1984; **52**(6): 597–601.

[36] Woolley F.R. Ethical issues in the implantation of the total artificial heart. *New England Journal of Medicine* 1984; **310**(5): 292–296.

[37] Morreim E.H. Surgically implanted devices: ethical challenges in a very different kind of research. *Thoracic Surgery Clinics* 2005; **15**(4): 555–563, viii.

[38] Jatene A.D., Fontes V.F., Paulista P.P. *et al.* Anatomic correction of transposition of the great vessels. *Journal of Thoracic and Cardiovascular Surgery* 1976; **72**(3): 364–370.

[39] Yacoub M.H., Radley-Smith R., and Hilton C.J. Anatomical correction of complete transposition of the great arteries and ventricular septal defect in infancy. *British Medical Journal* 1976; **1**(6018): 1112–1114.

[40] Ross D., Rickards A., and Somerville J. Transposition of the great arteries: logical anatomical arterial correction. *British Medical Journal* 1976; **1**(6018): 1109–1111.

[41] Bull C., Yates R., Sarkar D. *et al.* Scientific, ethical, and logistical considerations in introducing a new operation: a retrospective cohort study from paediatric cardiac surgery. *British Medical Journal* 2000; **320**(7243): 1168–1173.

[42] Hasan A., Pozzi M., and Hamilton J.R. New surgical procedures: can we minimise the learning curve? *British Medical Journal* 2000; **320**(7228): 171–173.

[43] Jacobs J.P., Cerfolio R.J., and Sade R.M. The ethics of transparency: publication of cardiothoracic surgical outcomes in the lay press. *Annals of Thoracic Surgery* 2009; **87**(3): 679–686.

[44] Jacobs M.L., Jacobs J.P., Jenkins K.J. *et al.* Stratification of complexity: the Risk Adjustment for Congenital Heart Surgery-1 method and the Aristotle Complexity Score--past, present, and future. *Cardiology in the Young* 2008; **18 Suppl 2**: 163–168.

[45] Shroyer A.L., Coombs L.P., Peterson E.D. *et al.* The Society of Thoracic Surgeons: 30-day operative mortality and morbidity risk models. *Annals of Thoracic Surgery* 2003; **75**(6): 1856–1864; discussion 1864–1865.

[46] Welke K.F., Shen I., and Ungerleider R.M. Current assessment of mortality rates in congenital cardiac surgery. *Annals of Thoracic Surgery* 2006; **82**(1): 164–170; discussion 170–171.

[47] O'Brien S.M., Jacobs J.P., Clarke D.R. *et al.* Accuracy of the Aristotle Basic Complexity Score for classifying the mortality and morbidity potential of congenital heart surgery operations. *Annals of Thoracic Surgery* 2007; **84**(6): 2027–2037; discussion 2027–2037.

[48] Ramsay S. Publishing cardiac surgeons' outcome data. *Circulation* 2006; **114**(5): f118–19.

[49] Prendergast T.J. and Luce J.M. Increasing incidence of withholding and withdrawal of life support from the critically ill. *American Journal of Respiratory Critical Care Medicine* 1997; **155**(1): 15–20.

[50] Way J., Back A.L., and Curtis J.R. Withdrawing life support and resolution of conflict with families. *British Medical Journal* 2002; **325**(7376): 1342–1345.

[51] GMC (ed.) *Withholding and withdrawing life-prolonging treatments: Good practice in decision-making.* London: GMC, 2002.

[52] Reeves R.B., Jr. The ethics of cardiac transplantation in man. *Bulletin of the New York Academy of Medicine* 1969; **45**(5): 404–412.

[53] Mehra M.R., Kobashigawa J., Starling R. *et al.* Listing criteria for heart transplantation: International Society for Heart and Lung Transplantation guidelines for the care of cardiac transplant candidates — 2006. *Journal of Heart and Lung Transplantation* 2006; **25**(9): 1024–1042.

[54] Zuckermann A., Dunkler D., Deviatko E. *et al.* Long-term survival (>10 years) of patients >60 years with induction therapy after cardiac transplantation. *European Journal of Cardiothoracic Surgery* 2003; **24**(2): 283–291; discussion 291.

[55] Demers P., Moffatt S., Oyer P.E. *et al.* Long-term results of heart transplantation in patients older than 60 years. *Journal of Thoracic and Cardiovascular Surgery* 2003; **126**(1): 224–231.

[56] Peraira J.R., Segovia J., Fuentes R. *et al.* Differential characteristics of heart transplantation in patients older than 60 years. *Transplantation Proceedings* 2003; **35**(5): 1959–1961.

[57] Trulock E.P., Edwards L.B., Taylor D.O. *et al.* Registry of the International Society for Heart and Lung Transplantation: twenty-second official adult lung and heart-lung transplant report — 2005. *Journal of Heart and Lung Transplantation* 2005; **24**(8): 956–967.

[58] Hosenpud J.D., Bennett L.E., Keck B.M. *et al.* The Registry of the International Society for Heart and Lung Transplantation: seventeenth official report — 2000. *Journal of Heart and Lung Transplantation* 2000; **19**(10): 909–931.

[59] Radovancevic B., McGiffin D.C., Kobashigawa J.A. *et al.* Retransplantation in 7,290 primary transplant patients: a 10-year multi-institutional study. *Journal of Heart and Lung Transplantation* 2003; **22**(8): 862–868.

[60] Collins E.G. and Mozdzierz G.J. Cardiac retransplantation: determining limits. *Heart Lung* 1993; **22**(3): 206–212.

[61] Nagele H., Kalmár P., Rödiger W. *et al.* Smoking after heart transplantation: an underestimated hazard? *European Journal of Cardiothoracic Surgery* 1997; **12**(1): 70–74.

[62] Orens J.B., Estenne M., Arcasoy S. *et al.* International guidelines for the selection of lung transplant candidates: 2006 update — a consensus report from the Pulmonary Scientific Council of the International Society for Heart and Lung Transplantation. *Journal of Heart and Lung Transplantation* 2006; **25**(7): 745–755.

[63] Mehra M.R., Uber P.A, Prasad A. *et al.* Recrudescent tobacco exposure following heart transplantation: clinical profiles and relationship with atherothrombosis risk markers. *American Journal of Transplantation* 2005; **5**(5): 1137–1140.

[64] Moore F.D. New Problems for Surgery. Drugs That Act on the Cell Nucleus Affect the Surgeon's Work on Cancer and on Transplantation. *Science* 1964; **144**: 388–392.

[65] Starnes V.A., Barr M.L., and Cohen R.G. Lobar transplantation. Indications, technique, and outcome. *Journal of Thoracic and Cardiovascular Surgery* 1994; **108**(3): 403–410; discussion 410–411.

[66] Abecassis M., Adams M., Adams P. *et al.* Consensus statement on the live organ donor. *JAMA* 2000; **284**(22): 2919–2926.

[67] Barr M.L., Bourge R.C., Orens J.B. *et al.* Thoracic organ transplantation in the United States, 1994–2003. *American Journal of Transplantation* 2005; **5**(4 Pt 2): 934–949.

[68] Ghods A.J. Renal transplantation in Iran. *Nephrology, Dialysis and Transplantation* 2002; **17**(2): 222–228.

[69] Gill M.B. and Sade R.M. Paying for kidneys: the case against prohibition. *Kennedy Institute of Ethics Journal* 2002; **12**(1): 17–45.

[70] Daar A.S. Xenotransplantation: recent scientific developments and continuing ethical discourse. *Transplantation Proceedings* 2003; **35**(7): 2821–2822.

[71] Nicholas J.M. Infectious risk in xenotransplantation. *Current Opinion in Organ Transplantation* 2006; **11**: 180.

[72] Obama, B. *Executive Order. Removing barriers to responsible scientific research involving human stem cells.* 2009. http://www.whitehouse.gov/the_press_office/Removing-Barriers-to-Responsible-Scientific-Research-Involving-Human-Stem-Cells [accessed 25 April 2014].

[73] McKneally M. Controversies in cardiothoracic surgery: should therapeutic cloning be supported to provide stem cells for cardiothoracic surgery research and treatment? *Journal of Thoracic and Cardiovascular Surgery* 2006; **131**(5): 937–940.

12

Obstetrics and Gynaecological Surgery: The Ethics and Law of Abortion and Sterilisation

Ariel Zosmer

12.1 Introduction

Sexuality and reproduction are central to the human existence and affect all of us as individuals directly or indirectly. Traditions around the world favour notions of fertility and procreation and no culture advocates the goal of a childless partnership. Procreation is a biblical duty — "God blessed them; and God said to them, 'Be fruitful and multiply, and fill the earth, and subdue it'" (Genesis 1:28). In the Hindu tradition — "The purpose of marriage was to beget children, particularly sons, who would carry on the lineage in a patriarchal society" [1: p. 134] and the Catholic Church teaches that the primary blessing of marriage and the primary purpose of sex in marriage is offspring [2: p. 62]. In Islam, children are considered the gift of God and are described in the Qur'an as the "decoration of life" [3: p. 110] and for the Yoruba people in West Africa, as in many sub-Saharan African countries, "…women generally attribute to God the number of children they have. Marriage and having children is viewed as a religious duty" [4: p. 168]. To be unmarried and childless is regarded "…as stopping the flow of life … and hence the diminishing of mankind upon earth" [5].

At the same time, unwanted pregnancies have always existed and fertility control has been practised throughout history. The Ebers papyrus (around 1500 BC) contained prescriptions in use in 2500 BC such as compounded acacia (which produces lactic acid which is still used in many spermicides) [6]. The Mishna (the early Jewish Talmudic period c 200 BC–AD 200) contains references to sterilising potions for both men and women [7: p. 32]. Pomegranate seeds were recognised as anti-fertility agents in Greek medicine and are still used in India, Africa, and some Pacific areas. Plato's laws referred to the "many devices available ... to check propagation" [6] and ferula (giant fennel) was used both as a contraceptive and as an early-term abortifacient according to the Roman writer Soranus (AD 98–138) who also explains the difference between contraception (before conception) and abortion (destruction of what has been conceived) and states that the former is safer than the latter [8]. There is evidence of the use of abortifacients in China in 3000 BC and abortion was widely practiced in Roman times [9]. Abortion (including during the third trimester) is discussed in early Jewish Talmudic scriptures and is allowed in cases where the pregnancy is endangering the life or physical health of the pregnant woman [10].

Although sexuality may be a completely private matter, our tendency to express and share our sexual needs and desires with others and the natural association between sexuality and reproduction makes it inevitable that — "Sexuality and reproduction are never solely self-regarded and merely private. They always have both social consequences and social dimensions" [11].

The expression of the fertile individual's sexuality in a heterosexual relationship will in most cases result in procreation. For both the individual and for the society, this may have direct psychological and emotional consequences but it is also a matter of survival, prosperity, and domination, a matter of economics and politics.

Togonu-Bickersteth tells us that the desire of the contemporary Yoruba people in west Africa for a large family stems from a number of factors such as the desire to ensure survival of sons to continue the lineage in the face of high infant and child mortality rates, the economic contributions of child labour to the household economy, and the expectation of assistance from adult children during old age as there is no formal public assistance [4: pp. 169–170]. Undoubtedly, such considerations are common in many present societies and may have been even more common in the past. According to Shaikh [3: p. 116], Islamic religious scholars oppose family planning as contradicting the need of the Muslim world to grow and as being — "…an external western conspiracy aimed at curtailing the growth and strength of the Muslim world". Undoubtedly, Islamic leaders are not the only religious leaders to consider procreation as the most effective way to expand the power and influence of what they regard as the true religion. In Europe, for hundreds of years, information about the natural contraceptive properties of various plants was passed down orally by generations of midwives [6: pp. 123–125]. It has been suggested that the association that was made between the practices of midwifery and witchcraft has been due to the pro-natalist agenda of certain religious and political leaders [12]. In 1484, Pope Innocent VIII issued a *summis desiderantes* against witchcraft, singling out as especially heinous the crimes — "to ruin and cause to perish the offspring of women and hinder men from begetting and women from conceiving" [6: p. 124]. This may be an early example of the state trying to control the fertility of its citizens.

In contrast, many Native American Indian religious traditions show concern with population size. The Cherokee sacred story tells us that animals introduced diseases into the world because humans were overpopulating the earth and treating them carelessly [13]. In the Navajo account of creation, Coyote warns the people — "If we all live, and continue to increase as we have done, the earth will soon be too small to hold us, and there will be no room for the cornfields" [14]. China's one-child policy which is opposed by large parts of China's citizens [15: p. 3] is a more recent example of the state trying to control population size.

In a democracy such as the UK, fears of population decline were central to the active prosecution of abortionists after World War II. Twenty years later, the perceived threat of a population explosion undoubtedly played an important role in campaigns for free access to safe legal abortion. In the US in November 1959, President Dwight Eisenhower said that — "so long as I am president, this government will have nothing to do with birth control". In August 1965, President Lyndon Johnson urged the American people to — "face forthrightly the multiplying problems of our multiplying populations" [16].

Potts [17] tells us that — "Over the past 25 years population policies have swung back and forth like a pendulum." But according to John Riddle [8] — "It is widely acknowledged that, since at least the second century B.C., populations in the West have been deliberately limiting their rates of growth and, at times, slowing them to below replacement rates. It is thought that this has been achieved through various means such as celibacy and sexual restraint, delayed marriages, suppositories, condoms, abortions, infanticide and child abandonment." It would seem that the back and forth swinging of the individuals' procreation objectives and that of the states' population policies is going on for much longer than Potts suggests, indeed for a very long time. In particular when dealing with the ethics and law of abortion and contraception (in our case sterilisation), it is important to emphasise that such swings in practices (by individuals) and policies (by states) are to a large extent influenced by external factors (e.g., disease, poverty, famine) and that the interests of the individual and that of the state as a representative of the society at large does not necessarily coincide.

12.2 Religion and Fertility Control

The word *philosophy* comes from the Greek "Philosophia" meaning "love of wisdom". In the ancient world there was no "general term for religion" thus, for example, "Judaism to the ancient world was a philosophy" [18] and presented itself as a source of wisdom — "you will display your wisdom and understanding to other people. When they hear about all these statutes (laws), they will say, 'what a wise and understanding people this great nation is'" (Deuteronomy 4:6). So, too, were other religions "philosophies of life" in a quest — "…for enlightenment and betterment. They contain ore from which rich theories of justice and human rights can be extracted" [19]. As many, if not most, people consider themselves to have a religious affiliation at least to some extent, and also because much of the contemporary secular arguments have strong overt or hidden religious roots, it is appropriate to start with an account of religious attitudes towards abortion and sterilisation.

Religions are concerned primarily with human life — "Fundamental to Catholic bioethics is a belief in the sanctity of life: the value of a human life, as a creation of God and a gift in trust, is beyond human evaluation and authority. God maintains dominion over it. In this view, we are stewards, not owners, of our own bodies and are accountable to God for the life that has been given to us" [20]. Because also in the Jewish tradition we are not owners of our life and body but stewards, some believe that we (both patient and doctor) have an obligation to treat illness — "We ... require man to take all reasonable steps to preserve life and health. When beneficence conflicts with autonomy, the former is given precedence" [21]. This extends not only to one's own body and life but to anyone's, to our neighbour, whom we shall treat as we expect to be treated.

Religious bioethics is usually concerned with the intrinsic rightness or wrongness of a particular course of action, and less with pragmatic considerations or consequences. Religions' ethics put less emphasis on individual autonomy than the secular one.

In Jewish traditional law (*Halaha*) procreation is a biblical duty (Genesis 1:28) and contraception is generally not allowed. However, according to most authorities, this duty is addressed to the man only, although the woman has an obligation towards childbearing. The man's biblical duty to procreate is fulfilled once he has two children. This implies that once these children are born, sexual relations may proceed without procreative intent, suggesting that birth control may be used [7: pp. 31–32]. Of course, the rabbinic advice is to continue to have children even after the biblical commandment has been fulfilled. But once the minimum requirements have been achieved, other concerns, such as the woman's health and ability to cope attract more weight.

Women may use contraceptives (*mokh* — a vaginal cotton pad) for personal and especially for health reasons. In fact, when a pregnancy endangers the woman's life or her child's life, contraception is mandated. This relates to the principle of *Pikuach Nefesh* (saving a life), whereby danger to life suspends all commandments (excluding idolatry, adultery, and murder) [22]. "The Bariata of the Three Women" (*Bariata* is a debate in the Gemora (late Talmudic period — AD 200–500) based on the oral tradition of the Mishna (early Talmudic period — 100 BC to AD 200)) describes three cases when contraception must be used as pregnancy must be avoided — "A minor, because she might become pregnant and die. A pregnant woman because she might cause her fetus to become a *sandal* (flattened and crushed by intercourse or, possibly, by a second pregnancy — superfetation). A nursing woman (because she might have to wean her child prematurely and the child would die)" [23]. Contraception may also be considered in other situations where a woman's physical or emotional well-being is in danger [24–26].

Self-mutilation is forbidden by the bible (Leviticus 22:24). This includes destruction of the reproductive organs i.e., sterilisation. Because it is the man's duty to procreate, the prohibition for men is stronger than that for women. Therefore, vasectomy is never permitted but, in extreme circumstances, a Halachic authority may permit tubal ligation in a specific case, where other methods cannot be used and pregnancy would be a serious health concern (including mental health) and every possible aspect of the situation has been considered.

Thus, despite the general ban on contraception, the Orthodox Judaism will allow female contraception, including, in very exceptional cases, sterilisation, in order to preserve the health and the well-being of the woman or that of an existing or a potential child.

Judaism does not ban abortion completely, nor does it allow indiscriminate abortion "on demand". The fetus is regarded as a full-fledged human being — but not quite. The fetus is not considered a *nefesh* (soul) until birth (of the head, or in breech until most of the body emerges) and the first 40 days of conception are considered "like water" in the Mishna. However, deliberately harming a fetus is forbidden and punishable. Both the person who performs the abortion as well as the woman who voluntarily allows it to be done are culpable. But killing a fetus is not equivalent to killing an adult — "And if men strive, and hurt a woman with child, so that her fruit depart and yet no harm follows, he shall be surely punished, according as the woman's husband will lay upon him; and he shall pay as the judges determine. But if any harm follow (to the woman), you shall give life for life" (Exodus 21:22–23). Thus, while killing an innocent adult is considered murder which carries the death penalty, the killing of the fetus (although still considered murder by many authorities despite the above biblical entry) is not a capital punishment.

Abortion is permitted only if there is a direct threat to the life of the pregnant woman by carrying the fetus to term or through the act of childbirth when no other alternatives exist (such as maiming the fetus but not killing it). In such a circumstance, the fetus is considered a *rodef*, a pursuer after the mother with the intent to kill her, and killing the fetus is allowed in self-defence [27]. The woman's mental health may be considered in some cases (such as incest or rape). Although abortion because of fetal or newborn child considerations (suffering or a lethal defect due to malformation or disease) is forbidden by most (but not all) authorities it may be allowed in exceptional cases to avoid harm to the woman on the grounds of mental health.

Contraception and abortion are strictly forbidden by the Catholic Church. The main reason for the ban on contraception is that God's intention in sex is procreation —

God has wisely disposed natural laws and rhythms of fecundity which, of themselves, cause a separation in the succession of births ... [This teaching] is founded upon the inseparable connection, willed by God and unable to be broken by man on its own initiative, between the two meanings of the conjugal act: the unitive meaning and the procreative meaning [28].

Thus, the primary purpose of sex in marriage is offspring and it is wrong to use God's gift of sexuality not for its divine intention. Sex is not to be enjoyed. Fertility control practices are associated with serious sins (fornication, adultery, and prostitution). The joy of sex is a sin that, however, is forgiven as the intention (procreation) is good. Moreover, using contraception is regarded as a decision against creating new life and therefore against a basic human good [29]. But —

When, in 1954, Pius XII approved the rhythm method (abstinence during the fertile period, called Natural Family Planning within Catholic circles) in his 1954 address to midwives, he approved contraceptive intent and result [2: p. 66].

Therefore, natural infertile time can be used to practice sex for reasons other than procreation (intimacy, pleasure). However, fertility may be controlled only by natural ways such as abstinence and breast feeding. Any other methods (e.g., condoms) are strictly forbidden.

The Catholic Church also strictly objects to sterilisation as in its teachings sterilisation is a mutilation of the body which leads to the deprivation of the natural function and which must therefore be rejected unless it is strictly therapeutic — for the physical health such as hysterectomy for cancer or excessive menstrual bleeding.

The Roman Catholic and many other Christian denominations have a very strong line against abortion which Pope Paul VI [30] called an "abominable crime". For them personhood begins at ensoulment — the moment an entity develops a soul [31] which since the nineteenth century is usually taken to be at conception although at different points in time Christian theologians pointed to different stages of pregnancy as being the moment of ensoulment (e.g., 40–80 days after conception or at quickening early in the fifth month) [2: p. 69]. The idea that the fetus is a human being "from the moment of conception" is a relatively new idea. Saint Thomas Aquinas followed Aristotle's view that the soul is the "substantial form" of man and therefore one can not have a soul until it acquires a human shape. In the seventeenth century scientists reported that under microscopes the fertilised ova looked like perfectly formed people which they called "homunculus". If the fertilised egg has a human form then it can have a soul from the start. This idea took hold [32]. Rachels goes on to say —

> Because the church did not traditionally regard abortion as a serious issue, Western law (which developed under the church's influence) did not traditionally treat abortion as a crime. Under the English Common Law, abortion was tolerated even if performed late in pregnancy. In the USA there were no laws prohibiting it until well into the 19th century [32].

The one concession that the Catholic Church is willing to make is that if there is a very serious threat to the mother's life then indirect abortion is permissible. Thus, in the case of an ectopic pregnancy, the removal of a ruptured fallopian tube with the fetus is allowed to save the woman's life. Although this will inevitably kill the fetus there is no intention to do so (as per the doctrine of double effect). A direct attack on the fetus is not allowed under any circumstances, including in cases of fetal malformations or life limiting serious disease or to save the mother's life (e.g., craniotomy in the case of a woman bleeding to death who is unable to deliver a large fetus, as we should not prefer one life instead of another).

The Anglican Church is also generally opposed to family planning and to abortion. However, the 2005 briefing paper on abortion states that —

> The Church of England encourages its members to think through issues themselves in the light of the Christian faith and in dialogue with the Christian community ... The Church of England combines strong opposition to abortion with a recognition that there can be — strictly limited — conditions under which it may be morally preferable to any available alternative ... That in situations where the continuance of a pregnancy threatens the life of the mother a termination of pregnancy may be justified and that there must be adequate and safe provision in our society for such situations ... That in the rare occasions when abortion is carried out beyond 24 weeks, 'Serious foetal handicap' should be interpreted strictly as applying to those conditions where survival is possible only for a very short period — and —
>
> The Synod has not attempted to resolve all the dilemmas which arise in this area, such as when the unborn child has been conceived as a result of rape or the foetus may be known to be at risk of serious handicap. In such cases Anglicans will be agreed on the need to have regard to 'compassion for the mother and a proper responsibility for the life of the unborn child' ... but they may come to different conclusions about the proper course of action in particular cases" [33].

This position differs significantly from that of the Catholic Church.

Unlike Catholicism, in Islam marriage is not exclusively linked to procreation (although this is the primary objective). Both men and women have the right to sexual pleasure, which is independent of one's choice to have children. Most of the various classic Islamic legal schools permitted *coitus interruptus*, called *azl*, as a method of contraception. As this is initiated by the husband the only condition is that the wife agrees. This is because she is entitled to full sexual pleasure and *coitus interruptus* may diminish her pleasure and because she may wish to conceive [3: p. 114]. Eight out of nine classical Islamic legal schools permit contraception [34]. Al-Ghazzali (d. 1111) supported the use of contraceptive practice for various reasons including to protect the life of the woman, her beauty (for the enjoyment of the marriage), and for economic factors. He reasoned that physical and emotional hardship brought about by a large family may push one to resort to crime [35].

Sterilisation is absolutely *Haram* (prohibited) in Shari'ah and most Muslim traditions object to sterilisation as it is a form of mutilation (which is forbidden) and because of the irreversible nature of the procedure which contradicts the primary purpose of marriage (the religious duty to have children). Only in exceptional circumstances when the woman's life or permanent health is severely threatened by pregnancy and no alternatives exist, sterilisation may be permitted by some under the principle that — "Necessities make prohibitions lawful" [36].

It is worth mentioning here that sterilisation of both male and female is allowed in some Muslim countries such as Iran, Turkey, and Tunisia (but not Egypt) reflecting ongoing debate within Muslim communities [37].

Islam strongly opposes abortion. The fetus has the right to life from conception and abortion is therefore considered as murder [38] (the death sentence to a pregnant woman has to be postponed until delivery). The abortion of a formed fetus (after 120 days when it is ensouled) is considered a criminal offence and prohibited by all Islamic legal schools [3: p. 119]. Exceptions include danger to mother's life, where the pregnancy is harming an already suckling child, or where the fetus is expected to be deformed. Abortion is wrong at any time but it may be permissible, or at least not punishable, early in pregnancy. Before 120 days there are different positions in classical Islam ranging from unconditional permission (Zaydi school and some Hanafi and Shafi'i scholars), through conditional permission because of an acceptable justification, to strongly disapproved (Maliki jurists), and complete prohibition (some Maliki, Zahiri, Ibadiyya, and Imamiyya schools). In Iran, Ayatollah Ali Khameni issued a fatwa in favour of abortion for fetuses under ten weeks that were affected by thalassemia and the Islamic Council of South Africa permits abortion up to 120 days for impairment of mental capacity and integrity of the woman or her ability and willingness to accept responsibility [3: p. 121].

In Hinduism the general approach is consequential. The preferred course of action is the one that will cause the least harm to the mother, the father, the fetus, and society. Therefore, although Hinduism generally opposes abortion as contravening the principle of non-violence (*ahimsa*), in some circumstances abortion is permitted. Hinduism is concerned with a scale or hierarchy of values, rather than with absolute values. Therefore, the life and well-being of the mother takes precedence over the rights of the fetus (on the basis of compassion — *daya*). This includes rape, incest, and the mental health of the mother. In India sterilisation and abortion is available practically on demand [1: pp. 129–143].

12.3 The Ethics of Abortion and Sterilisation

Unlike sterilisation that does not involve the termination of a viable pregnancy, abortion is one of the most controversial areas in medical ethics. The contemporary controversy focuses on two main positions: on one side are the "pro-choicers" for whom autonomy, in particular women's autonomy, is the main consideration; and on the other side stand the "pro-lifers" who emphasise the right to life of the fetus.

Before we examine the various arguments it is important to draw attention to the terminology used. The inherent power of the language used in any debate to affect outcome is stronger in our case because the words used in argumentation already imply the outcome. For example, referring to the pregnant woman as "mother" or to the fetus as "unborn child" implies a status which exists according to some (pro-lifers) but not according to others (pro-choicers).

Another thing to point out is that usually the starting question in the debate is — "In what circumstances, if any, is it legitimate for a woman to terminate an unwanted pregnancy?" [39: p. 587]. If this is the starting point the woman who wishes to terminate her pregnancy is already on the defensive. Thus, both the terminology used and the starting point have the potential to affect a rational debate.

12.3.1 *The ethics of abortion*

12.3.1.1 *Some statistics*

In 2003 there were an estimated 205 million pregnancies (live births, spontaneous miscarriages, stillbirths, and induced abortions) worldwide. Of those, about 42 million (20%) ended in voluntary induced abortion [40]. The induced abortion ratio (number of induced abortions per 100 live births) worldwide was 31 (Africa — 17 (range among regions 12–24), Asia — 34 (22–51), Europe — 59 (23–105), Latin America and the Caribbean — 35 (26–42), North America — 33, and Oceania — 22) [40]. The worldwide induced abortion rate (number of induced abortions per 1,000 women aged 15–44) was 29 (Africa — 29 (range among regions 22–39), Asia — 29 (24–39), Europe — 28 (12–44), Latin America and the Caribbean — 31 (25–35), North America — 21. and Oceania — 17) [40].

Of the estimated 42 million abortions induced in 2003, approximately 20 million (48%) occurred outside national legal systems. Illegal abortions are unsafe as they are often performed in clandestine by providers who lack the necessary skills and/or in unhygienic conditions. Over one in four women having an unsafe abortion will develop complications and an estimated five million women are hospitalised every year for treatment of complications related to unsafe abortion [41]. Management of these complications also has a significant cost implication. It was also estimated that in 2003 unsafe abortions resulted in 66,500 deaths (in 2000 this number was estimated at 68,000 or 12.7% of the worldwide maternal deaths) [42]. In Eastern Europe and central Asia, 8–16 per 100 procedures lead to post-abortion complications and 15–50% of maternal deaths are related to abortion [43]. Some of the high-risk abortions are illegal, whereas others are legal but done under poor conditions or using inappropriate methods.

In 2003 the case-fatality rate of unsafe abortion (deaths per 100,000 unsafe abortions) worldwide was estimated to be 300. In Africa, where abortion is highly restricted by law in nearly all countries, there were 650 deaths for every 100,000 procedures, compared with fewer than 10 per 100,000 procedures in developed regions [42].

In contrast, legal abortions are usually safe. In the US, less than 0.3% of women undergoing abortions have a complication that necessitates hospital admission [44]. The mortality rate for legally induced abortions in the US was 0.6 per 100,000 procedures [42]. Abortions (both spontaneous and induced) account for 4% of maternal deaths [45].

In 2008, the total number of abortions in England and Wales was 202,158 (195,296 were to residents and 6,862 to residents of other countries) [46]. This can be compared to an abortion rate of 18.2 per 1,000 resident women aged 15–44 and an abortion ratio (per 100 live births) of

28.5. Surgical abortions accounted for 62% of the total or 125,338. The complication rate was 0.2% [46]. The maternal mortality rate in the UK in 2003–2005 was 14 per 100,000 maternities (live births plus still births at more than 24 weeks' gestation). Maternal mortality rate attributed to legal abortions was 0.09 per 100,000 maternities [47].

12.3.1.2 *Arguments against abortion: the moral status of the fetus*

The main argument against abortion focuses on the moral status of the fetus. The religious view is that what makes an entity distinctly human is a soul. The Roman Catholic Church sees the fetus as ensouled from the moment of conception. The modern secular argument replaces ensoulment with personhood: when personhood may be attributed to an entity (in our case the fetus), this entity has the right to life as any other person and this right should not be violated. Various commentators with no religious affiliation argue for different points in the development of the human being as the demarcation mark, starting from the establishment of the zygote (the fertilised oocyte) through various developmental stages during pregnancy and up to some point after delivery.

Koop [48] argues that conception is the only possible point in time that can be clearly marked as the beginning of personhood — "My question to my pro-abortion friend who will not kill a new born baby is this: would you kill this infant a minute before he was born, or a minute before that, or a minute before that, or a minute before that?". Such an argument assumes that we need to clearly identify a point in time at which life, and personhood, begins. That unlike other relative concepts that gradually transform from one to the other and vice versa (such as day and night) we do need to determine precisely whether an entity is or is not a person and does or does not have a right to life [49].

It has been pointed out, however, that the creation of the new entity (the zygote) is not instantaneous but a process (fertilisation) that normally takes about 22 hours, making it difficult to pinpoint the beginning of life [50]. Second, the zygote has the potential to occasionally develop into two (or even more) distinct embryos, and it is only at the formation of the primitive streak that a completely genetically unique entity may be identified. Furthermore, when exactly the primitive streak is formed is not entirely clear.

Noonan [51] argues that the fetus is a person from conception because at that moment its genetic makeup is complete. A similar view is held by Finnis —

> …the unborn child is, from conception, a person and hence is not to be discriminated against on account of age, appearance or other such factors insofar as such factors are reasonably considered irrelevant where respect for basic human values is in question … (the zygote is) a unique genetic constitution … which thenceforth through its life, however long, will substantially determine the new individual's makeup. This new cell is the first stage in a dynamic integrated system that has nothing much in common with the individual male and female sex cells save that it sprang from a pair of them and will in time produce new sets of them. To say that this is when a person's life began is not to work backwards from maturity, sophistically asking at each point 'How can one draw the line here?' Rather it is to point to a perfectly clear-cut beginning to which each of us can look back … Judith Thomson thinks she began to acquire human characteristics 'by the tenth week' (when fingers, toes, etc. became visible). I cannot think why she overlooks the most radically and distinctively human characteristic of all — the fact that she was conceived of human parents [52].

It has been argued that this preference for humanity (termed speciesism) is as arbitrary as racism, sexism, or nationalism and a "culpable injustice" [53: p. 23]. But Warnock defends this approach —

> I would argue, on the other hand, that the concept of "speciesism" as a form of prejudice is absurd. Far from being arbitrary it is a supremely important moral principle. If someone did not prefer to save a human rather than a dog or a fly we would think him in need of justification … To live in a universe in which we were genuinely species indifferent would be impossible, or if not impossible, in the highest degree undesirable. I do not therefore regard a preference for humanity as "arbitrary", nor do I see it as standing in need of further justification than that we ourselves are human [54].

Some argue that although the embryo is not a person from conception it should be treated as a person because it has the potential to become one. The wrong in killing the embryo is in the deprivation of future life [55–57]. But the potentiality argument suggests —

> ...that we have to regard as morally significant anything which has the potential to become a fully fledged human being and hence have some moral duty to protect and actualize all human potential, then we are in for a very exhausting time of it. For it is not only the fertilized egg, the embryo, that is potentially a full fledged adult. The egg and the sperm taken together but as yet ununited have the same potential [58].

If this is the case, then abstinence may be immoral as it deprives someone of a future life [59]. Moreover, a medical student has the potential to become a doctor but no one treats him as being a doctor. I may have the potential to learn how to speak Albanian but no one treats me as if I actually spoke Albanian. Dworkin argues that —

> Whether abortion is against the interests of a fetus must depend on whether the fetus itself has interests at the time the abortion is performed, not whether interests will develop if no abortion takes place [60: p. 19].

Furthermore, it is questionable whether it is wrong to deprive someone of a future that they are unaware of [61]. McMahan [62] argues that killing someone who has no awareness of his future is not as bad as killing someone who is aware of his future, implying that killing a fetus may not be as wrong as killing a child or an adult (this may also imply that killing someone in a (temporary) coma may not be as wrong as killing someone who is conscious). The potentiality argument is also rejected by those who believe that the fetus is a person from conception — "he or she is a human being and human person with potential, not merely potential human person or potential human being" [63].

It has also been argued that because of the doubt as to when personhood starts it is better to be on the safe side and err in favour of life as it is better to treat a non-person as a person than to treat a person as a non-person —

> Perception of the status of the embryo derives in many cases from the presence or absence of religious belief … The dispute reaches stalemate … The humanity of the embryo is unproven and unprovable. But that acts both ways. Just as I cannot prove that humanity was divinely created and that each and every one of us possesses an immortal soul, so it cannot be proved that it is not so [64].

Tollefsen argues that it is not necessary to prove that embryos are persons. Because killing is such a serious wrong —

> The standards which must be met to permit killing must be pretty high — where there is reasonable doubt, where there is room for reasonable persons to disagree, the default position … should not be permissive [65].

It is therefore for those who wish to destroy embryos to show that they are not persons.

If we accept that a person has a right to life, a right that is not stronger or weaker than any other person's right to life, and that personhood starts at conception, then not only abortion but also some forms of contraception, including the contraceptive pill and the intrauterine contraceptive device, as well as embryo research and discarding spare embryos created by in-vitro fertilisation, are immoral. For many, this conclusion is clearly difficult to palate. It is no wonder, therefore, that various arguments have been put forward to justify different cut offs which will make at least some abortions (as well as contraception modalities and embryo handling) morally acceptable.

Some consider that the fetus becomes a distinct entity not at conception but when the primitive streak appears — at about 14–15 days [66]. Warnock explains the decision of the "Warnock Report" (The Report of the Committee of Enquiry into Human Fertilisation and Embryology) not to allow to keep or to use embryos after 14 days —

> Fourteen days was decided on as the limit because of the great change in the development of the embryo heralded by the development of the

primitive streak ... Even though before that an embryo has a genetic individuality, it has no pattern of human identity, any more than human tissue has. The history of each person who is born can be traced back to the development of the primitive streak and not before. Before that there could have been two or three people formed of the same material [67].

According to the Warnock committee, at this point in its development (14 days) the embryo acquires a moral status although not personhood. The committee, chaired by Mary Warnock, was faced with a most serious dilemma: how to make the cake without breaking the eggs. How to allow embryo research while at the same time providing a response against the slippery slope argument manifested in the moral position advanced by the committee itself that — "...every one agrees that it is completely unacceptable to make use of a child or an adult as the subject of research procedures which may cause harm or death" [68]. In this sense the line drawn by the Warnock committee is arbitrary. Nevertheless, according to Williams, it is reasonable to draw it —

It may be said that a line of this kind cannot possibly be reasonable since it has to be drawn between two adjacent cases in the range ... that are not different enough to distinguish ... But though the line is not, in this sense, uniquely reasonable, it is nevertheless reasonable to draw a line there (because) ... it is reasonable to distinguish in some way unacceptable cases from acceptable cases, (because) the only way of doing that in the circumstances is to draw a sharp line, (and) it cannot be an objection to drawing the line here that it would have been no worse to draw it somewhere else — if that were an objection, then one could conclude that one had no reason to draw it anywhere, and that is a style of argument that led to the death of Buridan's ass, who ... died of starvation between two piles of hay because neither pile had any characteristic that drew him to it rather than to the other [69].

The Committee of Inquiry into Human Fertilisation and Embryology chaired by Mary Warnock was commissioned to make recommendations on the regulation of fertility treatment and embryo research. While drawing the line at 14 days paved the way for fertility treatment and embryo research (while coincidently providing a moral justification for oral contraceptives and IUD) it does not solve the problem of surgical abortion as at 14 days the existence of the pregnancy is usually yet unknown.

For many years, "quickening" (the feeling by the mother of the fetal movements) was accorded moral significance, as it was perceived as the moment life begins. Today, with the benefit of ultrasound, we know that the fetus moves much earlier than was previously thought. This is another good example of knowledge, gained through technological advances, changing moral perceptions.

For some, personhood starts at viability (being born alive — currently about 22 weeks' gestation) [70: p. 17] as at this point the fetus is no longer exclusively dependent on the mother. As it may live independently (although with medical support) it is now "separate" and should therefore be regarded as a person. However, it has been pointed out that this may mean that the moral status of the fetus may depend on when (in history) or where (in the world) it exists [71]. While in some countries a 24 weeks' baby may survive with the aid of state of the art medical care, this may not be so in many other places. Moreover, technology may develop to such an extent that from conception the embryo is "viable" [72]. Such a definition of personhood also depends on the definition of viability as a premature baby is completely dependent on others and complete independence is in fact not possible until the child is several years old.

For others, the approach should be reversed: if we can determine when human life ends we will be able to determine when human life begins. As it is accepted by many that brain death marks death, then the beginning of brain activity marks the beginning of life [59]. The development of the brain provides the capacity for sentience and consequently some form of consciousness and self-awareness [73]. Therefore, at sentience (the ability to experience pain and pleasure), which may be around 26 weeks' gestation [74, 75], the fetus has interests and thus acquires a moral status [76: p. 5]. It has been argued, however, that sensation or sentience (that can be experienced by animals for example) is not enough to turn an individual into a person —

> I argue that the moral status of the embryo and indeed of any individual is determined by its possession of those features which make normal adult human individuals morally more important than sheep or goats or embryos [77].

For Harris a person is a "rational self-conscious being" and that does not start until some time after birth. This approach could in fact also lead to the view that personhood does not begin until some time after birth.

To some commentators personhood begins at birth. While until birth the fetus may be regarded as part of the woman's body, after birth it is an entirely separate entity. Furthermore, until birth the fetus is totally dependent on the woman while after birth the child may be cared for by others. The UK law is clear that only after birth is the child regarded as a person with independent legal rights [78]. Nevertheless, although birth is a dramatic event which is significant in terms of the relationship between the mother and her child and between the child and the rest of us, it is difficult to see why the place a 28 weeks' fetus/child is in (womb or incubator) should alter its moral status. Birth as a demarcation line seems as arbitrary as any other.

According to the gradualist approach the respect for the fetus grows with its development [79: p. 228]. This view sees the status of the fetus changing during pregnancy from being a human organism to a human being to being a human person. The Polkinghorne committee argues for —

a special status for the living human foetus at every stage of its development which we wish to characterize as a profound respect based on its potential to develop into a fully formed human being [80].

The gradualist view is the approach adopted by the British Medical Association and — "…is reflected in the current legislation which permits different time limits for different grounds for abortion" [70: p. 15]. This compromise between saying that the fetus has no moral status at all and regarding the fetus as having the full moral status of a person will probably appeal to many in both the pro-choice and the pro-life camps [81] as many in the former camp are uncomfortable with very late terminations (thus accepting that the fetus has at least some value) while many in the latter camp will accept abortions in cases of rape (thus accepting that the fetus does not have the moral status of an adult).

12.3.1.3 *Personhood, rationality, and self-consciousness*

In the seventeenth century the philosopher John Locke tried to define personhood —

> ...we must consider what person stands for: which, I think, is a thinking intelligent being, that has reason and reflection, and can consider itself, the same thinking thing, in different times and places; which it does only by consciousness which is inseparable from thinking and seems to me essential to it; it being impossible for any one to perceive without perceiving that he does perceive [82].

Thus, rationality and self-consciousness (or at least the ability to acquire a concept of itself) characterise a person and distinguish a person [83]. For Harris — "...a person will be any being capable of valuing its own existence" [53: p. 18]. And, following Locke, only rational and self-conscious beings have such capability [53: p. 15]. If so, neither a fetus nor a newborn infant are persons [84]. "We must recall however, that when we kill a new-born infant there is no person whose life has begun. When I think of myself as the person I now am, I realise that I did not come into existence until sometime after my birth" [85].

While in legal terms a person with rights exists only after birth, Gillon argues that morally a newborn baby is not different from a fetus immediately prior to birth —

> UK law, like that of many other jurisdictions, is explicit that a fetus is not legally speaking a person and does not have the legal rights of persons including the right to life enjoyed by (natural) persons, whereas a born child is a person and does have a right to life. While in practical terms the simple criterion of birth is generally easy to apply and corresponds to a stage when what was previously hidden and private inside another human being is now a revealed, public, and clearly separate social entity, as a criterion for moral differentiation of a human being's intrinsic moral status it seems highly implausible. Essentially it is a criterion of what might be dubbed biological geography, asserting that a human being does not have a right to life if it lies north of a vaginal introitus but has a right to life once it has passed south and has (entirely) emerged

from the vagina. What morally relevant changes can there have been in the fetus in its passage from inside to outside its mother's body to underpin such a momentous change in its intrinsic moral status? [86].

Warren argues that while the fetus may be human, it is not yet a person and its potential to become a person does not override the rights of the pregnant woman. She suggests the following criteria for personhood —

1) Consciousness ... and in particular the capacity to feel pain, 2) Reasoning (the developed capacity to solve new and relatively complex problems), 3) Self-motivated activity..., 4) The capacity to communicate..., 5) The presence of self-concept, and self-awareness... We needn't suppose that an entity must have all these attributes to be properly considered a person ... Neither do we need to insist that any one of these criteria is necessary for personhood ... All we need to claim, to demonstrate that a fetus is not a person, is that any being which satisfies none of 1–5 is certainly not a person. I consider this claim to be so obvious that I think anyone who denied it, and claimed that a being that satisfies none of 1–5 was a person all the same, would thereby demonstrate that he had no notion at all of what a person is — perhaps because he had confused the concept of personhood with that of genetic humanity ... If 1–5 are indeed the primary criteria of personhood, then it is clear that genetic humanity is neither necessary or sufficient for establishing that an entity is a person ... A fetus is a human being which is not yet a person, and which therefore cannot coherently be said to have full moral rights ... We have seen that a fetus does not resemble a person in any way which can support the claim that it has even some of the same rights. But what about its potential, the fact that if nurtured and allowed to develop naturally it will probably become a person? ... It is hard to deny that the fact that an entity is a potential person is a strong prima facie reason for not destroying it: but we need not conclude from this that a potential person has a right to life ... But even if a potential person does have some prima facie right to life, such a right could not possibly outweigh the right of a woman to obtain an abortion, since the rights of any actual person invariably outweigh those of any potential person, whenever the two conflict [87].

But if we follow this logic we have to conclude that infanticide is permissible [84], a conclusion that for many is not acceptable —

> We treat babies in certain ways and not in others: not for example, as if their lives were at our disposal. Bioethics demand for what reason we do so, but there is no reason — or, to put the same point differently, their being babies is the reason, all the reason in the world [88].

According to Abbott such definitions of personhood would exclude not only fetuses, but also a significant proportion of children and incapacitated adults —

> What makes one a person (or human in the moral sense)? Warren suggests five "traits" …Note how deftly Warren plies her trade. A fetus might be able to feel pain, but surely he or she is unable to reason, especially with developed capacity. What is shocking about this criterion (2) is that a two-year old may fail to meet it. What this means…, and let us be direct about it, is that we must restrain our emotions and come to regard an infant as not a person at all but a mere clump of genetic humanity. Are not then the comatose patient, the schizophrenic, the catatonic, the unaided mute, the paraplegic in danger of slipping into that awful category "genetic human"? We must ask what the consequences are of this collapsing humanity, this clarification of the "confusion" over the genetic and the moral senses of humanity … There are very few general laws of social science, but we can offer one that has a deserved claim: the restriction of the concept of humanity in any sphere never enhances a respect for human life. It did not enhance the rights of slaves, prisoners of war, criminals, traitors, women, children, Jews, blacks, heretics, workers, capitalists, Slavs, Gypsies. The restriction of the concept of personhood in regard to the fetus will not do so either … Warren approached the question "what is human?" in terms of "what characteristics must an entity have in order to claim right?" …To be human in any moral sense is to have the ability to be a holder of rights. To be a holder of rights one must pass a test of independence in order to establish that one is in a position to claim those rights [89].

12.3.1.3 *Autonomy and abortion*

On the other side of the debate stand the pro-choicers who emphasise the woman's autonomy and her right to bodily integrity. If the fetus is not a person or has no rights or interests at least until birth then the case against abortion is difficult to defend. But if the fetus is a person or has rights or interests then his interests are set against the interests of the woman.

One approach emphasises the woman's right to bodily integrity —

You wake up in the morning and find yourself back to back with an unconscious violinist. A famous unconscious violinist. He has been found to have a fatal kidney ailment, and the society of Music Lovers has canvassed all the available medical records and found that you alone have the right blood type to help. They have therefore kidnapped you, and last night the violinist's circulatory system was plugged into yours, so that your kidneys can be used to extract poisons from his blood as well as your own. The director of the hospital now tells you, "look, we're sorry the Society of Music Lovers did this to you — we would never have permitted it if we had known. But still, they did it, and the violinist is now plugged into you. To unplug you would be to kill him. But never mind, it's only for nine months. By then he will have recovered from his ailment, and can safely be unplugged from you [90: pp. 48–49].

The case that Thomson makes here is that even if the fetus is a person (an assumption she makes only for the purpose of the article) the fetus has no right to use the woman's body without her consent. Your right to bodily integrity means that you are under no moral obligation to remain attached to the violinist. You are under no obligation to act like a Good Samaritan. Therefore, you will be justified to unplug the violinist to whom you are attached against your will. Similarly, the woman is justified to have an abortion if she is unwilling to continue with the pregnancy.

Thomson's scenario works well in the case of rape but is not convincing in other cases. For women who have consensual intercourse and use contraception Thomson gives the following answer —

> Suppose it were like this: people-seeds drift about in the air like pollen, and if you open your windows, one may drift in and take root in your carpets or upholstery. You don't want children, so you fix up your windows with fine mesh screens, the very best you can buy. As can happen, however, and on very, very rare occasions does happen, one of the screens is defective; and a seed drifts in and take root. Does the person-plant who now develops have a right to use of your house? Surely not — despite the fact that you voluntarily opened your windows, you knowingly kept carpets and upholstery furniture, and you knew that screens were sometimes defective [90: p. 59].

But what about the woman who does not use contraception? Thomson [90: p. 58] does not give a convincing answer to this possibility as she compares the fetus to a burglar. This analogy does not work well as the womb is the natural place for the fetus that has no intention to invade or harm.

It has been argued, however, that as the woman knows that contraceptives are not 100% reliable and if she is prepared to take the risk she should also accept the responsibility [76: p. 78] —

> you joined the Society of Music Lovers and undertook to be plugged by lottery if necessary. If you are selected you are morally bound to remain plugged because you took on responsibility when you joined the Society [87].

Also, while the violinist is a stranger to the woman the fetus is not. She is his mother, and parents have a duty towards their children (pro-choicers reply that parents are not obliged to donate organs to save their child's life [91]).

Abortion has also been regarded as an act of self-defence against the bodily intrusion and pain caused by the pregnancy which has been compared to "rape, slavery, kidnapping and battery" [92] when it is done without consent. However, pregnancy does not usually pose a direct and imminent threat to life to justify killing. Moreover, the fetus is innocent and has no intention to harm.

It has been pointed out that in Thomson's violinist scenario the unplugging may be regarded as an omission while during a (surgical) abortion the fetus is actively killed (an act). Also, by unplugging the violinist there is no intention to kill (the doctrine of double effect, see Foot [93]) while during surgical abortion the intention is to kill the fetus.

A different approach is to see abortion in the context of the right of woman to equality with man — "Abortion promises to women sex with men on the same reproductive terms as men have sex with women" [94: p. 99].

Some in the pro-choice camp see abortion as a matter of privacy. Abortion involves very serious moral, social, and personal issues which are for the pregnant woman, and only for her, to decide [94: p. 99]. The husband, doctor, or society should have no say in a matter which concerns the individual woman only. The problem of the privacy argument is that it underplays the other arguments of bodily integrity and equality and only requires that the state should not restrict abortion but removes the obligation of the state to provide funding for abortion facilities [94: pp. 96–97]. McDonagh argues that —

> defining the problem of abortion as a problem of privacy and choice by the [US] Supreme court constitutionally and politically on the basis of a very traditional model of motherhood, one invoking cultural and ethical depictions of women as maternal, self sacrificing nurturers by pro-lifers and (as we might not expect) by pro-choice advocates. This resulted in a rigid, serious consequence — failure to obtain access to abortion services for women in the form of public funding of abortions ... In the case of abortion rights, therefore, we must confront the task of expanding ethical norms appropriate for women to include the norm of self-defence as a justification for the right to obtain an abortion. Only by so doing can we complete the agenda, in order to obtain both a constitutional and political guarantee of access to abortion services [95].

Some pro-choicers reject the emphasis on the woman's rights and prefer to focus on the relationship between the woman and her fetus —

> Their (rights) ultimate flaw resides in the inability of the liberal rights position to cope with caring, interdependent relationships. This means that a position which is based on the individual rights of the woman

alone inevitably appears self-centred and inhumane. Basing the claim for access to abortion on women's individual rights has forced feminists to maintain a hopelessly insensitive position on the status of the foetus [96].

Finally, it has been argued that it is wrong to concentrate on the moral status of the fetus in isolation from the woman as by doing so we are setting the interests of the fetus in conflict with those of the mother — "…The only point of recognizing fetal personhood, or a separate fetal entity, is to assert the interests of the fetus against the pregnant woman" [97]. Rather, the focus should be on the relationship between mother and fetus as —

> her fetus is not merely in her as an inanimate object might be, or something live but alien that has been transplanted into her body. It is "of her and is hers more than anyone's" because it is, more than anyone else's, her creation and her responsibility; it is alive because she has made it come alive [60: p. 55].

Interestingly, some feminists use the relationship model to argue against abortion as there is —

> …a prima facie inconsistency between an ethics of care and abortion. Quite simply, abortion is a failure to care for one living being who exist in a particular intimate relationship to oneself. If empathy, nurturance, and taking responsibility for caring for others are characteristics of the feminine voice, then abortion does not appear to be a feminine response to an unwanted pregnancy [98].

However, relationship argument can be used to support both sides of the debate —

> A feminist challenge to fetocentrism has to assert that, while some fetuses may become at some point transplantable, no fetus is actually viable. Fetuses are biologically dependent on a pregnant woman and will be physically and socially dependent on her after birth. This dependence provides the basis for both her moral obligation to regard the fetus with care and her moral right to decide whether to keep it [99].

12.3.2 *Ethical considerations of sterilisation*

Sterilisation is intended to be permanent and generally irreversible. The irreversibility of sterilisation is the focus of the ethical objection to such procedures as if the woman later changes her mind or her circumstances change the permanent loss of fertility cannot be reversed. It has also been argued that in many cases the decision to undergo sterilisation is not free from coercion or personal or social pressures. Nevertheless, apart from objection on religious grounds, sterilisation for a woman who wishes to be sterilised, is fully informed of the implications, and consents to the procedure is ethically acceptable. It has also to be remembered that in the era of in-vitro fertilisation, oocyte donation, and surrogacy, the irreversibility of sterilisation is no longer absolute.

The main ethical objections are in cases where sterilisation is non-consensual. National eugenic sterilisation programs were introduced not only in Nazi Germany but also in liberal democratic countries such as the US, Canada, Switzerland, France, Austria, and all Scandinavian countries where state sponsored sterilisations of, among others, people with mental illness or learning difficulties, or those convicted of criminal or sexual offences went on sometimes under the guise of voluntarism until the mid 1970s. In Japan people with mental illness, learning difficulties, or disabled were still sterilised against their will in the 1990s [100]. Although coercive sterilisation was always disputed by the Chinese government most reports suggest that more or less forced sterilisations took place mainly in rural areas until at least the mid 1980s [15: pp. 108–109] and possibly to this day.

Today the ethical problem concerns individual cases and focuses on the basic right to reproduce. Such a right can not be absolute as in normal circumstances it requires the cooperation of another person who is under no obligation to cooperate. In addition (or alternatively), such an absolute right to reproduce will mean unlimited access to assisted reproduction techniques including surrogacy which again is unacceptable. Alternatively, it has been proposed that the right to reproduce is the right to retain the capacity to reproduce [101]. It has also been argued that the definition of reproduction should be extended to include not only the pregnancy and delivery but also the subsequent care for the child as mentally handicapped persons who may be able to carry the pregnancy to the end and deliver may not be able to care for the child after its birth and such cases may justify interference with the right to reproduce [102].

Although today very few people openly support eugenics many support sterilisation of incompetent people in what is called "their best interests". In this context best interests should be interpreted in a broad sense — not just medical but also social, emotional, and psychological.

12.4 Legal Aspects

12.4.1 *Legal aspects of abortion*

The United Nations identified the grounds on which abortion is permitted by various countries' law:

1) to save the woman's life,
2) to preserve physical health,
3) to preserve mental health,
4) in case of rape or incest,
5) for foetal impairment,
6) for economic or social reasons, and
7) on request [103].

Almost all countries permit abortion to save the woman's life either explicitly or under the general criminal law principle of necessity. Some countries provide detailed lists of what is considered a life threatening situation while in most countries this is left to the physician's judgement. Five countries — Chile, El Salvador, Nicaragua, Malta, and the Holy See (the Vatican) — have provisions restricting the performance of abortion but even in these countries, it is unclear whether a defence of necessity would be rejected by the courts. In most countries the law permits abortion to preserve the physical (88% of countries in developed regions and 60% of countries in the less developed regions) or mental (86% and 57% respectively) health of the woman. Again, the definitions of physical or mental health vary: in some countries the term health is broadly defined allowing for interpretation or inclusion of both physical and mental health, while other countries have lists of conditions that are accepted as grounds for abortion. Abortion in cases of rape or incest is permitted in 84% of developed countries but only in 37% of countries in the less developed regions while on the grounds of foetal impairment abortions are allowed in 84% and 32% of countries respectively. Several countries specify the type and level of impairment necessary to justify an abortion. Abortion on economic or social grounds is permitted in 78% and 19% of countries respectively. Finally, in 67% and 15% of countries respectively the woman does not have to justify abortion or is only required to state that she is in a situation of crisis or distress (abortion on request) [103].

In many countries, before abortion may be legally performed, various procedural requirements must be met. These include gestational age limits, mandatory waiting period, parental or spousal consent, third-party authorisation, the categories of health providers permitted to perform abortions, the types of medical facilities where abortions may be performed, and mandatory counselling. Moreover, even when abortion is permitted, access to abortion services may be limited [103].

In the UK, under the common law, abortion was criminal only after quickening (around 16–18 weeks' gestation) when it was considered homicide or manslaughter but not murder. Abortion at any stage became a felony under the 1803 Act that also introduced the death penalty for abortion after quickening. The 1837 Offences Against the Person Act removed the distinction between abortion before and after quickening (as well as the capital punishment) [39: p. 595]. The Offences Against the Person Act 1861 which still applies prohibits unlawful abortion —

> Every woman, being with child, who, with intent to procure her own miscarriage, shall unlawfully administer to herself poison or other noxious thing, or shall unlawfully use any instrument or other means whatsoever with the like intent, and whosoever, with intent to procure the miscarriage of any woman, whether she be or not with child, shall unlawfully administer to her or cause to be taken by her any poison or other noxious thing, or shall unlawfully use any instrument or other means whatsoever with the like intent, shall be guilty of felony, and being convicted thereof shall be liable to be kept in penal servitude for life [104: pp. 1–2].

The word "unlawful" was intended to create an exception in cases where abortion was performed in order to save the life of the pregnant woman. Similarly, the Infant Life (Preservation) Act 1929 prohibits abortion unless it is done to save the woman's life —

Section 1: Punishment for child destruction — (1) Subject to hereinafter in this section provided, any person who, with intent to destroy the life of a child capable of being born alive, by any wilful act causes a child to die before it has an existence independent of its mother, shall be guilty of felony, to wit, of child destruction, and shall be liable on conviction thereof on indictment to penalty servitude for life. Provided that no person shall be found guilty of an offence under this section unless it is proved that the act which caused the death of the child was not done in good faith for the purpose only of preserving the life of the mother. (2) For the purpose of this Act, evidence that a woman had at any time been pregnant for a period of twenty-eight weeks or more shall be prima facie proof that she was at that time pregnant of a child capable of being born alive [104: p. 2].

(This act was introduced in order to close a legal loop as at that time it was a felony to kill the fetus in utero and it was murder to kill the child after it was born but there was no protection to the child during childbirth and before it was completely separated from the mother [39: p. 598].) In *R v Bourne* [105] the exception that allowed abortion to preserve the life of the mother was interpreted to include cases where continuation of the pregnancy will "make the woman a physical or mental wreck". Some doctors were prepared to interpret "mental wreck" broadly and terminate pregnancies of women who were distressed but not mentally ill. However, they risked prosecution and as a consequence their fees were high, making safe "legal" abortion inaccessible to most women.

Section 1 (1) of the Abortion Act 1967 provides a statutory defence to the criminal charges under the Offences Against the Person Act 1861 —

(1) Subject to the provisions of this section, a person shall not be guilty of an offence under the law [in] relation to abortion when a pregnancy is terminated by a registered medical practitioner if two registered medical practitioners are of the opinion, formed in good faith — (a) that the pregnancy has not exceeded its twenty-fourth week and that the

continuance of the pregnancy would involve risk, greater than if the pregnancy were terminated, of injury to the physical or mental health of the pregnant woman or any existing children of her family: or (b) that the termination is necessary to prevent grave permanent injury to the physical or mental health of the pregnant woman: or (c) that the continuance of the pregnancy would involve risk to the life of the pregnant woman, greater than if the pregnancy were terminated: or (d) that there is substantial risk that if the child were born it would suffer from such physical or mental abnormalities as to be seriously handicapped; (2) In determining whether the continuance of a pregnancy would involve such risk of injury to health as is mentioned in paragraph (a) or (b) of subsection (1) of this section, account may be taken of the pregnant woman's actual or reasonably foreseeable environment [104: p. 5].

Section 1 (3) of the Act provides that any such treatment (as above) must take place in a NHS hospital or in a place approved by the Department of Health [104: p. 5]. When the registered medical practitioner carrying out the termination is of the opinion, formed in good faith, that the termination is immediately necessary to save the life or to prevent grave permanent injury to the physical or mental health of the pregnant woman, Section 1 (3) and so much of Section 1 (1) as relates to the opinion of two registered medical practitioners shall not apply [104: p. 5].

The Abortion Act Section 1 (1) (a) as above, often referred to as the "social ground", is easily satisfied as, according to the Royal College of Obstetricians and Gynaecologists (RCOG), the definition of "health" is assumed to refer to the WHO definition of health as a state of physical well being, not merely the absence of disease or infirmity. Almost by definition, the mental heath of a woman who does not want to be pregnant will be promoted by an abortion. As abortion is less risky than pregnancy and labour, the woman's physical health will, also by definition, be promoted.

There is no list of conditions that satisfy Section 1 (1) (d) and the words "substantial" and "serious" are vague. The decision is left to the doctors who, nevertheless, have to form their opinion in good faith. In 2001 an abortion was performed on a fetus with a cleft palate after 24 weeks' gestation. Legal action was initiated by a member of the public, Reverend Joanna Jepson, on the grounds that the parliamentary debates prior to the

1990 amendments to the Abortion Act 1967 made clear that late abortions would be justifiable only for very serious conditions. Following a second police investigation, the Chief Crown Prosecutor decided that — "both doctors concluded that there was a substantial risk of abnormalities that would amount to the child being seriously handicapped. The evidence shows that these doctors did form this opinion and formed it in good faith … there was insufficient evidence for a realistic prospect of conviction … there should be no charges against either of the doctors" [106].

Medical personnel who have a conscientious objection to abortion are protected by Section 4 (1) of the Act and do not have to participate in any treatment unless the abortion is necessary to save the woman's life or to prevent grave permanent injury to physical or mental health [104: p. 6]. It is not clear whether signing the form confirming that the woman's circumstances satisfy the statutory grounds constitutes participation in treatment. However, referring the woman to another doctor does not constitute participation in treatment [107] and the RCOG advice is that when the woman's request of abortion meets the legal requirements doctors cannot claim exemption from giving advice or performing the preparatory steps to arrange an abortion including referral to another doctor.

The sexual partner or putative father has no right to prevent the woman from having an abortion [108, 109]. Regarding the possible challenge to abortion on the grounds of the right to life of the fetus it has been established by the European Commission of Human Rights that although the fetus has the potential to become a person and therefore should be protected as a matter of human dignity this does not make it a person with a right to life that should be protected by Article 2 of the European Convention on Human Rights [110].

Abortion is a legal medical treatment when performed according to the provisions of the Abortion Act 1967 and is governed by the general rules of consent. Incompetent patients such as minors or mentally incapacitated women can have an abortion which is in their best interests and according to good medical practice. Unlike sterilisation, for which court approval is required, abortion is not considered a special case [111].

It has to be emphasised that the Abortion Act 1967 does not accord the woman any legal right to demand an abortion. Rather, the Act gives the doctors the right to decide whether the woman's circumstances fall within the terms of the Act. It has been argued that because the public trusts and has confidence in the medical profession the medicalisation of abortion served to reduce the tensions surrounding abortion as, if the decision is taken by the doctor on medical grounds, it becomes difficult to challenge both the individual decision and the rules governing access.

The Abortion Act 1967 does not apply in Northern Ireland. A defence for abortion may exist under the Infant Life (Preservation) Act 1929 if the pregnancy is endangering the pregnant woman's life or for this purpose, following R v Bourne [105], is endangering her mental health so as to leave her a "mental wreck". Therefore, the decision has to be done on a case by case basis and each time the doctor is under potential threat of criminal prosecution. This situation, coupled with the lack of NHS funding, has the effect of reducing the number of abortions performed in Northern Ireland to less than 100 per year (the majority on the grounds of serious fetal anomalies) and forcing pregnant women to travel abroad for an abortion (1,173 abortions were performed in England and Wales in 2008) [112] which causes delay, inconvenience, and expense [39: p. 631].

The Offences Against the Person Act 1861 applies in Ireland and the Irish Constitution was amended in 1983 so that the unborn fetus and the pregnant woman have an equal right to life. Therefore, abortion is illegal except when the woman's life is in danger which includes suicide risk. As a consequence, many women travel abroad to have an abortion (4,600 to England and Wales in 2008) [112]. The legality of travel abroad was questioned in the case of a 14-year-old girl who was raped, conceived and wanted to travel to England for an abortion [113]. Following this case the Irish constitution was amended following a referendum in 1992 so as to limit the ability of the state to stop a woman from travelling abroad for abortion. The legality of providing information about arranging abortions in the UK was also questioned in courts and The Irish Supreme Court upheld an injunction granted by the High Court restricting the applicants from providing such assistance to pregnant women. It was argued that the restriction was justified because it pursued the legitimate aim of "the protection of morals of which the protection in Ireland of the right to life of the unborn is one aspect". This came before the European Court of Human Justice which held by majority that the restriction on provision of information was disproportionate [114]. In the 1992 referendum it was also decided that there should be a limited right to receive information on abortion services in England. The proposal that suicide risk should be excluded as a ground for life-saving abortion was rejected in the 1992 referendum and again by a very narrow margin in 2002 [39: p. 633].

In the US, it was only in 1973 that the US Supreme Court established that women had a constitutionally protected liberty to choose to have an abortion [115]. It was held that the right to privacy "is broad enough to encompass a woman's decision whether or not to terminate her pregnancy". The state could restrict this constitutionally protected liberty only in order to promote a compelling state interest. It was held that before viability the state had no such compelling interest in fetal life and therefore restrictions on the woman's right to decide would be unconstitutional. However, the state is under no obligation to provide funding for abortion. The Hyde Amendment, which prohibited federal Medicaid funding except in cases of life endangerment, has been renewed by Congress every year since its introduction in 1976. The Health Reform Bill was eventually passed by the US Congress in 2010 only after the initial provisions for federal funding for abortion were removed. Subsequent decisions of the Supreme Court further narrowed the scope of *Roe* v *Wade* when it held that restrictions on women's right to choose abortion would be unconstitutional only if they imposed an "undue burden", and even then, they might be justified by important state interests [116]. In Planned Parenthood v Casey [117] the US Supreme Court upheld restrictions on access to abortion imposed by a Pennsylvania statute including a mandatory 24-hour waiting period and parental consent required for minors (but not the spousal notification requirement as it was considered to represent an "undue burden" on women's right to choose abortion). It was argued that as the state had a "profound interest in potential life", it was entitled, throughout pregnancy, to —

> take measures to ensure that the woman's choice is informed, and measures designed to advance this interest will not be invalidated as long as their purpose is to persuade the woman to choose childbirth over abortion, provided that they do not impose an "undue burden on the right" [117].

It has been argued that although abortions in the US may be legal they are substantially unavailable, particularly to the poor, teenagers, and women living in rural areas —

> ...access has been undermined primarily through denial of public funding for abortion, parental involvement laws, and the loss of abortion services. Public funding ... was lost in 1976, just three years after Roe v Wade. The Hyde Amendment, which prohibited federal Medicaid funding except in cases of life endangerment, has been renewed by Congress every year since. Most States have followed the federal precedent and prohibit the use of state funds for abortions ... Nine out of ten abortion providers are now located in metropolitan areas ... ninety four percent of non-metropolitan counties have no services. Parental involvement laws requiring either parental consent or notification before minors can obtain abortions affect millions of young women [118].

12.4.2 *Legal aspects of sterilisation*

In the UK sterilisation is legal and is governed by the general rules of consent. For consent to be valid it has to be informed. It is therefore important that the patient will be well-informed regarding the consequences of sterilisation. If, for example, the doctor gives a guarantee that following sterilisation sterility will be achieved and subsequently the woman conceives, this will amount to a breach of duty of care and negligence may be established. The RCOG recommends full discussion of the small risk of failure following sterilisation [119].

The doctor has a duty to the patient and not to the partner or husband. Indeed, the routine search for the partner's agreement is now regarded by the BMA as inappropriate [79: p. 228] although it is good practice to encourage the patient to discuss it with their partner.

When the patient lacks capacity to consent but the sterilisation is therapeutic and required to treat a medical condition (e.g., excessive bleeding), the doctor may perform the sterilisation (provided this is the least intrusive way to proceed) if it is in the best interests of the patient according to the Mental Capacity Act 2005 [104: pp. 287–301]. If, however, the sterilisation is not therapeutic (e.g., to prevent pregnancy), a court declaration that the procedure would be lawful should be sought. If such a declaration is not sought the doctor may be in breach of professional guidelines. He will be acting unlawfully if it can be shown that the procedure was not in the best interests of the patient. The best interests of the patient will be interpreted by the court in a broad sense to take account not only of the medical considerations but also the welfare, psychological, emotional, and social aspects.

References

[1] Jain S. The Right to Family Planning, Contraception, and Abortion: The Hindu View. In D.C. Maguire (ed.) *Sacred Rights. The Case for Contraception and Abortion in World Religions*. Oxford: Oxford University Press, 2003.

[2] Gudorf C.E. Contraception and Abortion in Roman Catholicism. In D.C. Maguire (ed.) *Sacred Rights. The Case for Contraception and Abortion in World Religions*. Oxford: Oxford University Press, 2003.

[3] Shaikh S. Family Planning, Contraception, and Abortion in Islam: Undertaking Khilafah. In D.C. Maguire (ed.) *Sacred Rights. The Case for Contraception and Abortion in World Religions*. Oxford: Oxford University Press, 2003.

[4] Togonu-Bickersteth F. Family Planning and Abortion: Cultural Norma versus Actual Practices in Nigeria. In D.C. Maguire (ed.) *Sacred Rights. The Case for Contraception and Abortion in World Religions*. Oxford: Oxford University Press, 2003.

[5] Mbiti J. *Introduction to African Religion*. New York: Heinemann, 1991; p. 98.

[6] Riddle J.M. *Eve's Herbs: A History of Contraception and Abortion in the West*. Cambridge, MA: Harvard University Press, 1997.

[7] Zoloth L. Each One an Entire World: A Jewish Perspective on Family Planning. In D.C. Maguire (ed.) *Sacred Rights. The Case for Contraception and Abortion in World Religions*. Oxford: Oxford University Press, 2003.

[8] Riddle J.M. Oral Contraceptives and early term Abortifacients during Classical Antiquity and the Middle Ages. *Past & Present* 1991; **132**: 3–32.

[9] Hadley J. *Abortion: Between Freedom and Necessity*. London: Virago, 1997; p. 41.

[10] Spero A. A Talmudic overview of abortion. *Midstream* 1990; 20–22.

[11] Moskowitz E., Jennings B., and Callahan D. Long Acting Contraceptives: Ethical Guidance for Policymakers and Health Care Providers. In E. Moskowitz and J. Jennings (eds) *Coerced Contraception? Moral and Policy*

Challenges of Long-Acting Birth Control. Washington DC: Georgetown University Press, 1996; p. 6.

[12] Heinsohn G. and Steiger O. The elimination of medieval birth control and the witch trials of modern times. *International Journal of Women's Studies* 1982; **5**: 193–215.

[13] Mooney J. Myths of the Cherokee. In *Nineteen Annual Report of the Bureau of American Ethnology, 1897–98, Part I*. Washington, DC: GPO, 1900. [Re-print: Myths of the Cherokee. In *Myths of the Cherokee and Sacred Formulas of the Cherokees*. Nashville: Charles and Randy Elder, 1982; p. 250 of re-print].

[14] Mathews W. *Navajo Legends*. Boston: Houghton, Mifflin, 1897. [Re-print: Salt Lake City: University of Utah Press, 1994; p. 77 of re-print].

[15] Scharping T. *Birth Control in China 1949–2000, Population Policy and Demographic Development*. Oxon: Routledge, 2003.

[16] Chamie J. Trends, Variations and Contradictions in National Policies to Influence Fertility. In J. Finkle and A. McIntosh (eds) *The New Politics of Population: Conflict and Consensus in Family Planning*. Oxford: Oxford University Press, 1994; pp. 37–50.

[17] Potts M. The population policy pendulum. *BMJ* 1999; **319**: 933–934.

[18] Smith M. Palestine Judaism in the First Century. In M. David (ed.) *Israel: Its Role in Civilization*. New York: Harper and Brothers, 1956; 67–81.

[19] Maguire D.C. Introduction. In D.C. Maguire (ed.) *Sacred Rights. The Case for Contraception and Abortion in World Religions*. Oxford: Oxford University Press, 2003; p. 5.

[20] Warkwell H. and Brown B. Bioethics for clinicians: Catholic bioethics, *Canadian Medical Association Journal* 2001; **165**: 189–192.

[21] Glick S. A view from Sinai: A Jewish perspective on biomedical ethics. In E. Pellegrino, P. Mazzarella, and P. Corsi (eds) *Transcultural Dimensions*. Frederick, MD: University Publishing Group, 1992; pp. 76–77.

[22] Karo Y. Yore Deah. In *Shulkhan Aruch*. Zikhron Yaakov, Israel: Torah Education Center, 1966; **336**: 1.

[23] Babylonian Talmud, Yebamot, (Talman Inc., Jerusalem, 1981), 12b.

[24] Steinberg A. Hagisha Hayehudit Hakelalit Leminiyat Herayon. *Assia* 1983; **3**: 139–160.

[25] Aviner S.H.H. Tichnun mishpacha Uminiyat Herayon. *Assia* 1983; **3**: 167–181.

[26] Katan Y., Katan H., Baron A. Emtzai Meniya — Mabat Refui Hilchati. *Assia* 1994; **14**: 114–123.

[27] Maimonides M. *Mishneh Torah LeRambam. Hilkhot Rotzeah ve Shmirat Nefesh*. Jerusalem: Wagshell Inc, 1984; 1:9.

[28] Pope Paul VI, *Of Human Life. Encyclical Letter of His Holiness on the Regulation of Birth.* Vatican, 1968.

[29] Grisez G., Boyle J., Finnis J., May M. Every marital act ought to be open to new life. Towards a clearer understanding. *The Thomist* 1988; **52**: 365.

[30] Pope Paul VI, *Respect for Life in the Women.* Vatican, 1977.

[31] Morland J. and Rae S. *Body and Soul. Human Nature and the Crisis in Ethics.* Downer Grove, IL: InterVarsity Press, 2000.

[32] Rachels J. *The Elements of Moral Philosophy. Fifth Edition by Rachels S.* New York: McGraw Hill, 2007, pp. 66–67.

[33] Church of England. Abortion. A Briefing Paper. The General Synod's Mission and Public Affairs Division, 2005.

[34] Omran A.R. *Family Planning in the Legacy of Islam.* London: Routledge, 1992; pp. 145–167.

[35] Farah M. *Marriage and Sexuality in Islam: A Translation of Al-Ghazali's Book on the Etiquette of Marriage from the Ihya.* Salt Lake City: University of Utah Press, 1984; pp. 71–74.

[36] Ibn Nujaym Zayn al-'Abidin, *Al-Ashbah Wa'n-nazair* (Calcutta, 1270 H), 85.

[37] Boonstra H. The Guttmacher Report on Public Policy. Islam, Women and Family Planning: A Primer. The Guttmacher Institute, 2001; 4:6. http://www.guttmacher.org/pubs/tgr/04/6/gr040604.html [accessed 25 April 2014].

[38] Ebrahim A. Status of the embryo in the light of Islam jurisprudence. In A. Lewis and M. Freeman (eds) *Law and Medicine.* Oxford: Oxford University Press, 2000; pp. 245–256.

[39] Jackson E. *Medical Law: Text, Cases, and Materials.* Oxford: Oxford University Press, 2006.

[40] Sedgh G., Henshaw S., Singh S., *et al.* Induced abortion: estimated rates and trends worldwide. *Lancet* 2007; **370**: 1338–1345.

[41] Singh S. Hospital admissions resulting from unsafe abortion: estimates from 13 developing countries. *Lancet* 2006; **368**: 1887–1892.

[42] WHO. Unsafe Abortion: Global and Regional Estimates of the Incidence of Unsafe Abortion and Associated Mortality in 2003, 5th ed. World Health Organization, Geneva, 2007.

[43] Centers for Disease Control and Prevention (CDC) and ORC Macro, *Reproductive, maternal and child health in Eastern Europe and Eurasia: a comparative report.* CDC and ORC Macro, Atlanta and Calverton, MD, 2003 (revised 2005).

[44] Henshaw S.K. Unintended pregnancy and abortion: a public health perspective. In M. Paul, P.G. Stubblefield, D.A. Grimes, E.S. Lichtenberg, and L. Borgatta (eds) *A Clinician's Guide to Medical and Surgical Abortion.* New York: Churchill Livingstone, 2006; pp. 11–22.

[45] Chang J. Elams-Evans L., Berg C. *et al.* Pregnancy-related mortality surveillance — United States, 1991–1999. *MMWR Surveillance Summaries* 2003; **52**: 1–8.

[46] DoH, *Statistical Bulletin, Abortion Statistics, England and Wales: 2008, Bulletin 2009/01*, 2009.

[47] CEMACH. Saving Mothers' Lives: Reviewing Maternal Deaths to Make Motherhood Safer — 2003–2005. Seventh Report of the Confidential Enquiries into Maternal Deaths in the United Kingdom, December 2007, 8.

[48] Koop C. A Physician Look at Abortion. In R.L. Ganz (ed.) *Thou Shalt Not Kill: The Christian Case Against Abortion*. New York: Arlington House Publishers, 1978; p. 9.

[49] Boonin D. *A Defence of Abortion*. Cambridge: Cambridge University Press, 2002; p. 35.

[50] Williams G. The fetus and the right to life. *Cambridge Law Journal* 1994; **53**: 71–80.

[51] Noonan J.T. An Almost Absolute Value in History. In J. Noonan (ed.) *The Morality of Abortion: Legal and Historical Perspectives*. Cambridge, MA: Harvard University Press, 1970.

[52] Finnis J. The rights and wrongs of abortion: A reply to Judith Thomson. *Philosophy and Public Affairs*, 1973; **2**: 117–145.

[53] Harris J. *The Value of Life*. Oxon: Routledge, 1985.

[54] Warnock M. In vitro fertilisation: The ethical issues II. *Philosophical Quarterly* 1983; **33**: 238–249.

[55] Marquis D. Why abortion is immoral. *The Journal of Philosophy* 1989; **86**: 183–202.

[56] Marshall J. The case against experimentation. In A. Dayson and J. Harris (eds) *Experiments on Embryos*. London: Routledge, 1990; pp. 63–64.

[57] Wilkins B.T. Does the fetus have a right to life? *Journal of Social Philosophy* 1993; **24**: 123–127.

[58] Harris J. On the moral status of the embryo. In A. Dayson and J. Harris (eds) *Experiments on Embryos*. London: Routledge, 1990; p. 70.

[59] Savulescu J. Abortion, embryo destruction and the future of value argument. *Journal of Medical Ethics* 2002; **28**: pp. 133–135.

[60] Dworkin R. *Life's Dominion. An Argument about Abortion and Euthanasia*. London: Harper Collins, 1993.

[61] Brown M. The morality of abortion and the deprivation of futures. *Journal of Medical Ethics* 2000; **26**: 103–107.

[62] McMahan J. *The Ethics of Killing*. Oxford, Oxford University Press, 2002.

[63] Finnis J. Abortion and health care ethics. In R. Gillon (ed.) *Principles of Health Care Ethics*. Chichester: John Wiley and Sons, 1994; p. 548.

[64] Brazier M. The challenge for parliament. In A. Dyson and J. Harris (eds) *Experiments on Embryos*. London: Routledge, 1990; p. 134.

[65] Tollefsen C. Embryos, individuals and persons: An argument against embryo creation and research. *Journal of Applied Philosophy* 2001; **18**: 65–77.

[66] McMahan J. Cloning, killing, and identity. *Journal of Medical Ethics* 1999; **25**: 77–86.

[67] Warnock M. Experimentation on human embryos and fetuses. In H. Kuhse and P. Singer (eds) *A Companion to Bioethics*. Oxford: Blackwell, 1998; p. 394.

[68] Warnock M. Report of the Committee of Enquiry into Human Fertilisation and Embryology. Department of Health & Social Security, 1984; para. 11.12. http://www.hfea.gov.uk/docs/Warnock_Report_of_the_Committee_of_Inquiry_into_Human_Fertilisation_and_Embryology_1984.pdf. [accessed 25 April 2014].

[69] Williams B. Types of moral argument against embryo research. In Ciba Foundation Symposium (eds) *The Ciba Foundation, Human Embryo Research: Yes or No?* London: Tavistock, 1986; pp. 184–194.

[70] BMA. Abortion Time Limits: A Briefing Paper from the BMA, 2005. London: BMA.

[71] Watt H. *Living Together: Pregnancy and Parenthood*. Linacre Centre, 2002. http://www.linacre.org/AbortionDrHelenWatt.htm [accessed 25 April 2014].

[72] Gillon R. Editor's reply to Strong C. and Anderson G., The moral status of the near term fetus. *Journal of Medical Ethics* 1989; **15**: 25.

[73] Lockwood M. The moral status of the human embryo, *Human Fertility* 2001; **4**: 267–269.

[74] Glover V. and Fisk N.M. Fetal pain: Implications for research and practice. *British Journal of Obstetrics and Gynaecology* 1999; **106**: 881–886.

[75] RCOG, *Fetal Awareness. Report of a Working Party* (RCOG, London, 1997).

[76] Steinbock B. *Life before Birth*. Oxford: Oxford University Press, 1992.

[77] Harris J. *Clones, Genes and Immortality. Ethics and the Genetic Revolution*. Oxford: Oxford University Press, 1998; 79.

[78] *Re MB (Medical Treatment)* [1997] 2FLR 426.

[79] BMA. *Medical Ethics Today. The BMA's Handbook on Ethics and Law, 2nd ed.* London: BMJ Publishing Group, 2004.

[80] Polkinghorne J. *Review of the Guidance on the Research Use of Fetuses and Fetal Material*. London: HMSO, 1989.

[81] Quinn W. Abortion identity and loss. *Philosophy and Public Affairs* 1984; **13**: 24.

[82] Locke J. *An Essay Concerning Human Understanding.* London: Oxford University Press, 1964; book II, ch. 27.

[83] Lockwood M. When does a life begin? In M. Lockwood (ed.) *Moral Dilemmas in Modern Medicine,* Oxford: Oxford University Press, 1985; p. 10.

[84] Tooley M. Abortion and infanticide. *Philosophy and Public Affairs* 1972; **2**: 37–65.

[85] Kuhse H. and Singer P. *Should the Baby Live?* Oxford: Oxford University Press, 1985; p. 133.

[86] Gillon R. Is there a "New Ethics of Abortion"? *Journal of Medical Ethics* 2001; **27**: suppl. II, ii8.

[87] Warren M.A. On the moral and legal status of abortion. *The Monist* 1973; **1**: 43–61.

[88] Maclean A. *The Elimination of Morality. Reflection on Utilitarianism and Bioethics.* London: Routledge, 1993; p. 36.

[89] Abbott P. Philosophers and the abortion question. *Political Theory* 1978; **6**: 313–335.

[90] Thomson J.J., A Defense of Abortion, *Philosophy and Public Affairs* **1** (1971).

[91] Scott R. *Rights, Duties and the Body, Law and Ethics of the Maternal-Fetal Conflict.* Portland, Oregon: Hart Publishing, 2002; p. 90.

[92] McDonagh E. *Breaking the Abortion Deadlock.* Oxford: Oxford University Press, 1996; p. 169.

[93] Foot P. The problem of abortion and the doctrine of the double effect. *Oxford Review* 1967; **5**: 5–15.

[94] MacKinnon C. *Feminism Unmodified. Discourses on Life and Law.* Cambridge, MA: Harvard University Press, 1987.

[95] McDonagh E. Models of motherhood in the abortion debate: Self-sacrifice versus self-defence. In D.L. Dickenson (ed.) *Ethical Issues in Maternal-Fetal Medicine.* Cambridge: Cambridge University Press, 2002; p. 230.

[96] Himmelweit S. More than a woman's right to choose. *Feminist Review* 1988; **29**: 49.

[97] MacKinnon C. Reflections on sexual equality under the law. *Yale Law Journal* 1991; **100**: 1315.

[98] Wolf-Devine C. Abortion and the feminine voice. *Public Affairs Quarterly* 1989; **3**: 81–97.

[99] Petchesky R. *Abortion and Woman's Choice. The State, Sexuality, and Reproductive Freedom.* New York: Longman, 1984; p. xii.

[100] Kerr A. and Shakespeare K. *Genetic Politics. From Eugenics to Genome.* Cheltenham, Engalnd: New Clarion Press, 2002; **15**: 27–28, 46–61.

[101] McLean S.A.M. and Campbell T.D. Sterilisation. In S.A.M. McLean (ed.) *Legal Issues in Medicine.* Aldershot: Gower Press, 1981; pp. 176–190.

[102] Mason J.K. and Laurie G.T. *Mason and McCall Smith's Law and Medical Ethics, 7th ed.* Oxford: Oxford University Press, 2006; pp. 131, 134–135.

[103] United Nations. *World Abortion Policies 2007.* Department of Economic and Social Affairs, Population Division, United Nations, New York, USA.

[104] Jones A.M. and Morris A.E. Offences Against the Person Act 1861 (section 58–59). In *Blackstone's Statutes on Medical Law, 4th ed.* Oxford: Oxford University Press, 2005.

[105] *R* v *Bourne* [1939] 1 KB 697.

[106] CPS Press Release, Mar 2005. www. cps.gov.uk/news/pressreleases/117_05. html [accessed 25 April 2014].

[107] *Barr* v *Matthews* [2000] 52 BMLR 217.

[108] *Paton* v *Trustees of the British Pregnancy Advisory Service and Another* [1978] 2 All E.R. 987; [1978] Q.B. 276; [1978] 3 W.L.R. 687.

[109] *Paton* v *United Kingdom* [1980] 3 EHRR 408.

[110] *Vo* v *France* [2005] 10 EHRR 12.

[111] *Re SG (Adult Mental Patient: Abortion)* [1991] 2 FLR 329.

[112] DoH, *Statistical Bulletin, Abortion Statistics, England and Wales, 2008.* www. dh.gov.uk [accessed 25 April 2014].

[113] *Attorney General* v *X* [1992] 2 CMLR 277.

[114] *Open Door Counselling Ltd* v *Ireland*, The Times, 5 Nov 1992 (ECHR).

[115] *Roe* v *Wade* [1973] 410 US 113.

[116] *Webster* v *Reproductive Health Services* [1989] 492 US 490.

[117] *Planned Parenthood* v *Casey* [1992] 112 S Ct 2791.

[118] Gerber Fried M. Abortion in the United States — Legal but Inaccessible. In R. Solinger (ed.) *Abortion Wars: A Half Century of Struggle, 1950–2000.* Berkeley: University of California Press, 1998; pp. 214–215.

[119] RCOG. *Male and Female Sterilisation.* London: RCOG, 1999.

13

Ethical Issues in Plastic and Reconstructive Surgery

Ivo Pitanguy, Henrique Radwanski and Aris Sterodimas

13.1 Introduction

The Greek poet Pindar (474 BC) wrote about the mythical physician Asklepios, a competent physician who was induced by greed to perform a forbidden medical service, violated divine law, and paid the penalty. Medical ethics, then and now, is about the physician's attitude and dealings with the price of saving and healing life [1].

Over 2,000 years ago the foundation of medical ethics was defined clearly and classically by Hippocrates:

A physician should be an upright man, instructed in the art of healing, modest, sober, patient, prompt to do his whole duty without anxiety; pious without going so far as superstition, conducting himself with propriety in his profession and in all the actions of his life.

The wisdom of these words, as well as that of the modern principles of medical ethics, stem from one all-important basic principle: respect for the sanctity of human life [2].

By the nineteenth century, medical ethics emerged as a more self-conscious discourse. Thomas Percival wrote about "medical jurisprudence" and reportedly coined the phrase "medical ethics" [3]. Percival's guidelines have been criticized as being excessively protective of the home physician's reputation. In 1847, the American Medical Association adopted its first code of ethics, with this being based in large part upon Percival's work [4].

In the 1960s and 1970s, thinkers such as Joseph Fletcher [5] built upon liberal theory and procedural justice, dramatically shifting the discourse of medical ethics, largely reconfigured into bioethics. In 1979, Beauchamp and Childress published *Principles of Biomedical Ethics*, in which they presented "principles" that have since been adopted as the ethical basis for contemporary medical practice. These values included: respect for autonomy, beneficence, and non-maleficence [6]. At the same time that the principles were developed to guide physicians treating those suffering ill-health, they also provide the ethical framework which underpins modern surgical practice.

13.2 Respect for Patient Autonomy and Informed Consent

The historical model for the physician–patient relationship involved patient dependence on the physician's professional authority. Believing that the patient would benefit from the physician's actions, a patient's preferences were generally overridden or ignored; the concept of physician beneficence allowed this paternalistic model to thrive. During the second half of the twentieth century, the physician–patient relationship evolved towards shared decision making. This model respects the patient as an autonomous agent with a right to hold views, to make choices, and to take actions based on personal values and beliefs. Patients have been increasingly entitled to weigh the benefits and risks of alternative treatments, including choosing non-treatment and to select the alternative that best promotes their own values. These principles certainly apply to plastic and reconstructive surgery. In a phrase: the lucid body participates in the choices that are presented to it [7].

Providing patients are given sufficient information on which to make an informed decision, patients' wishes must be respected. Information must include the risks of surgery together with alternative options. Informed consent in ethics usually refers to the idea that a person must be fully informed about and understand the potential benefits and risks of their choice of treatment. An uninformed person is at risk of mistakenly making a choice not reflective of his or her values or wishes.

Informed consent is the process by which a fully informed patient can participate in choices about his healthcare. It originates from the legal and ethical right the patient has to direct what happens to his or her body and from the ethical duty of the plastic surgeon to involve the patient in his or her healthcare. The physician should put the health and safety of the patient first in deciding whether or not to accommodate a patient's request for a particular procedure. Ethics dictate that the surgeon would not perform any procedure without the written consent of the patient. Nor would the surgeon perform surgery on a minor without the consent of his or her legal guardian(s). The most important goal of informed consent is that patients have an opportunity to be an informed participant in their healthcare decisions. Informed consent must be obtained from the patient before any medical intervention. Well-informed patients will have fewer anxieties during surgery and better compliance with instructions. The success of informed consent is largely based on effective communication between doctor and patient and the ability of the patient to understand what is being communicated.

13.3 Beneficence

This principle requires medical practitioners to act in patients' "best interests". Undertaking surgery to improve a patient's self-image and esteem is acceptable. However, defining patients' best interests can be very difficult. Many people experience psychological pain, discomfort, social handicap, and suffering because they are self-conscious about their appearance. This group can benefit from aesthetic plastic surgery [8]. Beneficence means an ethical duty to maximize benefit. Plastic surgeons have a duty not only to avoid harm to the patient but also to weigh the risks of the surgery with the needs (or demands) of the patient and to offer a plan that will provide him or her with the maximum benefit. If benefit to the patient is not the ultimate outcome then the principle of beneficence has been violated. It is sometimes challenging to apply this principle with respect to aesthetic plastic surgery. Measuring benefits like long-term outcomes and quality of life is difficult and few studies on the long-term positive effects of aesthetic plastic surgery exist [9].

13.4 Non-maleficence

This principle ensures that doctors never act against patients' best interests or in a way that may harm a patient. Plastic surgeons may decline to operate on patients if they do not believe that surgery is in the patients' interests and should be reluctant to operate on those with unrealistic expectations, as the risks of surgery may outweigh any benefits. All such assessments need to be made on an individual basis. It is commonly said that a plastic surgeon is sometimes described as an artist who works with flesh. Body image, in our consuming societies, has become more and more important, and its new models have been magnified by the media, further burdening the plastic surgeon with ethic questions [10]. In the end, the plastic surgeon walks a fine line between the ideal of "doing no harm" and giving the patient what he or she asks for.

13.5 The Field of Plastic and Reconstructive Surgery

Plastic, reconstructive, and cosmetic surgery refer to a variety of operations performed in order to repair or restore body parts to look normal, or to enhance a certain structure or anatomy that is already normal. These types of procedures are highly specialized [11]. Reconstructive surgery developed out of the need to treat the amputated noses of unfaithful wives and the wounded soldiers in wartime, approximately 600 BC. Currently, abnormal structures of the body that are the focus of reconstructive surgery may be the result of birth defects, developmental abnormalities, trauma or injury, infection, tumors, or disease.

Every race, culture, and tribe has its own concept of beauty, and of what it considers to be normal. The judgments of normalcy lie on a continuum and may be viewed differently not only by the individual but also society. A cleft lip is certainly perceived as abnormal in appearance and corrective surgery will always be encouraged in such cases. On the other hand, a large nose may not be considered as an alteration of the norm, but for the individual, it may be unacceptable enough to prompt him or her to undergo surgery. Adolescents experience much emotional turmoil as part of their psychosocial development. When teased about physical qualities that do not conform to the average, such as prominent ears, they may experience sufficient suffering to consider surgery as a solution.

The motivation for cosmetic surgery is straightforward: to enhance beauty. Cosmetic surgery raises a considerable ethical problem: the balance of risks and benefits of operations without functional benefit [12].

Every analysis for potential surgery must weigh the following:

1. Purpose for surgery: Is the proposed surgery realistic? Does the patient seem competent to make the decision to have surgery? Patients must undergo thorough pre-operative evaluation and counseling before the operation. This may, in selected cases, require expert psychological assessment. Surgeons need to explain the likely benefits of surgery, alternative non-surgical options as well as the risks of surgery and anesthesia. The degree of success depends not only on the surgeon's skills but also inherent aspects of the patient, such as age, health, skin texture, bone structure, and the specific problems and expectations. In a final analysis, it would be unethical for any physician to guarantee the results of any treatment performed. The only guarantee that can be made is to do the best work possible for the patient.

2. Degree of deformity: Is the deformity noticeable? Are the patient's expectations for correction appropriate? Appearance and deformities are important to anyone who engages in social interaction. Distortions in body appearance can lower self-confidence and disrupt social acceptance. This can result in behavior difficulties, manifesting as aggression or withdrawal. Although improvement in appearance may be psychologically beneficial by increasing self-esteem and self-confidence, it is a caveat that cosmetic surgery is not the cure-all for all problems. Surgeons must ensure that patients' expectations are realistic. Particularly, if one blames his or her appearance for lack of success or happiness in life, the patient's expectations may be surgically unobtainable or too risky.

A word of caution must be dedicated to a particular type of patient. The dismorphobic patient should be firmly filtered away from surgery: he or she desires the correction of a minimal — or even non-existent — defect, placing all of life's frustrations on this supposed deformity. It has been proven that cosmetic surgery in this population will only lead to an unsatisfactory result or the creation of a different defect [13].

13.6 Training of the Plastic Surgeon

A plastic surgeon requires an extensive amount of education and training. Depending on the country, he needs to first complete his bachelor's degree in college and his medical school degree. Then he needs to undergo a complete residency in general surgery. Following this, a specialty training — either as a residency or a post-graduate program — to obtain the necessary skills in plastic surgery is undertaken[14]. Finally, the doctor must successfully pass exams to be board certified. He might even need more training for expertise in subspecialties. In all, the training past high school can take up to 16 years.

A plastic surgeon has to possess certain individual attributes as well. Competency in this specialty implies a special combination of solid basic knowledge, surgical judgment, technical expertise, ethics, and interpersonal skills in order to achieve satisfactory patient relationships and problem resolution [15, 16]. Unfortunately, in some countries, without any law prohibiting doctors to practice plastic surgery, any person with a medical degree can label himself as a plastic surgeon. With ever more attention being given to "aesthetic medicine" cosmetic procedures are sometimes learned through weekend workshops, official sounding "fellowships", or "videotapes".

13.7 Marketing, Media, and Plastic Surgery

Unfortunately, cosmetic surgery is too often treated as a commodity. False and misleading advertisements flourish in the media and on the internet in the fight for a share of the market, and the patient's welfare becomes second priority as procedures are promoted in the name of scientific development [17, 18]. A physician's clinical judgment and practice must not be affected by economic interest in, commitment to, or benefit from professionally related commercial enterprises or other actual or potential conflicts of interest. Disclosure of professionally related commercial enterprises and any other interests that may influence clinical decision making is required in communications to patients, the public, and colleagues. This disclaimer will allow the patient to assess whether there is any conflict of interest and if this affects the patient–physician relationship.

Cosmetic surgery has increased exponentially in the last decade; media coverage has matched this increase. Consumer pressure is responsible for the growth of both. To assist the public in obtaining medical services, plastic surgeons are permitted to make known their services through advertising. Ethical advertising permits public dissemination of truthful information about medical services, while prohibiting false, fraudulent, deceptive, or misleading communications, and restricting direct solicitation. The specific country's medical code of ethics often regulate what is, and what is not, correct in promoting plastic surgery to the public [19, 20].

13.8 Innovative Research and New Technologies in Plastic Surgery

Innovative research, and new technologies derived from such research, almost always raise ethical and policy concerns. Such efforts should be informed by the most current scientific evidence and should occur through a process that encourages broad involvement by all sectors of society. As in any medical and surgical specialty, plastic surgical procedures should be subjected to rigorous protocols before they are used on patients. Any clinical investigation in plastic surgery must adhere to the highest standards of research subject protection, safeguarding the health and welfare of the patients involved. Ethical committees exist to guide physicians who intend to research new procedures, technologies, or equipments.

The ethical and policy issues raised by stem cell research are unique and have received a significant amount of public attention and there is much to gain by open reflection on the implications of this sensitive area of research [21, 22]. Extensive media coverage has pushed stem cell research issues and applications in the field of plastic and reconstructive surgery into the spotlight [23].

13.9 Conclusion

The search for enhancement of physical traits has been documented throughout the history of man. It is an aspect that is found in all civilizations and cultures and represents, ultimately, the motivation for plastic and reconstructive surgery. The increased number of patients seeking aesthetic surgery is a hallmark of modern times and reflects the psychological, social, and cultural evolution of our society and our times. Surgical techniques are well established, with predictable results. Obtaining balanced and harmonious results is a consequence of a sound relationship between surgeon and patient and on accurate planning, indication, and performance of the vast array of existing procedures designed to improve physical appearance and hence self-esteem. In the final analysis, it is the ethical relationship between surgeon and patient that determines, to a very large part, the success of the planned procedure.

References

[1] Jonsen A.R. The fall of Asklepios: Medicine, morality, and money. *Plastic and Reconstructive Surgery* 1988; **82**(1): 147–50.

[2] Castañares S. Ethics in aesthetic surgery. *Aesthetic and Plastic Surgery* 1977; **1**(1): 209–212.

[3] Gregory J., Percival T., and Rush B. Medicine and Morals in the Elightenment (B.V. Rodopi ed.) Atlanta, GA: Rodopi BV Editions, 1997.

[4] Berlant J. (ed.) *Profession and Monopoly: A Study of Medicine in the United States and Great Britain.* CA: University of California Press, 1975.

[5] Fletcher J. (ed.) *Situation Ethics.* London: SCM Press, 1966.

[6] De Sousa A. Concerns about cosmetic surgery. *Indian Journal of Medical Ethics* 2007; **4**(4): 171–3.

[7] Sullivan D.A. *Cosmetic Surgery — the Cutting Edge of Commercial Medicine in America.* New Brunswick, NJ: Rutgers University Press, 2001.

[8] Haddad AM. Using principles of beneficence, autonomy to resolve ethical dilemmas in perioperative nursing. *Journal of the Association of Peri Operative Registered Nurses* 1987; **46**(1): 120, 122, 124.

[9] Sarwer D.B. and Crerand C.E. Body image and cosmetic medical treatments. *Body Image: An International Journal of Research* 2004; **1**(1): 99–111.

[10] Chavoin J.P. Aesthetic surgery and ethics. *Annals de Chirurgie Plastique et Esthetique* 2003; **48**(5): 273–8.

[11] Pitanguy I. Plastic surgery: Personal recollections, contributions, and some thoughts. The Ohmori lecture: 18th I.S.A.P.S. Congress, Rio De Janeiro — 2006. Aesthetic Plast Surg. 2007; **31**(6): 619–35.

[12] Goldwyn R.M. Unproven treatment: Whose benefit, whose responsibility? *Plastic and Reconstructive Surgery* 1988; **81**: 946–7.

[13] Honigman R.J., Phillips K.A., and Castle D.J. A review of psychosocial outcomes for patients seeking cosmetic surgery. *Plastic and Reconstructive Surgery* 2004; **113**(4): 1229–37. Review.

[14] Sterodimas A., Radwanski H.N., and Pitanguy I. Aesthetic plastic surgery: Junior plastic surgeons' confidence in a training program. *Aesthetic and Plastic Surgery* 2009; **33**(1): 131–2. Epub 31 Dec 2008.

[15] Klingensmith M.E. Teaching ethics in surgical training programs using a case-based format. *Journal of Surgical Education* 2008; **65**(2): 126–128.

[16] Ward C.M. Consenting and consulting for cosmetic surgery. *British Journal of Plastic Surgery* 1998; **51**: 547–50.

[17] Spilson S.V., Chung K.C., Greenfield M.L., and Walters M. Are plastic surgery advertisements conforming to the ethical codes of the American Society of Plastic Surgeons? *Plastic and Reconstructive Surgery* 2002; **109**: 1181–1186.

[18] Rohrich R.J. The market of plastic surgery: Cosmetic surgery for sale — at what price? *Plastic and Reconstructive Surgery* 2001; **107**: 1845–1847.

[19] Sarwer D.B., Grossbart T.A., and Didie E.R. Beauty and society. *Seminars in Cutaneous Medicine and Surgery* 2003; **22**(2): 79–92.

[20] Pearl A. and Weston J. Attitudes of adolescents about cosmetic surgery. *Annals of Plastic Surgery* 2003; **50**: 628–630.

[21] Walgenbach K.J., Voigt M., Riabikhin A.W. *et al.* Tissue engineering in plastic reconstructive surgery. *The Anatomical Record* 2001; **263**(4): 372–378.

[22] Sterodimas A., De Faria J., Correa W.E., and Pitanguy I. Tissue engineering in plastic surgery: An up-to-date review of the current literature. *Annals of Plastic Surgery* 2009; **62**(1): 97–103. Review.

[23] Outka G. The ethics of embryonic stem cell research and the principle of "nothing is lost". *Yale J Health Policy Law Ethics* 2009; **9** Suppl: 585–602.

14

Ethical Issues in Transplantation*

Miran Epstein

Transplant medicine is a huge ethical minefield. Virtually each and every one of its evolving aspects was at some point subject to a heated controversy. For more than five decades now it has challenged our conceptions of identity, personhood, autonomy, death, and the body. It has even called into question our time-honoured relations of solidarity, altruism, and love. And yet nothing in this field is philosophically challenging in itself. The only thing that accounts for its conceptual and ethical flammability is the enormous bearing it has on some of the most sensitive interests of so many social stakeholders.

This chapter expounds a systematic overview of the major ethical issues surrounding transplantation. It thus highlights the problems, the competing solutions, and the justifications for the latter. However, unlike similar overviews, it does not confine the discussion to the philosophical sphere alone, but draws attention to its social roots too. Let there be no mistake: a philosophical discourse about transplant ethics can certainly yield some interesting insights. However, it would be found seriously wanting if it were to be abstracted from its very own political economy, that is to say, the particular ecology of stakeholders, interests, and power relations from which it has emerged and evolved as such.

The benefits of discussing ethical ideas in their constitutive context are too important to pass up. This approach has a unique explanatory power: it can account for the emergence, the specificity, and the social status of

---

* This chapter was first published as Chapter 2 in N. S. Hakim (ed.) *Introduction to Organ Transplantation (2nd edition)*. London: Imperial College Press, 2012: pp. 21–57.

such ideas. It also has an acute explicatory power: it can shed new, possibly counterintuitive, light on their social role. Its critical power is particularly valuable: it requires us to not only consider the philosophical justifications of the ethical ideas, but also to question the morality of their very own political economy, a thing they would not normally do. These merits can be demonstrated, for example, on the argument supporting a market in organs (the pro-market argument) even without explicating it at all (a detailed discussion of the argument will be expounded later in this chapter).

Let us first consider the very emergence of the argument and its specificity. Could these be explained by the argument itself? No. Being philosophical in essence, the argument deals with justification, not explanations. Besides, it is the very thing to be explained. Can the social status of the argument be attributed to its veracity or falsity? Again, no. One cannot explain something that is changing, social status in this case, by something that is supposed to be immutable (veracity or falsity). Moreover, the social status of the criterion of veracity or falsity is subject to changes too, and thus becomes part of the object to be explained. A strictly philosophical argument cannot account for its own emergence, specificity, or social status.

The Darwinian metaphor can perhaps help us out here. This model has suggested that a biological mutation is a product of a particular ecology, and that its fate as such depends on its reciprocal interaction with the latter. The same, mutatis mutandis, could apply in the case of "ideic mutations", that is to say, ideas that are generated by society and then compete with each other for social status. The key to their specificity and social status can only be found in their interaction with their constitutive environment. The emergence, the specificity, and the social status of the pro-market argument could thus be understood only in light of the social interests in a market in organs and the circumstances that have bred these interests.

Now let us try to identify the role of the pro-market argument, that is to say, its reciprocal effect on the stakeholders. The argument purports to be in the interest of all stakeholders. This is implicit in its claim that its very own object — a market in organs — is in the interest of all stakeholders. Indeed, if a market in organs complies with some common interest, which is true as each stakeholder has some interest in a market in organs, then this must apply to its supportive argument too. But should we take all that at face value? Not necessarily.

The common interest in a market in organs, hence in its supportive argument, has a history that rests on a certain ecology of social interests, which, as we shall see, reveals a different picture. This ecology shows that buyers and vendors of organs, the main stakeholders who are supposed to benefit from a market in organs, would not have embraced the pro-market argument, let alone the market itself, if they had more appealing alternatives. Moreover, it also shows that the absence of such alternatives has been caused by other stakeholders who typically happen to have some interest in organ commercialism. This means that the common interest in a market in organs and in its supportive argument is a historical product of power relations. The market and the pro-market argument thus transpire to be doing more than they purport to be doing; while both appeal to a common interest as they say they do, they also conceal and thereby reaffirm the underlying power relations. This conclusion has a potentially disturbing and certainly counterintuitive implication; if we deem the appeal of the pro-market argument to some common interest to be ethical, but also believe the coercion that has generated that interest to be immoral, then we are bound to regard the pro-market argument as the ethics of the immoral. Conclusions of such kind are not just intellectually intriguing — they may have a critical implication as well.

Indeed, the last and by far the most important value of the suggested methodology is its potentially critical implication. Normally, ethical arguments, the pro-market argument included, deal with the morality of a certain solution to some problem. The methodology suggested here requires that we also question the morality of the circumstances that have created the problem and made us form and embrace a particular solution, rather than any other. For if the argument has indeed gained increasing popularity under coercive circumstances, then any attempt to criticize it could make sense only if it addressed those circumstances too. Indeed, the demand to ban commerce in organs would make little sense, and would most likely fail, if it did not also call for a ban on the social conditions that make such commerce so appealing in the first place.

Before we embark on this venture, however, some issues of terminology, scope, and classification need to be clarified. Strictly speaking, the term "transplantation" refers to a surgical intervention whereby solid tissue is removed from a biological source and subsequently implanted in a biological recipient. It differs from both "implantation", where the source is strictly synthetic, and "transfusion" — transplantation of non-solid tissue from a biological source, which is not an essentially surgical intervention.

Ideally, our discussion should cover ethical issues in transplantation, implantation, and transfusion, as these practices share many of their ethical issues. This book is about surgery, however. For this technical reason we shall have to confine the discussion to issues that involve transplantation and implantation only. Some attention will be given to issues involving prosthetic (artificial) and xenogeneic (animal) grafts. However, the better part of the discussion will be dedicated to the most contentious issues — those that involve organs from human sources.

How the ethical issues are to be sorted is another matter. Some overviews group them as donor-related versus recipient-related. This may be somewhat misleading, however, since the issues invariably involve and affect other stakeholders as well. Besides, implantation, for example, involves no donor at all, hence has no donor issues. An alternative categorization that drew on the specific nature of the different grafts could make sense; however, it would run the risk of obscuring the general themes. To tackle these concerns, we shall classify the issues according to the general practical contexts in which they arise (procurement of organs versus their distribution) and the general source of the graft to which they pertain (artificial, animal, human).

14.1 The Political Economy of Transplantation

A spectre is haunting transplant medicine, the spectre of the "organ crisis". Referring to a disturbing gap between demand and supply, this crisis seems to be getting worse. The US, for example, saw a 46% increase in the absolute number of donors between 1995 and 2008, but the patient-to-donor ratio has increased at a much faster rate (142%) and continues to grow. In 2009, the number of patients with end-stage renal disease (ESRD) listed for transplantation stood at just over 77,000 with only 16,000 receiving transplantation in that year. Another 25,000 patients were waiting for other organs, mainly heart, lung, liver, and pancreas [1]. The British experience is essentially similar. In March 2008, 7,500 patients were on the active transplant lists, and a further 2,000 were on the temporarily suspended transplant lists. This represents an increase of 6% and 10%, respectively, compared to the corresponding figures from the previous year [2]. The trend in Europe is somewhat different with a slight drop in the patient-to-donor ratio, but the number of patients on the waiting list saw a thirtyfold increase from 1969 to 2006.

The transplant discourse purports to account for the origins of this crisis by putting the blame on morbidity rates increasing faster than procurement rates. Albeit true, this explanation is not really informative. As a matter of fact, it is the very thing to be explained. A satisfactory explanation requires uncovering the conditions and the circumstances that have bred these trends. These should concern us here not so much because they can explain the evolution of the organ crisis, but rather because they happen to hold the key to understanding why its satellite ethical discourse looks as it does. Put differently, the political economy that has given rise to the problem and the political economy that has given rise to its competing solutions are one and the same.

14.1.1 *The demand for organs*

Like a demand for any other object, the demand for organs is a historical function of the technological ability to utilize them and the social interests in utilizing them (abilities and interests are historically interdependent: each is a product of preceding abilities and interests). Three general interests can be identified in this respect: interests in the technology of transplantation, interests in organs and transplantations, and interests in practices that create a demand for organs. The latter interests dominate the political economy of the demand.

The following sociological map is an abstraction: each stakeholder is described here as the holder of typical interests only. In reality, however, an individual stakeholder may have several interests, of which some may be in conflict with others. For example, a particular person may benefit and suffer from organ failure at the same time. The reader should bear this in mind and thus focus not on how individuals interact, but rather on how the different kinds of interests interact.

When speaking about the demand for organs in general, the interests that first come to mind are those of patients, organ donors, and doctors.

Each has a different interest in treating organ failure. However, they have developed their individual interests secondarily and subject to their failure to satisfy a more basic interest: avoiding or preventing the underlying morbidity in the first place. We often reduce the explanation of this failure to some biological pathophysiology. For example, we attribute the rising incidence of ESRD and end-stage liver disease (ESLD) to obesity, diabetes, and alcoholic liver cirrhosis. This is the truth, of course, but not the whole truth. These conditions have a social pathophysiology as well. Indeed, they are largely inflicted by certain forms of production and consumption, which are typically driven by profit. The political economy of the crisis would not be complete without mentioning the financial interests in such practices. As we shall see, the power relations between the beneficiaries of these practices and their victims have been reaffirmed by the ethical discourse: suggestions to manage the crisis have predominated in the discourse, while demands to eradicate its basic causes have been marginalized.

Some other players who have an interest in organs are driven by profit or funding, depending on whether the system in question is private or public, respectively. This group includes the hosting medical institution, the transplant system, its supporting technological and pharmaceutical industries, and, under certain circumstances, even organ brokers and the travel and tourism business.

Payers and purchasers of healthcare — states, insurers, providers, and taxpayers — are interested in organ transplants for their cost-saving effect. Their demand for organs tends to be selective, however, as some transplants are cost-effective compared to the alternatives, whereas others may not be cost-effective at all. Kidney transplant, for example, has the biggest cost-saving capacity, considering the relatively large number of patients with renal failure and the high cost of dialysis per patient. Although its cost per patient (around £46,000) is more than the annual cost of dialysis (around £25,000), once the transplantation has been done, annual treatment expenses drop to £7,000 each year, a saving of £18,000 per patient per annum. The overall saving is more than double, however. Thus every 2,400 kidney transplantations done in a certain year would save the taxpayer a total of one billion pounds over the next decade [3–5].

The cost-saving capacity of certain organ transplants is obviously compatible with the profit-maximizing interest of private sector payers, e.g., private healthcare insurers. The case of public-sector payers is different, though. Their need to control expenses is not essential to their nature. It has been imposed on them under certain historical circumstances. A comprehensive discussion of this point exceeds the scope of this chapter. However, suffice it to mention that the general funding problem of the public-sector payer has not been caused by any objective scarcity. On the contrary, it is the effect of unequal distribution and redistribution of social wealth that takes place within a rather affluent society. Here too, the domination of the interests of the beneficiaries of that system has been reaffirmed by the ethical discourse; suggestions to manage the crisis have pre-dominated in the discourse, while demands to eradicate its basic causes have been marginalized.

14.1.2 *The supply of organs*

The supply of organs has a political economy too. Some of the factors are already familiar to us, since they also play a role in the formation of the demand. In general, the pertinent vectors either enhance or hamper the supply, but some of them happen to have a double effect. The fact that there is some supply at all implies that the positive effect outweighs the negative one. However, this does not necessarily entail that the supply meets the demand. The very reality of the organ crisis implies rather the opposite.

Social conditions that breed solidarity and hence interests in mutual aid tend to increase organ donation. Religious and other cultural beliefs may play a positive role in this respect. Occasionally, they rather limit the supply. Some communities of Jewish Orthodox conviction, for example, forbid both deceased and living organ donation, but not reception [6]. In other societies, reluctance to sign a donor card or donate organs of deceased relatives may be secondary to cultural reluctance to receive cadaveric organs. Misunderstanding of the way death is established, distrust in the motivations of the medical authorities, and perhaps even awareness of the inferiority of cadaveric organs relative to organs from the living, are negative factors as well. In addition, reluctance to sign a donor card is commonly attributed to laziness, indifference, and unawareness. These phenomena are known to thrive in the absence of effective donor recruitment programmes. Indeed, the efficiency of such programmes has a direct bearing on the supply of organs.

The general social interest in protecting life may paradoxically limit the supply of organs. The legal ban on harvesting hearts from living donors demonstrates this point very well, and so does the drop in the rates of road traffic accidents. On the other hand, the very demand for hearts in itself has had a positive effect on their supply in a way that is arguably less concerned with protecting life. It has made an increasingly inclusive definition of death socially palatable. Hearts (and other organs) can now be harvested under circumstances that had been deemed unacceptable until not so long ago. As we shall see, both the formation and the reception of a broad definition of death have had little to do with its philosophical justifiability (although it may well be justified) and everything to do with its usefulness for the stakeholders. We shall also see that certain economic interests primarily drove this trend.

In fact, economic interests also play an important role in the political economy of the supply of organs. The following case is a rather subtle expression of this point. International data indicate that men are less likely to become organ donors and more likely to become recipients than their wives. Our intuition tends to attribute this gender bias to male chauvinism. However, this is an idealistic, and at any rate simplistic, explanation. It also fails to account for the fact that the phenomenon is more striking in poor communities. The different historical positions of men and women vis-à-vis the labour-power market are the fundamental factors in this case. In giving rise to the distorted conception that unpaid labour power has no value whatsoever, they normalize the idea among men and women alike that housewives ought to sacrifice their organs for their needy husbands [7]. Male chauvinism, which transpires to be an ideological epiphenomenon of these relations, may play a mediating role at best.

The profit drive, which has been shown to play an important role in the political economy of the demand for organs, also plays an important role in their supply. Its impact is complex, however: other factors ignored, it decreases supply from certain sources, but increases it from others. This double effect is mediated through an increasingly intensifying global economic competition in ways that are described in the following:

(1) A shift of interests.

Extreme economic competition is inclined to replace social solidarity with individualism. It transforms the social circumstances from such where the happiness of the individual depends on the happiness of others to such where the happiness of others becomes an obstacle to one's own happiness. One of the effects of this trend is a decline in the willingness to donate organs. Moreover, the competition also tends to force the competitors to reduce the value of any object they possess, the body included, to exchange value (a trend called "commodification") and all relations they have with each other to market relations (a trend called "commercialization"). This has an additional negative effect on the willingness to donate. Once a price tag has been attached to an object that had previously been given free of charge, a kidney, for example, the general willingness to donate it will tend to erode independently of the underlying commodification process.

The resulting shift from altruistic interests and relations of gift to egoistic interests and relations of commodity probably affects rich and poor equally, but its impact on the organ question generally varies according to the economic status of the player: the poor are more likely to sell their organs than the rich, the rich are more likely to buy organs than the poor, and both are less likely to donate them free of charge. All in all, this explains very well why ideas that support commerce in organs gain increasing popularity within the ethical discourse.

The specific effect of this shift on the actual supply of organs might be hard to assess, since the prevailing ethico-legal position that still rejects commerce in organs makes it difficult for the new motivations to express themselves freely. As a result, the increasing reluctance to donate organs may not be offset by the corresponding increase in the willingness to sell them. Moreover, such a problem may exist even in a system that allows commerce in organs. Those who can buy organs are unlikely to suffer from any shortage. However, those who cannot are likely to suffer even more because of the negative effect of the system on the willingness to donate organs free of charge. The phenomenon of "transplant tourism" — patients travelling from one country in which commerce in organs is effectively banned to another country where organs are commercially available — demonstrates a similar problem on a global scale. In decimating the rate of donations in both countries, it has created a problem for both non-commercial albeit funding-dependent transplant centres as well as patients who cannot afford to buy the organs [8].

(2) Increase in poverty.

Contrary to a common view, contemporary poverty is not a result of idleness or bad luck. Rather, it is a historical outcome of an increasingly unequal distribution and redistribution of resource, power, and opportunity, which has been brought about first and foremost by the profit interest. Intriguingly, this interest retains its compensatory potential for any drop in the supply of organs it might have caused also through its active impoverishing effect. As already suggested, the poor, more than anyone else, are likely to consider organ vending as a viable option. Increase in both the rate of poverty as well as its intensity is thus likely to augment the supply of commercial organs, all other things ignored.

(3) Decreased investments in donor programmes.

In giving rise to the cost-containing interest of governments, the economic competition may foster their reluctance to invest in donor programmes with a concomitant drop in donation rates. The new Israeli Transplant Law, for example, introduces financial incentives for donors, but fails to secure a budget to support donor programmes as previously proposed [9]. True, this apparent irrationality could be explained away by showing that the cost-effectiveness of the existing allocation of funding is greater than that of any other alternative, but an empirical support to this effect is still pending.

14.2 Two Great Solutions

We have seen that the organ crisis has been caused by its very own victim. Unsurprisingly, that victim — society — also seeks to resolve it. It has come up with two kinds of solutions: non-consensual and consensual. Virtually each and every one of the non-consensual solutions was defended at some point for being moral, and virtually each and every one of the consensual solutions was attacked at some point for being immoral. Since we have no Archimedean criterion of morality, the question cannot be decided philosophically. That said, it is decided socially: we may or may not embrace the "really" moral solution, but we universally regard the solution that we embrace as "really" moral, and brand the one that we reject as "really" immoral. Whether or not there is any moral difference between these categories is thus debatable. That said, there is a discernible sociological difference between them.

Non-consensual solutions do not conceal their partiality. They neither satisfy, nor do they purport to satisfy, any common interest. On the contrary, they blatantly serve some stakeholders at the expense of others. Solutions of that sort reflect some extreme imbalance of power, either real or desired. Accordingly, they are either imposed by overwhelmingly powerful stakeholders or proposed by weak stakeholders who would like to be overwhelmingly powerful. Examples of the former case include procurement of organs using various forms of violence against their original owners, whereas proposals to ban certain morbidity-inflicting forms of production and consumption are examples of the latter case. It is apparently easier to rob the organs of the have-nots than to impinge on the property rights of the haves.

In contrast, consensual solutions serve some common interest, that is, an abstract interest that is compatible with some concrete interest of each stakeholder. The debate about a market in organs, for example, demonstrates that consensual solutions can be in conflict with each other. Indeed, the pro-market argument and the anti-market argument are both consensual (or nearly consensual) solutions to the organ crisis. Each appeals to some common interest, albeit a different one.

Consensual solutions present a potential problem, however. In serving some common interest, they tend to give the impression that they serve each and every interest of each and every stakeholder. This is certainly possible, but only if the pertinent political economy is made of agonistic interests only, that is to say, interests that are compatible, or at least not incompatible, with each other. The consensus around the Euclidian geometrical axioms, for example, has so far rested on such a tranquil political economy [10].

In contrast, the political economy of transplantation is stormy: it contains both agonistic and antagonistic interests, the latter referring to conflicting interests. For example, the interest of the patient in avoiding organ failure is in conflict with any financial interests in organ failure or practices that tend to generate organ failure. In fact, the increase in morbidity rates reflects the dominance of the latter over the former. And yet neither the conflict of the interests nor the domination of some interests on others precludes the emergence of a common interest in organ transplants. On the contrary, they become its parents. Consensual solutions, so it appears, are possible even under coercive circumstances. They simply become hegemonic in that they address a common interest that has effectively been tailored by a dominant stakeholder to suit his own interests [11].

This point is worth remembering, as the ethical discourse about transplantation is almost entirely made of consensual solutions of the hegemonic type. The very fact that it embraces ideas that purport to increase the organ pool while marginalizing those that suggest ways of reducing the need for organs in the first place is its hallmark. The discourse is conservative, then. Instead of challenging the political economy that generates the crisis, it is largely concerned with where to draw the ethical line insofar as the procurement of organs is concerned. Moreover, as the crisis deepens, it is increasingly inclined to push that line to places that had previously been deemed utterly immoral.

14.3 The Ethical Discourse: Procurement of Organs

14.3.1 *Prosthetic implants*

Since whole, functioning, prosthetic organs are yet to be developed, the impact of this source on the organ crisis is still marginal. At any rate, the ethical discourse finds only the distribution of prosthetic implants potentially problematic (problems pertaining to their distribution will be discussed later on) [12]. In fact, it finds few problems (if any) in their production. This is not surprising, considering the fact that synthetic materials such as metal, plastic, or ceramic, which are meant to replace lost tissue, involve no donor and hence no donor issues. Nevertheless, even the production of inanimate objects may raise some ethical issues.

One of these rather marginalized issues concerns the justifiability of producing implants of low cost-effectiveness or clinical efficacy relative to available alternatives. Mechanical bridging devices such as a total artificial heart and left ventricular assist devices are good examples. Both their cost-effectiveness and their clinical efficacy are considerably low compared to hearts from human sources. The argument supporting such production appeals to the low, and at any rate decreasing, supply of transplantable hearts. It also reminds us that these devices purport to provide a temporary solution only until a suitable human equivalent is found. This makes sense.

In contrast, the argument that appeals solely to the "demand" or "the autonomous will of the customer" is problematic (interestingly, arguments in support of any commodity rarely appeal to the financial interest of the entrepreneur). If given the choice, autonomous customers would never prefer an inferior product to a superior one. A desire for an inferior product would necessarily imply diminished autonomy. Accordingly, the production and marketing of inferior products could be criticized for being necessarily manipulative.

A closely related issue concerns the nature of the need for certain implants, typically cosmetic implants and such that provide some enhanced function that goes beyond the normal. Here, the implants may not be inferior to any alternative. As a matter of fact, they are unlikely to have any equivalent alternative at all. Nonetheless, a need for such implants may have been induced and nurtured by a manipulative industry for the sake of its own profits. An industry that responds to autonomous needs of people is moral, whereas the one that implants heteronomous needs in their minds is not [13].

14.3.2 *Xenogeneic organs*

The potential benefits of a successful xenograft programme appear to be considerable. The supply of xenografts would in theory be unlimited. The organs could be tailored to the patient's needs. The transplantation could be performed as an elective procedure with therefore better preparation of the patient. There would also be more time to test the animal donor for potential infections compared to the current situation with human transplants.

That said, the scientific-technological obstacles to clinical xenotransplantation are still considerable, and, like prosthetic implants, this source of organs has so far had little if any effect on the crisis. Nevertheless, the ethical discourse was quick to identify its potential problems. Distribution and recipient issues will be discussed later on, but some of them need to be mentioned here, for they have bearing on the ethics of the preliminary scientific work that aims at making this source usable in the first place.

The pertinent issues are two fold: immunological hurdles and the risk of rejection, and the possible presence of already known and yet undiscovered animal viruses that may put individuals and populations at risk of serious infection.

14.3.2.1 *Clinical trials involving human research subjects*

Against the backdrop of these risks, the first ethical question is not whether it is moral to implant animal organs into humans (so long as the treatment is not viable, the answer is no), but rather whether it is moral to proceed with research, particularly clinical trials, into xenotransplantation.

Typically, the answer is positive. It draws on the argument that success in xenotransplantation would be the best hope for saving the lives of patients with end-stage organ disease, so that the importance of the research objective outweighs the potential risks, which are anyway speculative. Those who are not convinced are seen as fearmongers, blind to the benefits of technology and to human suffering.

This argument raises several objections. First, xenotransplants are currently not the best way to save lives. Transplantation of organs from human sources is available and is known to be relatively safer. Second, it is not justifiable to put individual patients at risk for some uncertain future benefit for other patients. Third, there is evidence that such trials have been driven by money, not by the needs of patients, and that this drive has distorted the scientific information deduced from such trials. In view of these points, it would be impossible to obtain adequately informed consent from research candidates. Moreover, given the fact that the research subjects were all desperately ill, and all transplants resulted in the death of the patients, this question needs to be raised about the past as well. Since the resolution of the ethical and scientific obstacles to xenotransplantation is not guaranteed, one may argue that resources now being directed to it would be better deployed elsewhere [14].

14.3.2.2 *The use or abuse of animals*

Another set of ethical questions that is not really unique to the issue of xenotransplantation refers to the use of animals in the present research phase and as a future source of tissues and organs.

The first question is about the morality of sacrificing one organism for the sake of another. The question, as it is put, presupposes the possibility that all organisms, or at least all those who have a central nervous system, have the same right to life and freedom from "unnatural" exploitation and suffering (such a claim is highly contentious, since it presupposes that human actions are essentially 'unnatural'). To be more specific, it presupposes the possibility that humans and other sentient animals have the same moral status. If this is the case, then any use of animals for human purposes that involves suffering and/or death for the former would be immoral and ought thus to be avoided. The same goes for the closely related question, whether it is morally acceptable to alter the genome of animals to make xenotransplantation possible. This question presupposes the possibility that interfering with nature or with God's creations is bad, even if this involves no particular suffering.

In essence, there are two general ways of tackling these questions: either by appealing to philosophy or by appealing to power (a combination of both may perhaps be seen as a third way, but it obviously gives primacy to power).

The classical philosophical argument that opposes abuse of animals for human needs, also called the "antivivisectionist argument" insofar as it involves research on animals, proceeds from the assertion that there is no essential biological difference between some animals and humans. Whether true or false, this assertion purports to be a fact. In themselves, however, facts do not entail any moral implications or values. For example, the fact that "Switzerland has a chocolate industry" does not in itself entail that "Switzerland is good or bad", or indeed that "chocolate is good or bad". By the same token, the factual assumption that humans and other animals are biologically similar does not in itself entail any moral conclusion. In order to draw any moral conclusion, a general moral assertion needs to be added to the alleged fact. For example, if we asserted that "countries that produce chocolate are good" or that "sweets are good", then we could draw some moral conclusions based on our previous knowledge that "Switzerland is a country" and that "chocolate is a sweet". Indeed, the antivivisectionist argument makes such a general moral assertion. It takes it for granted that "the same should be treated the same" and deduces that humans ought not to do to animals things they would not want animals to do to them, if they could [15].

The opposing argument may accept the claim about biological similarity, but it asserts that the moral status of humans is superior to that of all animals hence the former ought to exploit the latter if necessary. The argument is typically secular; however it may also draw on the Old Testament:

> And God said, Let us make man in our image, after our likeness: and let them have dominion over the fish of the sea, and over the fowl of the air, and over the cattle, and over all the earth, and over every creeping thing that creepeth upon the earth. So God created man in his own image, in the image of God created he him; male and female created he them. And God blessed them, and God said unto them, Be fruitful, and multiply, and replenish the earth, and subdue it: and have dominion over the fish of the sea, and over the fowl of the air, and over every living thing that moveth upon the earth (Genesis 1:26–28).

Like all philosophical debates, however, this one is also irresolvable. There cannot be any fundamental criterion that could tell us which of the opposing general moral premises is really true. This point is of great importance, for it actually entails that our choice to embrace one premise and reject the other was not made on the basis of any truth, but rather on the basis of our interests. The fact that, as a society, we do exploit animals reflects nothing but the dominance of those who have interests in the pertinent practices over those who have opposing interests.

This sociological conclusion sheds light on the second ethical question too: Ought animals to be protected from suffering while they are alive and when they are killed? Few would argue that we should not be concerned with the welfare of animals. Some may argue that our moral duty to protect them from suffering is derived from their innate rights. Others may argue that such a duty is derived solely from concerns about the face and future of humanity. Whatever the case, the fact that it is now universally agreed that animals ought to be protected from suffering should not be seen as a victory of goodness over evil. Nor should it be seen as a reflection of the dominance of the antivivisectionists, let alone the animals themselves. On the contrary, it reflects a social compromise that rather reaffirms the domination of those who have some interest in exploiting animals. This conclusion may not make the philosophical debate redundant, but it strongly suggests that we should be more aware and perhaps even critical of the pertinent interests and the circumstances that have bred them.

14.3.2.3 A financial bubble?

So far, the paucity of practical achievements of research into xenotransplantation is in stark contrast to the amount of funding which the area attracts. In this respect, xenotransplantation resembles some other biomedical research areas, such as stem cell research and perhaps even the Human Genome Project as well. Non-medical examples of practices that have had little value aside from increasing the GDP are well known, and are collectively called "bubbles". Of course, research into xenotransplantation may eventually prove to be fertile. However, its failure so far and the fact that it takes place when other alternatives are available should raise the questions whether it is not just another bubble and whether the money it absorbs should not be put to better use.

14.3.3 Human organs

At least as far as human organs are concerned, the history of transplant ethics is that of a continuous expansion. As mentioned above, the deepening organ crisis and the fact that the stakes are high for so many players explain why we have pushed, and continue to push, the ethical line to places that had previously been deemed immoral. Before we discuss the ethical debate around each of the historical ethical milestones, it may be useful to observe the general trend first.

In the beginning we allowed deceased donations only. To tackle insufficient supply from the dead we embraced an increasingly inclusive definition of death. This has made it possible for us to retrieve organs from patients who had been considered legally alive according to the old definition of death. We then came up with the idea of opt-out consent according to which the dead are presumed to have given their consent for using their organs unless stated otherwise. These steps have certainly helped, but as the crisis continued to deepen we went one step further: we allowed donations from the living. In this category, we first permitted related and non-directed unrelated (anonymous) donations only. These measures have expanded the organ pool, but not enough.

By that time we had already become aware that interests in organ commerce were constantly intensifying, and that those in need of organs or money were increasingly likely to turn to the black market or seek a legal loophole that would allow them to conceal the commercial transaction behind some legitimate gesture. Until recently, we haven't done much about the black market, but we have banned altruistic-directed living unrelated donations fearing that they would become that legal loophole. This fear did not last long, though. The increasing hunger for more organs has driven us to legitimize this category as well. Indeed, it has helped a lot, but it did not suffice either. And so, still in the name of altruism and solidarity, we allowed paired exchange and donor chains. The contribution of these barter deals to the organ pool has only been marginal, though.

Recently, attempts to increase donation by removing disincentives (e.g., reimbursement of costs and assurance of free healthcare) or by offering non-commercial incentives (e.g., giving the relatives of a deceased donor priority on the transplant waiting list) are being considered in several countries. A thin line crosses between such measures and organ commercialism. Indeed, being tired of partial solutions, we are now introducing a dual strategy, depending on the audience: to those who still need to fool themselves we peddle the idea of quasi-non-commercial incentives for both living and deceased donations, and to those who no longer need to fool themselves we offer the bare market.

An educated assessment of trends and possibilities requires us to go back to the political economy of transplantation. That said, the prevailing trend is pretty obvious even without knowing much about it: if things are to continue as they have, we shall sooner or later embrace organ commercialism as one of the legitimate solutions to the underlying needs. The ethical justifications will follow the interests, not the other way around.

14.3.3.1 *Organs from the dead*

For some time, the dead used to be the almost exclusive source of organs for transplantation. This rested on three ethical premises. First, it is morally acceptable to retrieve organs, mainly kidneys, from the dead, if, when the subjects were still alive, they expressed their consent to donate their organs upon their death by signing a donor card or by making another form of advance directive. Second, it is morally acceptable to retrieve organs from the dead even without any advance directive if their relatives gave their consent to donate their organs. Third, there is a fundamental moral difference between deceased and living donations: the former are morally acceptable, whereas the latter are not. There are two main reasons for this difference: the donation cannot harm the dead as much as it can harm the living, and the dead, unlike the living, are no longer at risk of donating their organs under coercion.

In an attempt to increase the organ pool without breaching the ethical premises of this category, ethical amendments were made in relation to the definition of death (in most countries) in relation to the legal doctrine of consent (in some countries). The reader should again bear in mind that it was the underlying motivation that necessitated these ethical amendments, not the other way around. That said, whether or not they are philosophically plausible is for the reader to decide.

14.3.3.1.1 An expanding definition of death

Until the mid 1960s, death had been defined as the irreversible cessation of circulatory-respiratory function. The need to replace that definition with another became urgent when two economic interests appeared on the scene: interests in reducing the financial burden incurred by an increasing number of chronically ventilated comatose patients, and interests in retrieving organs for transplantation [16]. Regardless of any philosophical justification, this need was based on the understanding that expansion of the definition of death could legitimize withdrawal of ventilation and retrieval of organs, respectively, in some patients hitherto considered alive. In particular, an appropriate change in the definition of death could, if embraced by the law, legitimize retrieval of hearts from patients who, according to the then prevailing definition had been considered alive, that is to say, brain-dead patients whose circulatory functions are maintained even if by mechanical means only.

The concept of "brain death" was canonized soon after the publication of the report of the Harvard Committee in 1968 [17]. In the opening remarks, the committee, on which two transplant surgeons sat, was very clear about the interests underlying its endorsement of the concept — meeting the increasing demand for organs and containing the financial crisis in intensive care and dialysis. These interests were later reiterated even more explicitly by the founder of the committee himself, the famous doctor Henry Beecher [18]. Interestingly, the report made no reference to any neurological research and was totally unclear about the very criteria of brain death. Moreover, it did not take the trouble to conceal the role of the new definition and its underlying interests behind any philosophical justi-fication. This was first done by the President's Commission in 1981, only following a heated public controversy [19]. The philosophical rationale underlying the new definition was simple: human life requires cognition; cognition, hence human life, resides in a functioning brain; hence brain death and only brain death means death.

Though the change in the definition of death initially increased the organ pool, its practical implications were limited. First, pronouncement of death based on brain death criteria could apply in certain hospital set-tings only. Second, the required neurological tests have proved to be expensive. Thus in order to overcome these limitations, an even more flexible definition of death was called upon: when pronouncing death, doctors are now encouraged to *choose* between brain death and circulatory-respiratory death, depending on the circumstances and the interests. Accordingly, the death of hospital patients who are not potential donors is established by the criteria of the old definition, and the same goes for non-hospital patients who are potential donors.

In 2007, the *Washington Post* reported that doctors were increasingly declaring patients dead within minutes after their heart stopped beating and without any evidence of brain death, so that surgeons could remove their organs [20]. This trend is openly supported by major figures in the American transplant community, notwithstanding claims that the presumption that the act of organ procurement has taken place after death (the "dead donor rule") is a legal fiction [21, 22].

The concept of "legal fiction" invites a brief explication, since, as we shall see, it plays a central role in several practices in transplantation where it raises some serious ethical questions.

With minor differences in formulation, most modern law dictionaries define legal fiction as a presumption taken to be true by the courts of law, irrespective of whether it is true or false, and even though it might knowingly be false. Not every presumption is a legal fiction, though. To be a legal fiction, the chances that a presumption be true must be significantly diminished. In principle, this may happen when the presumption does not lend itself to scrutiny, let alone serious scrutiny, and where circumstantial conditions that make it somewhat unlikely to be true apply [23].

In view of the underlying interests and the difficulty in establishing the facts, the presumption that "death has occurred prior to the retrieval of the organs" may indeed be a legal fiction. In strong words, it may become a legal loophole that conceals murder. Precisely for the same reasons, the presumption that "the pronouncement of death is done independently of the retrieval of the organs" also turns out to be legal fiction.

We may believe that there is nothing wrong with retrieving organs from cadavers. But in view of what's been said, wouldn't we feel more comfortable if we knew that our current definitions and criteria of death remained in place even under a political economy that contained no economic interests in death [24]?

14.3.3.1.2 Opt-out consent

The legal doctrine of informed consent provides the justification for retrieving organs from those who have the mental capacity to consent as long as they are informed and can make a free and voluntary choice. As long as these conditions apply, the doctrine is not concerned about whether the consent was explicit (opt-in consent) or implicit/presumed (opt-out consent).

In most cases, consent to donate one's organs when one dies or consent to donate the organs of a deceased relative is of the opt-in kind. The subjects involved must give their explicit consent to donate the organs. In other words, their organs will not be taken without such consent. However, several countries have introduced and others are considering introducing a system of opt-out consent. In such a system, people are presumed to have given their consent to become organ donors after death, unless they explicitly refused.

The effect of an opt-out system on deceased donation rates is difficult to establish, since so many other factors are also involved. Such factors include the non-existence or existence of efficient donor programmes, the level of public trust in the medical authorities and its motivations, and general cultural attitudes toward deceased donation. Indeed, in Spain and Greece, two countries that have an opt-out system in action, the trends are opposite: the donation rates in Spain are high while those in Greece are low. In fact, there is some evidence that under certain social conditions the opt-out system can have a detrimental effect on donation rates. The UK, for example, has recently rejected proposals to introduce such a system precisely because of such fears [25].

These are mainly empirical concerns, not ethical ones. The ethical rationale behind the opt-out system draws on the presumption that all people are willing to donate their organs after death, but some are simply too lazy to give their explicit consent. This presumption can be put in other words: those who did not sign a donor card would have signed it had they been less lazy. The aim of an opt-out system is thus to bypass the laziness of individuals, not their free will.

Interestingly, the idea of opt-out consent has only rarely attracted criticism for being immoral. This is notwithstanding the fact that the presumption upon which it is based is just another instance of legal fiction. Opt-out consent does not necessarily imply consent, let alone informed consent. It may increase the organ pool by recruiting many who are really willing to donate their organs, but it might also recruit those who are not. In part, then, this system is effectively based on deception.

14.3.3.1.3 State ownership of deceased organs

A far more extreme version of the opt-out system is the idea that deceased organs should be owned by the state and made use of regardless of the wishes of the subjects involved [26]. Like the opt-out system, such a proposal could be justified only if it rested upon a total social consensus. Such a consensus does not exist as of yet.

14.3.3.1.4 Deceased organ commercialism

Currently, commerce in deceased organs is illegal in all countries, and is thus confined to the black market. Nevertheless, proposals to legalize the practice have been made in an attempt to exhaust the procurement potential of this category. These proposals offer some material value to families who are willing to vend (the term "donate" is inappropriate in this case) their deceased relative's organs. This material value could be translated, for example, to life insurance, covering funeral costs, obtaining priority in the transplant waiting list for needy family members, and even cash payments.

Deceased organ commercialism poses some serious ethical issues. However, these shall be discussed in the next section that deals with, among others, living organ commercialism. The latter, so it will be argued, raises precisely the same issues [27, 28].

14.3.3.2 *Organs from the living*

The benefits of using organs from the living, mainly kidneys and liver, over deceased organs are prominent. This organ pool is potentially bigger; the transplantation may be planned in advance; the quality of the organ and its suitability for the particular recipient, hence the survival of the graft, are generally better. This general category raises two major ethical issues, however.

First, one should note that procurement of organs from the living is an act of medicalization, namely, an act that imposes the categories and practices of medicine on a non-medical object. Indeed, this act requires us to abandon the supreme Hippocratic principle according to which it is essentially unprofessional to turn a healthy person, i.e., the donor, into a patient, even if for a short time only. To justify this audacious step we appeal to the deontological principle of respect for the donor's autonomy and the legal doctrine of informed consent, and to the utilitarian premise of maximization of happiness (both the donor and the recipient are happier than before). Unfortunately, however, there is no fundamental philosophical criterion that could tell us which of the two ethics is "really" moral and which is "really" immoral (theoretically, both may be immoral, but if one is moral, then the other must be immoral). One thing should be clear, though: we have made the ethical choice on the basis of our historically evolving interests.

And yet a difficult ethical question should be raised in this context: if indeed it is morally acceptable for a doctor to take out the kidney of a healthy person based on a certain ethic, should it not be also morally acceptable to take out his or her heart based on the same ethic?

We currently say no. We believe that there is an essential difference between the cases as the latter inevitably entails death. We still feel that doctors ought not to deliberately kill people under any circumstances. On the other hand, there are signs that the idea of physician-assisted suicide is gaining popularity in many societies, and that in such cases the ethical justification appeals to the principle of respect for the patient's autonomy. Why then should a mother who wants to donate her heart to her son be treated differently?

The answer cannot be found in ethics, but in sociology. The political economy of assisted suicide is different from that of living heart donation. One day, if our interests dictate so, the stubborn remnant of the Hippocratic ethics, which still affects the latter category, may disappear.

The general category of living donation raises another ethical issue: the demand for organs may put healthy people at risk of losing their organs under some form of coercion. Organ robbery is an extreme example. However, coerced "donation" can also occur in the presence of the donor's informed consent. In other words, informed consent in itself does not rule out coercion. This unfortunate fact has been widely recognized, and attempts have indeed been made to ban practices that involve coercion even regardless of the presence of consent. Whether these attempts were effective or not is a completely different matter, however.

14.3.3.2.1 Related donation and non-directed unrelated (anonymous) donation

In order to prevent forms of coercion that might be concealed behind informed consent, we first allowed related donation and non-directed unrelated (anonymous) donation only. We have assumed that family ties and non-directedness preclude coercion and necessarily imply altruism. This assumption is another form of a legal fiction, however. In fact, the mechanisms that we installed to confirm that assumption are lax. They do not allow certain forms of coercion to interfere with the donor's consent. For example, the subtle forms of coercion that might occur within the family are often overlooked by the prevailing control mechanisms. The tendency of wives and husbands to become donors and recipients, respectively, which has been mentioned above, reflects this failure fairly well. A similar problem exists in the case of non-directed unrelated donations. Such donations seem to preclude coercion even better than related donations, but even they cannot preclude complex clandestine commercial ties, which as we shall see, pre-suppose and imply some sort of coercion. In this case too, the prevailing control mechanisms are usually unable to spot any commercial ties.

14.3.3.2.2 Altruistic-directed unrelated donations

This subcategory of living donation has been banned for a long time of fear that the presumption of altruism could become a legal loophole concealing clandestine commercial ties between vendor and emptor, hence some form of coercion. This fear is not baseless. The deepening organ crisis, the decline of social solidarity, and the evolving interests in organ commercialism are likely to turn this presumption into a legal fiction.

Nevertheless, the increasing demand for organs has made us abandon that fear. In most countries this subcategory is now acceptable [29]. Control mechanisms have indeed been installed, but they too are somewhat lax. For example, the control mechanisms in the US and in Israel are fairly similar in rigour [30]. However, comparisons of the socioeconomic profile of donors versus recipients in both countries suggest that these mechanisms are more likely to be fooled in Israel. This strongly suggests that the factors that determine whether altruistic-directed unrelated donation becomes a legal fiction or not should not be sought in the rigour of the control mechanism, but rather in the strength of the local social solidarity [31].

14.3.3.2.3 Paired exchange and donor chains

Related donations may not always be the best option even if potential coercion is not an issue. Indeed, donor-recipient incompatibility will rule out such donation. Recently, creative solutions were developed to bypass this problem. For example, if fathers X and Y want to donate their kidneys to their sons x and y, respectively, but their kidneys could only be given to y and x, respectively, then a paired exchange may take place. X will give his kidney to y, and Y will give his one to x. Similarly, an extended chain may be formed, involving more than two donors. Moreover, a donor chain may involve not just donors and their related recipients, but also altruistic donors who have no designated recipients and thus do not expect to receive anything in return [32].

Such enterprises obviously require meticulous technical logistics. However, they are also required to prevent breach of the group contract by one or more of the candidate donors. In the case of a paired exchange, such a breach could be prevented by having all four operations done simultaneously. Since simultaneity is almost impossible in the case of a long donor chain (the completion of the chain could sometimes take several months), the ethical challenge is more difficult and could be partly overcome by the recruitment of altruistic donors who have no designated recipients.

This subcategory of living donations has been hailed as a perfectly ethical solution, not just because it is based on the consent of the participants, but also because it increases social solidarity. Paradoxically, however, proponents of organ commercialism may argue that it serves as a pretext for the idea they wish to push through. Based on the claims that (1) paired exchange and donor chains are private instances of barter, (2) barter is ethically acceptable, and (3) money simply facilitates barter by giving the players more freedom, they could argue that all transactions that involve money, buying and selling of organs included, ought to be ethically acceptable too. Moreover, they could add that the risk of trading one's kidney for too little money is no greater than the risk involved in trading one's good kidney for one of lesser quality.

The analogy between barter in organs and commerce in organs may fall flat, however. In the former case one kidney is traded for another kidney, while in the latter case the kidney is traded for another commodity.

This difference in itself does not have a moral significance, but the difference in the circumstances underlying each of these transactions may indeed have a moral significance.

14.3.3.2.4 Organ commercialism

As we have seen, the political economy of the organ crisis breeds pressures to commercialize organ procurement. As a matter of fact, in the current situation each and every stakeholder has some interest in a market in organs. Both those who need the organs as well as those who need the money can expect the market to be able to meet their respective needs. At the same time, some of the stakeholders have opposing interests as well. For example, potential vendors who have an interest in trading their kidney for money also have an interest in not having to make such a choice in the first place. The same goes for patients who have an interest in buying a kidney. It is not a great pleasure to have to sell or buy body parts.

This conflict of interests is reflected in the global legal reality. On the one hand, almost all countries still forbid commerce in organs (Iran is currently the only exception) with a black market existing in some parts of the world. On the other hand, the voices that call for legalization of some form of organ commercialism intensify. Interestingly, however, both the opponents and the proponents of organ commercialism are unified on one point: transplant tourism, where a patient from a rich country travels to buy a kidney in a poor country, and other forms of the black market are not just immoral but also deleterious as far as local interests are concerned. This position has been asserted by several international bodies [33–35].

The current debate around organ commercialism takes place between those who oppose any form of organ commercialism and those who support some form of local commercialism. This debate reflects a conflict of interests within the political economy of transplantation, but it takes place in the realm of ethics.

1. The pro-market argument

The pro-market discourse maintains that, however efficient, a transplant donor programme that appeals to social solidarity and the goodwill of individuals will inevitably fail to meet the increasing demand for organs.

It asserts that letting patients suffer and die on the waiting lists, when so many organs are out there just begging to be harvested, is morally unacceptable, and so is wasting public resources. Non-commercial systems are thus both ineffective as well as immoral.

The pro-market discourse holds that, in contrast, the market, and only the market, can provide unlimited access to these organs and be moral at the same time. Not any market, though. A global organ market, for example, is not just counterproductive but also immoral. This is because it creates severe inequities in the distribution of power, benefit, and risk. Such faults, the discourse contends, result from the essentially unfettered nature of this market. A global organ market cannot be tamed and is thus bound to remain both counterproductive as well as immoral.

That said, an organ market that is free from any practical drawbacks and inequities is feasible within the bounds of a national market or an economic union. It must adhere to certain regulatory principles, though. As far as the protection of recipients is concerned, such principles include a single buyer, mechanisms assuring safety and quality, and systems that guarantee equitable, non-means-based allocation of the organs. The principles are no less attentive to the welfare of the vendors. In addition to the single buyer, they include mechanisms validating consent requirements, safeguards against buying organs from vulnerable people, strict prohibition of brokering, and systems assuring competitive remuneration, life insurance, continuous healthcare, and priority in transplant waiting lists [36].

Otherwise, the pro-market discourse sees no essential moral problem with trading in organs. First, body parts are private property. In the name of liberty, their owners should be free to do with them as they like. Second, both parties can make a free choice, at least in principle. The unpleasant nature of the dilemma each one of them is facing does not by itself make their choices unfree. On the contrary, it is rather the existing prohibition of commerce in organs that limits their freedom, often with dire consequences for both of them. Third, the generally accurate classification of buyers and vendors as rich and poor, respectively, may perhaps seem to reflect inequities and suggest relations of power and exploitation. However, this does not have to be the case. In the regulated market, the parties would maintain perfectly symmetrical relations vis-à-vis each other. Their complementary deficiencies and surpluses would guarantee "mutual exploitation" and hence equal distribution of benefits and risks. Fourth, many instances involving commerce in the body are already legitimate. Making the kidney an exception would be ethically inconsistent. Fifth, the real choice we are facing, and the only one, is between a regulated market and a black market. Considering the interests of buyers and vendors, the former is by far the better option.

2. The anti-market argument

The argument against a regulated market in organs makes two points. First, it casts doubt upon its feasibility and efficacy. It maintains that regulation would be counterproductive, if not altogether impossible. With so much money at stake, it posits, the regulatory mechanisms that purport to assure liberty, quality, and safety are bound to fail, doctor–patient relationships would be harmed, and people would start buying what they currently get for free, which would increase public spending.

Being empirical in nature, these claims have a clear advantage over ethical ones: they appeal to reason, not sentiment. They may even attempt to appeal to the reason of the proponents of the market themselves. Otherwise, they are disturbing. First, the political economy of transplantation indicates that some players have vested interests in the organ market regardless of whether it is regulated or not. These powerful players do not care about any other consequences. They are unlikely to be convinced. Second, such claims pre-suppose that there is actually nothing wrong with the ideally regulated market, hence with the fundamental principle of trade in body parts. As such, they effectively normalize and moralize the commercial idea. Finally, to argue that the regulated market is bound to fail when one believes that the experiment carries a high risk is a very dangerous thing to do. Indeed, empirical claims do not scare the proponents of the market. Rather, they invite them to try to prove their case, and they will not turn this invitation down.

To be robust, then, the anti-market discourse should not be concerned with the feasibility or the efficacy of a regulated market. On the contrary, it should take its premises at face value and direct its criticism at the very heart of the problem — the very principle of trade in body parts.

Indeed, the second point which the argument makes addresses the bare principle of trade in body parts. In attempt to identify its moral fault, it points at the payment as the source of evil. Indeed, it associates a greater payment with greater coercion and a smaller payment with greater exploitation. It uses this culprit to conclude that since the payment violates the human dignity of the vendor, a ban thereon would preserve that dignity.

However, this is fundamentally wrong. In the ideally-regulated organ market there is a complementary symmetry between emptor and vendor. Every buyer is also a seller, and every seller is also a buyer. One buys a kidney and sells money, while the other buys money and sells a kidney. Moreover, each of the commodities in question is the equivalent of the other. Under such circumstances it would be unreasonable to describe any one of the offers as being coercive, let alone more coercive than the other. Indeed, no one would describe an offer to sell one's kidney in terms of "undue inducement", so why should one describe an offer to sell one's money in such terms?

If this is still not convincing, one could make a different argument, such that is not based on assumptions about any symmetry, equivalence, or exchange. Imagine a worker in a meat factory whose hand has just got stuck in a giant mincer that threatens to devour him completely. The switch is located in another room, so that the machine could not be deactivated quickly enough to save the poor man's life. The only thing one could do is offer him the nearest knife so that he could choose whether he wants to cut himself free from his hand or not.

Now, would you describe this offer as coercive? Would you argue that the sharper the knife the more coercive the offer, or that the blunter it is the more exploitative the offer? Would your answers to these questions depend on the interests or motivations of the helper? Certainly not! What you could do is acknowledge that the offer gives the worker a choice, and that giving him that choice, however sad, is better than giving him no choice at all.

We shall return to this gruesome scenario in a moment, but let us first see that neither organ commerce nor an embargo thereon has anything to do with the human dignity of the vendor.

Anatole France (1844–1924), the French poet and novelist and the Nobel laureate for literature for 1921, wrote: "The law, in its majestic equality, forbids the rich as well as the poor to sleep under bridges, to beg in the streets, and to steal bread" [37]. Now let us portray a different law, such that allows both the rich and the poor to sleep under bridges, etc. According to the anti-market conclusion the former law respects the human dignity of the subjects in question, whereas the latter does not. The truth is that none of these laws is better than the other. If there is any problem with the respective social systems, then it resides in the difference between rich and poor as far as their available options are concerned, and in the fact that none of these laws addresses that difference.

But if payment for organs is not in itself morally problematic, what then is wrong with trade in body parts?

To answer this question, let us go back to our meat-factory scenario and look deeper into the context. We might perhaps discover that the calamity was neither the worker's own fault nor was it the result of any natural or supernatural decree. As a matter of fact, our worker, whether he be the rich patient who needs a kidney or the poor person who has nothing to sell but his kidney, was deliberately pushed into the mincer. Indeed, the political economy of our society shows that both kidney failure as well as poverty are largely the outcomes of certain social practices which are propelled by certain beneficiaries. Now, if this is where the evil lies, then the offer of the knife, and in our case the offer of money for a kidney and vice versa, will no longer seem moral. It will transpire to be just an ethical façade that conceals and reaffirms an underlying immorality.

To be robust, then, the anti-market argument should acknowledge the fact that the regulated market is ethical and reject it precisely on that ground. It should tell its audience that those who push some people into kidney disease and others into poverty ought not to be allowed to hide these wrongs behind any ethical veil. To those who are rightly concerned with the fate of the individual person who begs for an acute solution should explain that the suffering-preventing capacity of a kidney-disease-free and poverty-free world is considerably greater than that of any organ market.

To conclude this part of the chapter let us focus again on the difference between organ donation and organ vending. In the former case, the donor cares very much about the fate of the organ once it has been removed from his or her body. In the latter case, the vendor becomes *alienated* to the organ. He or she no longer cares about its fate; on the contrary, many vendors actually wish that it be rejected! Such alienation reflects heteronomy (the opposite of autonomy), hence some form of coercion.

This point has bearing on both living and deceased organ commercialism: in both cases, the vendors would not have sold the organs had they not been deprived of better options. Neither the problem nor its solution should be sought in the market ethics, but rather in the social factors that inflict this deprivation and thereby drive the victims to seek refuge in the market [38].

14.4 The Ethical Discourse: Distribution of Organs

14.4.1 *Prosthetic implants*

The distribution of prosthetic implants raises several general and specific ethical issues. Social equity is a general issue. It does not depend on the specific nature of the implant/organ but rather on whether its distribution is regulated by the free market or by the public healthcare system. With small differences in emphasis, a similar issue exists in the distribution of organs obtained from animal and human sources as well.

Distribution of implants and organs, which is regulated by market forces only, that is to say, by the purchasing capacity of the patients, would mean that only the relatively rich could have access to the treatment. This begs the general question whether such treatments ought to be treated like any other commodity or be given to the needy regardless of their financial status. The answer to this question requires a profound analysis of the prevailing political economy of production in general. This goes beyond the scope of this paper, but two central points can be made. If the analysis were to show that all goods, including implants, have been produced by society, one could argue that they should also be owned and distributed by society and not by private individuals who, because of class relations of power, happen to appropriate them. Equally, if the analysis were to show that the class of private owners of commodities were also responsible for the emergence of production- and consumption-related diseases, then it should take responsibility at least for treating the victims. If medical treatment is a human right, then this is only because of that reason.

But the distribution of implants and organs may raise an ethical problem even when regulated by the public. If implants and organs are scarce, how should we allocate them? The basic approach has been based on the principle of "first come, first served" (ignoring the need) and need (ignoring the place in the waiting list). Recently, however, criteria of outcome were also introduced. In some cases, these are replacing the criterion of need. For example, hip replacement, which requires an implant, is often allocated to those who are likely to show better outcomes, namely, those who are not obese. It is denied from those who need it most. This utilitarian value-for-money approach seems to be compatible with a good investment policy, but it is morally dubious. It discriminates against the obese, whose condition is now known to result from certain forms of social consumption. The system that has made these people ill exempts itself from responsibility for their care.

A different question that may emerge in the case of implants is if and when the device should be turned off. This question, which applies particularly to life-sustaining implants, belongs to the realm of end-of-life ethics.

Another ethical issue concerns the potential capacity of electronic implants to replace lost neurological functions or enhance human capabilities beyond normal levels. In the case of replacement of lost functions — cochlear and ocular implants, for example — problems of adaptation may exist. As far as the case of enhanced capabilities is concerned, this capacity is still largely fictional. However, mental changes and changes in personal identity have been named as potential risks. One may also argue that there should be a limit to any enhancement, but the real question is that of benefit and loss, beneficiaries and victims.

14.4.2 *Xenogeneic organs*

In the case of xenotransplantation, the issue of social equity receives a specific dimension, because the service might become available only within the confines of private healthcare, and yet it might expose the entire population to the risk of infection by known and unknown agents. This injustice is still more disturbing to the extent that public resources are being mobilized to develop xenotransplantation.

There may also be some cultural barriers, primarily religious, to receiving xenogeneic organs. However, these may be overcome by other alternatives, and possibly by reinterpretation of the underlying taboos.

14.4.3 *Human organs*

The problem of social equity is of primary concern in this area. In non-commercial settings, a combination of waiting list, need, outcome, tissue compatibility, and the quality of the available organs forms the acceptable way of allocating the organs. Even the idea of a regulated market in organs accepts this premise (in contrast, a "free" market in organs allocates them only according to the purchasing capacity of the customer). "Need" and "outcome" are very delicate issues, however. Are the young in greater need than the elderly? Should those whose prognosis is worse be discriminated against?

Let us consider one case only. Two patients are waiting for a liver transplant, but only one liver is available. One has an idiopathic liver disease and the other has alcoholic liver cirrhosis. Everything else is equal. We know that the prognosis of the latter patient is worse, let alone that he or she are likely to resume drinking. Who should receive the liver?

Currently, our common intuition would give the priority to the patient whose lifestyle has played no role in the pathophysiology of the underlying condition. This is not surprising, since we tend to think in categories of "outcome" and "personal responsibility". Alcoholism, however, is a social problem. In part it has cultural features, but in part it is also caused by profit-driven and perhaps even politically driven forms of consumption. If this is the case, then the latter patient should be seen as a victim of society. Denying the transplant from this patient would thus double the injustice.

A closely related issue concerns the effect of the time spent on the waiting list on the outcomes of transplantation. We know that the longer the wait, the poorer the prognosis. Criteria of outcome would therefore prioritize those who have entered the list just recently. In turn, those who have been waiting a long time would have to wait even longer.

Transplantation of organs from human sources raises two other issues of justice and fairness. The first issue concerns the suggestion that patients should receive a transplant only if they have been willing to donate their own organs upon their death. This idea is found seriously wanting, since it has the potential of discriminating against those who are unaware of donor programmes, and those who have some cultural or political (distrust in medical authorities) reason for not signing a donor card. Under such circumstances, the idea of conditionality becomes just another form of social victimization.

An extension of the idea of conditionality can be found in suggestions to give priority to relatives of a deceased donor. Such suggestions, which are usually marketed as non-commercial incentives for donation, have the capacity of discriminating against patients on the waiting list who have had no deceased donor in their family.

Another issue to be mentioned here concerns allocation of organs to foreigners. In the context of transplant tourism, such allocation is known to have a detrimental effect on non-commercial patients in both countries involved. In the context of some international agreement it is acceptable, however. For example, two or more countries may have an organ-sharing programme on the basis of equality. Equally, one country that has a developed transplant system may help another country that has no such system.

However, by far the biggest and the most disturbing problem concerns the global inequity in access to transplantation. We typically mention the numbers on the transplant waiting lists in developed countries. However, we tend to forget that most patients who suffer from organ failure can only dream of dialysis, let alone a waiting list. The solution to this problem will not be found in the globalization of commerce, but rather in the globalization of wealth and freedom.

References

[1] Organ Procurement and Transplantation Network. 2009. Available at: http://optn.transplant.hrsa.gov/ [accessed 9 August 2010].

[2] NHS Blood and Transplant. *Transplant Activity in the UK 2010–2011*. 2011. Available at: http://www.uktransplant.org.uk/ukt/statistics/transplant_activity_report/transplant_activity_report.jsp [accessed 27 July 2011].

[3] About Operations. *Organ Donation: Facts and Figures*. 2011. Available at: http://www.aboutoperations.co.uk/organ-donation-facts-figures.html [accessed 1 September 2010].

[4] Sagmeister M., Mullhaupt B., Kadny Z. *et al*. Cost-Effectiveness of Cadaveric and Living-donor Liver Transplantation, *Transplantation* 2002; **73(4)**, 616–622.

[5] NHS Blood and Transplant. *Cost-effectiveness of Transplantation*. 2009 Available at: http://www.uktransplant.org.uk/ukt/newsroom/fact_sheets/cost_effectiveness_of_transplantation.jsp [accessed 13 March 2011].

[6] Gal I. Heart Recipient's Father: We'll Never Donate Organs. *Israel Jewish Scene 2009.* Available at: http://www.ynet.co.il/english/articles/0,7340, L-3663653,00.html [accessed 12 May 2010].

[7] Scheper-Hughes N. The Tyranny of the Gift: Sacrificial Violence in Living Donor Transplants. *American Journal of Transplantation* 2007; **7**(3), 507–511.

[8] Budiani-Saberi D.A. and Delmonico F.L. (2008). Response to: Will Transplant Tourism Erode the Surgical Skills of Transplant Surgeons in Israel? *American Journal of Transplantation* 1964; **8**.

[9] Israel Transplant Law. (2008). [17/68, in Hebrew.] Available at: http://www. knesset.gov.il/privatelaw/data/17/3/68_3_1.rtf [accessed 1 March 2011].

[10] Hobbes T. *Leviathan.* Oxford University Press, Oxford. 1996[1651]; I.11.21.

[11] Gramsci A. *Selection from the Prison Notebooks.* Lawrence & Wishart, London 1971.

[12] Hansson S.O. Implant Ethics. *J Med Ethics* 2005; **31**, 519–525.

[13] Marcuse H. *One-Dimensional Man: Studies in the Ideology of Advanced Industrial Society.* Routledge, London, 2002 [1964].

[14] Collignon P. and Purdy L. Xenografts: Are the Risks so Great that We Should Not Proceed? *Microbes Infect* 2001; **3**, 341–348.

[15] Singer P. *Animal Liberation: The Definitive Classic of the Animal Movement.* Harper Perennial, New York, 2009.

[16] Wolstenholme G. and O'Connor M. (eds.) *Ciba Foundation Symposium. Ethics in Medical Progress* J & A Churchill Ltd, London, 1966.

[17] No author. Report of the Ad Hoc Committee of the Harvard Medical School to Examine the Definition of Brain Death: A Definition of Irreversible Coma, *Journal of the American Medical Association* 1968; **205**, 337–340.

[18] Beecher H. Scarce Resources and Medical Advancement: Ethical Aspects of Experimentation with Human Subjects. *Daedalus* 1969; **98**(2), 275–313.

[19] President's Commission on Ethical Problems in Medicine and Biomedical and Behavioral Research. *Defining Death: A Report on Medical, Legal, and Ethical Issues in the Definition of Death.* Washington, DC: US Government Printing Office, 1981.

[20] Stein R. New Trend in Organ Donation Raises Questions, *Washington Post,* 18 March 2007, A03. Available at: http://www.washingtonpost.com/wp-dyn/ content/article/2007/03/17/AR2007031700963.html [accessed 10 February 2011].

[21] Rady M.Y., Verheijde J.L. and McGregor J. Organ Donation After Cardiocirculatory Death and the Dead Donor Rule: What is the Evidence? *Canadian Medical Association Journal eLetters* 2006. Available at: http://www.cmaj. ca/content/175/8/S1/reply#cmaj_el_5442?sid=0ae6bf94-fd24-4f28-b90d-508d701126fe [accessed 25 January 2011].

[22] Steinbrook R. Organ Donation after Cardiac Death. *New England Journal of Medicine*, 2007; **357(3)**, 209–213.

[23] Epstein M. Legal and Institutional Fictions in Medical Ethics: A Common, and Yet Largely Overlooked, Phenomenon. *Journal of Medical Ethics* 2007; **33(6)**, 362–364.

[24] Epstein M. The Political Economy of Death and the History of Its Criteria. *Reviews in the Neurosciences* 2009; **20(3–4)**, 293–297.

[25] Department of Health. The Potential Impact of an Opt-Out System for Organ Donation in the UK: An Independent Report from the Organ Donation Taskforce. 2008. Available at: http://www.dh.gov.uk/en/Publicationsandstatistics/ Publications/PublicationsPolicyAndGuidance/DH_090312 [accessed 3 May 2011].

[26] Schönfeld M.R. Whose Tissues Are They Anyway? A Proposal for State Ownership of the Human Body and Its Parts. *Journal of Cardiovascular Diagnosis and Procedure* 1994–1995 **12(3)**, 145–149.

[27] Mayrhofer-Reinhartshuber D. and Fitzgerald R. Financial Incentives for Cadaveric Organ Donation. *Annals of Transplantation* 2004; **9(1)**, 25–27.

[28] Arnold R. *et al.* Financial Incentives for Cadaver Organ Donation: An Ethical Reappraisal *Transplantation*. 2002; **73**, 1361–1367.

[29] Directive 2004/23/EC of the European Parliament and of the Council of 31 March 2004 on Setting Standards of Quality and Safety for the Donation, Procurement, Testing, Processing, Preservation, Storage and Distribution of Human Tissues and Cells.

[30] Dew M.A. *et al.* Guidelines for the Psychosocial Evaluation of Living Unrelated Kidney Donors in the United States. *American Journal of Transplantation* 2007; **7**, 1047–1054.

[31] Epstein M. and Danovitch G.M. Is Altruistic Directed Living Unrelated Organ Donation a Legal Fiction? *Nephrology, Dialysis, Transplantation* 2009; **24**, 357–360.

[32] Rees M.A. *et al.* A Nonsimultaneous, Extended, Altruistic-Donor Chain. *New England Journal of Medicine* 2009; **360(11)**, 1096–1101.

[33] World Health Organization. *WHO Guiding Principles on Human Cell. Tissue and Organ Transplantation.* EB 123/5, 29 May.

[34] Steering Committee of the Istanbul Summit. Organ Trafficking and Transplant Tourism and Commercialism: The Declaration of Istanbul. *Lancet* 2008; **372**, 5–6.

[35] Epstein M. Sociological and Ethical Issues in Transplant Commercialism. *Current Opinion in Organ Transplantation* 2009; **14(2)**, 134–139.

[36] Erin C.A. and Harris J. A Monopsonistic Market: Or How to Buy and Sell Human Organs, Tissues and Cells Ethically. In Robinson I. (ed.) *Life and*

Death Under High-Technology Medicine. London: Manchester University Press in association with the Fulbright Commission, 1994; pp. 134–153.

[37] France A. *The Red Lily.* London, The Bodley Head 1930[1894]; Chapter 7.

[38] Epstein M. The Ethics of Poverty and the Poverty of Ethics: The Case of Palestinian Prisoners in Israel Seeking to Sell their Kidneys in Order to Feed Their Children. *Journal of Medical Ethics* 2007; **33**, 473–474.

15

Ethical and Legal Issues in Composite Tissue Allograft (Face, Arm, and Uterus) and Microsurgery

Richard Huxtable and Alice Guilder

15.1 Introduction

Composite tissue allografting involves transplanting a variety of tissues concurrently. In this chapter we seek to explore some of the ethical and legal issues to which a composite tissue allograft (CTA) gives rise, particularly those that have arisen in relation to hand transplants and, more recently, facial allograft transplantation (FAT). Although we will refer to the tissue donor in our analysis, we will be most concerned with the ethical dimensions pertaining to the (potential or actual) recipient of a CTA.

The analytical framework we employ is one that should be familiar to most (perhaps all) legal systems, since it organises the issues into one of three broad categories: individual choice, individual need, and public interest [1, 2]. Different legal systems and, indeed, people of diverse ethical commitments will attach different levels of importance to the questions arising — and answers provided — in each of these categories, but we suspect that they are all likely to feature in some way in the legal framework within which CTA is practised, regardless of exactly where one is practising.

Briefly to elaborate, medical law tends to draw a distinction between the patient or research participant who is capable of making healthcare choices (i.e., is autonomous or competent) and the patient or research participant who is not (i.e., is non-autonomous or incompetent). The former might have their autonomy respected, such that great weight may be attached to their choice for or against treatment or enrolment in a trial; the latter might have made their wishes known in advance, but might well not, such that a different criterion is required for deciding whether or not treatment should be provided or research undertaken. This criterion tends to be expressed in terms of the welfare of the individual or their "best interests", which may be judged according to an objective list of criteria, or might instead be more subjectively tethered to what the individual themselves might have chosen (the so-called "substituted judgement" approach).[1] Put simply, in terms of modern healthcare practices, the professional's approach could be led by considerations of *autonomy* or by considerations of *welfare*.

However, most legal systems would undoubtedly require more than (mere?) reference to a patient's perceived wishes or needs, and the interplay between the two will be subtler than the accounts just given. Fundamentally, even with an autonomous patient or participant, it is highly unlikely to be the case that a doctor must automatically accede to that individual's wishes without any regard to their welfare. It is more likely that the individual will be empowered to select an option from those which the doctor has already pre-selected in order to serve that person's interests. For this reason, we will start our analysis of CTA with considerations of welfare, in particular exploring the risks and benefits associated with the procedure. Only after exploring these will we return to consider the question of choice i.e., considerations of autonomy.

This will not be the end of the story; in addition, we discern a further boundary, which exists around every individual patient and, therefore, any consideration of their choices and interests. Crudely put, the individual exists within society and thus there will be considerations at the level of the "public interest" also to consider when appraising the legal and ethical

---

[1] For different examples of these sorts of approaches see the Mental Capacity Act 2005 (England) and *In re Quinlan* (1976) NJ 355 A 2d 647 (America).

dimensions of a phenomenon like CTA. We will, therefore, consider these too when assessing the merits (and de-merits) of such transplantation and microsurgical procedures. In order to undertake this assessment as fairly and accurately as possible, we start with an overview of the state of the science in this area.

15.2 Composite Tissue Allograft: Science Fact

The first (modern [3]) CTA, in the form of a hand transplant, was performed in Ecuador in 1963 [4]. Unfortunately, the graft was rejected and so the hand had to be removed within three weeks. However, by the late 1990s, developments in surgical and immunological expertise not only ensured the success of this procedure but also paved the way for other CTAs [5]. Amongst the notable successes are transplants of a larynx [6], lower limb and hindquarters [7], tongue [8], abdominal wall [9], uterus [10], testis [11], and penis [12].

The Louisville Hand Transplant Team, formed in 1996, spearheaded efforts to perfect the techniques for limb transplantation, which ultimately culminated in Lyon, France, with a hand graft undertaken by a team led by Jean-Michel Dubernard [13]. The recipient was Clint Hallam, an ex-convict from New Zealand. Initially the transplant appeared to be a success but Hallam reported difficulty adapting to his new hand and requested that it be removed. Amputation occurred in 2001, amidst criticism of the Lyon team for poor candidate selection [14].

Nevertheless, numerous hand transplants followed, including, in 1999, the first in the US, which was performed by the Louisville team [15]. By 2008, 38 hand transplants had been performed worldwide and registered with the International Registry on Hand and Composite Tissue Transplantation [16]. One of the more controversial hand transplants was performed on a one-month-old Malaysian girl, Chong Lih Ying. Born with a severely deformed arm, she received the arm and hand of her twin sister who died at birth [17]. More recently, Jeff Kepner received the US' first double-hand transplant in May 2009, the first having been performed in France, 2000. Evidence from the procedures so far conducted has been largely positive [18]; follow-up of the earliest American hand transplant recipients attests to the "long-term" (six to eight year) success of these grafts [19].

Whilst limb transplantation is therefore increasingly common, FAT is still in the early phases and has generated particular interest and, on occasion, controversy. The procedure was first mooted by Dr John Barker of the University of Louisville shortly after the hand transplant in 1998, and, in 2002, Dr Peter Butler's presentation on the topic to the British Association of Plastic Reconstructive and Aesthetic Surgeons sparked intense media interest [20]. The coverage prompted James Partridge, CEO of Changing Faces (a support group for people with facial disfigurement), to call upon the UK's Royal College of Surgeons (RCS) to intervene. The RCS convened a working party, comprising experts in ethics, reconstructive surgery, transplantation, and psychology, whose report concluded that "it would be unwise to proceed with human facial transplantation" [21].

The RCS report nevertheless invited further analysis of the phenomenon, to which a team from the University of Louisville responded by publishing their argument in favour of undertaking the procedure [22]. Alongside the publication of this paper in the *American Journal of Bioethics* were 15 commentaries, including contributions from Butler and colleagues in the UK [23], another American team, based in Cleveland, headed by Dr Maria Siemionow [24], and a French team led by Dr Laurent Lantieri [25].

In 2004, Lantieri's team submitted a proposal to the French government's advisory council on bioethics (Comité Consultatif National d'Ethique), prompting the council to issue a report in which it concluded that, although the ethical case for a full facial transplantation was not yet established, a partial transplant could be undertaken [26]. In the event, it was another French team, based in Lyon and led by Drs Jean-Michel Dubernard and Bernard Duvauchelle, who completed the first such procedure, in November 2005 [27]. The 38-year-old patient, Mme Isabelle Dinoire, had been mauled by her dog, which left her not only seriously disfigured but also compromised in her ability to eat and speak. The surgery was judged to be a success, in terms of the survival of the graft, its appearance, and Mme Dinoire's reportedly positive reaction. Yet, the success had been hard-won, since Mme Dinoire had endured several episodes of acute rejection — although each episode had been successfully tackled through adjustments to her immunosuppressive drugs [28, 29].

In the wake of this first case, Dr Butler was granted permission by an ethics committee to undertake transplants at the Royal Free Hospital in

London [30], but it was to be in China that the second transplant would occur. In April 2006, Dr Guo Shuzhong in Xi'an performed a procedure similar to Mme Dinoire's, in which he transplanted a cheek, upper lip, and nose to Li Guoxing, a 30-year-old farmer who had been mauled by a bear. Whilst the outcome initially looked good, Mr Guoxing reportedly ceased taking immunosuppressant drugs in favour of herbal medication, which ultimately caused the graft to fail and unfortunately appeared to cause his premature death [31, 32].

The third FAT again took place in France, in January 2007, this time led by Dr Lantieri [33]. The team had first to remove a large tumour, caused by neurofibromatosis type 1 (a genetic disorder), and thereafter to transfer a graft, which was three times the surface area of the one given to Mme Dinoire. Like his predecessors, the 30-year-old recipient, Pascal Coler, suffered several episodes of acute rejection, which were again dealt with by immunosuppression medications. By 2009 the patient was reportedly doing well [34].

Having been granted permission to proceed back in 2005 [30], Dr Maria Siemionow of the Cleveland Clinic (US) first undertook a partial face transplant involving a live recipient in December 2008. The patient was 46-year-old Connie Culp, whose husband had fired a shotgun in her face, in a failed murder-suicide bid [35]. The blast destroyed Mrs Culp's nose, upper jaw, and right eye, leaving her unable to speak or eat unaided. The 22-hour procedure involved a near-total face transplant, including (apparently for the first time) bones, alongside muscle, skin, nerves, and blood vessels. Once again, episodic rejection aside, Mrs Culp seemed to respond well.

Similar outcomes were reported for the fifth patient, a 28-year-old male whose lower face was also seriously disfigured by a shotgun blast [36]. Once more, Dr Lantieri and colleagues undertook the 15-hour procedure. One month later, in April 2009, an American team, based in Boston and led by Dr Bohdan Pomahac, completed a 17-hour procedure on James Maki, aged 59 [37]. Mr Maki had lost his nose, upper lip, cheeks, and the roof of his mouth when he fell onto the electrified third rail at a Boston train station in 2005. Mr Maki followed a similar post-operative course to his predecessors. The donor was named as Mr Joseph Helfgot, who was of a similar age and skin tone, and had died following a heart transplant.

Unfortunately, the seventh recipient of a face transplant, who also received two hands in the 30-hour operation, later suffered a fatal cardiac arrest during surgery to combat a serious bacterial infection. Lantieri, again leading the operation, reported that the initial signs had been good for the burns victim, who had received nearly a complete face, including functioning eyelids. It was thought that there was no correlation between the patient's death and the transplant [34].

The eighth transplant, conducted by Dr Pedro Cavadas in Valencia, Spain in August 2009, again broke new ground, since the 43-year-old recipient also received a new tongue and jaw [38]. The patient had lost part of his face a decade before following radiotherapy, while the donor was a 35-year-old who had died in a traffic accident. Early reports again appeared to be good, with the recipient reportedly smiling on first seeing his new appearance. In January 2010 Dr Cavadas also operated on an unnamed 30-year-old man with a serious degenerative malformation, providing him with the face of a road traffic accident victim. The families of the donor and recipient also met, at the request of the donor's mother. Initial coverage again indicated that the patient was responding "favourably" to the transplant [39].

A powerful indicator of the perceived success of FAT came in December 2009, with the announcement that the US Department of Defense was awarding $3.4 million for further FAT procedures at the Boston hospital [40]. However, in contrast to FAT, the first uterus transplant did not spur surgeons internationally on to attempting further procedures. In April 2000 a 26-year-old woman was the (to date, sole) recipient of a uterus transplant performed in Saudi Arabia [10]. She had undergone a life-saving hysterectomy six years prior to the transplant following post-partum haemorrhage. The living-donor was a 46-year-old woman who had her uterus removed following the discovery of benign ovarian cysts. Unfortunately, the recipient developed thrombosis within the uterine vessels, necessitating a hysterectomy 99 days post-transplantation. Nevertheless, in recent years there has been a renewed interest in the possibility of performing further uterine CTAs, particularly in America where the procedure has been viewed as another form of fertility treatment [41].

15.3 Best Interests: Balancing Benefits and Risks

In an early commentary on limb transplantation, Dickenson and Widdershoven referred to the view that "transplants cross technological frontiers but not ethical ones. They raise no ethical questions that have not been answered long since, in favour of transplantation" [42]. On this view, cadaveric hand transplantation could be permitted, subject to the team satisfying professional and procedural standards of competence, amongst them the need for open public evaluation [43]. The same opinion might be advanced in relation to other forms of CTA, and with good reason; after all, CTA necessitates engagement with familiar issues like the welfare of the recipient and respect for autonomy. However, like Dickenson and Widdershoven, we believe that CTA not only raises distinct concerns, but also requires particularly careful thinking about seemingly straightforward issues — not least the balance of benefits to risks.

Fundamentally, CTA is intended to benefit the patient, such as by restoring function or appearance. In their thorough review article, Gander *et al.* point out that CTA has a number of advantages over conventional reconstructive treatments [20]. Such conventional treatments include: reattaching amputated body parts using microsurgical techniques; transferring autologous tissues to reconstruct tissue defects; and using prosthetic materials to conceal the defect or disfigurement. (There has also been some debate about the relative merits of uterine CTA, as compared with, for example, surrogacy arrangements [44, 45].) Re-attachment provides the best results, since it involves working with the original tissue. However, this is impossible where the tissue either never existed (as in the case of congenital birth defects) or where the tissue in question has effectively been destroyed (by cancer or burns, for example). The other two treatments are capable of covering large wounds but they will not necessarily restore function and they are also susceptible to technical failure, infection, and rejection, in addition to requiring numerous follow-up procedures and a lengthy period of rehabilitation. The cost to the individual patient, their family and, indeed, society (if it must foot the bill) can be considerable. As such, Gander *et al.* feel that CTA, at least in the form of hand and face transplantation, "could eliminate many of these complications and drawbacks and provide superior functional and aesthetic outcomes and in doing so would revolutionize the field of reconstructive surgery" [20, 46].

There are certainly signs that CTA is realising its potential to do good. Thus, hand transplants have reportedly had good outcomes, in terms of both function and patient satisfaction [15, 18]. Over time, the grafts have acquired normal skin colour and texture, as well as normal hair and nail growth, and recovery of sensation has also been good. Furthermore, within two years of undergoing the procedure, the recipients have gained a sufficient level of motor function to enable them to return to work. Early reports of the outcomes of facial transplantation also appear to be positive. As commentators anticipated [47], the procedure is primarily concerned with improving appearance, although there are reports of improvement in function: for example, in August 2008, Dr Lantieri revealed that Pascal Coler, the third recipient, was now able to blink, "close his mouth completely, speak and eat", although "he still has some problems smiling because the way we set the muscles wasn't perfect" [33].

Yet, despite its capacity to do great good, CTA unfortunately also has the potential to inflict harm. Even its advocates recognise that immuno-suppression-associated risks present a significant barrier to the routine adoption of CTA [48]. Immunological risks are universal to all cases of organ transplantation. These risks are generated because the human body mounts an attack against foreign tissue, with the result that transplanted tissue is at constant risk of rejection. To avoid rejection occurring, transplant recipients are placed on a regimen of immunosuppressive drugs. Immunosuppression is necessarily a life-long precaution; without it, rejection would be inevitable. Unfortunately, this potentially carries a high price. In solid organ transplantation, over-immunosuppression tends to cause most complications, whether immunologic (such as malignancies and infection) or non-immunologic (where, for example, the drugs increase cardiovascular risk by affecting blood pressure or cholesterol levels). In other words, immunosuppression entails life-threatening risks, including hypertension, diabetes, and an increased susceptibility to both infection and cancer [49]. Indeed, one study estimates that transplant recipients on immunosuppressive therapy are subjected to a massive (100-times increased) risk of non-melanoma skin cancers, compared with an average individual [50].

Immunological problems have certainly presented with CTAs, with infection being the main complication arising in hand and face transplants [18]. Non-immunologic risks have also presented, including non-compliance (to which we shall return) and side-effects associated with corticosteroids. Such complications appear to have been tackled successfully. These are welcome findings. It nevertheless warrants emphasis that the risks associated with immunosuppression are sufficiently grave that their assumption would appear to require considerable benefits for the recipient of CTA before the ethical case can be made out. As Hettiaratchy *et al.* put it: "The crux of the matter is how much immunosuppression can be justified for a non-life-saving procedure?" [51]

The risks mount up once one appreciates that even immunosuppression cannot guarantee that transplanted tissue will not be rejected. Three phenomena warrant consideration: acute rejection; chronic rejection; and loss of the graft. Under-immunosuppression can lead to *acute rejection* of the transplanted tissue. In hand transplantation, acute rejection rates of 67% at one year have been reported, although anti-rejection therapy was successful in all of these cases and — unlike similar experiences with kidney transplants — the grafts survived [18]. *Chronic rejection* is less common, occurring, for example, two years after a transplant, when the patient ceased taking his immunosuppression medication. In that case, the hand was surgically removed [52]. Generally, though, Whitaker *et al.* attribute the low incidence of rejection to (*inter alia*) the visibility of the transplant (which enables action to be taken quickly), prompt follow-up, and the finding that CTAs (unlike kidney transplants) do not appear to be susceptible to vascular and parenchymal toxicity of immunosuppressive medication [48].

These are also encouraging findings — although, of course, we cannot overlook the high acute rejection rates, which appear to correspond to the greater immunogenicity of skin tissue [48]. This phenomenon arguably assumes even greater importance in the context of facial transplantation, where similar experiences have been reported. There too attempts to reverse acute rejection have been successful. But what if such efforts were to fail? As we just noted, graft loss is not unprecedented following limb transplantation [48], although it seems likely that alternative arrangements can be made in such cases (perhaps even, as one unlucky recipient hoped, another attempt at transplantation) [53]. Can similar solutions be found if it is the face which is rejected?

The apparent dearth of satisfactory fall-back positions certainly troubled some early commentators, thus, in their view, tipping the benefits/risks balance away from proceeding [47]. Such caution is understandable when we remember that, unlike much routine transplantation, facial transplantation is not intended to prolong or save life, such that would appear to make it reasonable to run the risk of graft loss. However, we would also do well to remember that, in routine transplantation, the choice is not necessarily between surgery and death. Kidney transplants, for example, might be performed in order to release a patient from their dependence on dialysis. Moreover, the surgeons are increasingly confident that not only will they be able to detect rejection promptly, but they will also be able to deal with it. Butler and colleagues, for example, propose three options: re-transplant (assuming a matched donor can be found); using an artificial dermal substitute (either while awaiting a donor or as a final option); and re-grafting, using standard reconstructive techniques [54]. The (literal) risk of "losing face" has therefore receded — but, on this account, the recipient is still bound to return to the clinic for further procedures.

The procedures, accompanying regimen of drugs and, we might add, current levels of publicity combine to suggest that there is another dimension to the benefits/risks calculation: the psychological impact of undergoing FAT — or, indeed, any form of CTA. Amongst the psychological challenges associated with transplantation (generally) are concerns about viability, rejection, immunosuppressive treatment, and the donor, to whom the recipient might feel responsible or grateful [55]. These challenges are no less present in CTA. Mr Hallam, recipient of the first successful hand transplant, stopped taking his immunosuppressant medication, resulting in chronic rejection of his transplanted hand, which was then surgically removed [14]. Mr Li Guoxing, who received the second face transplant, suffered episodes of acute rejection having decided to take herbal alternatives in place of his immunosuppressant medication [32]. Although these episodes of acute rejection were effectively treated, Li Guoxing died in 2008; no autopsy was performed to determine the cause of death but it was reported that this was due to Guoxing having ceased his immunosuppressant medication [31]. Evidently, there is a considerable psychological dimension to CTA, which requires careful assessment in any decision to proceed.

But is there, in principle, good enough reason for proceeding? Put differently, should the burdens and risks associated with CTA require us to place a moratorium on the practice? Although caution is advisable, we believe that there are still sound arguments for undertaking such procedures. Notwithstanding the considerable risks that seem to come with CTA [56], we cannot lose sight of the intended contributions that might be made to a recipient's quality of life. This begins to suggest that there is a relatively simple way of determining the matter: turn the decision over to the potential recipient — albeit with the vital caveat that due account is taken of the aforementioned psychological aspects of CTA.

15.4 Respecting Autonomy, Consent, and Personal Identity

If we are to turn the final decision about CTA over to the potential recipient, then we must engage with the recipient's autonomy, i.e., his or her capacity for self-rule. Respect for patient autonomy is a firmly established principle in modern medicine [57]. However, as one might anticipate, the application of this concept to CTA raises some complex dilemmas about consent to the procedure and personal identity.

15.4.1 *Autonomy and consent*

In practice, observance of appropriate consent procedures ensures that individual autonomy is respected and protected. Generally, consent (or a suitable substitute, such as proxy consent) is a fundamental requirement for any medical intervention and is particularly crucial where significant risks are posed. Consent not only carries ethical force, but also has a substantial legal dimension, since in many jurisdictions failure to obtain consent might result in criminal or civil proceedings, for such wrongs as assault, trespass to the person, and negligence [57].

In light of the significant risks associated with CTAs of the face, limb, and uterus, efforts must be made to ensure that a recipient's autonomy is respected, through articulation of and adherence to rigorous consent criteria. However, concerns have been expressed about the validity and limitations of any consent that is obtained. These concerns can be broken down into two main arguments: first, valid consent is an unrealisable goal; and, second, even assuming that valid consent can be obtained, those (less than maximally autonomous?) individuals who do consent to the procedure may be less well-equipped to manage the associated physical and psychological burdens.

Let us first consider the components of valid consent and how these are satisfied (or not) in the case of CTAs. Consent tends to comprise three integral elements: the person consenting must decide *voluntarily*, when *competent* and fully *informed* about the procedure in question [58]. These criteria are common to many legal systems, and they also feature frequently in philosophical accounts of respect for autonomy, such that the absence of any one of these elements would remove (or at least undermine) the individual's ability to make an autonomous decision [57]. The extent to which each of these elements is satisfied in the case of CTA has been challenged. These challenges merit careful scrutiny, given the potential threats not only to ethical practice but also to lawful permission.

The voluntariness of consent has been most rigorously questioned in the case of face transplants. In today's materially and aesthetically conscious society, argue Huxtable and Woodley, it is possible that social hostility towards any deviation from the norm may be so great that individuals with facial disfigurement may experience severe pressure from society to "normalise" [59]. Similarly, in the case of uterine CTA, it is possible that a woman without a uterus may perceive herself to be inadequate by reference to social expectations upon women to bear children. If undue influence is exercised over an individual's decision, then their voluntariness is impaired and consent is potentially vitiated. The key question here is whether society itself is capable of coercing vulnerable individuals into undergoing risky surgery. Certainly, a society's values will inevitably influence its members, but Brassington and White claim that beauty *is* indeed an advantage and choosing to undergo a procedure like facial transplantation ought not to be construed as submitting to social pressure any more than is seeking a more successful career [60]. While we are situated within a society we are necessarily exposed to its values, yet we do not (and should not) consider all our decisions to be coerced. On the other hand, we cannot wholly dismiss the pressure exerted by popular portrayals of beauty and their impact on individuals' perceptions of themselves. At the very least, it seems to us that the motivation and expectations of potential transplant recipients should be thoroughly explored prior to surgery.

Commentators including Morris *et al.* also fear that the competence of those seeking facial transplantation will be questionable, raising further questions about the validity of their consent [49]. The potential recipient may be suffering considerable distress as a result of their disfigurement, and so too might the individual who has lost a limb or uterus. The criteria for determining competence vary across legal jurisdictions but typical features include the need to understand pertinent information, retain it for a suitable period of time, and use it to reach a decision [57]. Amongst the concerns cited about recipients of CTA are the possibility that severe risks may be overlooked or underplayed, and the potential for unrealistic expectations [49]. However, the ethical relevance of these concerns remains open to question. Is it appropriate to prohibit CTA merely because some candidates *might* be incompetent to consent? Indeed, even if an individual's competence is compromised, in many countries it will still be possible for treatment to proceed on the basis of protecting the patient's best interests (and maybe even research too, where this is at least not contrary to the incompetent participant's interests). Of course, such a solution reopens the benefits/risks conundrum, which we considered in the previous section (and will not address further here). What we nevertheless should recognise is that there are opportunities for maximising competence and also viable alternative ethical frameworks, such that threats to competence need not present a wholly insurmountable obstacle.

Finally, the possibility of *informed* consent in radical CTA procedures has been contested. In 2004, the French committee for ethics suggested that informed consent for face transplantation is an illusion: "the information needed so that informed consent can become a reality is just not available" [26]. This conclusion reflected the fact that, due to its infancy and experimental nature, extremely limited evidence is available concerning the outcome and long-term prognosis for face transplant recipients. As we saw earlier, the evidence is now emerging. However, some points of principle still remain, which hinge on the definition of "informed consent" and in particular *how* "informed" consent needs to be.

Beauchamp and Childress identify two models of informed consent, the first involving sufficient information to enable autonomous authorisation, and the second abiding by institutional rules of disclosure [61]. The first model is more demanding and requires that the patient has *substantial information* and positively *authorises* the doctor to perform a *specific* procedure; this model focuses on the need for adequate information to facilitate autonomy. The second model is determined by the particular legal requirements for consent which operate in the state. This second model is not always sufficient to facilitate autonomous authorisation, since really it exists to protect doctors from liability or culpability in (for example) trespass to the person or battery. Due to a (probably understandable) preoccupation with the legal dimensions of informed consent, doctors may neglect the moral value of autonomy by falling short of the requirements contained within the first model.

Neither model quantifies or specifies how much information is needed for informed consent. In medical procedures generally, the level of information required by law tends to be determined according to one of three standards: that which is reasonable, according to responsible professional practice; that which a reasonable person would expect to be told; and that which the individual patient would want to know, in line with their individual circumstances [61]. In the case of CTA, and in line with the first model of consent to which Beauchamp and Childress referred, there is good reason for insisting upon substantial disclosure, at least while the evidence base itself is not yet substantial. Indeed, while facial and uterine transplants retain their status as research procedures, rigorous criteria for acquiring valid consent are demanded by the Declaration of Helsinki [62]. Provided that the potential recipient is furnished with all available information on a procedure, including information about the uncertainty of possible outcomes, then they will be in the best position to make an informed decision, particularly when we remember that it is their body undergoing the procedure. By factoring the uncertainty surrounding these novel transplants into the benefits/risks ratio, we ensure that an autonomous decision, in virtue of being maximally informed, is attainable in practice. Indeed, the imposition of high standards for disclosure arguably meets the requirements of respect for autonomy both now and in the future by not only respecting current participants but also, in generating new knowledge, enhancing the information that will be available to future participants and patients. After all, "medical science only advances by performing procedures at the limit of current knowledge" [42].

Having suggested that, in theory at least, all three elements of a valid consent can be satisfied for face, limb, and uterine CTAs, there still remains the autonomy-affecting concern described by Huxtable and Woodley as the "Catch-22 of facial transplantation" [47]. The difficulty, which might have wider relevance, concerns the potential recipients of radical transplants: those who want the operation might also be the very people least able to cope with the associated burdens. Presumably the individuals seeking radical surgery will have had particular difficulty adjusting to loss or disfigurement and are suffering as a result. While these candidates might be considered most in need of transplantation to alleviate their distress, they may accordingly be less able to cope with the long-term consequences of the surgery and potentially have diminished autonomy on account of their distressed state [47]. Thus the potential problem with more vulnerable potential recipients is twofold: first, there may be an inadequate capacity to cope post-transplantation; and second, any consent provided might be vitiated by diminished competence and therefore compromised autonomy.

Some commentators dismiss this Catch-22: White and Brassington deny the alleged correlation between seeking a face transplant and suffering from a reduced coping ability, and they claim that it is "fallacious" to assume that distress in response to disfigurement will predispose an individual to less robust coping mechanisms post-transplant [60]. They do accept that distress might undermine an individual's autonomy and ability to give consent — but they also point to a simple solution to this dilemma, in the form of the transplant itself, which should reduce that individual's distress and effectively restore their autonomy. There is something to be said for this stance. Nevertheless, we still think caution is advisable: to dismiss a probable connection between an individual's reaction to one psychological burden and their ability to cope with further psychological and physical burdens is to risk overlooking the potential adverse reactions of a recipient post-transplant.

An individual's ability to cope with the burdens of transplantation is undoubtedly crucial to the success of the transplant and to the recipient's subsequent emotional and physical well-being. Yet, if we have concerns about those seemingly most in need of a proposed procedure, then surely we must rule out such a procedure?[2] But this conclusion thrusts us onto the horns of a fresh dilemma: now, the people most in need are being denied the benefits of a procedure that might best tackle those needs. Fortunately, a simultaneously principled and pragmatic position is available, which should answer most of these concerns.

First, all candidates should be thoroughly informed of all the known (and any anticipated) consequences. Second, candidates should undergo rigorous psychological screening, as indeed Butler *et al.* have advised in the case of facial transplantation:

> [t]he patient would have to be determined and resolute in adhering to the prolonged rehabilitation and the need for chronic immunosuppression. The patient must be robust enough to cope with these challenges and the psychological effects involved [23].

Furthermore, the consent provided by the candidate must be sustained over a period of time, so as best to ensure that (however unlikely) the transplant has not been sought on a whim. Third, the doctor should be inclined towards the protection of autonomy in the long-term [63], maybe even in a manner one might describe as "weakly paternalistic". Here, the doctor's responsibility to their patient would be paramount and he or she would have to consider thoroughly the candidate's best interests and attempt to reinstate their autonomy in the long-term, whether by accepting them as a transplant recipient or by recommending alternative treatment. Effective application of these precautions ought to tackle the main features of the Catch-22 pitfall, whilst also ensuring that the science — which, lest we forget, is aimed at doing good — is able to progress.

Although we have suggested that valid consent can be obtained for these radical transplant procedures and have indicated possible ways to avoid any Catch-22 problems, face, limb, and uterine CTAs are not rendered ethically viable merely because an individual *can* autonomously

---

[2] Unless, following another argument detected by Huxtable and Woodley to its troubling conclusion, we are willing to proceed on the basis that this will be for the good of society.

authorise the surgery. The question remains whether these surgeries *should* be an option in the first place. Not only do the benefits/risks ratios remain finely balanced in relation to these transplant procedures, but they also raise complex ethical questions associated with personal identity, to which we will now turn.

15.4.2 *Personal identity*

Illness can (re)shape an individual's identity [64], and so too can medical intervention, as ongoing debates about advance directives and the possible applications of pre-implantation genetic diagnosis attest [65]. There is also evidence that solid organ recipients can experience difficulty in adapting to new tissues and resolving their identity [66, 67]. Viewed against this backdrop, the potential for CTA to impinge significantly on personal identity may be a cause for concern. There are accounts of identity, such as those which concern the lived-body and narrative, which offer some support for this view. However, as we hope to demonstrate, CTA also has the capacity to reinstate a transplant recipient's misplaced sense of identity and raise their potentially compromised self-esteem.

The link between CTA and identity appears reasonably easy to establish, when we consider the organs and tissues in issue. Facial transplantation, in particular, has generated great interest in questions of identity. How will a recipient react and adapt to having another person's facial tissue replace their own? Will the recipient find their sense of identity overwhelmed? Certainly, the face is a unique structure of the human body to which immense symbolic worth is attached; it is the feature by which most people will identify both themselves and others, and unwanted changes in facial appearance can have devastating effects, as the neurophysiologist Jonathan Cole has explained [68]. Early reports from the recipients of FAT also include some telling observations. Notice, for example, Isabelle Dinoire's description of her post-transplant visage, when, speaking of the donor, she commented:

> It's not hers, it's not mine, it's somebody else's ... Before the operation, I expected my new face would look like me but it turned out after the operation that it was half me and half her [69].

Similarly, there are indications of the contributions limbs make to personal identity, not least in the (aforementioned) reactions of Mr Hallam to the hand transplant from which he had reportedly become "mentally detached" [42]. Hands appear closely associated with individual identity: we use hand gestures regularly to help us communicate; our manual dexterity enables us to develop and refine unique skills (for example, as artists and musicians); and our hands are the highly sensitive instruments through which we explore and appreciate our environment and engage in more intimate behaviours. This latter point undoubtedly also applies to the penis: witness, here, the fact that the first penis transplant was rejected not by the recipient or his body, but by his wife [70]. Of course, the penis further contributes to the construction and preservation of identity in its association with maleness and masculinity. The uterus, meanwhile, although not externally visible, assumes an essential functional role in childbearing and is closely associated with femaleness and femininity. As Bean *et al.* have reported, a diagnosis of Mayer-Rokitansky-Küster-Hauser Syndrome (a congenital absence of the uterus) can represent "a threat to a woman's self-concept" [71].

The various organs and tissues with which CTA is engaged therefore appear intimately entangled with notions of personal identity. But how are we to understand the idea of "personal identity", and what light, if any, could this shed on the ethics of performing CTA? Despite (or perhaps because of) considerable philosophical interest, there is no single answer to the question "What makes me *me*?" As Huxtable and Woodley explain, the question is

> often considered along spatio-temporal lines, in terms of re-identification, where the quest is to discover the conditions that make a person at time T1 the same person as at time T2 [47].

Various answers are available, but it is helpful to start with the two most extreme positions, which emphasise psychological and biological features respectively.

The psychological account of personal identity, famously articulated by John Locke [72], states that our minds define us as individual people and dictate that we are the same person across a period of time. By extension, our memories, thoughts, knowledge, and other mental attributes determine our identity. A strict application of this psychological account maintains that a psychological connection between beings in a different space and time is both necessary and sufficient to conclude continuity of identity. As such, our physical body parts here make no contribution to our individual identity, which means that CTA poses no problems (and, indeed, makes no promises) in this regard.

Advocates of the psychological account maintain that it supports popular conceptions of an afterlife and reincarnation: provided there is continuity of psychological elements, a person's identity can potentially persist in the absence of their physical being. Furthermore, we are told that this account is consistent with intuition: if X's brain was transplanted into Y's head we would, apparently, conclude that X now existed in Y's body. However, in both of these examples, the psychological account overlooks the fact that the mind appears inextricably linked to the bodily substance that is the brain. A similar blind-spot exists at the other extreme, in the biological account of identity (such as that presented by Eric Olsen [73]), which seems to deny the link between our mental make-up (our minds) and our make-up *per se* (our identities).

Rather than adopt either of the apparently deficient extreme positions, we prefer a lived-body account of identity. On this account, our minds — by virtue of us being human — are "by definition embodied and enworlded" [74, 75]. In contrast with the psychological account, a phenomenological lived-body account highlights the significance of the body in personal identity. Maurice Merleau-Ponty was a prominent figure in interpreting personal identity in association with the body [76]. Merleau-Ponty argued that our identity is constructed through our perception of the world and, as our body is the medium via which we experience the world, it must be an essential determinate in our identities: "The body is the vehicle of being in the world, and having a body is, for a living creature, to be intervolved in a definite environment, to identify oneself" [76].

A supporter of the lived-body account might attempt to persuade a psychological advocate that, while psychological characteristics are key to identity, these characteristics are established through the sensory input provided to the mind by virtue of the body's intimate experiences of its surroundings, thus the body also plays a role in identity. However,

Merleau-Ponty does not wish the body to be conceived as *contingently* connected with identity by virtue of its relationship with the mind, but rather as fundamentally *essential* to identity.

It is therefore clear that, according to the lived-body account, the body plays a crucial role in establishing personal identity. It is through our bodies that we perceive the world, and through this perception that we develop our unique first-person experiences of our surroundings. This account is particularly relevant in relation to how our limbs may be perceived as integral to our identities: our limbs play a vital role in situating and engaging us with our environment, thus facilitating our relationship with the surrounding world in which we exist and interact.

An alternative, philosophically derived account of personal identity can be seen in the work of Ricoeur [77]. Ricoeur strives for a more biographical account of personal identity constructed from narrative, which weaves the importance of individual life stories into the fabric of identity. This narrative account highlights the role of relational context in identity, such that physical experiences and relationships are major constituents of identity.

In a discussion of the impact of FAT on personal identity, Edgar draws on lived-body and narrative accounts of identity in order to develop a theory that encompasses an "embodied" and a "social" self [78]. These two theories of self recognise that the body plays two distinct roles in establishing identity. First, as in Merleau-Ponty's lived-body account, our bodies are the vehicle through which we are situated in and interact with our world. Second, Edgar recalls a more Sartrean theory, in which the body is an object available for others to observe. In this manner, not only does our body influence how others immediately perceive us, but we also become aware of others' perception of ourselves and we begin to internalise and reflect this impression — thus constructing a social role for ourselves shaped by the perception of others. Edgar illustrates this theory by indicating the manner in which a child will observe how their mother judges their actions and uses this information to inform their behaviour and eventually their own values [78]. From this hypothesis, Edgar suggests that if the body becomes damaged or disfigured then this will alter our social communication and roles. Indeed, unforeseen changes to an individual's facial appearance can have devastating effects on their self-esteem, particularly when confronted with social situations [79].

The dramatic physical changes associated with facial disfigurement, loss of limbs, and the removal of a uterus can be readily perceived as a profound change in identity or even a *loss* of identity. But the question then arises: is further change, in the form of CTA, a good or a bad thing? Of particular concern is whether the physical changes associated with CTA are in any way better than those initiated by the original injury. The initial changes are often accompanied by a loss of self-esteem, which may provoke a lack of confidence in social situations, impair communication, and diminish overall quality of life. Facial disfigurement, for example, causes individuals to lose part of their identity, either through loss of their unique facial characteristics or through loss of function in the facial muscles which exhibit emotions. By comparison, FAT offers some individuals the chance to gain a new identity. Swindell frames the difference between FAT and facial disfigurement as "gaining an identity", as opposed to "losing an identity" [80]. Furthermore, not only is the change in identity presented by FAT positive in the sense that it involves *gaining* a sense of identity, it is also significant that individuals undergo transplantation *voluntarily*. This contrasts with the *involuntary* change in identity associated with traumatic causes of facial disfigurement, limb losses, unplanned hysterectomy, and other unwanted incursions. The voluntariness of change is important because it enables an individual to retain or resume authorship of their identity, which contributes to self-understanding and enables them be involved in the evolution of their narrative identity.

We suggest that the self and the body are inextricably linked, such that facial, limb, and uterine CTAs — as operations that dramatically alter the body — have an unavoidable impact on a recipient's identity. Nevertheless, the damage that these CTAs seek to remedy may already have challenged personal identity and these operations can offer an individual the opportunity to take (or resume) control over their identity. Of course, in a sense, identity is inherently unstable — our physical appearance changes considerably during our lifetime as we grow from a baby to an elderly adult, and so too our personalities alter with experience. In short, changes in identity *per se* are inevitable and need not necessarily be considered ethically problematic — rather, it is the nature of the change that is most important. Crucially, provided that CTAs are voluntarily sought by recipients, then we can best enable recipients to be actively involved in constructing their narrative identity.

15.5 In the Public Interest?

So far we have seen how CTA raises difficult questions about the balance of risks to benefits that might legitimately be anticipated by (or inflicted upon?) a recipient, and about the extent to which it is acceptable to turn the ultimate choice about undergoing CTA over to that individual. Despite favouring a degree of caution, we feel that on balance there is a good case for allowing CTA, provided that robust procedures are in place for tackling the concerns we have raised. However, before concluding our analysis, we feel it important to consider some of the wider ramifications of CTA, which might otherwise be obscured by too narrow a focus on the rights and interests of the proposed recipient and the associated obligations of the professional providing them with care.

The central question we wish to ask here is: is CTA in the public interest? To begin to answer this question we think it instructive to step back from the specifics of the procedure, and consider in a very general sense the legal and ethical basis for surgery *per se.* As one of the leading judges in England once said:

> Many of the acts done by surgeons would be very serious crimes if done by anyone else, and yet the surgeons incur no liability. Actual consent, or the substitute for consent deemed by the law to exist where an emergency creates a need for action [i.e. acting in the best interests of the patient], is an essential element in this immunity; but it cannot be a direct explanation for it, since much of the bodily invasion involved in surgery lies well above any point at which consent could even arguably be regarded as furnishing a defence. Why is this so? The answer must in my opinion be that proper medical treatment, for which actual or deemed consent is a prerequisite, is in a category of its own [81].

This account offers little explanation about what it is that enables "proper medical treatment" to stand alone (leaving aside the fact that it also fails to define "proper medical treatment"). However, what the statement does do is signal that surgery, and indeed healthcare more generally, performs a socially worthwhile role. This sort of justification seems to exist at the level of the "public interest".

The "public interest" is an amorphous concept, which (in the worst light) might promote the suppression of the individual for the alleged benefit of the majority. However, there are sincere and sustained attempts to explicate the particular interests at stake, and rank them appropriately, for the good of individuals and the community at large. The work of John Stuart Mill, with its emphasis both on liberty and on utilitarianism, is a case in point [82]. As Mill appreciates, liberty — or what we nowadays more often think of as respect for autonomy — is likely to be placed alongside the public "good" inherent in healthcare. Indeed, some legal systems could seek to remove or reduce any potential tension between the individual and society simply by making respect for autonomy the gold standard. However, we suspect there are still likely to be difficulties. For one thing, we need to consider what we mean by "respect for autonomy" and which account thereof is to be our guide [2]. But even if this can be settled, there will still be tensions between values, including occasions when what appears to be an individual's choice is instead more a reflection of a given society's prejudices.

The public interest questions that attend CTA should therefore be reasonably easy to discern. Although we have focused primarily on the benefits potentially accruing to the individual recipient of CTA, the public interest would also require us to consider the position of the donors, and the policies and practices in place for ensuring that their rights and interests are protected [83]. Moreover, a fully inclusive account of the "public" interest should require us also to consider the benefits to future recipients and to patients more generally. Advances in immunosuppressive and microsurgical techniques paved the way for FAT; what unforeseen benefits might FAT in turn promote?

Of course, we must resist any temptation for taking this argument beyond its proper limits (wherever they are). Some commentators already fear the presence of social contamination in the choice ostensibly made by the individual who opts to undergo CTA. These fears are most pronounced in relation to FAT, probably because this procedure is not only (or not necessarily) directed at improving function — it also strives to provide the recipient with a new appearance. Freeman and Jaoudé contend that individuals with facial disfigurement are only "disfigured" by virtue of their deviation from a "normal" appearance; if there was no expectation for individuals to conform to a socially perceived norm, then the notion of a "disfigured" face would not exist [84]. So, who is really the "patient" here — the proposed recipient or the society in which they find themselves? [47].

Medicalising the perceived problem adds an additional layer of complexity and controversy, since it opens the transplant team to charges of complicity, by endorsing (even perpetuating) society's intolerance of deviation from the norm. Such intolerance might not be overtly malicious, but teasing and the like will undoubtedly have an adverse impact on the person who is disfigured [85]. Of course, the team is highly unlikely to inflict such indignities on the proposed recipient — but is there not a sense in which, by performing the procedure, they are complicit in the underlying attitudes and prejudices?

According to Little, to be an accomplice is "to bear some improper relation *to the evil* of some practice or set of attitudes" [86]. Writing about cosmetic surgery, he argues that the surgeon is required to recognise the "limit to the suffering we require victims of the norm to bear before taking measures to escape that suffering" [86]. Agich and Siemionow similarly contend that individuals with disfigurement ought not to be left to suffer the consequences of society's insensitivity [87]. Yet, Little also acknowledges that the surgeon is duty-bound to consider the social context, and to avoid reinforcing suspect norms. As Strauss observes, "When something is correctable, our willingness to accept it untouched is reduced" [88]. Viewed in this light we should be wary of any detrimental effects on society's willingness to invest in alternative means of supporting people who are disfigured (such as counselling and programmes for educating society at large) and, indeed, the possible effects on those coming to terms with recently acquired disfigurement [89].

There are other components to the public interest of undoubted relevance to CTA, not least the questions associated with funding (who should fund these costly procedures?) and media reporting (when should that which is only *interesting to* the public be kept from them, in the public *interest*?). Sensitivity, rather than sensationalism, must point the way forward [59]. Rather than explore these ideas further, we hope to have said enough about the need for vigilance, so as best to ensure that the individual's interests are not sacrificed in pursuance of scientific progress or some other, rather more ambiguous and arguable goal. We also hope not to have overstated such concerns, but we maintain that it would be remiss not to consider the wider context in which CTA is performed.

15.6 Conclusion

It is to the credit of all the surgical teams involved that not only has CTA generally proceeded carefully, but also many of those procedures which have been undertaken have secured significant successes for their recipients. Among the reported achievements are improved functioning, a reduction in the number of procedures that might otherwise be anticipated, and enhanced quality of life. However, the successes have not come free from cost. Aside from the undoubted financial commitment required, CTA also necessitates careful monitoring of the considerable physical risks associated with immunosuppression and rejection, as well as of the psychological impact on the recipient of the graft. The benefits/risks ratio may be finely balanced but we believe it can tip in favour of undertaking CTA, provided that the recipient is capable autonomously of consenting thereto. Here too there will be challenges arising in relation to the extent to which any consent can be judged voluntary, competent, and informed — but in principle such hurdles can be overcome. A model of autonomy which is capable of encompassing concerns about a patient's welfare and their ability to self-govern could help here; in other words, a commitment to protecting and preserving the recipient's autonomy in the long-term seems to point us in the right direction. Our bodies are our vehicles for interacting with the world and for our perception by others. Changes in the body, including through CTA, will therefore effect changes in our social roles and communication, but such changes need not be malign provided that due care is taken with the benefits/risks assessment and in ensuring that the change is wanted (i.e., fully consensual). In short, we find no problem in principle with CTA, but we do encourage more sustained consideration of the public (or social) dimension of these procedures.

15.7 Post-script: Science Future?

Agich and Siemionov have complained about "sensationalistic" discussions of FAT, which have relied unduly upon "film and science fiction where the procedure is used for cosmetic or nefarious purposes" [87]. We remarked earlier on the need for sensitive and informed debate, and so to some extent share their disquiet. However, by way of a post-script, we think it important to add two brief points to the foregoing analysis. First, in response to Agich and Siemionov, we see nothing intrinsically wrong with such a method of analysis, when analogies, metaphors, and similes can help to bring into focus the salient features of an emerging technique [59]. Second, some of the comparators introduced in the debates do not seem so fanciful on reflection. The move from therapeutic FAT to cosmetic applications, for example, is not one that can be ruled out decisively, not least given the difficulties in delineating "needs" and "wants". We would do well to distinguish between whether, say, a criminal mastermind *could* adopt another's face [90] and whether uterine transplantation *could* enable a man to bear children [91, 92] from whether such developments *should* be embraced. As numerous scientific developments attest, we cannot always predict whether the currently impossible will become possible *in practice*, but we should be able to say whether the impossible should remain so as a matter *of principle*.

Acknowledgements

Thanks to Professor Ruud ter Meulen, who supervised the dissertation prepared by A. Guilder as part of the BSc (Hons.) in Bioethics, in which some of the arguments herein were first aired. The usual caveat applies.

References

[1] Chong S.A., Huxtable R., and Campbell A.V. Authorising psychiatric research: Principles, practices and problems. *Bioethics* 2011; **25**(1): 27–36.

[2] Huxtable R. Whatever you want? Beyond the patient in medical law. *Health Care Analysis* 2008; **16**(3): 288–301.

[3] Da Varagine J. *Leggenda aurea*. Florence, Italy: Libreria Editrice Fiorentina, 1952; p. 648.

[4] Gilbert R. Transplant is successful with a cadaver forearm. *Medical Tribune and Medical News* 1964; **5**: 20–22.

[5] Dubernard J.M., Owen E., Herzberg G., *et al.* The first transplantation of a hand in humans. Early results. *Chirurgie* 1999; **124**: 358–365; discussion, 365–367.

[6] Strome M., Stein J., Esclamado R., *et al.* Laryngeal transplantation and 40-month follow-up. *New England Journal of Medicine* 2001; **344**: 1676–1679.

[7] Zuker R.M., Redett R., Alman B., *et al.* First successful lower-extremity transplantation: technique and functional result. *Journal of Reconstructive Microsurgery* 2006; **22**: 239–244.

[8] Birchall M. Tongue transplantation. *Lancet* 2004; **363**: 1663.

[9] Levi D.M., Tzakis A.G., Kato T., *et al.* Transplantation of the abdominal wall. *Lancet* 2003; **361**: 2173–2176.

[10] Fageeh W., Raffa H., Jabbad H., and Marzouki A. Case report: Transplantation of the human uterus. *International Journal of Gynecology and Obstetrics* 2002; **76**: 245–251.

[11] Silber S.J. Transplantation of a human testis for anorchia. *Fertility and Sterility* 1978; **30**: 181–187.

[12] Hu W., Lu J., Zhang L., *et al.* A preliminary report of penile transplantation. *European Urology* 2006; **50**: 851–853.

[13] Dubernard J.M., Owen E., Herzberg G., *et al.* Human hand allograft: report on first six months. *Lancet* 1999; **353**: 1315–1320.

[14] Altman L.E. A pioneering transplant, and now an ethical storm. *The New York Times*, 6 December 2005.

[15] Francois C.G., Breidenbach W.C., Maldonado C., *et al.* Hand transplantation: comparisons and observations of the first four clinical cases. *Microsurgery* 2000; **20**: 360–371.

[16] Petruzzo P., Lanzetta M., Dubernard J.M., *et al.* The international registry on hand and composite tissue transplantation. *Transplantation* 2008; **86**: 487–492.

[17] Ahmad A.R. Medical history made. *New Straits Times*, 11 June 2000.

[18] Lanzetta M., Petruzzo P., Margreiter R., *et al.* The international registry on hand and composite tissue transplantation. *Transplantation* 2005; **79**: 1210.

[19] Breidenbach W.C., Gonzales N.R., Kaufman C.L., *et al.* Outcomes of the first 2 American hand transplants at 8 and 6 years posttransplant. *The Journal of Hand Surgery* 2008; **33**: 1039–1047.

[20] Gander B., Brown C., Vasilic D., *et al.* Composite tissue allotransplantation of the hand and face: a new frontier in transplant and reconstructive surgery. *Transplant International* 2006; **19**: 868–880.

[21] Royal College of Surgeons of England. Facial Transplantation: Working Party Report. Royal College of Surgeons, London, 2003; 20.

[22] Wiggins O.P., Barker J.H., Martinez S., *et al.* On the ethics of facial transplantation research. *The American Journal of Bioethics* 2004; **4**: 1.

[23] Butler P.E., Clarke A., and Ashcroft R.E. Face transplantation: when and for whom? *The American Journal of Bioethics* 2004; **4**: 16.

[24] Agich G.J. and Siemionow M. Facing the ethical questions in facial transplantation. *The American Journal of Bioethics* 2004; **4**: 25.

[25] Petit F., Paraskevas A., and Lantieri L. A surgeon's perspective on the ethics of face transplantation. *The American Journal of Bioethics* 2004; **4**: 14.

[26] Working Group-Comité Consultatif National d'Ethique (CCNE). Composite Tissue Allotransplantation of the Face (Full or Partial Facial Transplant). France, Opinion 82, 2004. http://www.ccne-ethique.fr [accessed 15 February 2010].

[27] Châtelet N. *Le Basier d'Isabelle* [Isabelle's Kiss]. France: Seuil, 2007.

[28] Dubernard J.M, Lengelé B., Morelon E., *et al.* Outcomes 18 Months after the first human partial face transplantation. *New England Journal of Medicine* 2007; **357**: 2451–2460.

[29] Follain J. Face transplant patient Isabelle Dinoire reveals her new life. *The Sunday Times*, 17 January 2010.

[30] Okie S. Facial transplantation: brave new face. *New England Journal of Medicine* 2006; **354**: 889.

[31] AFP. China face transplant patient dead: doctor. 19 December 2008. http://www.google.com/hostednews/afp/article/ALeqM5i34T5A86agA7wuh5pD-mAU_n7zs7w [accessed 17 February 2010].

[32] Chenggang Y., Yan H., Xudon L., *et al.* Some issues in facial transplantation. *American Journal of Transplantation* 2008; **8**: 2169–2172.

[33] Coghlan A. Two more face transplant triumphs. *New Scientist*, 22 August 2008.

[34] Coghlan, A. Face-transplant pioneer to carry on after patient's death. *New Scientist*, 17 June 2009.

[35] Associated Press. Recipient of Face Transplant Shares Her Story and Results. *The New York Times*, 6 May 2009. http://www.nytimes.com/2009/05/06/science/06face.html [accessed 17 February 2010].

[36] AFP. French doctor performs world's fifth face transplant. 28 March 2009. http://www.france24.com/en/20090328-french-doctor-performs-worlds-fifth-face-transplant- [accessed 17 February 2010].

[37] Hines N. American face transplant patient James Maki recalls hermit-like existence before operation. *The Times*, 22 May 2009.

[38] Heckle H. Spain's 1st face transplant patient can smile now. *The Washington Post*, 22 August 2009.

[39] Anonymous. Second face transplant of Spain takes place in Seville. 3 February 2010. http://www.euroweeklynews.com/2010020372353/news/heart-of-andalucia/second-face-transplant-of-spain-takes-place-in-seville.html [accessed 17 February 2010].

[40] Kowalczyk L. Brigham gets $3.4 m for face transplants. *The Boston Globe*, 21 December 2009.

[41] Pearson, H. Infertility researchers target uterus transplant. *Nature* 2007; **445**: 466–467.

[42] Dickenson D. and Widdershoven G. Ethical issues in limb transplants. *Bioethics* 2001; **15**(2): 110–124, 111.

[43] Siegler M. Ethical issues in innovative surgery: Should we attempt a cadaveric hand transplantation in a human subject? *Transplantation Proceedings* 1998; **30**: 2779–2782, 2782.

[44] Nair A., Stega J., Smith J.R., and Del Priore G. Uterus transplant: Evidence and ethics. *Annals of the New York Academy of Sciences* 2008; **1127**: 83–91.

[45] Stein R. First US Uterus Transplant Planned. *Washington Post*, 15 January 2007.

[46] Barker J., Vossen M., and Banis J. The technical, immunological and ethical feasibility of face transplantation. *International Journal of Surgery* 2004; **2**: 8.

[47] Huxtable R. and Woodley J. Gaining Face or Losing Face? Framing the Debate on Face Transplants. *Bioethics* 2005; **19**(5–6): 505–522.

[48] Whitaker I.S., Duggan E.M., Alloway P.R. *et al.* Composite tissue allotransplantation: A review of relevant immunological issues for plastic surgeons. *Journal of Plastic, Reconstructive and Aesthetic Surgery* 2008; **61**: 481–492.

[49] Morris P., *et al.* Face transplantation: A review of the technical, immunological, psychological and clinical issues with recommendations for good practice. *Transplantation* 2007; **83**(2): 109–128.

[50] Lindelöf B., Sigurgeison B., Gäbel H., *et al.* Incidence of skin cancer in 5356 patients following organ transplantation. *British Journal of Dermatology* 2000; **143**: 513–519.

[51] Hettiaratchy S., Butler P., and Andrew Lee W.P. Lessons from hand transplantations. *The Lancet* 2001; **357**: 494–495.

[52] Kanitakis J., Jullien D., Petruzzo P., *et al.* Clinicopathologic features of graft rejection of the first human hand allograft. *Transplantation* 2003; **76**: 688–693.

[53] Press Release. Nation's Fourth Hand Transplant Recipient Has Hand Removed. 21 April 2009. http://www.handtransplant.com/ForNewsMedia/tabid/59/Default.aspx?GetStory=1055 [accessed 17 February 2010].

[54] Butler P.E., Hettiaratchy S., and Clarke A. Managing the risks of facial transplantation. *Lancet* 2006; **368**: 561–563.

[55] Johnson S.E. and Corsten M.J. Facial transplantation in a new era: what are the ethical implications? *Current Opinion in Otolaryngology & Head and Neck Surgery* 2009; **17**: 274–278.

[56] Regan J.A. *Is it ethical to proceed with full face transplant research?* Keele University, unpublished DMedEth dissertation, 2010.

[57] Dickenson D., Huxtable R., and Parker M. *The Cambridge Medical Ethics Workbook, 2nd ed.* Cambridge: Cambridge University Press, 2010; Chapter 9.

[58] Faden R. and Beauchamp T. *A History and Theory of Consent.* New York: Oxford University Press, 1986.

[59] Huxtable R. and Woodley J. (When) will they have faces? A response to Agich and Siemionov. *Journal of Medical Ethics* 2006; **32**: 403–404.

[60] White B.E. and Brassington I. Facial allograft transplants: where's the catch? *Journal of Medical Ethics* 2008; **34**: 723–726.

[61] Beauchamp T.L. and Childress J.F. *Principles of Biomedical Ethics, 6th ed.* New York and Oxford: Oxford University Press, 2009.

[62] WMA Declaration of Helsinki Ethical Principles for Medical Research Involving Human Subjects 2013. Available from the World Medical Association website: http://www.wma.net/en/30publications/10policies/b3/index.html [accessed 17 February 2010].

[63] Coggon J. Varied and principled understandings of autonomy in English law: Justifiable inconsistency or blinkered moralism? *Health Care Analysis* 2007; **15**: 235–255.

[64] Barnard D. Healing the damaged self: identity, intimacy, and meaning in the lives of the chronically ill. *Perspectives in Biology and Medicine* 1990; **33**(4): 535–546.

[65] Degrazia D. *Human Identity and Bioethics.* New York: Cambridge University Press, 2005.

[66] Sharp L.A. Organ transplantation as a transformative experience: Anthropological insights into the restructuring of the self. *Medical Anthropology Quarterly* 1995; **9**(3): 357–389.

[67] Lock M. Human body parts as therapeutic tools: Contradictory discourses and transformed subjectivities. *Qualitative Health Research* 2002; **12**: 1406–1418.

[68] Cole J. *About Face.* Cambridge, MA: The MIT Press, 1998.

[69] Allen P. Face transplant woman struggles with identity. *The Daily Telegraph*, 2 November 2008.

[70] Hu W., Lu J., Zhang L., *et al.* A preliminary report of penile transplantation: Part 2. *European Urology* 2006; **50**: 1115–1116.

[71] Bean E., Mazur T., and Robinson A. Mayer-Rokitansky-Küster-Hauser Syndrome: Sexuality, psychological effects, and quality of life. *Journal of Pediatric and Adolescent Gynecology* 2009; **22**(6): 339–346.

[72] Locke J. *An Essay Concerning Human Understanding*. New York: Oxford University Press, 2008; Book II, pp. 203–219.

[73] Olson E. *The Human Animal: Personal Identity without Psychology.* New York: Oxford University Press, 1999.

[74] Carel H. *Illness*. Durham: Acumen, 2008; p. 13.

[75] Campbell A.V. *The Body in Bioethics*. London: Routledge-Cavendish, 2009.

[76] Merleau-Ponty M. *Phenomenology of Perception, 6th ed.* Translated by C. Smith. London: Routledge and Kegan Paul, 1974.

[77] Ricoeur P. *Oneself as Another*. Translated by K. Blamey. Chicago: University of Chicago Press, 1992.

[78] Edgar A. The challenge of transplants to an intersubjectively established sense of personal identity. *Health Care Analysis* 2009; **17**: 123–133.

[79] Rumsey N. and Harcourt D. Body image and disfigurement: issues and interventions. *Body Image* 2004; **1**: 83–97.

[80] Swindell J.S. Facial allograft transplantation, personal identity and subjectivity. *Journal of Medical Ethics* 2007; **33**: 449–453, 451.

[81] *R v Brown et al.* [1993] 2 All ER 75 109–110.

[82] Mill J.S. *Utilitarianism, On Liberty, Essay on Bentham (by John Stuart Mill), together with selected writings of Jeremy Bentham and John Austin* (edited by Warnock, M.). London: Collins, The Fontana Library, 1962.

[83] Baylis F. Changing Faces: Ethics, Identity, and Facial Transplantation. In D. Benatar (ed.) *Cutting to the Core: Exploring the Ethics of Contested Surgeries*. Maryland: Rowman and Littlefield Publishers, 2006, pp. 155–167.

[84] Freeman M. and Jaoudé P.A. Justifying surgery's last taboo: The ethics of face transplants. *Journal of Medical Ethics* 2007; **33**: 76–81.

[85] Turner S.R., Thomas P.W.N., Dowell T., *et al*. Psychological outcomes among cleft patients and their families. *British Journal of Plastic Surgery* 1997; **50**: 1–9, 4.

[86] Little M.O. Cosmetic Surgery, Suspect Norms, and the Ethics of Complicity. In E. Parens (ed.) *Enhancing Human Capacities: Conceptual Complexities and Ethical Implications*. Washington: Georgetown University Press, 1998; 162–176, 170.

[87] Agich G.J. and Siemionow M. Until they have faces: the ethics of facial allograft transplantation. *Journal of Medical Ethics* 2005; **31**: 707–709, 709.

[88] Strauss R.P. Ethical and social concerns in facial surgical decision making. *Plastic and Reconstructive Surgery* 1983; **72**: 727–730, 727.

[89] Rumsey N. Psychological aspects of face transplantation: Read the small print carefully. *American Journal of Bioethics* 2004; **4**(3): 22–25, 24.

[90] *Face/Off*. Directed by Woo J., Touchstone Pictures, 1997.

[91] Radford B. Male pregnancy. *Skeptical Inquirer* 2007; **31**(2): 22–23.

[92] Caplan A.L., Perry C., Plante L.A., *et al*. Moving the womb. *Hastings Center Report* 2007; **37**(3): 18–20.

16

Ethical and Legal Issues in Trauma Medicine

Rebecca C. H. Brown

16.1 Introduction: Why Trauma Medicine?

This chapter will consider some of the ethical and legal issues arising in trauma medicine. As with any area of medicine, there are numerous areas of ethical debate, and as the techniques and practices of trauma medicine develop, so too do the context and parameters of the bioethical discussion. Rather than seek to cover too much ground, this chapter will discuss just a few areas where trauma raises particularly acute difficulties for ethical practice and legal regulation.

Trauma medicine covers the treatment of patients who suffer injuries as a result of accidents or violence. The kind of injury, location, and severity can vary widely, and surgical intervention may or may not be immediately necessary. The Advanced Trauma Life Support (ATLS) course, which provides additional trauma medicine training for physicians internationally, has chapters covering thoracic trauma; abdominal and pelvic trauma; head trauma; spine and spinal cord trauma; musculoskeletal trauma; and thermal injuries. It also covers paediatric and geriatric trauma and trauma in pregnancy [1, 2].

A key insight from trauma research is the description of a "trimodal death distribution", whereby deaths from injury cluster into three groups: there is a first peak in deaths seconds to minutes after injury; a second peak minutes to several hours after injury; and a third peak days to weeks after injury. This has lead to the concept of the "golden hour" where care soon after injury can have a significant (including life-saving) impact on the patient's health. The ATLS course manual informs us:

> Historically, the approach to treating injured patients, as taught in medical schools, was the same as that for patients with a previously undi-agnosed medical condition: an extensive history including past medical history, a physical examination starting at the top of the head and pro-gressing down the body, the development of a differential diagnosis, and a list of adjuncts to confirm the diagnosis. Although this approach was adequate for a patient with diabetes mellitus and many acute surgical illnesses, it did not satisfy the needs of patients suffering life-threatening injuries. The approach required a change.
>
> [1: p. xxviii]

The focus, therefore, of modern trauma care is to make a rapid assessment of injuries and conditions and to provide life-preserving treatment in the first instance (which may occur during pre-hospital care) with further investigation and appropriate care to follow. Given that the form of care required by trauma is so different to that of other medical specialities, it is perhaps unwise to assume that the ethical issues that arise in such care, and the principles and regulations that should guide trauma care, will follow those developed in other areas of medical ethics.

There is, unfortunately, little by way of detailed philosophical treat-ments of the ethical issues arising specifically in the context of trauma medicine. This leaves trauma medicine covered, in terms of ethical analy-sis, only by quite general medical ethics. The modern discipline of medical ethics has been hugely influenced by a mood of anti-paternalism and a need to protect patients and research participants, encouraged largely by appalling examples of cruelty and exploitation involved in research "trials" in Nazi Germany and Tuskegee[1] towards the beginning of the twentieth

---

[1] The Tuskegee study involved monitoring the progression of syphilis in 400 black men. In the 1940s antibiotic therapy was found to be a safe and effective means of treating the disease, yet participants were not given access to this treatment. The study ran from 1932 until it was unveiled in the popular media in 1972 [6].

century. The Nuremberg Code and the Declarations of Helsinki and Geneva were part of the response to the Nazi experiments in particular, and the need for more to be done to ensure the protection of research trial participants [3–6]. In the 1970s, patient autonomy emerged as a dominant value in medical ethics, in no small part due to the influential work of Ruth Faden, Tom Beauchamp, and James Childress [7–9].

This focus on patient autonomy (and anti-paternalism) has been supported with reference to procedures such as informed consent (a central requirement of medical practice and one which I discuss later in this chapter) and offering patients more opportunities for "choosing" what healthcare they receive, where, and from whom. There has, however, been an increasing volume of criticism directed at the reliance on autonomy to justify much medical ethical guidance and legal regulation. Some of this has come about due to a dissatisfaction with the philosophical basis of autonomy-centric bioethics and the neglect of other, potentially important values (see, for instance, O'Neill [10]; Dawson [11]). Other criticism has arisen due to the development of sub-disciplines of bioethics, in particular the sub-discipline of public health ethics, where the usefulness of individual autonomy as a guiding principle seems to be minimal and potentially unduly restrictive of healthcare interventions [11–14].

Trauma medicine seems like another example where a focus on patient autonomy is likely to miss the point: much care delivered in this context will be delivered under conditions where the promotion of autonomous control in the patient is unlikely to be plausible and will not be a helpful goal. Rather, values such as the preservation of life, relief of suffering, or provision of reassurance are more appropriate candidates for carers to focus on. Such a thought need not entail the dismissal of autonomy as holding a valuable position in the context of trauma care, but rather should lead us to doubt that it ought to hold a central and overriding position when considering what actions will be ethically laudable or criticisable.

The topics I will cover in this chapter will consider a number of different values that might be promoted through successful trauma care. I will begin by discussing the role of informed consent and judgements about the capacity of patients to makes decisions about their care. As mentioned above, informed consent is a well-established ritual of healthcare, and sometimes comes under criticism for its reliance upon autonomy for justification. There are, however, other reasons for engaging with informed consent practices and I shall discuss these and how they might be better suited to justifying informed consent in trauma care.

There are a number of issues arising in trauma medicine which relate to difficulties in balancing the best interests of the patient with the interests of others and of society at large. In particular, the need to conduct clinical research in order to progress medical practice and a great shortage in organs available for transplantation into people who are unwell create such conflicts. I will discuss how ethical issues surrounding medical research and organ donation arise and are made more acute in the trauma context.

The confidentiality afforded to patients is a key safeguard to ensure a trusting relationship between a patient and her carers. There are, however, circumstances where physicians are required to share privileged information about a patient, and sometimes it is not possible for informed consent to be sought for such a disclosure. In this section, I will summarise when physicians are obliged to share information about a patient with others, what the expectations are with regards to seeking consent or bypassing consent, and how this may create a conflict for the physician's role as a carer for her patient.

In the final section, I will discuss the practice of triage. This involves prioritising treatment to some patients at the expense of others and occurs when resources are limited. Triage is a routine part of emergency care and is undertaken by a variety of individuals both in hospitals and at accident sites. I will outline some of the main different triage systems and identify some of the key ethical questions posed by any system of resource distribution which will, by necessity, require decisions to be made about who ought to be prioritised for treatment.

16.2 Informed Consent and Capacity

Informed consent procedures are incorporated into most aspects of patient care and participant involvement in medical research. As discussed in the introduction, this stems in large part from a need to protect patients and research participants from deception, coercion, paternalism, and similarly impermissible actions. The formalisation of informed consent procedures has developed in response to various ethical and philosophical developments, as well as historical events such as the Nazi medical experiments and Tuskegee study [3, 4, 6, 7, 10, 15].

As noted elsewhere (see, for example, Manson [4]; Manson and O'Neill [15]), there are a variety of bases for adopting informed consent practices in medicine. The influential work of Beauchamp, Faden, and Childress has tended to stress the importance of certain moral principles in bioethics, particularly the principle of respect for autonomy and hence how informed consent procedures might promote patient autonomy [7, 8]. More recently, autonomy justifications for informed consent practices have come under criticism, particularly from Neil Manson and Onora O'Neill, who point out that the *requirement* for patients to be "informed" to the standard required by informed consent removes from them the option of remaining uninformed and/or trusting physicians to make decisions on their behalf (and in their interests) [4: p. 302]. The point stressed by Manson and O'Neill is that we ought not to equate mere choice-making with autonomy promotion, and that sometimes informed consent procedures will not only fail to promote autonomy, but will actively undermine it.

This need not be problematic if we understand informed consent as having a number of virtues. Importantly, the giving of consent can act as a waiver to make what would otherwise be impermissible actions (in the case of medicine this will include assault and battery) permissible. Thus, seeking consent and having a record of it being given can provide important protection for medical practitioners to guard against potential litigation. The "informed" part of informed consent may also protect against deception and exploitation by specifying the extent to which patients and research participants need to be given certain information and be judged to have understood that information in order to make certain procedures permissible. To the extent that individuals are generally thought to be good at judging what is in their interests, informed consent procedures place decisional power in the patient's hands and thus may generally be successful at promoting well-being.[2] Informed consent

---

[2] Clearly, the extent to which people really are good at promoting their own interests may vary across time and individual, and so informed consent, to the extent it promotes patient control, will not always succeed in well-being promotion.

practices also have the further virtue of promoting trust in the medical profession more generally, as well as in the physician at hand, by providing the patient with assurance that she will be consulted about what care she receives and kept informed about her condition.

On the face of it, it may appear that the benefits bestowed by informed consent procedures in general medicine will also be valuable in the context of trauma. But there are relevant differences between care provided in trauma compared to other situations. In trauma, treatment is often urgent, with the need for it arising unexpectedly as the result of an accident or violence. Patients are also likely to be unfamiliar with their care providers and the place of care, and may not have any friends of relatives around to support them or with whom they can discuss their options, depending on the timescale of treatment.

In order for informed consent to successfully promote values such as patient autonomy and well-being, it will be important that the patient really is well-informed about her condition and treatment options and is able to deliberate carefully about the advice she is given by practitioners and her own preferences and values. This may be possible for some instances of trauma care, but not always. For instance, patients who require emergency surgical procedures, who are distressed or in a lot of pain may be little able to deliberate about their treatment in a way that makes following informed consent procedures likely to promote their autonomy. Similarly, decisions patients make under such conditions may not be in their best interests and thus may fail to promote their well-being.

A study of patients undergoing orthopaedic surgery found that trauma patients were significantly poorer at recalling complications associated with their surgery than elective patients [16]. The authors cannot say with certainty why this is the case, but suggest "poor recall may be expected in patients who have acute admissions and were previously well, are in pain and have little time to absorb complicated information" [16: p. 781]. If trauma patients were unable to process the information they were given before surgery then informed consent will not have lived up to its claims as a tool for promoting autonomy and well-being insofar as this requires quality patient deliberation. If recall is not related to the quality of deliberation (rather, it may be that the stress of trauma affected patients' capacity to retain the information, but not to process it in the first place), then informed consent may be more successful than the authors' interpretation suggests. Lack of recall still seems problematic, however, given the importance of self-identification with one's decisions for autonomy. If patients are unable to self-identify with decisions they made pre-operatively, despite apparently giving informed consent, then this will hinder the extent to which informed consent can be thought to promote their autonomy.

16.2.1 *Capacity*

It is precisely in recognition of the potential for informed consent practices to fail to promote autonomy and well-being that a requirement of capacity is built into consent procedures. According to the General Medical Council (GMC) guidelines for practice in the UK, there is a presumption of capacity for patients unless "having been given all appropriate help and support, they cannot understand, retain, use or weigh up the information needed to make that decision, or communicate their wishes" [17: p. 27]. The British Medical Association and Law Society's joint account states that capacity requires the individual is able to:

> Understand in simple language what the medical treatment is, its nature and purpose, and why it is being proposed;
> Understand its principal benefits, risks and alternatives;
> Understand in broad terms what will be the consequences of not receiving the proposed treatment;
> Retain the information for long enough to use it and weigh it in the balance in order to arrive at a decision.
>
> [18: p. 120]

This is closely related to the Mental Capacity Act 2005 which identifies understanding, retaining, and weighing information, and the ability to communicate a decision, as the key to capacitous decision making [19: p. 2]. Plenty more explications of what should be required for decisional capacity have been described elsewhere (see, for further examples, Jonas [20]). It is clear, however the conditions are spelled out, that trauma medicine will regularly involve patients who are incapable of meeting the requirements for capacity due to their condition or pre-existing factors.

Thus, trauma medicine must contend with patients who may lack capacity in some way, due to distress, pain, unconsciousness, or some other factor; who are suffering from significant injuries which require urgent, invasive surgical care; who are isolated from friends and family members who might have access to some information about the patient's wishes; and who have no pre-existing relationship with the medical team caring for them. In such contexts it may be impossible to achieve any form of informed consent.

The need for informed consent is particularly stressed where the recommended treatment is invasive and where there are significant potential complications [17]. However, in some circumstances, bypassing consent is permitted,

> provided the treatment is immediately necessary to save [the patient's] life or to prevent a serious deterioration of their condition. The treatment provided must be the least restrictive of the patient's future choices [17: p. 32].

In deciding whether or not a patient lacks capacity and, if so, what treatment should be pursued, a lot of emphasis is placed on the physician's judgement. Although the guidelines laid out in the Mental Capacity Act 2005 and by the GMC may seem neat, applying the tests of understanding, retaining, deliberating, and communicating will rest with the physician and her interpretation of the patient in front of her. Similarly, protecting the "best interests" of an incapacitous patient and judging what qualifies as life-sustaining treatment, or what treatment will most effectively restore the patient's capacity to make decisions for herself, will depend on the physician's judgement. This could involve opting for the least invasive treatment, or the treatment associated with the fewest risks of complications, or that with the greatest chance of restoring the patient to full health.

Aside from the professional guidelines, there have also been common law rulings which shape how individuals and institutions approach the treatment of patients who may or may not lack capacity (and other aspects of seeking informed consent). In the UK, influential cases in include *Re C* (1994) and *Re T* (1992) amongst others [17: p. 39], [21, 22]. Such cases can influence future practice and clarify the way guidelines should be interpreted, but in emergency and trauma situations the time available for considering the capacity of an individual and what treatment she ought to receive will often be limited and decisions may need to be made based more on judgement and instinct than in-depth consideration of previous cases.

16.3 Research Ethics in Emergency Contexts

Providing trauma care in emergency circumstances where informed consent is not possible can be readily justified since it will be necessary for minimal well-being. Critics that complain that to do so undermines autonomy or fails to respect the individual somehow can be readily dismissed since crippling injury or death is likely to be far more destructive to autonomy than life-sustaining medical care: to provide such care for people is in no way disrespectful of their status as human agents.

To conduct clinical research in such contexts is much more difficult to justify and, as such, is hard to get approved by research ethics committees. Where it is possible for individuals to consent (including their meeting the necessary criteria for capacity, as discussed above), then, beyond the standard informed consent guidelines for all medical care, there is a focus on the likelihood that the patient will benefit from the procedure and the minimising of the risks to which she is exposed.

The GMC has specific guidelines relating to good practice and consent in research, and state that "[physicians] must make sure that the safety, dignity and wellbeing of participants take precedence over the development of treatments and the furthering of knowledge" [23: p. 3]. Seeking consent is essential where the patient has the capacity to give consent, and in the case of children or the incapacitated, consent must be sought from a valid authority (such as a parent, carer, or legally appointed proxy). Since emergency medicine may require research under circumstances where such consent cannot be sought (for instance, if a child's parents are uncontactable), the possibility of going ahead with involving the patient in the research continues so long as a research ethics committee has approved such practice or a physician not involved in the research agrees [19], [23: p. 14]. If an adult recovers capacity then consent must immediately be sought for their continued participation in the research.

Elsewhere, the GMC guidelines appear slightly more restrictive with regard to involving patients who lack capacity in research. For instance, on p. 3 of the *Good Practice* guidelines it states, in the case of people capable of consenting, "the anticipated benefits must outweigh the foreseeable risks, or the foreseeable risks to participants are minimal if the research only has the potential to benefit others more generally." The guidelines relating to adults incapable of consenting state "[physicians] must only undertake research involving an adult who lacks capacity if it is related to their incapacity or its treatment." Similarly to the with-capacity situation, the guidelines do permit research on those without capacity who are unlikely to benefit from the research, so long as the risks are minimal.[3]

Difficulties regarding consent and the need to urgently treat trauma patients in order to relieve pain or preserve life mean that research in trauma settings is difficult. Thus, for the most part, trauma-related research will often be retrospective, limiting the potential for progress in this area.

There is also a concern that involvement of people in research who have suffered traumatic injuries risks further distress to those individuals, particularly where the research involves questioning participants about the traumatic event and requires them to "re-live" the experience in some way. Newman *et al.* explored this in a 2006 study of the distress trauma-related research causes participants. The kind of research focused on here was that concerned with reducing future traumatic events and their ill conse-quences, using interviews, challenge tasks, biological samples, role plays, and other methods to gather data [24: p. 30].

The conclusion of these researchers was that, whilst some participants experience distress from participating in trauma-related studies, this is generally tolerable and the research is often linked with positive outcomes for most of the participants [24: p. 36], [25–28]. Though it is important to be aware of the limitations of this kind of research, which seeks an empir-ical route for "measuring" the ethics of research in trauma patients (and thus overwhelmingly focuses on ethically salient features that are easily measurable), it is worth noting the emphasis on the potential *positive* out-comes of research participation. Much focus in research ethics tends to be

---

[3]"Minimal" is clearly an ambiguous term open to interpretation, though is often taken to mean not more than the risks one faces in one's normal life [24].

on discovering the extent of potentially *harmful* effects, assuming that people such as those involved in trauma are particularly vulnerable and likely to be too fragile to participate in research, to the neglect of considering the wider benefits that might arise from feeling involved in interesting and valuable research.

16.4 Organ Donation

There are a number of different, sometimes conflicting, values and stakeholders in the domain of organ donation, and it is an area of healthcare which attracts extensive philosophical discussion [29–32]. I am concerned here with *deceased* organ donation (either heart beating donors or non-heart beating donors), not live donors.[4] Procedures for acquiring donor organs and allocating them to recipients need to balance the interests of the (deceased) donor; the donor's partner, family, and friends; the recipient and those close to her; the medical staff involved; and society at large. Organ donation demands consideration as part of a discussion of trauma-related ethico-legal issues because a considerable number of organ donors are trauma patients: in the US around 30% of all deceased organ donations are from trauma patients, with 21% dying after motor vehicle accidents [33]. Since this is an issue covered in detail elsewhere, particularly with regards to critical and end-of-life care, I shall keep the discussion here fairly brief.

One of the main and continuing debates surrounding organ donation relates to whether opt-in or opt-out ("presumed consent") systems are preferable (see, for instance, [34–37]). Opt-in systems are where potential donors are presumed *not* to consent to donation unless they have explicitly said otherwise; opt-out systems are where potential donors are presumed to consent unless they explicitly remove consent.

It seems, however, that the dominance of the opt-in/opt-out question in the discussion may have distracted from other important features affecting donation rates. An important paper by Fabre *et al.* seeks to illustrate how the "presumed consent" aspect of the system in Spain (which has the highest

---

[4] Many interesting ethical issues arise in the context of live organ donation but these are not relevant to trauma medicine.

rates of deceased donation globally) is, to some extent, an irrelevance [35]. In fact, in Spain as in the UK (and most countries), a "double veto" system is in place. This means that either the potential donor or her family can refuse transplantation and this will be respected. In the UK the National Organ Donor Register is intended to indicate to family members and medical staff what preferences an individual holds regarding her donor status, but this will only act to inform the family's decision, which (assuming the family are available) will always determine whether donation is made.

Organ donation rates in the UK are some of the lowest in Western Europe, with around 13 donors per million of population (pmp), compared to Spain's 35 pmp [37]. Comparing systems between different countries in order to identify means of improvement is tricky, since numerous socio-cultural factors will impact on donation rates. Fabre *et al.*, however, identify a number of areas (apart from presumed consent) where Spain and the UK differ and which might explain the disparity in donation rates. The authors emphasise the introduction in 1989 of a "comprehensive, nationally organised organ donation system", since which the donation rates in Spain have gradually risen, with the refusal rate falling from about 30–40% to 15% over 20 years. Key features of the Spanish system include a higher capacity on intensive care units and therefore a greater number of potential donors; transplant coordinators (most of whom are intensive care physicians) placed at every procurement hospital;[5] a nationally organised training programme; and efforts to construct a "positive social climate for donation and [generate] trust in the donation system" by paying careful attention to media and communications, including a 24-hour phone line [35: p. 923].

This final point is worth emphasising: trust in the healthcare system in general, and individual physicians in particular, is vital for the system to function effectively. A cautionary tale comes from Brazil, where, in 1997, the government was forced to abolish a presumed consent law which was badly received by both the public and the medical profession. One of the most damaging effects of the law's introduction was the distrust of the medical profession it seemed to create [35,38].

---

[5] Transplant coordinators' roles include identifying potential donors and approaching potential donors' families.

In trauma medicine, then, there is a great deal of pressure to identify potential donors as early as possible (ideally at the emergency department stage). It is vital, however, that such actions are not perceived as "jumping the gun", and that perceived conflicts of interest are dealt with openly and effectively. This means that decisions not to continue treatment in a patient suffering catastrophic injuries is clearly made on the basis of what is in the best interests of that patient, and emphatically *not* influenced by a desire to harvest the patient's organs. There are guidelines regarding the decision that continuing treatment is not of overall benefit to the patient and to initiate the organ donation process [39]. However, it is essential that the attending physician is seen and understood by the potential donor's family to not be subject to conflicts of interest and to be acting entirely within the law. Practice in Scotland is governed by the Human Tissue Act 2006, and in the rest of the UK by the Human Tissue Act 2004. Although provided for in legal regulation and professional guidance, the concept of "clinical death" can be problematic with potential beating heart donors since it does not cleanly overlap with ordinary understandings of "death".

The role of consent with regards to organ donation seems to be more about preserving trust in the medical profession and relationships between patients' families and physicians (than, for instance, fulfilling the potential donor's wishes). The report from the UK Organ Donation Taskforce emphasises:

> All patients who are potential organ donors are in hospital under the care of clinicians whose primary objectives and responsibilities are to provide the best possible treatment, in the best interests of the patient, in the hope or expectation that the patient will survive. The change of emphasis to possible organ donation can only occur when death of the patient is to be confirmed following clearly defined tests of the brain stem, in which case Donation after Brain Death (DBD) may be possible, or when a decision has been taken — again in the best interests of the patient — that no further treatment options are available or appropriate and active treatment should be withdrawn, in which case Donation after Cardiac Death (DCD) may be possible once death has been certified following cardio-respiratory arrest.
>
> [37: p. 22].

The "change of emphasis" is illuminating here, for there is also a need, as mentioned, to identify potential donors as early as possible, and trauma physicians will be expected to be in communication with transplant coordinators if they are treating potential donors. A specialist organ donation nurse, who may eventually be involved in the approach to a potential donor's family to ask for consent for donation, may be present early in the process. The National Institute for Health and Clinical Excellence (NICE) guidance recommends involvement of the specialist nurse as soon as intention to withdraw treatment is confirmed. On the one hand, having trained staff who are able to support family members and be on hand to offer information and comfort may help the process of introducing the possibility of donation in a sensitive and compassionate way, reduce the likelihood of refusal, and speed up the process. However, the early involvement of specialist nurses is contentious, particularly if family members are not initially aware of the role of specialist organ donation nurses when they are first introduced [40: p. 11].

To summarise, procedures to facilitate organ donation must be sensitive to the wishes of both organ donor and her family, and avoid compounding distress at this time. Yet improving donation rates will also have the great benefit of improving the well-being of those who require organs and may die without them. Emphasis is now turning to early identification of potential donors and specialist staff who are experienced in making approaches to potential donors' families. From an ethical and legal standpoint, such practices will be permissible (and desirable) insofar as they do not create (the appearance of) conflicts of interest in medical staff. This further requires excellent communication with family members and time taken to explain in appropriate detail the procedure, the significance of brain death, and so on. Trauma medics must coordinate with others involved in the organ donation process, treating the interests of their patients first and foremost, whilst ensuring the early identification of potential donors and facilitating consent approaches should they arise.

16.5 Confidentiality and Mandatory Reporting

Trust is an important feature of good relationships between physicians and patients. In order to encourage both the seeking of treatment and honest discussions about the nature of the health problem an individual is experiencing, patients need to have confidence that their doctors will not disclose sensitive personal information to others. It may also be argued that confidentiality (and respecting of patients' privacy) is important as a means of promoting other important values in healthcare, such as respect for autonomy and well-being [41, 42].

Informed consent, again, can play an important role in determining when sharing information about a patient is permissible and when to do so would be a breach of trust and may directly harm the patient in some way. In terms of confidentiality, patients may give consent for information to be shared with specific others. This indicates to the physician that the patient is comfortable with the disclosure of information and can act as a kind of "waiver", making disclosure no longer wrongful (as with consent to medical interventions).

Informed consent to disclosure of information faces the same issues as other informed consent requirements relating to capacity: what degree of "informed" is necessary; and how to determine the extent and limits of consent. Where information sharing and confidentiality is concerned, this may become particularly tricky because it is necessary for at least *some* information about the patient to be shared amongst the medical care team in order for treatment to be possible. The GMC's guidance describes "appropriate information sharing" as "essential to the efficient provision of safe, effective care, both for the individual patient and for the wider community" [43: p. 6]. It is assumed that a certain amount of information sharing within the care team is expected and that explicit consent need not be sought for this. Beyond this, however, patients must be informed where personal information is to be shared with those the patient would not normally expect. This is, of course, not decisive, since different patients will have different expectations and it is left to the individual physician's judgement as to what will count as within "reasonable expectations".

In trauma (and other) medicine, however, information disclosure may be requested by individuals not involved in the immediate care of the patient, where it is not possible to get consent from the patient either because she lacks capacity, refuses consent, or where there are strong reasons not to approach her for consent at all. In the case of a medical emergency, where it is not possible to approach the patient for consent, it is accepted that to act in the patient's best interests by proceeding with treatment is appropriate. The GMC guidance stresses that the patient should be informed of how her personal information was used if and when she regain capacity.

Disclosure without consent will sometimes be permitted without an overriding need to protect the interests of the patient (such as in medical emergences). There are two general instances where this is the case:

1. Where disclosure is required by law.
2. Where disclosure is justified in the public interest.

Physicians must disclose personal information when ordered to do so by a judge or presiding officer of a court, though she may object if the information requested is irrelevant to the case. Disclosure is also required in accordance with the statutory powers of various regulatory bodies (for example, the GMC is permitted access to medical records in order to investigate fitness to practice of practitioners). Finally, there are specific requirements for hospitals to inform authorities about patients suffering from, for instance, certain notifiable diseases and, of particular relevance to trauma, knife or gunshot wounds [43, 44]. This is extended to cases of serious crime where others may be at risk of injury and it will be in the public interest to report crimes to the police. In cases of disclosure on legal or public interest grounds it is advised that physicians only disclose "factual information [they] can substantiate, presented in an unbiased manner, relevant to the request" [43: p. 15].

Any injury resulting from a gunshot, even where this is accidental and the individual is licensed to possess a firearm, must be reported to the police. In the case of injuries caused by knives or other sharp objects, disclosure may only be necessary when the injury is the result of an attack or where there is a risk of injury to a minor due to improper access to knives, for instance [44]. There are further requirements to report injuries resulting from serious crime (though the definition of this is poorly specified and rests largely on the physician's judgement).

In many instances, it may not be clear to a physician whether disclosure of personal information to the police, regulatory organisation, or some other body or individual, is required by law or necessary in the public interest. There is, after all, a clear public interest in maintaining a healthcare system where patients are able to share information with their physicians without worry that it will be disclosed to third parties. Degrading trust in medical practitioners can make it less likely that people will seek treatment when they need it, and that they may withhold important information from their practitioners to the detriment of their health [10]. Beyond this, the fiduciary relationship between physicians and patients places an additional duty on physicians not to disclose personal information about their patients when it is not in the patient's interests, when consent to disclosure is refused, and especially if disclosure is likely to bring about harm to the patient.

This fiduciary relationship may obstruct a straightforward weighing up of the "public interests" argument. For instance, trauma patients who arrive at hospital distressed, confused, and in pain may say things to their carers which have wider implications relating to crime, and which might merit reporting to the police. A physician's duty to the public interest may be fulfilled both by disclosing information in such a scenario (by providing the police with information relevant to their investigation) and by the opposite action of not disclosing the information in order to protect the relationship of trust between her and her patient (and thus protect systemic trust). But we should distinguish between the duty to protect the patient's interests as a means of protecting the public interests, and the duty *directly* to the individual, where the physician ought not to disclose because of her fiduciary relationship with the patient (and not because such relationships are, in general, a good thing).

The onus on physicians to promote both the instrumental and intrinsic value of trust is a burdensome one. Guidelines provided by, for instance, the GMC and legal requirements only go part of the way to instruct physicians when disclosure without consent or where consent is expressly withheld is appropriate.

It might be thought that, in the case of trauma medicine (and other specialties where there is no pre-existing relationship between the patient and her physician), the obligations of trust are weaker. This would suppose, for instance, that it would be worse for a patient's general practitioner (GP) to share sensitive information about her since she holds a long-standing relationship with the GP, than it would be for a physician she had never encountered before to do the same. I think this is an interesting possibility, but it seems that trusting relationships between medical practitioners and patients should not be dependent on establishing relationships over time in the way that, say, friendships are. There may be a personal sense in which one feels it more deeply if a familiar person (including a GP) betrays one's trust than if a stranger (such as a trauma physician) does. But in order for the physician–patient relationship to be viable, it seems that a large degree of trust must be established from the first encounter.

16.6 Triage

Triage is a system used to allocate healthcare provision where resources are scarce, prioritising the treatment of some above others. Rather than considering population level distribution questions, triage refers to acute, micro-allocation problems, such as at the site of accidents where there are multiple traumas, in hospital emergency departments, and on battlefields (where the practice of "triaging" originated) [45]. Depending on the context in which triaging takes place, the "scarce resources" may include medical equipment and supplies, expertise, and time. The pressure on these resources will be greater in some circumstances than others. Iserson and Moskop provide a table of different triage settings including emergency departments, intensive care units (ICU), multi-casualty accidents, battlefields, localised disaster, and widespread disaster (such as weapons of mass destruction) [45: p. 276]. Alongside are some of the associated features of these situations, including resources available (e.g., relatively plentiful to sparse); state of the social order (from intact to chaos); resource-to-patient ratio; patient arrival pattern (either linear or grouped); and the triage methods adopted.

This last category is important to ethical analysis, since the actual triage system will determine the practice of triage and how resources are allocated. Triage systems may be broadly different according to their aims. For instance, military triage (more so historically than recently) may be more directed towards returning soldiers to the front line, and so may focus efforts on treating those with minor, quickly fixable injuries. Other systems are more likely to be geared towards treating the sickest first or maximising the best outcomes.

Any system of triage is troubled by the pressure on those providing care to fulfill different needs: to maximise utility; to uphold duties of non-abandonment to the individual; to try to maintain standards of privacy and confidentiality; to communicate with patients to keep them informed; to treat people justly; and so on [46,47]. It is the scarcity of resources that makes triage necessary, and the need to choose between fulfilling the needs of different individuals that makes it problematic, and an interesting case for bioethicists to consider.

Some of the different triage systems in use in the UK and overseas are:

- Australian Triage Scale
- Canadian Triage and Acuity Scale
- Emergency Severity Index
- Manchester Triage Score
- Sacco Triage Method
- SALT (Sort, Assess, Life-saving interventions, Treatment and/or transport)
- START (Simple Triage and Rapid Treatment)

These systems vary with regards to the triage levels available and the criteria used to judge which level a given individual should be assigned to. Most of those listed above have five different levels which may be indicated by different coloured tags. Often each level will have an associated time scale within which the patient needs to receive treatment. For instance, the Manchester Triage Score has red, orange, yellow, green, and blue tags which indicate immediate through to non-urgent levels, where "immediate" level patients need to be seen within one minute and non-urgent patients may wait up to 240 minutes [46]. Apart from physiological measures and standard observations that can contribute to triage scoring, the time and medical resources that treatment of a person would absorb may also be a factor. One of the most unpalatable aspects of triage scoring is the sometime inclusion of an "expectant" category: this is for people whose injuries are so catastrophic that either they cannot be saved or to do so would divert too many resources where these are extremely scarce.

Due to a need for efficient prioritisation of patients arriving at emergency departments, triage is carried out routinely by nurses. In the UK, patients are examined to get a general idea of their health, taking, for instance, blood pressure, heart rate, and temperature measurements, and making general observations about their condition. They are then divided into majors and minors (and paediatrics): majors will go straight into a bay on the ward where they will be seen by a doctor relatively quickly, whilst minors remain in the waiting room and will have to wait longer until they are seen. Patients arriving at hospital by ambulance will be triaged en route and will generally skip the sorting stage and go straight into a bay. People who suffer significant trauma, such as multi-trauma where a number of traumatic injuries are sustained, should be taken directly to a trauma centre if possible. It is important that the triaging undertaken by both first responders transporting patients to hospital and nurses at the receiving hospital is accurate and consistent: failure to do so can mean that seriously ill patients are not attended to quickly enough.

In the case of trauma, training emphasises the need to establish facts about the circumstances of the trauma [1]. Particularly in young, previously healthy people, serious injuries may not be immediately apparent as they may effectively compensate and so be conscious, appear relatively lucid, and not in great pain. Yet, especially in the case of blunt trauma, this can mask serious internal injuries which may be life threatening, making it necessary to assess the degree of kinetic energy hitting the body in the accident. Poor triaging (even where resources are not particularly scarce) can therefore delay treatment with disastrous consequences. This places an emphasis on the quality of training received by carers who are not qualified doctors, since they will play an important role in the early (and influential) treatment of trauma patients.

Even where triaging is "successful" it raises ethical questions. Prioritising treatment to those most in need seems sensible, but it may directly harm others. Such harm may mean increased duration of pain or a slightly longer recovery period, but in multi-casualty trauma the stakes may be extremely high, and diverting treatment from one individual to another may effectively mean allowing one person to die so that another may be saved. Triage is generally thought to approach such questions of "who to save" according to a utilitarian outlook: aim for the greatest good for the greatest number. But it may also adopt other principles of distribution, such as "maximin". Maximin refers to allocating resources so as to maximise the well-being (or some other value) of the worst off. In triage contexts, this requires that those who are worst injured should receive medical care before those with lesser injuries do so. This might, however, instruct carers to use huge resources attempting to save someone with very poor prospects of survival, whilst neglecting patients who stand a better chance (and diminishing their chances in so doing).

The World Medical Association (WMA) describes it as ethical

> for a physician not to persist, at all costs, in treating individuals "beyond emergency care", thereby wasting scarce resources needed elsewhere. The decision not to treat ... is justified when it is intended to save the maximum number of individuals [48].

The WMA adopts an explicitly utilitarian position here, with a focus on life-saving (although later, the statement also mentions keeping morbidity to a minimum). It is noteworthy that Iserson and Moskop, in referencing the WMA statement, quote the WMA as saying that "It is unethical for a physician to persist, at all costs, at maintaining the life of a patient beyond hope, thereby wasting to no avail scarce resources needed elsewhere" [45: p. 279].

The WMA statement was revised in 2006 and so, presumably, this sentence was altered during the revision. This change may be illuminating: the difference in wording hints at an asymmetry between action and inaction. In one case, actively *using* resources on an individual who cannot be saved is described as *unethical*; in the other case, *not using* resources on an individual who cannot be saved is described as *ethical*. The latter form is weaker since we generally emphasise the need to avoid wrongdoing, and the fact that one action is ethically justified does not mean that another action is ethically unjustified. Roughly, the newer wording makes it explicit that one is justified in not treating someone who cannot be saved, but it stops short of saying that to treat such a person is wrongful or unjustifiable.

This is important, for it acknowledges that other values (aside from utilitarian maximisation) may also be important to consider. In fact, the WMA statement further states

> Rescue workers and physicians are confronted with an exceptional situation in which their normal professional ethics must be brought to the situation to ensure that the treatment of disaster survivors conforms to basic ethical tenets [48].

Consent, along with treating people respectfully and fairly (not discriminating based on irrelevant factors), are mentioned, with the caveat that consent may be unachievable under the circumstances.

Certain situations where triage is required, therefore, place demands on physicians (and other carers) that mean the full range of normal ethical requirements, such as informed consent and non-abandonment, are not achievable. Yet this does not mean that values such as compassion and autonomy have no place in such circumstances, just that they may slide down the priority order. Effectively, room must be left open for actions which are motivated by compassion or other values, such as trying to offer comfort to a catastrophically injured individual. The alternative, of coldly following a utilitarian maximising principle, would effectively instruct emergency carers to divorce themselves from ordinary human emotions and instincts, and is quite problematic in so doing.

16.7 Concluding Remarks

In this chapter, I have discussed a number of areas where ethical issues may arise in trauma medicine. This is far from a comprehensive account of such issues, but instead I have focused on just a few areas that seem particularly pertinent and where trauma medicine seems to raise distinct problems from those arising in general medicine. I began by discussing the requirement to seek informed consent from patients before performing examinations or interventions, and how this is dependent upon judgements relating to capacity. In trauma medicine, informed consent procedures may be unusually problematic given time constraints and the level of capacity patients suffering traumatic injuries will have. While it still seems important to make an effort to keep patients informed about their condition, and to seek agreement from them regarding treatment, when this is not possible due to incapacity it should not be considered an affront to autonomy. Communicating well with patients and respecting their wishes serves purposes other than autonomy promotion, and so should be attempted, alongside efforts to safeguard patients' well-being, even where they lack capacity (and hence autonomy appears an unsuitable value to focus upon).

Very much related to issues of consent and capacity are questions of how research in trauma contexts should be regulated and how organ donation should be approached. Research in trauma medicine is made difficult by the high standards of informed consent generally required in medical research as a means of protecting participants from exploitation and harm. In discussing the guidance intended to protect potential participants as well as facilitate research, I sought to emphasise the often neglected possibility of *positive* experiences of research participation which some participants, trauma patients included, experience. In discussing organ donation, I summarised some of the conflicting interests of the different parties involved, and the high profile question of whether opt-out systems of consent are more effective at increasing donation rates. I suggested that some persuasive evidence suggests that factors other than opt-out are influential when it comes to donation rates in certain countries, particularly Spain, and that other values (such as trust in the healthcare system) may be vulnerable to destruction by perceived heavy-handed policies by the state. This is a tricky area, but policies and practices of organ donation need to be sensitive when it comes to approaching families to seek consent, and the appearance of subjugating the potential donor's interests in favour of the recipient's must be avoided.

In trauma, as with other areas of medicine, it will be important to respect patients' privacy and not to share confidential information in ways that are not implicitly or explicitly consented to. There are, however, exceptions when to disclose information without consent may be justified in the public interest or because it is legally required. In this section, I summarised the sorts of cases where guidelines permit or require the disclosing of information about patients; in particular in the mandatory reporting of knife and gunshot wounds. Respecting confidentiality as far as possible will, however, be important as a means of fostering trust in the healthcare system in general, and also in the relationship between a given patient and her physician. It is therefore preferable that physicians question the necessity of any instance where the release of confidential information is requested in the public interest in order to protect those values and relationships.

The final section considered the practice of triage and the particular ethical issues this raises. I discussed some of the varieties of triage system and how they might promote different things, such as lives saved or minimising morbidity. I emphasised the importance of leaving room in such triage systems for ordinary human responses and obligations in the face of suffering: that to demand *only* that utilitarian principles of maximisation are followed may not be appropriate or even possible (considering how this may demand triage officers to behave).

In summary, trauma medicine presents, to some extent, an exceptional form of medicine where ethical and legal guidelines need to be tailored to take account of the demands of the care required. Traditional accounts of medical ethics which focus on informed consent and autonomy promotion will be unsatisfactory here, since the former will often be impossible and the latter irrelevant. We must adopt an approach to bioethics and legal regulations which is flexible to the circumstances and acknowledges the variety of values at play in different contexts of healthcare.

References

[1] ATLS. *Advanced Trauma Life Support, 9th ed.* Chicago: American College of Surgeons, 2012.

[2] Davis M. Should there be a UK based advanced trauma course? *Emergency Medicine Journal* 2005; **22**(1): 5–6.

[3] Annas G.J. and Grodin M.A. *The Nazi Doctors and the Nuremberg Code: Human Rights in Human Experimentation.* Oxford: Oxford University Press, 1992.

[4] Manson N.C. Consent and Informed Consent. In R.E. Ashcroft, A.J. Dawson, H. Draper, and J.R. McMillan (eds) *Principles of Health Care Ethics.* Chichester: John Wiley & Sons, 2007; pp. 297–303.

[5] Ashcroft R.E. The Ethics and Governance of Medical Research. In R.E. Ashcroft, A.J. Dawson, H. Draper, and J.R. McMillan (eds) *Principles of Health Care Ethics.* Chichester: John Wiley & Sons, 2007; pp. 681–687.

[6] Caplan A.L. When Evil Intrudes. *Hastings Center Report* 1992; **22**(6): 29–32.

[7] Faden R.R., Beauchamp T.L., and King N.M.P. *A History and Theory of Informed Consent.* Oxford: Oxford University Press, 1986.

[8] Beauchamp, T.L. and Childress J.F. *Principles of Biomedical Ethics.* Oxford: Oxford University Press, 2001.

[9] Gillon R. Ethics needs principles, four can encompass the rest, and respect for autonomy should be "first among equals". *Journal of Medical Ethics* 2003; **29**(5): 307–312.

[10] O'Neill O. *Autonomy and Trust in Bioethics.* Cambridge: Cambridge University Press, 2002.

[11] Dawson, A.J. The future of bioethics: Three dogmas and a cup of hemlock. *Bioethics* 2010; **24**(5): 218–225.

[12] Dawson, A.J. and Verweij M. Public health ethics: a manifesto. *Public Health Ethics* 2008; **1**(1): 1–2.

[13] Coggon, J. *What Makes Health Public?* Cambridge: Cambridge University Press, 2012.

[14] Rudnick, A. (ed.) *Bioethics in the 21st Century*. Rijeka: InTech, 2011.

[15] Manson N.C and O'Neill O. *Rethinking Informed Consent in Bioethics*. Cambridge: Cambridge University Press, 2007.

[16] Bhangu A., Hood E., Datta A., and Mangaleshkar S. Is informed consent effective in trauma patients? *Journal of Medical Ethics* 2008; **34**(11): 780–782.

[17] General Medical Council. *Consent*. London: General Medical Council, 2008.

[18] British Medical Association and The Law Society. *Assessment of Mental Capacity*. London: BMJ Books, 2005.

[19] Stationery Office. *Mental Capacity Act 2005*. London: The Stationery Office, 2005. http://www.direct.gov.uk/prod_consum_dg/groups/dg_digitalassets/@dg/@en/@disabled/documents/digitalasset/dg_186484.pdf [accessed 25 April 2014].

[20] Jonas M.F. Competence to Consent. In R.E. Ashcroft, A.J. Dawson, H. Draper, and J.R. McMillan (eds) *Principles of Health Care Ethics*. Chichester: John Wiley & Sons, 2007; pp. 255–261.

[21] Re C [Adult, refusal of treatment] [1994] 1 All ER 819.

[22] Re T [Adult] [1992] 2 All ER 649.

[23] General Medical Council. *Good Practice in Research and Consent to Research*. London: General Medical Council, 2010.

[24] Newman E., Risch E., and Kassam-Adams N. Ethical issues in trauma-related research: a review. *Journal of Empirical Research on Human Research Ethics: An International Journal* 2006; **1**(3): 29–46.

[25] Ruzek, J.I. and Zatzick D.F. Ethical considerations in research participation among acutely injured trauma survivors: an empirical investigation. *General Hospital Psychiatry* 2000; **22**(1): 27–36.

[26] Kassam-Adams N. and Newman E. Child and parent reactions to participation in clinical research. *General Hospital Psychiatry* 2005; **27**(1): 29–35.

[27] Galea S., Nandi A., Stuber J., *et al.* Participant reactions to survey research in the general population after terrorist attacks. *Journal of Traumatic Stress* 2005; **18**(5): 461–465.

[28] Griffin M.G., Resick P.A., Waldrop A.E., and Mechanic M.B. Participation in trauma research: Is there evidence of harm? *Journal of Traumatic Stress* 2003; **16**(3): 221–227.

[29] Lamb D. Organ transplants, death, and policies for procurement. *The Monist* 1993; **76**(2): 203–221.

[30] Price, D. *Legal and Ethical Aspects of Organ Transplantation.* Cambridge: Cambridge University Press, 2000.

[31] Nuffield Council on Bioethics. *Human Bodies.* Nuffield Council on Bioethics, 2011.

[32] Fabre, C. *Whose Body Is It Anyway?* Oxford: Oxford University Press, 2008.

[33] Finger, E.B. 2013. Organ Procurement Considerations in Trauma. www. medscape.com. http://emedicine.medscape.com/article/434643-overview [accessed 17 December 2013].

[34] Hamm D. and Tizzard J. Presumed consent for organ donation. *British Medical Journal* 2008; **336**(7638): 230.

[35] Fabre J., Murphy P., and Matesanz R. Presumed consent: a distraction in the quest for increasing rates of organ donation. *British Medical Journal* 2010; **341**: c4973–c4973.

[36] Hitchen L. No evidence that presumed consent increases organ donation. *British Medical Journal* 2008; **337**: a1614–a1614.

[37] Department of Health. 2008. Organs for Transplants. http://www.nhsbt.nhs. uk/to2020/resources/OrgansfortransplantsTheOrganDonorTaskForce1stre-port.pdf [accessed 5 March 2014].

[38] Csillag C. Brazil abolishes "presumed consent" in organ donation. *Lancet* 1998; **352**(9137): 1367.

[39] NHS 2010. Donor Identification in Emergency Medicine. *Organ Donation — NHS UK.* https://www.organdonation.nhs.uk/about_us/professional_development_ programme/pdf/donor_identification_emergency_medicine.pdf [accessed 17 December 2013].

[40] NHS 2013. Approaching the Families of Potential Organ Donors. http:// www.odt.nhs.uk/pdf/family_approach_best_practice_guide.pdf [accessed 5 March 2014].

[41] Bennett R. Confidentiality. In R.E. Ashcroft, A.J. Dawson, H. Draper, and J.R. McMillan (eds) *Principles of Health Care Ethics.* Chichester: John Wiley & Sons, 2007; 325–332.

[42] Goold S.D. and Lipkin M. The doctor–patient relationship. *Journal of General Internal Medicine* 1999; **14**(S1): 26–33.

[43] General Medical Council. *Confidentiality.* London: General Medical Council, 2009.

[44] General Medical Council. *Confidentiality: Reporting Gunshot and Knife Wounds.* London: General Medical Council, 2009.

[45] Iserson K.V. and Moskop J.C. Triage in medicine, Part I: Concept, history, and types. *Annals of Emergency Medicine* 2007; **49**(3): 275–281.

[46] Aacharya R., Gastmans C., and Denier Y. Emergency department triage: an ethical analysis. *BMC Emergency Medicine* 2011; **11**(1): 16.

[47] Moskop J.C. and Iserson K.V. Triage in medicine, Part II: Underlying values and principles. *Annals of Emergency Medicine* 2007; **49**(3): 282–287.

[48] World Medical Association. 1994. WMA Statement on Medical Ethics in the Event of Disasters. www.wma.net. http://www.wma.net/en/30publications/10policies/d7/index.html.pdf?print-media-type&footer-right=%5Bpage%5D/%5BtoPage%5D [accessed 20 December 2013].

Index